Malicious Objects,
Anger Management, and the
Question of Modern Literature

Malicious Objects, Anger Management, and the Question of Modern Literature

Jörg Kreienbrock

FORDHAM UNIVERSITY PRESS   *New York*   2013

ML | the modern language initiative

THIS BOOK IS MADE POSSIBLE BY A COLLABORATIVE GRANT FROM THE ANDREW W. MELLON FOUNDATION.

Copyright © 2013 Fordham University Press

All rights reserved. No part of this publication may be reproduced, stored in a retrieval system, or transmitted in any form or by any means—electronic, mechanical, photocopy, recording, or any other—except for brief quotations in printed reviews, without the prior permission of the publisher.

Fordham University Press has no responsibility for the persistence or accuracy of URLs for external or third-party Internet websites referred to in this publication and does not guarantee that any content on such websites is, or will remain, accurate or appropriate.

Fordham University Press also publishes its books in a variety of electronic formats. Some content that appears in print may not be available in electronic books.

Library of Congress Cataloging-in-Publication Data

Kreienbrock, Jörg, 1969–
  Malicious objects, anger management, and the question of modern literature / Jörg Kreienbrock. — 1st ed.
    p. cm.
  Includes bibliographical references and index.
  ISBN 978-0-8232-4528-4 (cloth : alk. paper)
  ISBN 978-0-8232-4529-1 (pbk. : alk. paper)
  1. Anger. 2. Emotions. 3. Anger in literature. 4. Emotions in literature. I. Title.
BF575.A5K74 2013
809'.93353—dc23
                        2012027145

Printed in the United States of America

15 14 13   5 4 3 2 1

First edition

To Ella, with all the love in the world

CONTENTS

Acknowledgments ix

Introduction: How (Not) to Do Things with Doors 1

1. "When Things Move upon Bad Hinges":
   Sterne and Stoicism 22

2. Annoying Bagatelles: Jean Paul and the Comedy
   of the Quotidian 67

3. Malicious Objects: Friedrich Theodor Vischer
   and the (Non)Functionality of Things 122

4. Igniting Anger: Heimito von Doderer
   and the Psychopathology of Everyday Rage 172

   Epilogue 225

   Notes 245
   Bibliography 279
   Index 305

ACKNOWLEDGMENTS

The writing of this book profited immensely from conversations with my friends and colleagues Michal Ginsburg, Marcus Moseley, Helmut Müller-Sievers, Rainer Rumold, Thomas Schestag, Samuel Weber, and Kirk Wetters. Peter Fenves should receive special recognition. Without his valuable insights and comments the writing of this book would not have been possible. Paul Fleming's and John Hamilton's careful reading of the manuscript helped to shape its central arguments. I am especially thankful to Benjamin Robinson, Robert Ryder, and Christian Pinawin, who worked with me on the translation of such difficult authors as Jean Paul, Friedrich Theodor Vischer, and Heimito von Doderer.

The completion of the manuscript was made possible by a faculty fellowship from Northwestern University's Kaplan Institute for the Humanities for the 2010–11 academic year.

Introduction

How (Not) to Do Things with Doors

---------------------- *Shut the door.* ----------------------
—LAURENCE STERNE, *Tristram Shandy*

FROM RECALCITRANCE TO MALICE

This study focuses on the obstinate obtrusiveness of what Martin Heidegger calls *Zeug*, a recalcitrant term that so thoroughly defies translation that only colloquial terms give some handle on what Heidegger is after. Often translated by "equipment," the term is probably better understood as the underlying stuff of everyday life,[1] the tools and equipment that are at one's disposal. Malicious objects refuse to disappear into their automatic, unconscious functionality and instead remain stubbornly conspicuous. Endowed with agency, these cunning and perfidious intruders into the lifeworld of the subject seem to actively interrupt his or her intentions, unleashing anger and rage against the object. The malicious object in any case is something the subject experiences as recalcitrant, obtrusive, and vexing. The very possibility of this experience is one of the constitutive features of experience in general: the possibility, that is, that the object will not simply be thrown out there, as the term *ob*-ject suggests, but will, instead, be thrust into the sphere of activity that is most fully the subject's own, the place where the subject feels most fully its sovereignty. And the realization of the experience in question, this study argues, gives direction to some of the most probing texts of literary modernity.

By focusing on the minute details of everyday human life, as they are reflected in the literary texts under consideration, this study argues for a reevaluation of the seemingly irrational, that is, affective, qualities of things. Why does the encounter with recalcitrant objects trigger such violent emotions as anger and rage? How is it possible to get angry at a tool, curse an instrument, or smash an object in rage? And what does this anger say, in general, about the affective character of the modern individual, who may have secured a certain freedom from social or political constraints but is then—ironically or pathetically—bound to the very objects that are the sign and seal of this freedom?

The object's recalcitrance, which resists the subject's intentions and calls into question the very idea of subjecthood, brings out the subject's anger, exposing a precarious junction of literature, epistemology, psychology, and ethics. This study concentrates on texts by four authors from the eighteenth through the twentieth century: Laurence Sterne, Jean Paul, Friedrich Theodor Vischer, and Heimito von Doderer. Despite their engagement with the philosophical and scientific thought of their respective times—ranging from Locke and Hume through Kant and Hegel to Freud and Heidegger—each of these writers represents a type of *literary knowledge* of the object in question,[2] an object that stubbornly resists integration into a discursive, systematic order. Thinking about malicious objects as a specific *poetics of knowledge* not only problematizes the relationship between the animate and the inanimate but undercuts clear divisions between different categories of discourse, so that fiction and science, literature, and philosophy meld into each other.[3] The advantage of literature—or, more exactly, certain exemplary forms of literary representation—lies in its positive acceptance of a situation in which the distinctions between categories of discourse, like the difference between subject and object, tend either to disappear or to be reordered in an unfamiliar, disturbing, and often comical manner. In this sense, all of the novels discussed, insofar as they not only describe but also perform the object's malice on the formal level through digressive and fragmented narration, mixtures of different genres, or explorations of the visual characteristics of writing, could be described as *malicious literature*, the basic characteristics of which this study seeks to capture even as it acknowledges from the beginning that this literature conforms to the character of the object under investigation. In resisting an immediate, straightforward understanding, this form of writing produces frustrations and irritations for the reader that resemble those of encountering tools, instruments, and everyday objects that block, thwart, and upset the human subject's intentions. These tendencies culminate in Heimito von Doderer's "Short Preface to a Literary Conversation"

(Kleine Vorbemerkung zu einer literarischen Unterhaltung), in which he defines his writings as irritants: "Here the only aim is to present a basic foundation, made up of irritants and stimulants, i.e., medicines, irritants in the sense of to anger, to annoy."[4]

CLOSING DOORS, OPENING THE OBJECT TO ITS HISTORY

In the reflection "Do Not Knock," part of *Minima Moralia: Reflections from Damaged Life*, Theodor W. Adorno discusses technology's influence on human gestures and the impossibility of establishing a world of human interactions that would not be affected by the "demands of objects." The example Adorno chooses is modern humanity's inability to close doors properly:

> Technology is making gestures precise and brutal and with them men. It expels from movements all hesitation, deliberation, civility. It subjects them to the implacable, as it were a-historical demands of objects. Thus the ability is lost, for example, to close a door quietly and discreetly, yet firmly. Those of cars and refrigerators have to be slammed, others have the tendency to snap shut by themselves, imposing on those entering the manners of not looking behind them, not shielding the house which receives them. The new human type cannot be properly understood without awareness of what he is continuously exposed to from the world of things around him, even in his most secret innervations.[5]

The inability to close a door properly shows the objectification of the subject in advanced capitalist society. Equipment does not facilitate and improve life but imposes limitations and restrictions. Hence the relationship between subjects and objects as well as the relationship between subjects is, in Adorno's view, reduced to one of "mere operation," equaling a loss of freedom. In modernity, according to Adorno, the "law of pure functionality" governs things as well as human beings.[6] The inability to close doors deliberately is a symptom of the loss of a specific type of experience: a door snapping shut "precisely expresses the objectification of the subject, the reality of reification."[7] At the heart of Adorno's brief reflection—and of the ensuing study—is the dismantling of the notion that objects such as doors are ahistorical because they are simply at the mercy of whosoever chooses to use them. The point is not, then, to develop a history of the object but to see the precise place where a door is opened to its historicity. One name for this door is *annoyance*.

Another is what Bruno Latour calls *object agency*.[8] His essay "Where Are the Missing Masses? The Sociology of a Few Mundane Artifacts," while attentive to the tradition of critical theory that culminates in Adorno's *Minima Moralia*, attempts to delineate a history of things and their relation to humans that does not simply mourn the loss of the thing in processes of objectification, reification, and commodification; instead, it emphasizes those instances in which the thing returns as something grander than any mere thing, a thing that is forever unruly, resisting its domination and domestication, preventing what Adorno calls the "realization of peace" among subjects,[9] which depends on a prior and often only implicit peace between subjects and the objects that they deploy without further reflection.

Latour introduces the notion of the recalcitrant object in his theory of the distribution of agency between subjects and objects, living human beings and inanimate things. Like Adorno, he argues for a conception of subject-object relations that would, in Adorno's words, "neither [be] the undistinguished unity of subject and object nor their antithetical hostility."[10] It is perhaps no accident that Latour also uses the example of a door to explicate the stakes of his theory: "On a freezing day in February, posted on the door of La Halle aux Cuirs at La Villette..., could be seen a small handwritten notice: 'The Groom is On Strike, For God's Sake, Keep The Door Closed ('groom' is the Frenglish for an automated door-closer or butler)."[11] For Latour, the automated door is an example of a technological setup characterized by a *"distribution of competences* between humans and nonhumans" that does not discriminate between either side.[12] The act of opening and closing the door has been delegated from a human being, a real groom or butler, to a nonhuman, technological actor. As long as this network of relations between human and nonhuman actors functions without interruption, it can be described as "the technologist's dream of efficient action."[13] But it becomes visible when the electric door malfunctions and won't open and close properly, when equipment shows its "recalcitrance" and appears as a "disturbing object" or as a "troublemaker," to use Latour's terms.

For Martin Heidegger, whose late notion of the thing as "gathering" informs Latour's actor-network theory, even as it exasperates Adorno, using a door properly exemplifies "the way in which everyday Dasein always *is:* when I open the door, I use the latch."[14] As long as the door, as "an item of equipment," functions, it does not appear thematically; it is "ready-to-hand."[15] In the famous sixteenth chapter of *Being and Time*, entitled "How the Worldly Character of the Environment Announces Itself in Entities within-the-World," Heidegger examines how equipment discloses itself. The "non-thematic circumspective absorption in references or assignments constitutive for the readiness-to-hand of a totality of equipment" appears *"when an assignment has been disturbed*—when something is unusable for some purpose—then the assignment becomes explicit."[16] The assignment of a thing to serve a certain purpose is disrupted when it shows recalcitrance. It "loses its readiness-to-hand" and announces itself as an object per se.[17] This announcement of unusability takes place in the modes of "conspicuousness, obtrusiveness, and obstinacy" (Auffälligkeit, Aufdringlichkeit, Aufsässigkeit).[18] Heidegger's vocabulary seems to denote, not just resistance or recalcitrance, but almost an antagonistic intention by the failing or missing equipment. Obtrusive objects represent obstacles to Dasein, triggering not theoretical reflection but "circumspection of the dealings in which we use" them.[19] This circumspection is highly ambivalent: on the one hand, it is the precondition of thinking the phenomenon under consideration as the very phenomenon it is; on the other, it tends in the direction of the theoretical attitude, which, in attempting to grasp the thing in itself, misses its own comportment and thus confuses the recalcitrance of the object for the obduracy of the world.

Heidegger's peculiar use of the word *Aufsässigkeit* points to Friedrich Theodor Vischer's by now proverbial phrase "die Tücke des Objekts." Vischer introduced this expression to illustrate the anthropomorphic projections taking place when humans ascribe agency to inanimate objects at moments when they appear as conspicuous, obtrusive, and obstinate. As Grimm's *Wörterbuch* points out, the noun *Tücke,* which can be translated as "malice" or "perniciousness," is derived from an act of personification when used for inanimate objects: "*Malice* denotes the harmful behavior of various types of things, which the subject therefore experiences as malevolent. Originally based on a type of personification that is barely conscious anymore, *malice* [Tücke] maintains the meaning of lurking, ambushing mischief, ruin, bad luck, danger."[20]

In contrast to Ludwig Wittgenstein's dismissal of the phrase "die Tücke des Objekts" as a "stupid anthropomorphism," this study examines the philosophico-historical condition in which objects acquire agency and subjects engage in ever more "stupid" forms of personification and anthropomorphism in response.[21] According to Latour, anthropomorphism must be understood not as a sign of a primitive animism or as mere psychological projection but as a moment of translation that renders precarious the boundary between what is considered animate and inanimate. This study pursues Latour's work by asking: What projections—that is, "fictions invested with affect" (Freud)—translations, and rhetorical transfigurations in an assembly of animate and inanimate agents are necessary to ascribe malice to an object?[22]

Equipment, appearing not only on the uncontrollable periphery but at the center of the human being's *Lebenswelt,* not only facilitates life but also adds another dimension of possible failures and disturbances. Therefore, the rise of technology and instrumental reason, cultivating the cause of enlightenment and rationality, also creates new mythologies. The disenchantment of everyday life goes hand in hand with its constant reenchantment. From this perspective, technology is neither a manifestation of a utopian promise nor an antagonistic force undermining any true human sociability. Latour condenses this insight and its implicit rejection of traditional histories of modernity into the statement that furnishes the title for one of his books, "We have never been modern." "Our world," writes Latour, "ceased to be modern when we replaced all essences with the mediators, delegates and translators that gave them meaning. . . . It has taken on an ancient aspect, with all those delegates, angels and lieutenants."[23] The interaction between human beings and the contingencies of their environment needs acts of mediation, translation, and projection. On the basis of rhetorical modes of anthropomorphism and personification that ascribe agency, equipment appears to be possessed by vital forces responsible for its malice. The modern subject dealing with the disturbances of technology resembles a primitive, believing in spirits, demons, and other mediating agents between the realm of the physical and the metaphysical.

MANAGING ANGER, CARING FOR ONESELF

Already in Greek antiquity, a malfunctioning door could ignite a sudden emotional outburst. In *The Diagnosis and Cure of the Soul's Passions*, the Greek physician Galen of Pergamon remembers his youth and his training in anger control: "When I was still a youth and pursuing this training," he writes, "I watched a man eagerly trying to open a door. When things did not work out as he would have them,

Introduction

I saw him bite the key, kick the door, blaspheme, glare wildly like a madman, and all but foam at the mouth like a wild boar."[24] In ancient Greece and in contemporary Paris, a dysfunctional door leads to sudden fits of rage. The everyday routines of human beings—from Galen's childhood to the unknown person pinning his plea "The Groom is On Strike, For God's Sake, Keep The Door Closed" onto the electric door—are being disrupted. For Galen, this episode leads to a moral reflection on the inappropriateness of anger: "When I saw this, I conceived such a hatred for anger that I was never thereafter seen behaving in an unseemly manner because of it."[25] Latour, on the other hand, uses the "description of a door" (the electric door with the nonfunctioning groom) to discuss the relation of subject and object in epistemological terms as an example of the delegation of actions to nonhuman actors in modern everyday life.[26] This study attempts to bring the epistemological and the ethical discourse represented by Latour and Galen into conversation. All authors discussed in this study ask, not only *What is a thing?*, but also *How can one live with a thing?*

Jacques Lacan introduces the psychology of affects in relation to the breakdown of an artifact that produces anger in the moment of the "failure of an expected correlation between a symbolic order and the response of the real."[27] Negotiating the precarious relations between the realms of the symbolic and the real is the task not only of psychology but also of ethics. It is no coincidence that Lacan's brief reflections on anger can be found in a seminar entitled *The Ethics of Psychoanalysis*. Discussing Heidegger's notion of "das Ding," Lacan claims that anger is "essentially linked to something expressed in a formulation of Charles Péguy's— . . . It's when the little pegs refuse to go into the little holes."[28] To live the good life in a world of recalcitrant objects requires specific "technologies of the self" to cope with disruptions and the passions they arouse. Michel Foucault defines "technologies of the self" as practices and techniques that "permit individuals to effect by their own means or with the help of others a certain number of operations on their own bodies and souls, thoughts, conduct, and way of being, so as to transform themselves in order to attain a certain state of happiness, purity, wisdom, perfection, or immortality."[29] In view of the "little pegs"—whatever their symbolic or semiotic valence may be—otherwise uncoordinated theoretical inquiries find a common object: whatever resists the subject can be considered the object of theoretical study par excellence, the object to which every theoretical inquiry must attend, even if only in the form of a passing glance of recognition.

Laurence Sterne's depiction of the Shandy household in *Tristram Shandy*, as analyzed in the first chapter of this study, marks the historical starting point for an analysis of different forms of anger management, understood as "technologies of the self," in a world of recalcitrant objects. The exponential increase of objects in bourgeois households of the eighteenth and nineteenth centuries amplifies the chance of accidents as well as the opportunities to encounter malicious objects.[30] The more tools, instruments, and gadgets populate the domestic sphere, the more likely it is that life in the bourgeois household will suffer from the possible breakdown and malfunction of these different pieces of equipment. Not just large natural catastrophes like the Lisbon earthquake from 1755—which established the context for Voltaire's *Candide* and set the young Kant into a turbulence of activity that eventually gave rise to the *Critiques*—but the small incidents and confrontations of everyday life, abetted by a certain Humean-inflected skepticism, lead Sterne to a reevaluation of traditional concepts of morality, as anchored in the idea of divine duty, where every adversity can be understood as a divinely sanctioned trial of faith. Learning to live in an environment of accidents, mishaps, and calamities requires a new form of moral management.

For Tristram, Walter, Uncle Toby, and Dr. Slop the question of what is an accident cannot be separated from the question of how human beings deal with the painful, enraging effects of these disturbances of everyday life. Roy Porter characterizes the world of *Tristram Shandy* as one "where, in anthropomorphic parody of human disasters, window sashes lack counter-weights, knives sever thumbs not string, parlour doors creak on their hinges, medical bags, mimicking their owners, get tied up fast in knots."[31] To live in this recalcitrant environment means being exposed to the contingencies of falling, cutting, and piercing objects. For Sterne, the small world of Shandy Hall represents the paradigmatic site to stage the emotional effects of contingency on the *Lebenswelt* of the individual. Hence the novel presents an ever-expanding range of methods to deal with these afflictions in order to remain in an emotional equilibrium. The novel's characters display a wide array of strategies—from Stoic programs of self-control, to ritualized curses of the object, to the venting of anger through whistles—in coping with the accidents of everyday life in England at the beginning of the industrial age. In this context,

Introduction

this study undertakes an analysis of the novel with these questions in mind: What "therapies of desire" can be used to make living bearable while one is exposed to the demands of objects? How, in general, can one live the good life in a house of recalcitrant objects?[32]

During the eighteenth century, moral management as a type of psychotherapy began to differentiate itself from the Galenic model of bodily humors as well as from purely mechanical models in the tradition of Descartes and la Mettrie.[33] Instead it perceived the human as defined by an interaction between mental and physical processes. It looked at the patient from the standpoint of an "anthropological physician," who treats the *whole* human being.[34] Consequently, psychiatric treatment began to take into account the various interactions between body and mind, the physiological and the psychological. Treating a mentally disturbed person, for example, therefore involved the utilization of imagination. Michel Foucault, in *Madness and Society*, calls this method "theatrical representation": "Insofar as it is of the essence of the image to be taken for reality, it is reciprocally characteristic of reality that it can mime the image, pretend to the same substance, the same significance. . . . If illusion can appear as true as perception, perception in its turn can become the visible, unchallengeable truth of illusion. Such is the first step of the cure by 'theatrical representation': to integrate the unreality of the image into perceived truth, without the latter seeming to contradict or even contest the former."[35] In the realm of the imaginary the subject can create different strategies of self-control, self-governance, and self-regulation. Both anger and its management function according to the same principles as theatrical performances on stage. The irrationality of excessive passions is not simply extirpated from the human psyche; it is performed and enhanced, creating new images that are supposed to heal the rift between the real and the imaginary.

THE ETHICAL DIMENSION OF HUMOR

Why do we—and this is especially true of the German reception of Steune[36]—laugh at Walter Shandy? Throughout the eighteenth and nineteenth centuries *Tristram Shandy* presented a crucial model for various theories of the aesthetic in general and the comic in particular. This study not only explores Sterne's influence on Jean Paul, which by now is commonly accepted,[37] but traces a tradition of humorous representations of malicious objects in literature from Sterne, to Jean

Paul, Vischer, and, finally, Doderer.[38] All of these authors not only give lucid and highly comical accounts of malicious objects but also depict the failure of various types of anger management. The reader laughs at the subject's desperate and eventually failed attempts to bridge the gap between the symbolic and real. Hence what is being perceived as comical is irreducible to the mere malfunction of equipment. Laughter—as well as anger—is the result of specific forms of projections, namely anthropomorphisms and personifications that allow the object or technical device to display malice and obstinacy.

One of the main sources of Sterne's humor consists in its repeated demonstration of the impossibility of applying abstract, scholarly knowledge of Stoic anger control to the concrete situation of the bourgeois household. Sterne quotes the philosopher, poet, and cleric John Norris, who, in *Practical Discourses upon Several Divine Subjects*, elaborates on the Stoic doctrine of the difference between inflictions that can be changed by the subject and inflictions that cannot. It is man's "inconsistent soul," according to Norris, that adds to the miseries of life. Sterne writes: "Inconsistent soul that man is!—languishing under wounds, which he has the power to heal!—his whole life a contradiction to his knowledge!—his reason, that precious gift of God to him—(instead of pouring in oyl) serving but to sharpen his sensibilities,—to multiply his pains and render him more melancholy and uneasy under them!—poor unhappy creature, that he should do so!"[39] Reason and knowledge stand in stark contrast to the urgencies of everyday life. Reason increases the vexations of everyday life instead of offering methods to alleviate them: the "sharper the sensibilities" of the subject, the greater the pain. The second chapter of this study discusses several literary as well as theoretical works of the German writer Jean Paul, who not only describes in minute detail the variety of interruptions and afflictions that anger the protagonist of his novel *Siebenkäs* but also considers the pleasures as well as the pains of anticipation.[40] What disturbs the writer Siebenkäs is not so much the actual noises of his wife working alongside him within the cramped confines of a petit bourgeois household but his own imagination anxiously reflecting back upon the last interruption and eagerly anticipating the next. As is the case for Laurence Sterne, man is an "unhappy creature" not only because of external pressures but even more because of a heightened form of attentiveness, a sharpening of reason that cannot be integrated into a practical ethics. Despite his intentions to oil the bad hinges, Walter Shandy cannot enjoy his

Introduction

sleep because he constantly anticipates being awakened by the creaking door:

> But the thing was morally speaking so very impracticable, that for the many years in which this hinge was suffered to be out of order, and amongst the hourly grievances my father submitted upon its account,—this was one; that he never folded his arms to take his nap after dinner, but the thoughts of being unavoidably awakened by the first person who should open the door, was always uppermost in his imagination, and so incessantly step'd in betwixt him and the first balmy presage of his repose, as to rob him, as he often declared, of the whole sweets of it.[41]

What is more vexing than the actual disturbances are thoughts of a disturbance, or what Norris calls "Phantastick and Imaginary Goods." Famously, the novel *Tristram Shandy* begins with a motto from Epictetus's *Enchiridion:* "We are tormented with the opinions we have of things, and not by the things themselves."[42] Again, as in the case of *Siebenkäs*, opinions, imagination, and fantasy introduce moments of interruption, misery, and sorrow instead of providing relief. Laurence Sterne and Jean Paul deconstruct the belief in a harmonious accord between humans and things, subjects and objects, nature and culture, based on art or philosophy: "There was not a subject in the world upon which my father was so eloquent, as upon that of door-hinges—And yet at the same time, he was certainly one of the greatest bubbles to them, I think, that history can produce: his rhetoric and conduct were at perpetual handy-cuffs.—Never did the parlour-door open—but his philosophy or his principles fell a victim to it;—three drops of oyl with a feather, and a smart stroke of a hammer, had saved his honour for ever."[43] Neither philosophy nor rhetoric nor scholarly knowledge guarantees an undisturbed handling of the door. They are impractical, exposing a rift between theory and practice, knowledge and conduct, the symbolic and the real. None of Walter Shandy's seemingly endless discourses can replace the simple application of "three drops of oyl."

Ridiculous figures like the failing writer Siebenkäs in *Siebenkäs,* the prison chaplain Süptitz in *The Comet,* and the bailiff Freudel in *The Libel of Bailiff Josuah Freudel against His Accursed Demons (Des Amts-Vogts Josuah Freudel Klaglibell gegen seinen verfluchten Dämon)* exemplify, in a similar way to *Tristram Shandy,* how difficult it is for the modern subject to exist happily in a world populated by objects interfering with his intentions. Life, for Jean Paul's tragicomic heroes, is a constant struggle to establish an idyllic space of happiness. In this context, humor functions as one mode of reducing contingency. Laughing at the world enables human beings to distance themselves from the persistent, uncontrollable intrusions of reality. Humor allows them to turn quotidian annoyances into sources of pleasure by applying Epictetus's doctrine of treating life as if it were a play. In an addendum to *Life of Quintus Fixlein* entitled "On the Natural Magic of Imagination," Jean Paul offers a rewriting of the Stoic doctrines of ataraxia and eudaimonia, introducing a theatrically based "steadfastness" in the face of a recalcitrant world of objects that is "more sublime, rarer and sweeter than Stoic apathy."[44] In his reflections on the doctrines of the seventeenth-century neo-Stoic Alfons Anton de Sarasa, rendered as "Little Book of Joy or *Ars Semper Gaudendi*," Jean Paul explicitly relates poetics to ethics. For Jean Paul, the most originary poetic figurations are those of personification and anthropomorphism. They project the subject onto inanimate objects, thereby animating them. It is this "poetic animism" that relieves humans from the obtrusiveness of their surroundings—it soothes pain through the pleasures of fantasy.[45] But these pleasures, embodied in the trope of the idyllic and figurations of the comical, are always threatened by moments when animated objects aggressively turn against man's intentions, leaving "disturbed idylls."[46] Imagination functions as a pharmakon, in the double sense of poison and remedy.[47] What is supposed to heal the rift between subject and object and alleviate the human's vexations turns out to increase and intensify the painful antagonism between living human beings and inanimate objects.

For Albert Einhardt, the choleric protagonist of Friedrich Theodor Vischer's novel *Another One* (1878), a creaking door not only interrupts his concentration but actually speaks to him, uttering the Latin phrase *eo ipso*: "Now I do not have to listen to the creaking of my office door anymore. Lubricating was difficult and rarely successful. The whistling creak always spoke clearly: Eo Ipso!"[48] The creaking door speaks Latin. Einhardt's imagination, rather than providing the means for coping with the disruption, increases his pain and misery. He obsesses about the squeaking door, listening for meaning. His anger, therefore, stems not from the actual sound but from an act of signification.

In the belief that objects are possessed by antagonistic demons actively impeding the subject's intention, as in the case of Vischer's

Introduction

novel *Another One*, the border between paranoia, primitive animism, and modern scientific thought becomes porous. In the mode of projection, which creates a "fiction invested with affect," human beings anthropomorphize and personify those contingent forces that threaten their lives.[49] For Einhardt, objects are possessed by malicious demons trying to counter his plans and intentions. The third chapter of this study interprets this metaphysics of malicious objects as the ironic reformulation of Vischer's aesthetics and theories of the comical, which are based on the concept of projection. Einhardt does not represent a merely pathological case. His mythology of demonic spirits who possess objects pushes the universal human activity of symbolization, that is, anthropomorphization and personification, to a grotesque extreme. It seems that the more objects a subject possesses, the more possessed they appear; Albert Einhardt is being "possessed by possessions."[50]

In "My Autobiography" (Mein Lebensgang), Vischer relates his theory of projection as an act of "infusing manufactured objects with a metaphysical dimension" to its poetical incarnation in the figure of Albert Einhardt:[51] "If one slightly increases and intensifies that foisting, lending, personifying play of imagination, which every living human being can recognize within him- or herself, then play almost turns into earnestness. It is as if someone who gets angry with a disruption almost believes in a lurking gremlin [lauernder Kobold] responsible for it. A. E. resembles such a figure halfway believing in the earnestness of imagination."[52] Not only does Vischer's doctrine of projection, using the terms *anthropomorphization, personification,* and *symbol,* develop directly out of Jean Paul's *School for Aesthetics* (*Vorschule der Ästhetik*), but it also partakes in an intense discussion of the notion of projection in such diverse fields as psychology, philosophy of technology, theology, ethnology, aesthetics, and literature during the nineteenth century.[53] All of these discourses are characterized by what Derrida calls "hermeneutical compulsion," that is, a specific form of ascribing meaning to randomness and contingency.[54] Derrida's example is Freud's study *The Psychopathology of Everyday Life*, which, not surprisingly, narrates several instances of erroneously carried-out actions dealing with the difficulty of opening a door. Freud writes: "In former years I visited patients in their homes more frequently than I do at present; and on numerous occasions when I was at the front door, instead of knocking or ringing the bell, I pulled my own latch key out of my pocket, only to thrust it back again in some confusion."[55] For Freud, this type of error is no coincidence but, upon further analysis, reveals an underlying desire. Hence, "The parapraxis was a symbolic representation of a thought which was not after all really intended to be accepted seriously and consciously."[56] Derrida identifies in Freud a "reintroduction of determinism, necessity, [and] signification."[57] Parapraxis, for Freud, is always a meaningful event. There is no erroneous action performed by the subject that does not signify. When it comes to human actions, there are no accidents, only symptoms. Freud, in an attempt to distinguish psychoanalysis from superstition, differentiates between external chance and internal determinism: "I believe in external (real) chance, . . . but not in internal (psychical) events."[58] It appears that Vischer's insistence on personification and anthropomorphism as anthropological necessities points directly to the difficulty of clearly distinguishing internal and external, randomness and necessity. In this sense, one could ask with Derrida, "What is the difference between superstition, paranoia, or animism and their literary representations on the one hand, and science on the other, if they all mark a compulsive tendency to interpret random signs in order to reconstitute a meaning, a necessity, or a destination?"[59] Is it possible, in encountering malicious objects, to maintain Freud's distinction between external chance and internal necessity? Does the creaking door speak? And what does it say?

CATHARTIC ERUPTIONS

In an essay discussing the significance of technology for Edmund Husserl's concept of *Lebenswelt*, entitled "Lebenswelt und Technisierung unter Aspekten der Phänomenologie," Hans Blumenberg points to the invention of the electric doorbell as an example of a specifically modern experience of technology. While older mechanical bells still guaranteed an immediate relation between the human hand and the creation of a sound, the electric bell, triggered by a button, introduces a different mode of causality: "There are old mechanical bells that need to be pulled or turned. Because there is an adequate nexus between hand and sound, their usage creates the immediate feeling of producing a specific effect. . . . This is different in the case of the electric bell, which is rung by pressing a button: the hand's activity and effect are unspecific and heteromorphic— one does not produce the effect anymore, one merely triggers it."[60] Advanced technology dissolves the immediate nexus between cause and effect. The user of a mechanical doorbell knows not only what to do but also why and how his or her action creates a certain effect. This insight, according to Blumenberg, is lost for the modern user of an electric doorbell. Technology induces a "withdrawal of insight."[61] This lack of knowledge leads to various *parapractic* actions: "In a world that is increasingly characterized by igniting functions [Auslösefunktionen], not only the interchangeability of persons performing unspecific actions increases, but also the interchangeability of the triggers themselves. To stay with the example of the doorbell: How often does one press the doorbell in the stairwell when one actually 'meant' to switch on the light?"[62] Technology tends to hide its inner workings, its "secret of construction and principle of function."[63] The more functional, that is, straightforward and effortless, a tool or instrument becomes, the more it appears merely as a surface offering triggers, and the more prone to mishaps, dysfunctions, and accidents it becomes. Human actions and gestures become, to use Adorno's vocabulary, unspecific, homogenous, interchangeable, and thereby susceptible to interruptions and disturbances. An increase in functionality equals an increase in disturbances.

Blumenberg's usage of the verb "to ignite" (auslösen) to elucidate an action that cannot be integrated into a standard model of cause and effect points to Julius Robert Mayer's short but influential essay "On Ignition" (Über Auslösung) from 1876. Mayer, a physicist and physician, is best known for formulating what was soon thereafter called the first law of thermodynamics, that is, the law of the conservation of energy. In "On Ignition," published shortly before his death, Mayer introduces a new explanation of processes like ignitions, explosions, or catalyses that seem to contradict the law of *causa aequat effectum*, of cause equaling effect: "In the case of ignitions one speaks of cause and effect in a very different sense. Here, not only are cause and effect not equal or proportionate, but there is no quantitative relationship between cause and effect; instead, the cause in relation to effect generally has to be considered as a vanishingly small measure."[64] The electric doorbell in Blumenberg's description functions like a trigger in Mayer's sense. The quantity of energy necessary to ignite an action seemingly lacks any direct relation to its outcome. The examples Mayer discusses include physical ignitions like explosions but also the psychological effects of "exploding anger": "As much as mourning is a passive condition, rage is an active pain of the soul. Venting it enormously increases ignition tendencies [Auslösungstendenz], especially those of the tongue."[65]

In the second half of the nineteenth century, Mayer's doctrine of energetic ignitions appears, reconfigured as catharsis, in such diverse discourses as aesthetics (Bernays, Nietzsche), and psychology (Freud, Breuer). In the short study "On Catharsis: From Fundamentals of Aristotle's Lost Essay on the 'Effect of Tragedy'" (Grundzüge der verlorenen Abhandlung des Aristoteles über Wirkung der Tragödie) from 1857, Jacob Bernays interprets the notion of catharsis in terms of an ignition that affords the abreaction of affects. He analyzes tragedy in decidedly medical (i.e., pathological) terms. Arguing against Lessing's moralistic reading of cathartic effects in the experience of drama, Bernays stresses the alleviating qualities of tragedy in terms of a "solicitation" of affects. Drama causes a sudden abreaction of affective energies of the audience that equals a cleansing and purification. Bernays describes this cathartic solicitation as follows: "The way fire lights up when in proximity of a combustible agent, tragic action, made up of sad and horrible events, must trigger in every healthy audience member an outburst of these affects."[66] Hence Bernays defines the notion of *katharsis* as follows: "*Katharsis* is a term transferred from the physical to the emotional sphere, and used of the sort of treatment of an oppressed person which seeks not to alter or to subjugate the oppressive element but to arouse it and draw it out, and thus to achieve some sort of relief for the oppressed."[67]

Freud, the son-in-law of Bernays, uses a similar model of energetic discharge in his early studies on hysteria and in his work on the joke and its relation to the unconscious. For him, laughter as well as anger is conceptualized in terms of a sudden release of psychic energies. As in Mayer's theory of ignition and Bernays's doctrine of "solicitation," Freud posits the possibility of a disproportionate relation between cause and effect in comic situations. A small cause that itself has little effect can, if it is aided by other causes, create great pleasure (i.e., trigger an abreaction).

For Freud, the tendentious joke provides the often minute amount of psychic energy necessary to release otherwise blocked desires.[68] Freud cites the example of angry cursing to show how jokes can release repressed urges and desires:

> Let us assume that there is an urge to insult a certain person; but this is so strongly opposed by feelings of propriety or of aesthetic culture that the insult cannot take place. . . . Let us now suppose,

Introduction

> however, that the possibility is presented of deriving a good joke from the material of the words and thoughts used for the insult—the possibility, that is, of releasing pleasure from other sources which are not obstructed by the same suppression. This second development of pleasure could, nevertheless, not occur unless the insult were permitted; but as soon as the latter *is* permitted the new release of pleasure is also joined to it. Experience with tendentious jokes shows that in such circumstances the suppressed purpose can, with the assistance of the pleasure from the joke, gain sufficient strength to overcome the inhibition, which would otherwise be stronger than that. The insult takes place, because the joke is thus made possible. But the enjoyment obtained is not only that produced by the joke: it is incomparably greater. It is so much greater than the pleasure from the joke that we must suppose that the hitherto suppressed purpose has succeeded in making its way through, perhaps without any diminution whatever. It is in such circumstances that the tendentious joke is received with the heartiest laughter.[69]

In tendentious jokes laughter is symptomatic of repressed urges. The strength of the affect of laughter is caused, not by the joke itself, but by the sudden release of those psychic energies that were not allowed to manifest themselves in cursing. The decorum of "aesthetic culture" does not allow angry energies to appear as invectives; therefore the joke transforms these energies into a socially acceptable form. Freud calls the surplus of comic pleasure that allows for the repressed angry energies to be released "fore-pleasure" that succeeds in lifting "suppressions and oppressions."[70] Laughter, to quote Samuel Weber's reconstruction of Freud's theory of the joke, must "'break out' or 'explode.'"[71]

USING ANGER

The explosiveness of passionate outbursts in anger or laughter characterizes Friedrich Nietzsche's existence as a philosopher who radically questions traditional ideas of subjectivity.[72] His self-fashioning as a highly volatile catalyst for a new philosophy of the self that would destroy conventional (i.e., metaphysical) concepts of epistemology and ethics culminates in the infamous proclamation from *Ecce Homo*: "I am no man, I am dynamite."[73] In *The Gay Science*, Nietzsche explicitly relates the experience of energetic discharges in music to the ancient theory of catharsis. Music "was credited with the power of discharging the emotions, of purifying the soul, of easing *ferocia animi*."[74] Abreaction, purification, and alleviation, for Nietzsche, are elements of a medico-ethical therapy. Musical trance makes life bearable; it offers a treatment for the miseries of life.

For this "therapy of desire" (Nussbaum) to be successful, passionate discharges have to be activated, not suppressed. The first step in this treatment consists in intensifying and increasing the passions: "One sought to push the exuberance and giddiness of the emotions to the ultimate extreme."[75] According to Nietzsche, the result of this escalation after its final eruption is soothing.

Nietzsche's interest in the utility of psychic energies as an important element of the *art of living* stems to a large degree from his reading of Mayer's essay "On Ignition."[76] Living the good life, in this sense, would mean, not following abstract doctrines of morality that preach the extirpation of passions and drives, but igniting oneself.[77] Self-ignition consists in the proper discharge of energies. This release is experienced as pleasurable; it relieves the pain of blocked energies and ultimately creates happiness. Self-ignitions initiate not only a new "gay science" but also a cheerful, energetic morality. Letting off steam in a controlled, directed fashion therefore becomes the central principle of what the chemist and philosopher Wilhelm Ostwald, editor of Mayer's "On Ignition," in 1911 calls the "energetic imperative."[78] Its main rule: "Don't squander any energy, exploit it!"[79] With Ostwald's energetic imperative, self-government and self-regulation as forms of caring for the self become, under the guise of self-improvement, modes of self-rationalization. The subject must submit to the same mechanisms of efficient action as machines. To reach a state of happiness one has to turn oneself into a technological artifact. Self-ignitions, instead of producing a sovereign and autonomous self, as imagined by Nietzsche, are put into the service of the human being's subjugation to the demands of modern technological society.

The final chapter of this study analyzes the Austrian writer Heimito von Doderer's description of psychological as well as medical therapies from the first half of the twentieth century dealing with the anger aroused by malicious objects in similar terms of self-ignition, self-governance, and self-fashioning. Doderer's conception of anger as the paradigmatic psychopathology of modernity finds it most concise representation in one of the mottos of his 1962 novel *The Merowingians, or The Total Family*: "The wrath of the age is deep."[80] *The Merowingians* focuses on variations of anger management that rely on artificially igniting outbursts of anger. The characters Dr. Horn and Dr. Schajo both develop forms of treatment that, in contradistinction to psychoanalysis, do not attempt to determine (i.e., hermeneutically decipher) the causes of anger. Rather, they insist on purely mechanical forms of cathartic abreaction, relieving the patient of his or her distress, yielding to the *groundlessness* of rage. In *Repertory*, Doderer writes: "Fits of rage without apparent reason [grundlose Wutanfälle] have their reason [Grund] exactly in this lack of reason [Grund]. Therefore they are characterized by an abysmal lack of reason [abgründiger Grundlosigkeit]."[81] Fits of rage without apparent reason/ground have their reason exactly in this lack of reason/ground. Therefore they are characterized by an abysmal lack of reason/ground. Groundless rage, like the phenomenon of ignition, questions the possibility of establishing a relation between cause and effect because it seems to contradict the model of *causa aequat effectum*.[82] In contrast to hermeneutically based therapies, which read symptoms to determine the reason for psychic disorders, for Doderer the reason for pathological rage is indeterminable. What is the abysmal groundlessness of rage? How can anger be controlled if its eruptions appear to be groundless, without reason?

Doderer explicitly ties his grotesque phenomenology of anger ignition to contemporary moral and political discourses. For him, rage caused by malicious objects impedes the open, unprejudiced perception of concrete reality, which he calls *apperception*, and the ability to organize one's life accordingly. Exposed to the thrusts of contingency and blinded by rage, the subject is unable to distinguish between the essential and the merely accidental; he or she is unable to determine causes, reasons, and grounds. The angry individual enters a "pseudological space" that manifests itself either as a perversion (on the level of the individual) or as a totalitarian state apparatus (on the level of the collective). For Doderer, in "Sexuality and the Total State," the pathologies of the individual and politics are inextricably linked.[83] Hence anger management is an epistemological, an ethical, and a political imperative.

Doderer's notion of a "pseudological space," understood as a condition characterized by the universal inability to *apperceive*—that is, by the urge "to impose a preconceived picture on the world"— resembles Heidegger's rejection of a definition of the thing based on its utility.[84] While the analysis of equipment within the fundamental ontology of *Being and Time* focused on equipment that was produced to be used in a specific way, Heidegger's later texts equate this usefulness of tools—their "serviceability, conduciveness, usability, manipulability"—with an "assault upon the thing."[85] The thing in Heidegger's thought after the so-called "turn" (Kehre) is not the product of a *techne*, understood as a technology of producing purposeful tools. In the epilogue to *The Merowingians,* the figure of Doctor Döblinger (a thinly veiled self-portrait of Doderer) quotes from Heidegger's essay "The Thing": "What does the philosopher say? 'Aus dem Dingen des Dinges ereignet sich und bestimmt sich auch erst das Anwesen des Anwesenden,' and: 'Wie aber west das Ding? Das Ding dingt. Das Dingen versammelt.'"[86] While for Heidegger the thing, defined as a form of peaceful gathering, guarantees a smooth, uninterrupted experience of the world, Doderer conceives of it as a malicious object, triggering groundless fits of rage.

The separation of form and matter, privileging the former, induces, according to Heidegger, a technological philosophy of subjectivity and intentionality that can be overcome only by a different thinking of the thing. According to Doderer, Heidegger's notion of the thing as a form of assembly not only "give[s] in utmost brevity and pregnancy a complete theory of the total family" but also allows for a grounding of ethics in the encounter of humans and things.[87] This different relationship between human beings and objects would not reduce things to objects—that is, perceive of them as means to ends— and thereby remain "committed to the precincts of representational thinking."[88] Instead, answering the question "What is a thing?" leads to the "beginning of a change of questioning and assessment, of seeing and deciding, in short: of Da-sein in the midst of beings."[89] It furthermore establishes a different relationship of human beings to equipment: that is, tools, instruments, and technical devices. In his *Discourse on Thinking (Gelassenheit),* Heidegger asks how, in a world that has lost its grounding and rootedness, human beings can cope with the intrusion of technical artifacts. Instead of cursing and demonizing objects, Heidegger proposes a different attitude: "Still we can act otherwise. We can use technical devices, and yet with proper use also keep ourselves so free of them, that we may let go of them any time. We can use technical devices as they ought to be used, and also let them alone as something which does not affect our inner and real core. We can affirm the unavoidable use of technical devices, and also deny the right to dominate us, and so to warp, confuse, and lay waste our nature."[90] Being able to both affirm and deny technology makes possible a "releasement towards things."[91] Treating things as things in the mode of *Gelassenheit*—that is, "no longer viewing things in

Introduction

a technical way"—lets them remain effectual without triggering destructive affects: they are part of the human *Lebenswelt* without disrupting it.[92] If the *"releasement towards things"* as a form of anger management succeeds, objects will lose their malice and "our relation to technology will become wonderfully simple and relaxed."[93]

Yet this wondrous tranquillity of a "new autochthony" can be described as the result of a technology, namely a technology of the self in Foucault's sense.[94] The ability to use objects freely without submitting to their demands is the result of a specific way of questioning and interrogating the self. Despite Heidegger's attempt to ground a new relationship to technology in an explicitly nontechnological, almost pastoral way that involves actively forgetting equipment's conspicuousness, obtrusiveness, and obstinacy, he has to rely on specific quasi-technological procedures of self-governance and self-regulation.[95] Technology returns. The *"releasement towards things"* remains inscribed in the techno-energetic imperative of rationalizing self-improvement. For Heidegger, there is no restoration of a "natural" relationship of humans and things; the recalcitrance of objects cannot simply be erased. As a form of "meditative thinking," *Gelassenheit* attempts not to deduce the essence of things from a notion of functional equipment but instead to create a disposition of serenity, composure, and imperturbability. In this regard, the disappearance of obstinacy and malice in Heidegger's late philosophy—although not based in cathartic laughter—surprisingly resembles the two educational mottos of "Hulesch & Quenzel" (an organization that industrially produces malicious objects) from Doderer's *The Merowingians*: "POST RABIEM RISUS" and "Take it easy!"[96]

CHAPTER ONE

"When Things Move upon Bad Hinges"

Sterne and Stoicism

"Unhappy *Tristram*! child of wrath! child of decrepitude! interruption! mistake! and discontent!"

—LAURENCE STERNE, *Tristram Shandy*

"WHEN THINGS MOVE UPON BAD HINGES"

Laurence Sterne's novel *The Life and Opinions of Tristram Shandy, Gentleman*, published in nine volumes between 1759 and 1767, describes the life of its protagonist as constantly threatened by accidents. "I have been the continual sport of what the world calls Fortune," Tristram exclaims; "and though I will not wrong her by saying, She has ever made me feel the weight of any great or signal evil; — yet with all the good temper in the world, I affirm it of her, That in every stage of my life, and at every turn and corner where she could get fairly at me, the ungracious Duchess has pelted me with a set of as pitiful misadventures and cross accidents as ever small Hero sustained."[1] Falling and cutting, pelting and piercing objects perpetually disturb the everyday life in Shandy Hall. It unfolds in "one of the vilest worlds that ever was made" (10). This chapter attempts to analyze some of these disturbances to the bourgeois household as they relate to questions of the relationship between necessity and contingency, regularity and irregularity, wholeness and interruption, body and soul. What exactly is it that makes life for Tristram, Walter, Uncle Toby, and the other members of the Shandy household so vexing, and what strategies do they develop to cope with these vexations, irritations, and aggravations? The epistemological question "What is an object?" in *Tristram Shandy* cannot be separated from the anthropological investigation of how, as a human being, one can live in an environment populated with recalcitrant, accident-prone objects.

The rise of consumer society during the seventeenth and eighteenth centuries goes hand in hand with a considerable increase in the number of household items and other objects of everyday life.[2] The more tools, instruments, and gadgets populate the household, the more likely it is that the life of its human inhabitants will suffer from the breakdown and malfunction of these different pieces of equipment. The disruptions and catastrophes of the world (the earthquake of Lisbon 1755 took place only four years before the publication of the first two volumes of *Tristram Shandy*), and with them their disorienting, anxiety-inducing effects, reappear within the limited space of the household *en miniature*. The most famous example of this miniaturization and domestication is Uncle Toby's reenactment of the battles of the war between England and France in his backyard. Since skeptical Enlightenment philosophy radically questioned the security of all forms of religious and dogmatic worldviews, earthly disturbances could no longer be integrated into an overarching salvation plan. As part of the "secularization of accidents," the small world of Shandy Hall becomes the site for Sterne to present, perform, and stage the emotional effects of the contingency of the individual's *Lebenswelt*.[3]

One piece of equipment in Shandy Hall that constantly fails is the parlor door. Tristram uses this piece of furniture to teach a moral lesson and to exemplify Walter Shandy's philosophical principles and his rhetorical eloquence. "In mentioning the affair of door-hinges," he aims to show how Walter's "rhetoric and conduct were at perpetual handy-cuffs" (183). Life in Shandy Hall consists of a constant struggle between abstract principles and the concrete realities of everyday life. In response to the dysfunctional door hanging on bad hinges, the philosopher Walter experiences anxiety, pain, and melancholia. "His philosophy or his principles fall a victim" to the parlor door hinges (183). From this collision of philosophical principle and recalcitrant world Tristram learns to question whether systematically organized knowledge can produce pragmatic prescriptions for living well. Man's soul is "inconsistent," torn between reason and the unavoidable accidents of the quotidian:

> Inconsistent soul that man is!—languishing under wounds, which he has the power to heal!—his whole life a contradiction to his knowledge!—his reason, that precious gift of God to him—(instead of pouring in oyl) serving but to sharpen his sensibilities,—to multiply his pains and render him more melancholy and uneasy under

them!—poor unhappy creature, that he should do so!—are not the necessary causes of misery in this life enow, but he must add voluntary ones to his stock of sorrow; struggle against evils which cannot be avoided, and submit to others, which a tenth part of the trouble they create him, would remove from his heart for ever? (183)

Instead of eloquently reasoning on the nature of doors and hinges as practiced by Walter—"There was not a subject in the world upon which my father was so eloquent, as upon that of door-hinges" (182)—Tristram recommends "three drops of oyl with a feather, and a smart stroke of a hammer" (183). Despite all his eloquence and sharpened sensibility of reason, Walter is unable to cope with the mostly unnecessary annoyances of everyday life. In his resistance to repair the door hinges, he shows his whole life to stand in contradiction to his knowledge. Scholarly erudition does not lead to happiness but instead can multiply the stock of sorrows. Walter recognizes the faulty door, and "every day for at least ten years together did my father resolve to have it mended" (182). Yet his eloquent reasoning undermines proper action. His theoretical acumen does not solve any problems but diverts and consequently complicates matters, never arriving at a pragmatic solution or bringing a project to an end. Like his *Tristrapedia*, an encyclopedic attempt to provide a scholarly and theoretical foundation for the education of young Tristram, his plan to mend the door is never fully realized. Against this form of abstract reasoning that leads only to anguish and pain, Tristram suggests differentiating between those causes of anger that cannot be avoided and those that can be avoided. He does not simply apply the Stoic doctrine of *ataraxia*[4]—a passive, detached endurance—but calls for the active elimination of those sources of sorrow that lie within the subject's abilities. Tristram understands living the good life to consist in not struggling "against evils that cannot be avoided" and in removing the voluntary ones: "By all that is good and virtuous! if there are three drops of oyl to be got, and a hammer to be found within ten miles of Shandy-Hall,—the parlour-door hinge shall be mended this reign" (183). He promises to mend the door and hence heal the wounds and unhappiness caused by it. It would take only "three drops of oyl," a small amount of lubrication, to reduce friction among the hinge's parts and thereby to restore order and make things work properly again. The door, as the element that connects inside and outside, the realm of the Shandy family and that of the servants, of private and public, would function without creaks.

During the eighteenth and nineteenth centuries the increasing complexity of machines and their interaction with human users required equipment that could reduce friction and wear so as to make things work smoothly. Hence the rise of tribology as a *science of friction*. Tribology, as defined by Bharat Bhushan, is "the interdisciplinary science and technology of interacting surfaces in relative motion and associated subjects and practices."[5] "The most effective means of controlling friction and wear is by proper lubrication, which provides smooth running and satisfactory life for machine elements."[6] What oil is to the hinges, rhetorical affect control is to the social relations between the different members of the Shandy household. While lubrication eases the movement of tools, instruments, and mechanical gadgets in relation to each other, *technologies of the self* in the sense of Michel Foucault allow human beings to exist in an environment made up of inanimate objects as well as other human beings. The interaction of subjects and objects is threatened by the resistance of matter, appearing as friction and wear, possibly making things stick, breaking down movement and communication.

In Shandy Hall "things move upon bad hinges" (184), and the sound of the squeaking hinge that no one ever repairs wakes Walter just in time to discover that Trim has used Walter's jackboots to create two mortar pieces for Uncle Toby's fortification models. Furthermore, Walter's sleep—under constant threat of being disturbed—does not put his imagination to rest; he is permanently prevented from entering a state of peacefulness and tranquillity. Even during his sleep, imagination incessantly attacks and occupies Walter's body and mind: "He never folded his arms to take his nap after dinner, but the thoughts of being unavoidably awakened by the first person who should open the door, was always uppermost in his imagination, and so incessantly step'd in betwixt him and the first balmy presage of his repose, as to rob him, as he often declared, of the whole sweets of it" (184). In the form of the creaking door hinges the possibility of a contingent disturbance and interference appears. Consequently, Walter has to be on constant guard against the intrusive forces that might enter through the creaky door. Because Walter has not mended the hinges, as proposed by Tristram, he constantly anticipates the creaking door and thus remains restless and frustrated, always inventing new and different forms of protection and fortification against the "infirmities of ill health, and other evils of life" (3). The door, instead of protecting Walter's sleep, stirs his imagination.

In volume 4, chapter 7, however, Walter envisions "hidden resources" that allow human beings to cope with the irritating accidents of life: he remarks to Toby that "when one runs over the catalogue of all the cross reckonings and sorrowful items with which the heart of man is overcharged, 'tis wonderful by what hidden resources the mind is enabled to stand it out, and bear itself up, as it does against the impositions laid upon nature" (25). Walter, very much in the tradition of the Enlightenment, believes in the human being's ability to withstand and finally overcome nature's impositions by the exercise of reason. He rejects Toby's invocation of the power of religion in these matters, since this would equal "cutting the knot . . . instead of untying it" (250). The alternative of untying the knot involves slowly and analytically retracing the threads that lead to the causes of misery, thereby solving the "riddles" and "mysteries" of life. The act of untying reverses the temporal sequence of the original drawing up of the knot. The knot, as a result, must be connected to a cause, and the connection between cause and effect can be established only by analyzing the intricate makeup of that knot. In discussing the knots that make Dr. Slop's bag of instruments unusable, Tristram also notes the necessity of slowly and patiently untying them: "In the case of these knots then, and of the several obstructions, which, may it please your reverences, such knots cast in our way in getting through life—every hasty man can whip out his penknife and cut through them.—'Tis wrong. Believe me, Sirs, the most virtuous way, and which both reason and conscious dictate—is to take our teeth or our fingers to them" (151). Reason and virtue demand the slow undoing of the obstacles and disturbances of everyday life. Like knots, they need to be dissolved by a method of analytical disentanglement. Analysis attempts to separate and define the cause for every effect, priority and posteriority, by reducing chaotic contingencies to distinct and unequivocal determinations. It turns "accident into design."[7] Every knot, or obstacle, can be traced back to its moment of creation. And it is this knowledge of cause and effect, excluding any accidental occurrences, that allows human beings to overcome all obstacles and disturbances.

But while Tristram grounds his morals in virtue, reason, and practical knowledge, Walter, after rejecting Toby's belief in the redemptive powers of religion, surprisingly depicts the "hidden resources of the mind" as a "secret spring" (251). He represents the faculty of the human mind that can cope with the many causes of trouble as a purely mechanical device. It merely absorbs the shocks, thereby "counterbalancing" evil forces: "But the spring I am speaking of, is that great and elastic power within us of counterbalancing evil, which like a secret spring in a well-ordered machine, though it can't prevent the shock—at least it imposes upon our sense of it" (251). Man equals an elastic machine, absorbing the shocks of the real. What is lacking in this concept of the shock-absorbing secret spring within us is the possibility of differentiating between necessary and unnecessary evils or the rational analysis of its causes as proposed by Tristram. In Walter's vision of the human mind as a secret spring, there is no reason and no element of rational choice. Each shock—from the smallest irritation to the greatest catastrophe—is dealt with in the same mechanical way. In effect, Walter is not untying the knots but, much like Toby with his faith in God, cutting them by not paying attention to the heterogeneity of the "catalogue of all the cross reckonings and sorrowful items with which the heart of man is overcharged" (250). In passive reception and springlike absorption, Walter fails, at least in Tristram's view, to actively change the conditions of his existence. He endures—depending on the elasticity of his mind—more or less dispassionately, but none of his calculations provide protection from the shocks of an antagonistic environment. Instead, his success in existing happily lies in a mechanized application of learned and merely recited knowledge. Walter does not perceive the uniqueness of any given disturbance; rather, he immediately relates and explains its occurrence by quoting a philosophical or scientific authority. He thereby effectively erases its singularity and avoids reckoning with contingency.[8] Even the greatest accidents and disasters can easily be integrated into Walter's stable system of knowledge.

The metaphor of the spring and the machine reappear in the description of the Shandy family as a whole: "Though in one sense, our family was certainly a simple machine, as it consisted of a few wheels; yet there was thus much to be said for it, that these wheels were strange principles and impulses,—that though it was a simple machine, it had all the honour and advantages of a complex one,— and a number of as odd movements within it, as ever were beheld in the inside of a Dutch silk-mill" (323). It is exactly the door with bad hinges that turns the seemingly simple machine of Tristram's family into a complex one. The springs of "strange principles and impulses," situated in this passage between parlor and kitchen, do not work properly. Bad hinges leave the door "somewhat a-jar" (323), neither fully open nor closed, and thereby allowing for sudden disruptions and misunderstandings. The door, "intersecting access and closure," contradicts the French proverb that a door is either open or closed.[9] When the door is ajar, it is open but not open enough to let a person through, and not closed enough to block out unwanted entry or exit, leaving only voices and sounds to pass through. The governing of the house rests on a fault, the slight opening of a passage, which creates "a number of . . . odd movements within," leaving it entirely ambiguous who the real head of the household is. The door can control neither the passage of bodies nor that of sounds, complicating the distinction between inside and outside, the real and the imaginary: "In its nature, the door belongs to the symbolic order, and it opens up either on to the real, or the imaginary, we don't know quite which."[10]

In the crooked architecture of Shandy Hall, the door moving upon bad hinges functions as a passage between parlor and kitchen, the realm of the head of the household and the realm of the servants. The dysfunctional door creaks and never fully closes: "'Twas the rule to leave the door, not absolutely shut, but somewhat a-jar—as it stands just now,—which, under covert of the bad hinge, (and that possibly might be one of the many reasons why it was never mended) it was not difficult to manage; by which means, in all these cases, a passage was generally left, not indeed as wide as the Dardanells, but wide enough, for all that, to carry on as much of this windward trade, as was sufficient to save my father the trouble of governing his house" (323). The bad hinges (mis)manage the opening of a passage through which the kitchen can partake in the governing decisions of the parlor room. "Any thing worth knowing or listening to" (i.e., every thought of Walter under discussion) is being noticed and commented upon in the realm of the kitchen, where his wife and the servants rule: "Whatever motion, debate, harangue, dialogue, project, or dissertation, was going forwards in the parlour, there was generally another at the same time, and upon the same subject, running along parallel along with it in the kitchen" (323). The most prominent and sorrowful of these discussions deals with the death of Tristram's brother Bobby. After delivering the fatal letter imparting Bobby's death to his master, Obadiah walks through the passage of the parlor door into the kitchen and distributes the sad news among the gathered servants. Obadiah's delivery is only one of several intrusions through the slightly opened door that permanently interrupt Walter's efforts to calculate a journey's expenses, provoking a "mixed motion betwixt accident and anger" (315). Opening the door again and again, Obadiah—as the messenger of bad and irritating news—*attacks* the poorly guarded parlor of the household's head. While on the one hand the doors allows the servants to listen in and for information to leak out, on the other it simultaneously opens the parlor to the contingencies of the outside world.

Questions of position, placement, and orientation recur in Tristram's rejection of Descartes's theory of the pineal gland as the organ that mysteriously bridges mind and body, as well as Borri's placement of the soul within the liquid of the cerebellum. Walter, and consequently Tristram, agree with the Dutch anatomists who define the location of the soul within the body not as a place but as a square: "What, therefore, seem'd the least liable to objections of any, was, that the chief sensorium, or head-quarters of the soul, and to which place all intelligence were referred, and from whence all her mandates were issued,—was in, or near, the cerebellum, — or rather somewhere about the *medulla oblongata*, wherein it was generally agreed by Dutch anatomists, that all the minute nerves from all the organs of the seven senses centered, like streets and winding alleys, into a square" (132). To locate the soul in one singular place overlooks its "streets and winding alleys," its various dimensions, constituting an "incomprehensible contexture in which wit, fancy, eloquence . . . do consist" (132). Space is not a well-ordered grid of rectangular directions but a textured web resembling the crooked, winding streets of a city. It is slanted and uneven, slightly deviating from straight paths and right angles. Like a garment, the place of the soul, origin of wit, fancy, and eloquence, makes up a "delicate and fine-spun web" (133). Delicacy of thinking and speaking can be achieved only by protecting the "infinitely fine and tender texture of the cerebellum" (133). This protection consists of filling gaps by pulling together single threads that tend to break or displace the whole of the network. Otherwise the integrity of the "intellectual web" is threatened and it appears to be "rent and tatter'd" (134). In preserving and protecting the complex intellectual web from accidental piercings and perforations, man can avoid appearing as a "puzzled skein of silk,—all perplexity,—all confusion within side" (134). Walter Shandy, elaborating on the philosophy of Zeno and Chrysippus, explains: "Error, Sir, creeps in thro' the minute-holes, and small crevices, which human nature leaves unguarded" (130).

One method of defending oneself against the attacks of a malicious environment consists in maintaining a sturdy, protective barrier around the human body. Proper clothing, in this context, is not only a sign of proper decorum; it also guards the interior against hostile, exterior forces. The protection of Phutatorius's clothing, for example, is breached because of a "neglect of . . . punctilio," a gap in his breeches. The infamous hot chestnut enters via "that particular aperture, which in all good societies, the laws of decorum do strictly require, like the temple of Janus (in peace at least) to be universally shut up. The neglect of this punctilio in Phutatorius (which by the bye should be a warning to all mankind) had opened a door to this accident" (288). Neglecting proper decorum opens the door to accidents; it allows the breeches to be breached. If Phutatorius had followed the rules of decency and clothed himself according to the laws of decorum—had he drawn or buttoned up his breeches—the hot chestnut could not have penetrated his attire and hurt his genitals. Missing the proper protection opens breaches and the possibility of being afflicted by even small trifles.

Holes in garments, breaches in breeches, gaps in decor and decorum invite the penetration and consequently destruction of the moral, intellectual, and emotional equilibrium of the human being. Tristram's description of Phutatorius's reaction to the small chestnut further elaborates on the trifle as a passionate disturbance of the mind's composure: "It is curious to observe the triumph of slight incidents over the mind:—What incredible weight they have in forming and governing our opinions, both of men and things,—that trifles light as air, shall waft a belief into the soul, and plant it so Immoveably within it, that Euclid's demonstrations, could they be brought to batter it in breach, should not at all have power to overthrow it" (290). The triumph of slight and minute disturbances over the subject's rational mind is typical for many comical representations of the contingent and accidental in relation to necessity, as David Wellbery points out: "No representation of contingency can dispense with this topos: The smallest perturbation has the greatest effect."[11] The smallest trifle causing the greatest pain exemplifies the human's inability to connect highly significant events with seemingly insignificant causes. This perceived disproportion between a slight incident and its often overwhelming consequences not only allows for comically overestimating the small but also for ridiculing the great. Even Euclid's geometry cannot be protected from the intrusions of things moving in unpredictable curves, influencing one's opinions about the nature of things. Nothing can prevent something slight from becoming a slight. Therefore, one cannot live the good life merely by establishing and applying abstract ethical theories; these doctrines must prove their value in the altercations and contentions with the minute vexations of everyday life. The good life requires attention to the small and neglected that can at any minute attack the physical and psychological integrity of the human being. According to Juliet McMaster, Sterne "is always seeking the right metaphor for the relation of mind and body, one that will not convey simple equivalence, but the discontinuities and contiguities of flesh and spirit."[12] Through the metaphors of skin, clothes, and covers, the precarious dialectics of connection and discontinuity, unity and disruption, essence and accident comes to the fore. Throughout the novel, its main figures discuss as well as practice different modes of protecting the fragile human body from adverse influences. As Brian Michael Norton comments, "Sterne employs sartorial metaphors to illustrate his characters' never-ending struggles to shield themselves from external evils. The novel speaks of buttoning and unbuttoning vexations, and of being 'hemm'd in' by distress."[13]

In volume 4, chapter 4, Tristram addresses the readers as follows: "A man's body and his mind, with the utmost reverence to both I speak it, are exactly like a jerkin, and a jerkin's lining;—rumple the one—you rumple the other. There is one certain exception however in this case, and that is, when you are so fortunate a fellow, as to have your jerkin made of a gum-taffeta, and the body-lining to it, of a sarcenet or thin Persian" (144). For Tristram, in this passage there is a direct connection between body and soul just as there is a direct connection between the jerkin—a type of jacket—and its inner lining. Only when the jerkin is made of gum-taffeta (so that it is stiff on the outside) and its lining made of sarcenet (so that it is flexible on the inside) does the garment function as a protective cover for the delicate and frail human body. In another section, the narrator Tristram lists a number of "*Shandean* people," among them Zeno, Cato, Varro, Seneca, Pantenus, and Montaigne, whose constitution is that of a jerkin made of gum-taffeta with a sarcenet lining, combining stiffness and flexibility. Their stoic appearance is based on their ability to be steadfast and unwavering on the outside and elastic on the inside: "Shandean people . . . all pretended that their jerkins were made after this fashion,—you might have rumpled and crumpled, and doubled and creased, and fretted and fridged the outsides of them all to pieces,—in short, you might have played the very devil with them, and at the same time, not one of the insides of 'em would have been one button the worse, for all you had done to them" (144–45). The choice of mostly Stoic philosophers as examples of a *Shandean* mode of dealing with the vexing attacks of the real shows that for Sterne questions of epistemology such as the Cartesian mind-body dichotomy cannot be separated from ethical questions regarding the possibility of living the good life. Not only the greatest representatives of Stoic philosophy but also "good honest, unthinking, Shandean people" have devised strategies to protect the inside from the outside and not be perturbed by accidental and contingent occurrences. Like a jerkin made of gum-taffeta or a machine with secret springs, members of the Shandy family like Walter and Uncle Toby are able to absorb shocks mechanically, unthinkingly. They are simultaneously rigid and flexible, thereby appearing to be ridiculous and serious at the same time. It is this automatic, unreflective reaction that, following Henri Bergson's theory of the comic, makes them appear ridiculous but nonetheless guarantees their steadfastness and resolve in the face of pain and sorrow.[14]

ZOUNDS! PHUTATORIUS'S BREECHES

One mode of coping with passions aroused by unruly and recalcitrant objects consists in cursing. This section and the next will examine two instances of this form of speech act: Phutarius's outcry "ZOUNDS!" in volume 4, chapter 27, and Dr. Slop's recitation of the curse of Ernulphus in volume 3, chapter 11. In both cases Sterne, by establishing the connection of rhetorical devices and Stoic programs of self-government, asks how one can govern oneself and one's passions in the face of an unruly, recalcitrant environment. "Cursing has the capacity," according to Kate E. Brown and Howard I. Kushner, "to sponsor fantasies of immunity to circumstance."[15] Therefore, the speech act of the curse functions as a specific *technology of the self*. *Tristram Shandy*, like several other literary and philosophical texts of the eighteenth century, is "concerned with self-improvement or self-formation. In that sense, [it] continued the tradition of the spiritual exercise in an increasingly secular guise."[16] In the last lines of volume 4, chapter 26, Tristram interrupts his description of a conversation between Yorick and Didius on the proper preaching of the Gospel, warning the reader of a word that he, the author, is ashamed to write down. This "illegal" and "uncanonical" word, which nevertheless "must be written—must be read" (286), appears at the beginning of the chapter: "ZOUNDS!" This "word of all others in the dictionary the last in that place to be expected" (286) was a common oath of the eighteenth century, a contraction of the phrase "God's wounds," referring to Christ's wounds on the cross. "ZOUNDS" is followed by a long dash, covering two and a half lines, before the word is repeated in a slightly modified version: "Z-ds!" The contraction *Zounds,* used to avoid formally swearing and uttering the name of the Lord in vain, is further transformed into a word split by a dash, hiding its profanity without becoming unreadable. Must this mutilation be interpreted as Tristram's attempt to adhere to the rules of decency and decorum? The Profane Oaths Act of 1746, after all, threatened penalties for swearing in public.[17] Why, one could ask, does Sterne use capital letters and no dash in the first utterance, while in the second he uses a dash, as if to hide its profane nature? Is the second exclamation just a repetition of the first, and is the person uttering the oath "ZOUNDS!" the same as the one who cries out, "Z-ds!"? The beginning of chapter 27 reads as follows: "ZOUNDS! --------- ------------------ Z-ds! cried Phutatorius, partly to himself—and yet high enough to be heard—and what seemed odd, 'twas uttered in a construction of look, and in a tone of voice, somewhat between that of a man in amazement, and of one in bodily pain" (286). It seems difficult to integrate "ZOUNDS!" into the context of the narration because it remains unclear who utters the word. The long dash between the curses simultaneously connects and separates. If the dash is read in its connecting function, "ZOUNDS!" and "Z-ds!" are both spoken by the same person (Phutatorius), but if the dash is read as a paratextual marker of separation, both utterances do not have the same origin. Maybe it is not Phutatorius but Tristram pronouncing "ZOUNDS!," cursing the task of having to write a curse: the curse of having to write a curse word creates such vexation in the narrator that he "forgets" the rules of decorum and the Profane Oaths Act and utters the oath without any covering, "point blank" (286). The long dash would thus mark the difference between two levels of narration, between the cursing figure (Phutatorius) and the narrator relating the curse of Phutatorius. Émile Benveniste argues, in "La blasphémie et l'euphémie," that blasphemy cannot, as the essay's title indicates, be separated from euphemism.[18] The blasphemous character of swearing by God's wounds is simultaneously highlighted and erased by the euphemistic abbreviation of "God's wounds" to "Zounds" and further to "Z-ds." Blasphemous cursing and its euphemistic veiling in

Tristram Shandy are inextricably intertwined. The act of uncovering and laying bare cannot be separated from its immediate covering. The contraction "Z-ds" allows the curse to be written without becoming indecent. It represents the discreet translation of the spoken curse of everyday life into the written language of literature.

After Phutatorius's identification as the one who utters "Z-ds!," Tristram reports on the various interpretations that the sound "Z-ds!" induces. The first explanation, proposed by "one or two who had very nice ears" (286), focuses on the tone of voice, unsuccessfully reading the "Z-ds!" as a musical expression. In this analysis, Phutatorius's interjection, pronounced "somewhat between that of a man in amazement, and of one in bodily pain" (286), is perceived as a "mixture of the two tones as plainly as a third or a fifth, or any other chord in musick" (286). But although the "two tones" can be clearly distinguished, they are "quite out of key, and no way applicable to the subject started;—so that with all their knowledge, they [the musical critics] could not tell what in the world to make of it" (286). Knowledge of tone and voice does not provide enough information to make sense of "Z-ds!" Differing from this purely acoustic interpretation, other members of the dinner party perceive "Z-ds!" not merely as a sound but as a meaningful word. For them, "who knew nothing of musical expression, and merely lent their ears to the plain import of the word" (286), Phutatorius's exclamation marks the beginning of a speech, "the exordium to an oration" (286) supporting Didius's attack on Yorick.

The lack of a continuing speech after the exordium leads to another possible elucidation. According to this interpretation, the oath "Z-ds!" is voiced without intent. It is "no more than an involuntary respiration, casually forming itself into the shape of a twelve-penny oath—without the sin or substance of one" (286). Therefore, it is not a curse in the strict sense but a sheer bodily manifestation, an "involuntary respiration," which therefore has no content. Void of meaning, Phutatorius's outcry of "Z-ds!," understood as a mere interjection, randomly coincides with a twelve-penny oath. "Z-ds!" as an empty signifier lacks intention and thus does not fall under the category of punishable public swearing.

Other listeners at the table, in contradistinction, identify "Z-ds!" as a meaningful curse directed against Yorick: "Others, and especially one or two who sat next to him [Phutatorius], looked upon it on the contrary, as a real and substantial oath propensly formed against

Yorick" (287). "Z-ds!," according to this interpretation, is neither a musical expression, nor the exordium to an oration, nor an involuntary respiration, but an oath directed against a specific person. The cause for its utterance is Phutatorius's dislike of Yorick in general and his theory of preaching in particular. The oath "lay fretting and fuming at that very time in the upper regions of Phutatorius's purtenance; and so was naturally, and according to the due course of things, first squeezed out by the sudden influx of blood, which was driven into the right ventricle of Phutatorius's heart, by the stroke of surprise which so strange a theory of preaching had excited" (287). This passage proposes a quasi-medical explanation for the curse of Phutatorius. The concept of a "real" and "substantial" oath positions it as a part of the human body that follows the laws of circulation of bodily fluids. "Z-ds!" is flushed out of the body by blood rushing into the heart. As an oath it has a material reality that is affected by the physiological changes of the human body. Surprised and excited by Yorick's sermon, Phutatorius's body reacts and expresses the oath in the literal sense of the word. Substance in this context is conceived as a form of matter, not as the semantic content of the signifier *Z-ds!* What makes the oath "real" and "substantial" is its cathartic materiality that follows the due "course of things" in physical reality. Excitation manifests itself in increased blood pressure, driving out the "fretting and fuming" oath. Cursing happens naturally and cleanses the body of angry, vexing elements. Benveniste, in a similar fashion, stresses the pure "emotional discharge" taking place in blasphemy: blasphemy "does not communicate any message, it does not start a dialogue, it does not provoke a response."[19] It constitutes an "eruptive voice,"[20] a foreign body within the human purtenance.

In the recent study *The Sacrament of Language: An Archaeology of the Oath*, conceptualized as a part of *Homo Sacer*, Giorgio Agamben relates the curse to a specific type of speech act that is void of meaning. Taking up Benveniste's analysis of blasphemy, originating in mere interjections, Agamben observes a split between words and things in the act of cursing: "If the connection that unites language and the world is broken, the name of God, which expressed and guaranteed this connection based in blessing [bene-dicente], becomes the name of the curse [male-dizione], that is, of a word that has broken its truthful relation to things.... The name of God, released from the signifying connection, becomes blasphemy, vain meaning becomes available for improper and evil uses."[21] Curses like "Zounds," for example, "constitute not a semantic element but rather a purely semiotic one."[22] They become empty signifiers, resembling interjections and exclamations. Agamben quotes Benveniste: "As he [Benveniste] writes, 'blasphemy manifests itself as an exclamation and has the syntax of interjection, of which it constitutes the most typical variety.' Like every exclamation, blasphemy also is a 'word that one "lets slip out" under the pressure of a sudden and violent emotion.'"[23] In a direct address to his readers on the purpose of his writing, Tristram points out the cathartic qualities of laughter. As a physiological process of purging the body of unhealthy passions, laughing resembles cursing: "If 'tis wrote against any thing,—'tis wrote, an' please your worships, against the spleen; in order, by a more frequent and a more convulsive elevation and depression of the diaphragm, and the succussations of the intercostals and abdominal muscles in laughter, to drive the *gall* and other *bitter juices* from the gall bladder, liver and sweet-bread of his majesty's subjects, with all the inimicitous passions which belong to them, down into their duodenums" (271).[24] Sterne uses the same verbs *fretting* and *fuming* to describe Phutatorius's and Tristram's psycho-physiological disposition. From a merely physiological point of view, curses serve the same function as laughter. They both work "against the spleen." Eruptive laughter, like the curse, allows for a purging of the body and the reestablishment of its humoral as well as its emotional balance.

Walter Shandy, who puts forward the speculation on the physiological origins of cursing, explicitly refers to the classical model of humors, claiming distinct physiological causes for human emotions. An imbalance between the four different bodily fluids, blood, phlegm, black bile, and yellow bile, is responsible not only for diseases of the body but also for mental instabilities and illnesses. In this view, it is the prevalence of yellow bile that defines the choleric character. Roy Porter has pointed out that in the field of life sciences the tradition of the theory of temperaments was, despite the rise of the "New Science," still very much standard knowledge throughout the eighteenth century.[25]

In contrast to the varying explanations of Phutatorius's exclamation "Z-ds!," Tristram asserts that the "true cause" (287) has nothing to do with the argument about Yorick's theory of preaching but lies "at least a yard below" (287). What for the observer appears to be an interpolation into the ongoing conversation between Yorick and Didius,—"and indeed he looked first towards the one, and then towards the other, with the air of a man listening to what was going forwards" (287)—is really caused by an accident that requires "all imaginable decency" (287) and knowledge of the "laws of decorum" (288) to describe: a hot chestnut falling into Phutatorius's breeches and the consequent injury to his genitals:

> But the truth was, that Phutatorius knew not one word or one syllable of what was passing—but his whole thoughts and attention were taken up with a transaction which was going forwards at that very instant within the precincts of his own Galligaskins, and in a part of them, where of all others he stood most interested to watch accidents: So, that notwithstanding he looked with all the attention in the world, and had gradually skrewed up every nerve and muscle in his face, to the utmost pitch the instrument would bear, in order, as it was thought, to give a sharp reply to Yorick, who sat over-against him—Yet I say, was Yorick never once in any one domicile of Phutatorius's brain—but the true cause of his exclamation lay at least a yard below. (287)

Phutatorius's outburst of rage must be traced not only to the physical intrusion of the chestnut into the breeches but also to the psychological process it triggers within Phutatorius's mind. While the warmth of the chestnut is gradually changing to painful heat, Phutatorius's attention is drawn toward the origin of this perception. But his intellectual abilities are unable to determine the cause of his pain: "With the best intelligence . . . Phutatorius was not able to dive into the secret of what was going forwards below, not could he make any kind of conjecture, what the devil was the matter with it" (289). Despite this ignorance regarding the true causes of pain, Phutatorius, like a Stoic, decides to bear it without showing any signs of perturbation. Within the context of the assembled members of the dinner party, he deems it prudent not to breach social decorum by displaying his pain directly. But this doctrine of Stoic imperturbability fails, since the "sallies of imagination" disturb Phutatorius's mind:

> However, as he knew not what the true cause might turn out, he deemed it most prudent, in the situation he was in at the present, to bear it, if possible, like a stoick; which, with the help of some wry faces and compursions of the mouth, he had certainly accomplished, had his imagination continued neuter—but the sallies of imagination are ungovernable in things of this kind—a thought instantly darted into his mind, that tho' the anguish had the sensation of a glowing heat—it might, notwithstanding that, be a bite as well as a burn; and so, that possibly a Newt or an Asker, or some such detested reptile, had crept up and was fastening his teeth. (289)

The ungovernable powers of imagination threaten the ability to bear pain stoically. It is not merely the physical sensation of the hot chestnut that causes anger but the imagination's attempts to uncover the true cause of pain. As Jonathan Lamb points out: "Phutatorius' imagination is incapable of staying neutral; it must fasten an image to the sensation."[26] A "thought darted" into Phutatorius's mind, turning the "anguish" of the "glowing heat" into a feeling of a "bite as well as a burn." Imagination personifies the pain—it ascribes an agent, in this case a newt or an asker. Already Aristotle in the *Rhetoric* defines anger in terms of a connection between a physical disturbance and an intellectual assent. Martha Nussbaum reconstructs Aristotle's discussion of anger in terms of the difference between appearance and belief.[27] She argues that "emotions have a rich cognitive structure. . . . They are not mindless surges of affect, but discerning ways of viewing objects."[28] For an impression, like that of heat, to become a feeling, "an element of conviction and acceptance" is required.[29] Passions are defined as cognitive responses to physical impressions.

Controlling anger, for Aristotle as well as the Stoics, consists in one's ability to govern and mediate the way the mind handles physical disturbances. Not coincidentally, the frontispiece of the second edition of the first two volumes of *Tristram Shandy* famously quotes as a motto the *Enchiridion* of the Stoic philosopher Epictetus: "We are tormented with the opinions we have of things, and not by things themselves" (599). The real causes of torment and anguish are opinions,[30] which, in the case of Phutatorius, appear to be ungovernable, thereby calling into question the main argument of the Stoics' concept of anger management. As Nussbaum notes: "What is stressed is the fact that it is the way things are seen by the agent, not the fact of the matter, that is instrumental in getting emotions going. Intentionality, not absence of commitment, is the issue."[31] For Aristotle and the Stoics, the mind intentionally assents to the impression, giving it meaning and causing anger to rise. Therefore the temperate man refuses this assent to the physical sensation he or she experiences. In the case of Phutatorius, this assent is not given consciously; rather, the "sallies of imagination" dart into his mind instantaneously. A sudden, uncontrollable rush that—very much like wit, which according to Locke represents an "irrational combination of ideas" quickly draws together the impression with a possible meaning.[32] For Phutatorius, the pain is caused not by heat but by the bite of an adversary reptile. Since anger cannot be directed against a physiological impression, he needs to determine a responsible agent. Who or what is behind his pain? If anger by Aristotle's definition is a "longing . . . for a real or apparent revenge for a real or apparent slight, affecting a man himself or one of his friends, when such a slight is undeserved," then it is necessary to determine what the slight is and who is responsible for it.[33] In the case of Phutatorius, the "sallies of imagination" intervene and provide a cause and an agent (a newt or an asker), upon which he can project a future revenge. What he feels is not simply heat but the bite of a malicious reptile.

The desire to determine the true cause of an event also appears with regard to whether the fall of the hot chestnut into the open breeches of Phutatorius was accidental or represented a judgment, an avenging punishment for the publication of his obscene treatise *de Concubinis retinendis*. In discussing this matter, Tristram states:

> Accident, I call it, in compliance to a received mode of speaking,— but in no opposition to the opinion either of Acrites or Mythogeras in this matter; I know they were both prepossessed and fully persuaded of it—and are so to this hour, That there was nothing of accident in the whole event—but that the chestnut's taking this particular course, and in a manner of its own accord—and then falling with all its heat directly into that one particular place, and no other—was a real judgment upon Phutatorius, for that filthy and obscene treatise *de Concubinis retinendis*, which Phutatorius had published about twenty years ago—and was that identical week going to give the world a second edition of. (288)

It is impossible for the narrator Tristram to decide between accident and judgment, although by mentioning the imaginary philosophers Acrites and Mythogeras, who defend the event's necessity, he shows his skepticism toward the possibility of explaining the fall of the chestnut as punishment for Phutatorius's obscenity. According to Joan and Melvyn New's notes, the philosopher's names Acrites and Mythogeras translate as "confused, undiscriminating" and "tale-bearer" (668). Hence the interpretation of the particular course of the chestnut as revenge for an earlier slight is ridiculed as that of confused, undiscriminating talebearers. It is a *mythos*, a story, created by the "sallies of imagination," that Phutatorius's breach of decorum was the cause of the breach of his breeches. Philosophy and science, as modes of reason attempting to eliminate the accidental by determining a cause for every event, appear ridiculous. They represent forms of confused, undiscriminating talebearing. For the philosopher nothing happens without a reason—there is no contingency and no such thing as an accident—so, according to David Hume, "in this respect he might be compar'd to those angels, whom the scripture represents as covering their eyes with their wings."[34] Tristram describes as a natural impulse the desire to search for explanations and causes in dealing with the contingencies of reality: "When great or unexpected events fall out upon the stage of this sublunary world—the mind of man, which is an inquisitive kind of a substance, naturally takes a flight, behind the scenes, to see what is the cause and first spring of them" (290–91).

Tristram denounces this ascription of "mystical meaning" (291) as being as "groundless as the dreams of philosophy" (291). For him, there is no ground for the breach of breeches and no secret intention to the slight incident. Belief in an agency behind the scenes of the sublunary world of man is merely a dream. It is a confused and undiscriminating worldview, founded in an inability to differentiate between reality and imagination. As in myth, man's inquisitive mind looks for hidden causes, thereby projecting meaning and intention onto natural objects and "turning accident into design."[35] What otherwise seemed random and chaotic now appears caused and ordered by a transcendent agency. Life becomes bearable, and its contingencies, if not controllable, at least interpretable.[36]

When Yorick picks up the chestnut, he does so only because it is a piece of food that should not be wasted, but Phutatorius interprets his action differently:

> Yorick, I said, picked up the chestnut which Phutatorius's wrath had flung down—the action was trifling—I am ashamed to account for it—he did it, for no reason, but that he thought the chestnut not a jot worse for the adventure—and that he held a good chestnut worth stooping for.—But this incident, trifling as it was, wrought differently in Phutatorius's head: He considered this act of Yorick's, in getting off his chair, and picking up the chestnut, as a plain acknowledgment in him, that the chestnut was originally his, —and in course, that it must have been the owner of the chestnut, and no one else, who could have plaid him such a prank with it. (290)

Phutatorius's inability to cope with slight, trifling incidents "like a stoick" stems from ungovernable opinions. For him, opinions are like "sallies of imagination" constantly threatening to invade the mind, breaking down its defenses against hostile attacks. Not only are his breeches not properly buttoned up, but his mind is also vulnerable to disturbing, ungovernable opinions: "the horrid idea" that the hot chestnut is actually an aggressive reptile, along with a fresh glow of pain arising that instant from the chestnut, seized Phutatorius with a sudden panick, and in the first terrifying disorder of the passion it threw him, as it has done the best generals upon earth, quite off his guard" (289). The Stoic governs his passions and his opinions like a general, fending off all possible disturbances of his emotional equilibrium, but Phutatorius, who is "somewhat of a cholerick spirit," fails in this form of defending himself. His upper region, at the time considered to be the site of the rational part of man, is "empty as a purse" (289).[37] Hence he is unable to rule over his lower part, from where his passions originate. The poorly protected openness of his mind, under constant attack by the "sallies of imagination," is not guarded by judgment, resolution, or deliberation.[38] Phutatorius is unable to keep wit (imagination) and judgment in balance, instead letting his ideas about the origin of the pain run their irregular and uncontrolled course.

ERNULPHUS'S CURSE: THE INSTITUTE OF SWEARING

Walter Shandy retraces the genealogy of all "oaths and imprecations" (165) to one original curse. It is an extract from *The Book of the Church of Rochester through Bishop Ernulf [Textus de Ecclesia Roffensi per Ernulphum Episcopum]*, written between 1122 and 1124:

> I will undertake to prove, that all the oaths and imprecations, which we have been puffing off upon the world for these two hundred and fifty years last past, as originals,—except St. Paul's *thumb,—God's flesh and God's fish*, which were oaths monarchical, and, considering who made them, not much amiss; and as kings oaths, 'tis not much matter whether they were fish or flesh;—else, I say, there is not an oath, or at least a curse amongst them, which has not been copied over and over again out of Ernulphus, a thousand times: but, like all other copies, how infinitely short of force and spirit of the original! (165)

Curses are not inventions but quotations. Whoever utters a curse or an oath repeats and reenacts a preceding one. Since Ernulphus, all curses are nothing but copies, lacking the original "force and spirit." By referring to the force of Ernulphus's curse, Walter points toward the performative character of all curses. Ernulphus's speech represents "a formal ecclesiastical censure or anathema: a sentence of excommunication."[39] In curses, as in oaths, maledictions, and excommunications, words perform a certain action. According to Brown and Kushner, "Cursing takes the form of malediction (*male* [badly] + *dicere* [to speak]), a category of speech that makes an unusually powerful claim for the efficacy of utterance. Like blessings or marriage vows, the malediction is what J. L. Austin calls a performative speech act."[40] When the malediction is domesticated through its transfer from the realm of theology into that of everyday life, cursing loses its performative efficacy as a sacred speech act.[41]

For Walter, Ernulphus's anathema is nothing but a collection of all laws of swearing. It constitutes an "institute of swearing, in which, as he [Walter Shandy] suspected, upon the decline of swearing in some milder pontificate, *Ernulphus*, by the order of the succeeding pope, had with great learning and diligence collected together all the laws of it" (165). Already the original curse of Ernulphus is a collection and compendium of earlier practices of swearing. Not only does Walter ironically refer to Quintilian's *Institutio Oratoria*, but he also compares Ernulphus's *Textus Roffensis* to Justinian's codification of Roman law. According to Walter, Ernulphus collected the laws of swearing "for the same reason that *Justinian*, in the decline of the empire, had ordered his chancellor *Tribonian* to collect the *Roman* or civil laws all together into one code or digest,—lest through the rust of time,—and the fatality of all things committed to oral tradition, they should be lost to the world for ever" (165).

Ernulphus's *Textus Roffensis* resembles a digest, recording and preserving an oral tradition in writing. Cursing after Ernulphus, which, for Walter is always an act of speaking, consists of the act of returning the maledictory utterance back into the realm of the spoken word. Brown and Kushner point out the crucial role of the voice in acts of maledictory cursing: "Like maledictory and coprolalic eruptions, then, curse words are not owned but are only *voiced* by the speaker. In vocalizing them, we lay claim to the word's autonomy, thus disavowing the circumstances that have rendered us helpless or ridiculous."[42] The curse always transcends the intentions of the one who curses; there is something "unattributable to any autonomous speaking self. The voice becomes eruptive rather than expressive, something that *happens to* a subject."[43] Every curse uttered comes from somewhere else, from a time and place that is not proper to the subject. For Walter, everyone who curses simply quotes from Ernulphus; thus his or her speech act lacks originality.[44] Nonetheless, he and Toby insist that Dr. Slop recite Ernulphus's curse in full. But while in the ecclesiastical tradition a malediction was used to avenge a sin or a malfeasance, Walter Shandy uses the curse for purely medical, that is cathartic, purposes:

> They [curses] serve, continued my father, to stir the humours—but carry off none of their acrimony:—for my own part, I seldom swear or curse at all—I hold it bad—but if I fall into it, by surprise, I generally retain so much presence of mind (right, quoth my uncle *Toby*) as to make it answer my purpose—that is, I swear on, till I find myself easy. A wise and a just man however would always endeavour to proportion the vent given to these humours, not only to the degree of them stirring within himself—but to the size and ill intent of the offence upon which they are to fall. (151–52)

Walter uses swearing to vent his angry humors. Coleridge uses the same metaphor of venting to explain the speech act of swearing. For him, curses function as "escape-valves to carry off the excess of . . . passions, as so much superfluous steam that would endanger the vessel if it were retained."[45] Humans and steam engines work in similar ways, insofar as the danger of high pressure and passionate imbalance needs to be contained for the whole body/machine to function properly. The psychologist G. T. W. Patrick, in a 1901 article entitled "The Psychology of Profanity," also stresses the venting, that is, cathartic, function of curses. He comes to conclusions similar to those of Sterne and Coleridge: "We are thus able to account for the 'katharsis' phenomenon of profanity. It seems to serve as a vent only in the sense that it brings to an end the intolerable period of inner conflict, of attempted inhibition, of repression and readjustment."[46]

As for most cathartic models of venting anger (and laughter), there is an inherent paradox in Walter Shandy's model of the curse as a method to achieve a state of emotional equilibrium. On the one hand, Walter conceptualizes the curse as a quasi-automatic, physiological discharge of humors. On the other hand, it requires the reason and wisdom of a "just man." Cursing belongs simultaneously to the lower realm of the passions and the corporeal and to the higher realm of the rational mind. Paul Ricoeur, discussing "the epistemological problem in Freudianism," works in the context of psychoanalysis to discuss a tension between an energetic and a hermeneutical mode of explanation in Freud. He asks: "What is the status of representation or ideas in relation to the notions of instinct, aim of instinct, and affect?"[47] Cursing, as Walter Shandy discusses it, oscillates in a similar fashion between an explanation of anger stressing the representational character of emotions and an explanation focusing on its physiological aspects. How, in the case of Walter Shandy's model, can one simultaneously "stir the humours" and "retain so much presence of mind . . . as to make it answer" one's "purpose"? How can one vent in the right proportion to the occasion without a breach of decorum? How does a "just man" vent his anger?

For Walter Shandy, one way of overcoming this tension between discharge and meaning in cursing consists in stressing its repetitive, quotational character. Walter "swear[s] on" until he is calm. Again, the curse affects not only the accursed, as the ecclesiastical tradition would have it, but also the one who curses. Uttering Ernulphus's curse as a performance has a calming effect on the orator; it functions as a therapy. Hence it can be used in any vexing situation independently of the specific circumstances. "I have the greatest veneration for that gentleman," says Walter, "who, in distrust of his own discretion in this point, sat down and composed (that is at his leisure) fit forms of swearing suitable to all cases, from the lowest to the highest provocations which could possibly happen to him" (152). By quoting the bilingual republication of Ernulphus's curse, Sterne stresses this general suitability by adding the proper name Obadiah (against whom Dr. Slop's curse is directed) to the English translation of the Latin pronoun *illum*. "Maledictus sit ubicunque fuerit" (158), for example, becomes "May he (Obadiah) be damn'd where-ever he be" (159).[48] Encompassing all possible occasions of anger, the universality of Ernulphus's curse allows the cursing subject to resort to it as a useful tool to reclaim his or her own emotional balance. According to Walter, Ernulphus (and consequently himself) kept the compendium of curses "ever by him on the chimney piece, within his reach, ready for use" (152). Later on, he differentiates between reading and using the template of Ernulphus's curse: "I was reading, though not using, one of them to my brother *Toby* this morning, whilst he pour'd out the tea" (152). Again, it is the performative character of the curse that is of interest for Walter. Only when it is being used, instead of being merely read, can it deploy its calming function. Cursing is essentially a social act, relying on spoken language and a specific listening audience (who can be the curser him- or herself) to be successful.

To further elucidate the curse as a performative, Walter and Toby discuss the actor Garrick reciting a soliloquy. What distinguishes Garrick's performance is its irregularity: "And how did *Garrick* speak the soliloquy last night?—Oh, against all rule, my Lord,—most ungrammatically! Betwixt the substantive and the adjective, which should agree together in *number, case* and *gender*, he made a breach thus,—stopping, as if the point wanted settling;—and betwixt the nominative case, which your lordship knows should govern the verb, he suspended his voice in the epilogue a dozen times, three seconds and three fifths by a stop-watch, my Lord, each time" (163–64). Garrick's performance is characterized by its breaches, breaks, and suspensions. The listener of the soliloquy, who narrates his observations to Walter and Toby and who is never clearly identified, pays attention solely to the grammatical and prosodic aspects of Garrick's speech. Very much like cursing, performance "lends force to the aspects of language that exceed message, including, for example, volume, timing, tone, rhythm, emphasis, and patterns of sound repetition."[49] Not only must this passage be understood as a satire of pedantic, merely mechanical reviews of Garrick's recitations, but it also shows how the performative force of a speech act "exceeds" its meaning. By focusing only on the ungrammaticality of the soliloquy, the observer does not pay any attention to its content: "Admirable grammarian!" Walter exclaims and continues to ask: "But in suspending his voice—was the sense suspended likewise? Did no expression of attitude or countenance fill up the chasm?—Was the eye silent? Did you narrowly look?—I look'd only at the stop-watch, my Lord.—Excellent observer!" (164). Whether the speaker tries to "fill up the chasm" and cover the breaches in his speech is of no importance to the listener. Garrick's performance is convincing despite the audience's ignorance regarding its content. As a parody of, for example, Thomas Fitzpatrick's *An Enquiry into the Real Merit of a Certain Popular Performer* (1760), this passage points toward a possible incommensurability between the semantic and the performative aspects of language. While Fitzpatrick criticizes Garrick's "improprieties, in respect of speaking" and his "faults" (640), he misses the performative force of the soliloquy. For Sterne, a friend and admirer of Garrick's, the unruliness of his performance, the breaches and suspensions, not only resemble his own style of writing but also exemplify the efficacy of curses. Their felicity, to use Austin's terminology, relies on the "gusto" (165) of the one who swears. In addition to his copiousness, it is his enthusiasm and vigor that distinguishes Garrick from less talented actors and Ernulphus from other, less powerful cursers: "He is more copious in his invention,—possess'd more of the excellencies of a swearer,—had such a thorough knowledge of the human frame, its membranes, nerves, ligaments, knittings of the joints, and articulations,—that when *Ernulphus* cursed,—no part escaped him.—'Tis true, there is something of a *hardness* in his manner,—and, as in *Michel Angelo*, a want of *grace*,—but then there is such a greatness of gusto!" (165). As a good orator, the swearer Ernulphus, like the actor Garrick, is able to stir passions. The aim of the curse, as of the orator's speech in court and the actor's performance on stage, is primarily persuasion. Success or failure depends, not on the correct communication of a message, but on its passionate appeal, its ability to persuade the listener.

Rhetoric as a mode of producing affect always unifies auto- and hetero-affection. It is directed not only toward someone else but also always to oneself. For speakers or actors to be convincing and able to arouse emotions, they must create these passions within themselves. If, for the curse to be successful, it is enough to create and abreact passions, then its content is of lesser importance. The appeal to a higher order, be it God or the devil, is merely rhetorical. Walter has suspended the belief in an immediate, magical intervention of a higher, metaphysical power. In this sense, the practice of cursing undergoes a process of secularization and profanation. In the sixteenth and seventeenth centuries the Reformation attacked the belief in the quasi-magical powers of curses, incantations, and similar speech acts: "Protestantism thus presented itself as a deliberate attempt to take the magical elements out of religion, to eliminate the idea that the rituals of the Church had about them a mechanical efficacy, and to abandon the effort to endow physical objects with supernatural qualities by special formulae of consecration and exorcism."[50] Malediction in this view does not belong to religion proper but is considered to be a primitive, magical remnant that needs to be extirpated from religious practices.

Walter uses Ernulphus's curse as a template, arousing and simultaneously controlling affects. While for orthodox Protestantism ritualistic enunciations addressing God move from an "automatically effective" to a "petitionary" mode, Walter Shandy suspends any communication with a transcendent order, reducing the curse to a merely rhetorical device.[51] Its performative force derives, not from a magical or religious sphere, but from its utterance within an institute of (oratory) swearing as a ritualized speech act. While Protestant dogma calls for a real emotional appeal to God, rejecting the idea of purely mechanical recitations of formulas, Walter ironically stresses the curse's automatic, universally applicable character. For him, reciting Ernulphus's curse is effective only as a rhetorical and psychological method of alleviating anger, not as a religious, that is, magical, speech act. He becomes a swearing machine of formularity, turning malediction's aggression "from fight into game, savor the rhetoric."[52] The curse becomes a *technology of the self*, a mode of dealing with an obstinate, recalcitrant environment. Walter's address to God and the litany of saints, apostles, and so on merely quotes from Ernulphus; he does not attempt to persuade God of the worthiness of his appeal. Instead, in the rhetorical mode of self-affection, he persuades and affects himself. The curse as the quotation of a ritualized formula that in turn quotes passionate exclamations functions as a form of secularization insofar as the belief in the magical powers of language is reduced to a rhetorical performance of auto-affection.[53] Cursing is stripped of its religious transcendence and magical efficacy. Leaving its linguistic structure intact, it in return gains the performative force of an auto-affective speech act. The following sections will examine the specific rhetorical operations that turn passions into expressions,[54] thereby creating emotional equilibrium and providing protection for the frailty of human existence.

YORICK: DRAWING UP BREECHES

In volume 3, chapter 14, of *Tristram Shandy* the narrator claims that the decay of contemporary eloquence, including a proper technique of swearing, is due to the disappearance of proper garments for it. In antiquity, orators during the performance of their speeches, could produce—out of the folds of their mantles—the discussed matter as material objects and not just as words: "It is a singular stroke of eloquence (at least it was so, when eloquence flourished at Athens and Rome, and would be so now, did orators wear mantles) not to mention the name of a thing, when you had the thing about you, in petto, ready to produce, pop, in the place you want it" (167). Wearing a mantle allows the speaker to replace words—the name of things—with the things themselves. Veiling and unveiling objects becomes a rhetorical device, a technique to produce evidence, to "put things in front of the eyes" of the listeners, with the orator placing "himself and his audience in the position of the eyewitness."[55]

Sterne's treatment of words as things—a rhetorical practice deeply rooted in the rhetorical tradition—has become a commonplace in the commentary on the narrative structure of *Tristram Shandy*.[56] The chapter referred to as "the chapter of THINGS" (302) mentions a list of things the narrator must do with things: "I have a thing to name—a thing to lament—a thing to hope—a thing to suppose—a thing to declare—a thing to conceal—a thing to chuse, and a thing to pray for.—This chapter, therefore, I name the chapter of THINGS—" (302). Not surprisingly, the condition of the possibility of representing things is again related to a feature of a piece of clothing: buttonholes. The identity of Jenny, the narrator's friend and addressee, "is the thing to be concealed—it shall be told you the next chapter but one, to my chapter of button-holes,—and not one chapter before" (303). Identifying Jenny is—in the tradition of classical rhetoric—deferred to the proper moment, the correct place within the novel: a place that explicitly deals with opening and closing, veiling and unveiling. Ironically, the promised chapter on buttonholes, which would reveal Jenny's identity, is constantly being postponed until it is finally abandoned for good. Tristram's ideal orator argues *ad rem* in the strictest sense, basing his speech on the actual appearance of the discussed subject. Oscillating between absence and presence, appearance and disappearance, the orator's mantle is more than a mere prop or an ornament; it is the device that allows for things to be put in their proper place. Eloquence equals having a thing *in petto*, "ready to produce, pop, in the place you want it." It allows placing, making the object appear at the right time and place.

Today, says Tristram, the fashion of "short coats" and the "disuse of trunk-hose," or the loose-fitting breeches of the previous century (which, as Melvyn and Joan New explain, were sometimes stuffed with wool), and the adoption instead of tight-fitting breeches that cannot conceal objects means that antiquity's feats of successful oratory cannot be replicated (167).[57] "Mantles,—and pretty large ones too, my brethren, with some twenty or five and twenty yards of good purple, superfine, marketable cloth in them,—with large flowing folds and doubles, and in a great stile of design" (167), could be stuffed with an ax, a pound and a half of pot-ashes in an urn, even a toddler,[58] and loose-fitting breeches, while less capacious, still had some capacity for concealment. On the contrary the tight-fitting breeches of Tristram's time do not allow their wearer to conceal or reveal anything: "We can conceal nothing under ours, Madam, worth shewing" (168). Garments, to be rhetorically useful, need places that fold and double, where things can appear and disappear. The surface of men's clothes must allow for wrinkled and perplexed spaces, crevices and slits, interrupting the clear-cut opposition of inside and outside. What plainly shows itself lacks the eloquent power of persuasion; it does not produce evidence in the most productive way. But opening and closing are intertwined on a mantle's folded, flowing surface. Rhetoric becomes a technique to control and govern this space of veiling and unveiling by methodically organizing the interplay between presence and absence. Decor and decorum are more than just expressions of fashion or ornament. They are the sites where—in the form of the *Latus Clavus*, buttonholes, or breeches—inside and outside connect, psyche and society interact, things and words coincide. This site must be understood, not as a stable place, but as an unstable play of open positions.

The most prominent figure in *Tristram Shandy* who embodies the dialectics of veiling and revealing in its rhetorical as well as ethical context is the parson Yorick. His appearance on a "lean, sorry, jackass of a horse value about one pound fifteen shillings" (17) is perceived as a "breach of decorum" (17). Maimed—not being a "horse at all points" (18)—Yorick's horse is the "true point of ridicule" (19). Yorick could improve the appearance of his horse by adorning it with "a very handsome demi-peak'd saddle, quilted on the seat with green plush, garnished with a double row of silver-headed studs, and a noble pair of shining brass stirrups, with a housing altogether suitable, of grey superfine cloth, with an edging of black lace, terminating in a deep, black, silk fringe, poudrè d'or, . . . ornamented at all points as it should be" (18). But he refuses to "banter his beast" and thereby commits a "breach of all decorum . . . against himself, his station, and his office" (17). Decorum demands that the horse be outfitted properly, thereby diverting attention from its true character, that is, its emaciated state. In choosing a plain bridle and saddle, Yorick refuses to take part in the rhetorical strategies of decoration and decorum, thereby risking being perceived as ridiculous. While the ancient orator takes full advantage of the rhetorical capabilities of veiling/unveiling gowns and the eloquent clothing of things and ideas, the modest, "nice-tempered" parson shows himself to be "above the temptation of false wit" (19). There is a direct, clearly visible resemblance between Yorick and his horse; both are lean and lanky. The outside constitutes an immediate representation of the inside. Modesty and humility show themselves openly, "since he [Yorick] never carried one single ounce of flesh upon his own bones, being altogether as spare a figure as his beast" (19). Yorick's horse resembles Don Quixote's Rozinante, known "to be a Horse of that Sobriety and Chastity, that all the Mares in the Pastures of Cordova could not have rais'd him to attempt an indecent thing."[59] Rozinante's decency and knowledge of decorum shows itself in his figure: "Rozinante was so admirably delineated, so slim, so stiff, so lean, so jaded, with so sharp a Ridge-bone, and altogether so like one wasted with an incurable Consumption, that any one must have owned at first Sight, that no horse ever better deserved that Name."[60] Sobriety and chastity are not veiled under an elaborate garment, hidden under ornaments; rather, they appear "admirably delineated" in a distinct, "spare figure."

This resistance to rhetorical decorum, ornament, and exuberance in Yorick comically contradicts his vocation. As a parson, he is, by definition, an orator.[61] Yorick defends his style of riding and oration because on the back of a "meek-spirited jade of a broken winded horse . . . he could sit mechanically, and meditate as delightfully *de vanitate mundi et fuga sæculi*, . . . that he could draw up an argument in his sermon, or a hole in his breeches, as steadily on the one as in the other;—that brisk trotting and slow argumentation, like wit and judgment, were two incompatible movements" (19–20). Riding "mechanically" on the back of a slow, unspirited horse, Yorick is able to compose a sermon characterized by "slow argumentation" and judgment. These qualities he opposes to the wit of "brisk trotting." The antagonism of wit and judgment and the call for their complementarity was a commonplace in seventeenth- and eighteenth-century philosophy. The *locus classicus* is Locke's *Essay concerning Human Understanding*, which in book 2 claims:

> And, hence, perhaps, may be given some Reason of that common Observation, That Men who have a great deal of Wit, and prompt Memories, have not always the clearest Judgment, or deepest Reason. For Wit lying most in the assemblage of ideas, and putting those together with quickness and variety, wherein can be found any resemblance or congruity, thereby to make up pleasant Pictures, and agreeable Visions in the Fancy: Judgment, on the contrary, lies quite on the other side, in separating carefully, one from another, Ideas, wherein can be found the least difference, thereby to avoid being misled by Similitude, and by affinity to take one thing for another.[62]

Wit, in the Lockean sense, consists of quickly drawing associations and ideas together, creating pleasant images, while judgment slowly and carefully separates ideas, uncovering false affinities and similitudes. Wit "is a mere recognition of superficial congruence among ideas, without exhaustive analysis."[63] Sterne cites Locke in volume 3, "The Author's Preface": "Wit and judgment in this world never go together; inasmuch as they are two operations differing from each other as wide as east is from west.—So, says Locke" (174). Sterne's rejoinder, "So are farting and hickuping, say I" (274), is typically ironic in that it remains unclear whether the paralleling of wit and judgment with two vulgar physiological phenomena must be considered an affirmation or a criticism of the two faculties' antagonism. Sterne emphasizes this undecidability by referring to an invented compendium, entitled *De fartandi et illustrandi fallaciis,* by the imaginary "Didius, the great church lawyer" (174).[64] The mixing of high with low, the learned scholarship of the Christian tradition personified by Didius with low and distasteful physiological reactions, leaves open how to interpret the author's comment on Locke. Does he agree or disagree? Because farting and hiccupping have aspects in common— they are undesirable and uncontrollable "natural" discharges that breach decorum—but also differ in many respects—coming from different orifices and aiming in different directions—this illustration is unreadable. Is Sterne's relationship to Locke one of wit or judgment? Does he quickly establish resemblances and congruity, or does he distinguish between ideas and concepts? Does he fart or hiccup?[65]

Yorick overcomes the (in)compatibility of wit and judgment by drawing up his breeches and his sermon, composing his speech and his cough: "Upon his steed—he could unite and reconcile every thing,— he could compose his sermon,—he could compose his cough,—and, in case nature gave a call that way, he could likewise compose himself to sleep" (20). Yorick coughs up his sermons, uniting wit and judgment, dissociation and association. The emaciated parson riding a "broken-winded" horse, the incarnation of breached decorum and respectability, becomes the site of rhetorical composition. Composing in this context should be read in terms of pulling together, drawing up, and ordering. The rhetorical and the physiological coalesce, allowing for wit and judgment to be reconciled and united in a grotesque way. While the composition of a sermon consists in combining and joining words and phrases, ending a cough or putting oneself to sleep implies a move toward a state of calm and repose. Differences and antagonisms are composed, put to an end. Yorick's appearance— although seemingly ridiculous—is one of serenity and composure.[66]

PUTTING TRISTRAM SHANDY INTO BREECHES

The well known opening chapter of *Tristram Shandy* discusses the scattering and dispersion of animal spirits in the moment of Tristram's interrupted conception. Sterne mentions the need for the homunculus (little man), a fully developed prefiguration of the human being contained in the male sperm for which the female womb provides only a nourishing environment, to be protected in order to develop properly. In Sterne's appropriation of the "animalculist" theory of procreation, the animal spirits have the task of escorting and conducting the homunculus safely "to the place destined for his reception" (6). It is Tristram's mother's question, interrupting intercourse, that leaves Tristram prone to accidents, threatening the "happy formation and temperature of his body, perhaps his genius and the very cast of his mind" (5). His constitution is, like an old garment, "worn down to a thread;—his own animal spirits ruffled beyond description" (7).[67] From this interrupted conception on, Tristram's life is affected by a seemingly never-ending onslaught of accidents. None of Walter's attempts to protect his son is successful. Paradigmatic for these failed attempts to safeguard the body and soul of young Tristram is the project of putting the boy Tristram into breeches. To find the right breeches Walter consults—as usual—the (pseudo)canonical scholarship of his time. His primary source is, according to Tristram's narration, Albertus Rubenius, son of the Flemish painter Peter Paul Rubens, and his work *Of the Clothing of the Ancients, Particularly of the Latus Clavus (De Re Vestiaria Veterum, Praecipue de Lato Clavo)*. But Rubenius does not provide sufficient answers to the question of which breeches to choose for Tristram. Far from enabling Walter to make a well-informed choice, Rubenius's extensive list—the "Toga, or the loose gown. The Chlamys. The Ephod. The Tunica, or Jacket. The Synthesis. The Paenula. The Lacerna, with its Cucullus. The Paludamentum. The Praetexta. The Sagum, or soldier's jerkin and the Trabea"—produces the opposite result, overwhelming him and preventing any resolution. Hence Walter is unable to "extract a single word out of Rubenius upon the subject" (397). Especially the *Latus Clavus* seems to be a point of dissent among the learned. Lefèvre de Morsan, a possible source for Sterne's discussion of ancient garment, describes this item of traditional Roman clothing as follows: "The Senators had under [the Praetexta] a tunic ample enough, called Latus-clavus, which was long taken literally for an habit adorned with large studs of purple like nail-heads, but has since been discovered to signify only a stuff with large stripes of purple" (696). Despite this rather precise description, Walter's research on the topic brings up only vastly differing and partly contradictory results: "That Egnatius, Sigonius, Bossius Ticinensis, Bayfius, Budaeus, Salmasius, Lipsius, Lazius, Isaac Causabon, and Joseph Scaliger, all differed from each other,—and he from them: That some took it to be the button,—some the coat itself,—others only the colour of it:—That the great Bayfius, in his Wardrobe of the Ancients, chap. 12.—honestly said, he knew not what it was,—whether a fibula,—a stud,—a button,—a loop,—a buckle,—or clasps and keepers" (398).[68] A discussion about proper breeches for a toddler digresses into a historical debate about an obscure piece of Roman clothing. Neither the breeches nor the *Latus Clavus* can be defined or clearly identified. Instead, Walter creates lists of circumlocutions, never coming to a final, definite answer. He is informed about everything but breeches and their relation to the *Latus Clavus*, becoming more and more entangled in a web of esoteric and impractical textual knowledge that cannot be applied in the concrete situation. Finally, in a purely decisionistic manner that is not grounded in the accumulated knowledge at all, Walter declares the *Latus Clavus* to consist of "hooks and eyes" (399) and orders for Tristram's breeches to be made in this fashion.

According to de Morsan, a "loose gown" is the "mark of dissolute manners" (696). Walter's question "And what was the Latus Clavus?" (398) can thus be translated into "And what did the term *Latus Clavus* mean?" For Walter, as a parody of a modern scholar, this meaning is forever lost. The *Latus Clavus* as a sign of distinction in Roman society, separating slaves and masters, cannot be identified, remaining an empty signifier, pure *distinction* and difference, thereby affording different ascriptions of meaning. It—the *Latus Clavus*—can be anything from a coat to a button or a buckle. David Wellbery calls it an ornament that simultaneously signifies "all and nothing."[69] The *Latus Clavus* opens and closes the garment, it veils and unveils, pointing toward the aporetic status of textual signification and oscillating undecidably between weaving and unweaving, tying and untying. For Wellbery, the *Latus Clavus* marks "the point of intersection of language and contingency."[70] Sterne's witty play with the discrepancy between place and meaning, position and signification, according to Wellbery, shows "the structure of language as such."[71] The empty signifier of the *Latus Clavus* initiates a play with the empty position. This is not meant to be an ellipsis of representation, which the reader fills imaginatively, but a place of differentiation, to which no element can be assigned. The empty position, one could say, is the excessive position, without which there would be no lability in the system; it is the condition of metonymy, of semantic mobility.[72]

Putting Tristram into breeches is a protective act that can be compared to a coping mechanism, dealing with the symbolic loss of the phallus. The breeches, as a piece of clothing as well as a social signifier, cover an empty place. They function like a "covered way," veiling the unspeakable. Jacques Lacan, in *The Language of the Self: The Function of Language in Psychoanalysis*, discusses the word occupying an open position in terms of a dialectics between presence and absence: "Through the word—already a presence made of absence—absence itself comes to giving itself a name in the moment of origin."[73]

Walter's resolution to put Tristram into breeches must be read as an attempt to arrest the indistinctiveness and openness of the empty place. It is an attempt to define the meaning of the word *Latus Clavus* and to assign a definite (i.e., male) gender to his circumcised and possibly castrated son.[74] Volume 6, chapter 15, positioned between the report of the sash-window accident and a long digression on the (non)relation of the *Latus Clavus* to breeches, consists of nothing but Walter's exclamation: "I'll put him, however, into breeches said my father,—let the world say what it will" (391). Walter decides to assign Tristram the male gender, despite his possible loss of procreative powers (i.e., his being neutered by the falling window sash). While the *Latus Clavus* in ancient Rome marked a social difference, for Walter putting Tristram into breeches (adorned with hooks and eyes) guarantees the designation of a definite gender despite the questionable status of Tristram's sex. It becomes an attempt to deal with a cut, a gap, a lack.[75] The narrator Tristram cannot put this empty placeholder into words because it veils/unveils something "bawdy"— the male genitals—but also hides the fact of their injury and impotence/dysfunction. Sterne's text performs this oscillation between veiling and unveiling the empty place of the phallic lack with a series of dashes and asterisks: "Doctor Slop, like a son of a w-, as my father called him for it,—to exalt himself,—debased me to death,—and made ten thousand times more of Susannah's accident, than there was any grounds for; so that in a week's time, or less, it was in every body's mouth, That poor Master Shandy ******** entirely.—And fame, who loves to double every thing,—in three days had sworn

"When Things Move upon Bad Hinges" 55

positively she saw it,—and all the world, as usual, gave credit to her evidence—'That the nursery window had not only ********;—but that *******'s also'" (391). Walter fears not only Tristram's possible circumcision/castration but also the effects of public opinion, which exaggerates the "real" event of circumcision, leaving "poor Master Shandy" in the eyes of the public a dismembered, castrated, impotent man. The unspeakable of the real, once it has entered the public discourse of the imaginary, is "doubled" and made "ten thousand times more." That which is supposed to be veiled and covered doubles and multiplies, initiating an excess of signification that cannot be controlled. Neither silent disregard of the rumors triggered by Tristram's accident nor an explicit denial can retroactively limit the signifying effects of the open, empty place.[76] Walter reasons: "And yet to acquiesce under the report, in silence—was to acknowledge it openly, at least in the opinion of one half of the world; and to make a bustle again, in contradicting it,—was to confirm it as strongly in the opinion of the other half" (391). This aporetic situation is expressed in Walter's outcry "Was ever poor devil of a country gentleman so hampered?" (391), which can refer either to Tristram's impediment or to his—Walter's—inability to control the effects of public opinion about the empty place created by the sash-window accident.[77] What is left for Walter, however, is to put Tristram in breeches, attempting to regain a sense of decorum—that is, to re-cover and re-veil what has been revealed. He rejects Toby's suggestion of showing the evidence directly as ineffectual: "I would show him [young Tristram] publickly, said my uncle Toby, at the market cross.—'Twill have no effect, said my father" (391). Exposing Tristram's injury in public would be unsuccessful because there is nothing to point at directly. The cut, as a purely structural mark of difference, escapes deictic representation. It leaves nothing but an open place.

Walter's concern regarding the false perception of Tristram in a world that is an "inextricable labyrinth of debts, cares, woes, want, grief, discontent, melancholy, large jointures, and lies" (390) stems not only from a skeptical view of public opinion and the structural impossibility of representing Tristram's lack but the fact that the actual event of his injury is in itself already multiplied. After the "misadventure of the sash" (339), which the maid Susannah equates with a murder, the treatment of the wound is hampered and eventually prevented by another accident: Susannah sets Dr. Slop's wig on fire while he is trying to administer a cataplasm to Tristram's wound. Dr. Slop erupts in a fit of anger, using the cataplasm, instead of applying it to Tristram, as an instrument of revenge:

> Slop snatched up the cataplasm, Susannah snatched up the candle;— a little this way, said Slop; Susannah looking one way, and rowing another, instantly set fire to Slop's wig, which being somewhat bushy and unctuous withal, was burnt out before it was well kindled.— You impudent whore! cried Slop,—(for what is passion, but a wild beast)—you impudent whore, cried Slop, getting upright, with the cataplasm in his hand;—I never was the destruction of any body's nose, said Susannah,—which is more than you can say:—Is it? cried Slop, throwing the cataplasm in her face;—Yes, it is, cried Susannah, returning the compliment with what was left in the pan. (372)

Tristram, after being hit by the falling sash, does not receive proper treatment because the raging Dr. Slop misuses the healing compress to angrily punish Susannah. Dr. Slop lacks the ability to control his temper and gives in to his passions. Cases of rebellious maids and misbehaving and unruly servants and slaves are a constant throughout almost all Stoic treatises on the control of anger and other disruptive passions. In *De Ira*, for example, Seneca argues that anger against servants is as mad as anger against animals or inanimate objects. He asks rhetorically: "For why is it that we are thrown into a rage by somebody's cough or sneeze, by negligence in chasing a fly away, by a dog's hanging around, or by the dropping of a key that has slipped from the hands of a careless servant?"[78] By Seneca's lights, Dr. Slop's body and mind have been corrupted by his temper; he acts, in the words of Tristram, like a "wild beast," adding injury instead of mending it and escalating the situation. Such conduct leads to the disintegration of the strict separation between master and servant that the *Latus Clavus* would uphold. Walter, paraphrasing Albertus Rubenius, explains that "persons of quality and fortune distinguished themselves by the fineness and whiteness of their cloaths . . . but . . . the inferior people . . . generally wore brown cloaths, and of a something coarser texture,—till towards the beginning of Augustus's reign, when the slave dressed like his master, and almost every distinction of habiliment was lost, but the Latus Clavus" (398). By becoming angry with Susannah, Dr. Slop treats her like an equal. A hierarchical relationship turns into a reciprocal one: she returns the compliment and throws the contents of the pan in his face. Overwhelmed by their angry passions, master and servant become indistinguishable. The law of decorum in the household is broken. William

Harris, commenting on Plutarch's treatment of anger, states that, for the Roman household, "decorum, apparently, is what requires one not to terrorize the servants while guests are present. It was clearly embarrassing if a visitor to the house encountered a slave who was being whipped—decorum again."[79] Decorum and decor, social aptitude and appearance, mirror each other. By wearing the *Latus Clavus* as well as controlling his passions the eudaimonistic, stoic master distinguished himself from mere servants, wild beasts, and inanimate objects. In *Tristram Shandy*, this strict stratification between different social and ontological realms breaks down.

In this context it is not surprising that the cause of Dr. Slop's fit of rage can be traced to a "scruple of decorum" (372). It was not necessarily Susannah's clumsiness or a dysfunctional tool that led up to the aborted attempt to cover Tristram's wound. She questioned whether it was appropriate for her to assist in the application of the cataplasm: "When the cataplasm was ready, a scruple of decorum had unreasonably rose up in Susannah's conscience, about holding the candle, whilst Slop tied it on; Slop had not treated Susannah's distemper with anodines,—and so a quarrel had ensued betwixt them" (372). For Susannah, looking directly at the site of Tristram's wound would be a breach of decorum—a concern that is characterized by Tristram as "unreasonable," coming at the wrong time. Her concept of decorum requires all the crevices and openings of the human body to be covered. This is a sentiment shared by Tristram, who, while commenting on Walter's and Toby's discussion about the "right end of a woman," claims: "But who my Jenny is—and which is the right and which the wrong end of a woman, is the thing to be concealed" (303). Decorum requires concealment and cover. Susannah's scruples about an immediate approach to Tristram's genitals are similar to those voiced by Walter and Toby earlier in the novel as they attempt to rhetorically avoid mentioning their sister's buttocks:—"'My sister, mayhap, quoth my uncle Toby, does not choose to let a man come so near her ****' Make this dash,—'tis an Aposiopesis.—Take the dash away, and write Backside,—'tis Bawdy.—Scratch Backside out, and put Cover'd-way in, –'tis a Metaphor" (90). Like Tristram's open wound, his aunt's backside cannot be represented literally without breaching decorum.[80] This sense of aptness leads to a series of rhetorical placeholders ranging from asterisk to metaphor, yet none of these properly fill the empty space, and each placement immediately and almost compulsively forces its replacement. The representation of Tristram's aunt's backside consists in continuous scratching out and rewriting, circumscribing the bawdy place of (sexual) difference.[81] Susannah's scruples hint at a similar question of how to properly deal with an opening that should be kept under wraps. How can one point toward an empty place? The circumcision can only be circumvented: that is, the gap/cut created by the falling window can only be represented metaphorically in a bawdy, figural way or by paratextual markers like dashes and asterisks, all allowing for a possibly infinite sequence of replacements and substitutions.

TRISTRAM'S RHETORIC

The logic of veiling and unveiling, absence and presence, literal and figural speech as it manifests itself in Sterne's discussion of the *Latus Clavus* also informs his appropriation of rhetorical devices. He combines concepts like *perspicuitas* or *gravitas* with Locke's seminal distinction between wit and judgment, producing a style of writing that, in its blending of progressive and regressive tendencies, performs an ironic critique of traditional narratologies based on ideas of linearity and directness. In the "Author's Preface," Tristram draws up his argument using metaphors and similes, replacing "opake words" that threaten to hinder the reader's comprehension of the author's intentions. Images, taking the place of learned and incomprehensible concepts, can "clear the point at once" (180). Tristram, quoting Rabelais, asks what "hinderance," "hurt," or "harm" can come from the desire to know, even if it is caused by lowly everyday objects like "a sot, a pot, . . ., or a cane chair" (180). Seated on a cane chair, Tristram illustrates the relationship between wit and judgment by comparing these two concepts to the ornamental knobs on his chair: "Will you give me the leave to illustrate this affair of wit and judgment, by the two knobs on the top of the back of it,—they are fasten'd on, you see, with the two pegs stuck slightly into two gimlet-holes, and will place what I have to say in so clear a light, as to let you see through the drift and meaning of my whole preface, as plainly as if every point and particle was made up of sun beams" (180). Plain objects allow the creation of a lucid and distinct discourse in which the discussed issues not only appear clearly but become transparent themselves: every point and particle is made of light. Things become lucid; the reader can see right through them. In addition to *latinitas*, *aptum*, and *ornatus*, ancient rhetoric identifies *perspicuitas* as a necessary stylistic quality of a good speech. It serves to increase intellectual comprehensibility by making the issues transparent. Quintilian notes: "I regard clearness [perspicuitas] as the first essential of a good style: there must be propriety in our words, their order must be straightforward, the conclusion of the period must not be long postponed, there must be nothing lacking and nothing superfluous. Thus our language will be approved by the learned and clear to the uneducated."[82] Avoiding obscurity results from "propriety in the use of words."[83] Propriety in this context "means calling things by their right names,"[84] whether the thing in question is a sot, a pot, or the knob of a cane chair. If the speaker steers clear of ordinary language completely, his discourse will become purely ornamental and incomprehensible. "Tall, opake words" (180) and false witticisms cover and veil the true meaning of things, leaving nothing but empty, meaningless phrases. Transparency of oratory aims simultaneously at the learned and the uneducated; it speaks plainly, in the language of proper names. This language of proper names is to be avoided, following Quintilian, if it is "obscene, unseemly or mean."[85] The orator has to negotiate *aptum* and *perspicuitas*, neither sinking "beneath the dignity of the subject and the speaker" nor shying away from using "words that are in ordinary use."[86] Speaking clearly and properly is always threatened by the possibility of a breach of decorum by "obscene," "unseemly," or "mean" words. A good orator negotiates the demands of clarity and decorum, literal explicitness and figural circumscription. It is this balance that scholarly erudition, according to Tristram, cannot achieve: "I hate set dissertations,—and above all things in the world, 'tis one of the silliest things in one of them, to darken your hypothesis by placing a number of tall, opake words, one before another, in a right line, betwixt your own and your readers conception,—when in all likelihood, if you had looked about, you might have seen something standing, or hanging up, which would have cleared the point at once" (180).[87] Scholarly works tend to put unintelligible words between writer and reader. They are dark and incomprehensible, veiling the point, while ordinary objects "clear the point," unveiling and enlightening it. Speaking in plain and proper words equals clearing a point, explicating an issue, but also opening an empty place where every "point and particle" (180) loses its opaqueness. Placing words "in so a clear light" (180) allows them to be perceived in a transparency that exposes and reveals; it lets the reader "see through the drift and meaning of the whole preface" (180). Tristram conceives of words as resembling things, elements occupying a specific place. By looking at the specific arrangement of words and things—as "something standing, or hanging up"—the author can initiate a witty game with the cleared point. Words become placeholders. The scholarly discourse of "set dissertations" cannot enter this language game because it attempts to arrest the flexible game of deferral and dislocation centered on the open gap of the cleared point. Its method of following a right line is blind to the interruptions, openings, and crevices that appear if one looks at words as placeholders that shift and move along curved, eccentric lines.

Yorick, in defense of his style of oratory, also uses the metaphor of an empty, blank space in his comparison of words to bullets: "To preach, to shew the extent of our reading, or the subtleties of wit—to parade it in the eyes of the vulgar with the beggarly accounts of a little learning, tinseled over with a few words which glitter, but convey little light and less warmth—is a dishonest use of the poor single half of our week which is put into our hands—'Tis not preaching the gospel—but ourselves—For my own part, continued Yorick, I had rather direct five words point blank to the heart" (285). Yorick favors a form of eloquence that comes from the heart and aims point blank for the heart. Its direction is straightforward, without digressions or interruptions. It is a knowledge of the "point de blanc," the white, open spot of the target. The term *point blank* is used in archery to designate a specific technique of aiming: "In target archery, one sighting technique is 'point of aim.' The archer notes the spot associated with his line of sight over the tip of his arrow while he is at 'full draw,' or ready to release the arrow. At a certain distance, that point will correspond to the target itself. When the point falls on the white target, while aiming, it is 'point de blanc.'"[88] In other words, the orator must go ballistic. The points of sight and the white target must coincide for the projectile to hit the target. Aiming directly at the heart means aiming at a blank point, pointing toward an empty white piece of cloth. It requires a technique of determining the proper moment of release that is based on the knowledge of how and when to pull the trigger and to ignite emotions. To hit the mark, to enter the heart and breach the souls of his parishioners, the priest, with a singular "stroke of eloquence," must hit their "point de blanc." He must negotiate horizontal and vertical forces of motion. Even antirhetorical gestures and speeches like that of Yorick rely on rhetorical devices. Words become projectiles, resembling arrows and bullets that pierce and breach. It is

"When Things Move upon Bad Hinges" 61

no coincidence that Toby immediately associates Yorick's pronouncement of the term *point blank* with ballistics: "As Yorick pronounced the word point blank, my uncle Toby rose up to say something about projectiles" (287).

The "graver gentry" of philosophy cannot aim simultaneously with wit and judgment. Hence their approach, always shooting straight, will always miss the point, lacking proper balance: "Now your graver gentry having little or no kind of chance in aiming at the one,—unless they laid hold of the other,—pray what do you think would become of them?" (181). The combination of wit and judgment can only be aimed at, pointed to, in a way that resists the serious *gravitas* of "your *graver gentry*." The ideal orator uses words as projectiles moving between speaker and listener, author and reader, along the "line of GRAVITATION" (427). Writing and speaking become parabolic. In an essay entitled "Tristram Shandy's Law of Gravity," Sigurd Burckhardt asserts that "words, unlike ideas, have body. . . . Having body, they are subject to gravity, so that nothing is surer to make a man miss his target than the philosopher's notion that the only requirement is to aim straight."[89] Philosophizing, for Tristram, despite all its *gravitas*, asks for a method of aiming that takes into account—in a world where everything is exposed to gravitational pull—the impossibility of pointing straight ahead, of hitting the mark without digression and aberration. True *gravitas* consists in the ability to perceive words as objects that have weight and therefore not to confuse a straight line with the line of gravity: "Pray can you tell me . . . by what mistake—who told them so—or how it has come to pass, that your men of wit and genius have all along confounded this [straight] line, with the line of GRAVITATION?" (427). To act properly, showing "moral rectitude," means to ballistically calculate the *point de blanc*. It means to project in the literal sense—to throw words like stones toward an open space—in order not to miss the point. This includes forecasting the tendency of words and things to fall and err from a straightforward path.[90] The line of argument is curved, its progression "similar to the projectile's parabola."[91]

Tristram's journey through southern France exemplifies his idea regarding the relationship of wit and judgment, writing and morality, words and things. Having "the whole south of France . . . at my leisure" (481), Tristram decides to slow the speed of his journey and ride his mule "as slowly as foot could fall" (482). The decision for deceleration and delay aims at "managing plains," (481) which pose a serious problem for the writer: "There is nothing more pleasing to a traveler—or more terrible to travel-writers, than a large rich plain; especially if it is without great rivers or bridges; and presents nothing to the eye, but one unvaried picture of plenty" (482). What is pleasing for the traveler turns out to be terrible for the travel writer. The monotony of "unvaried . . . plenty" poses a predicament for its proper representation. For the writer, to simply list the abundant beauties "is the most terrible work" (482). After having described the richness of the large plain, travel writers "know not what to do with it" (482). It "is of little or no use to them but to carry them to some town; and that town, perhaps of little more, but a new place to start from to the next plain—and so on" (482). Plains offer no marks or distinctions that the writer can grasp. They lack "handles" guiding and structuring his work. No place is distinct from the others. In its abundance the plain resembles a desert, a space without distinctions. To manage the plains better—that is, not to perceive them as just a passage on the way to another town—the writer has to change his mode of traveling and writing. The plain is not made for a plain style. Moving ahead quickly and in a straightforward motion "presents nothing to the eye" and carries the traveler to the next city, neglecting the abundance of nature. Under the title "Plain Stories" Tristram lays out a different approach to managing plains that does not aim straight but instead turns the plain into a city. How does one transform the monotony of a plain into the diversity of a city? Tristram's strategy is characterized, not by following a planned route, but "by seizing every handle, of what size or shape soever, which chance held out to me in this journey" (484). This ability to perceive "every thing" that time and chance present to the traveler is detailed by Sterne in *A Sentimental Journey*, where he writes: "What a large volume of adventures may be grasped within this little span of life by him who interests his heart in every thing, and who, having eyes to see, what time and chance are perpetually holding out to him as he journeyeth on his way, misses nothing he can fairly lay his hands on."[92] Tristram creates variety by communication and association: he stops his ride at every intersection, lets every encounter delay his progress. He does not ride faster than he could walk, instead "stopping and talking to every soul who was not in full trot—joining all parties before me—waiting for every soul behind—hailing all those who were coming through cross roads—arresting all kinds of beggars, pilgrims, fiddlers, fryars—not passing by a woman in a mulberry-tree without commending her legs, and tempting her into conversation with a pinch of snuff" (483–84). Deceleration allows for the creation of communities, for "joining," "hailing," and "talking." Applied wit in the sense of yoking disparate elements brings Tristram in contact with the various travelers he meets during his slowed-down trot and allows chance encounters to turn into conversation. He thereby is "always in company" (484). The plain becomes the ground on which the witty traveler creates a community of diverse outcasts. Tristram's company consists of beggars, pilgrims, fiddlers, and friars, existing on the fringes of bourgeois society. The plain turned into a city is one of loners, outsiders, and pariahs. Chance appears in the form of figures who do not fit the proper decorum of learned "graver gentry." Instead, Shandy's company is of "that sprightly frankness which at once unpins every plait of a Languedocian's dress—that whatever is beneath it, looks so like the simplicity which poets sing of in better days—I will delude my fancy and believe it is so" (484).

Plain, rural Languedoc is characterized by a frank (i.e., direct and immediate) form of discourse that unveils and uncovers. Conversation "unpins every plait of the dress"; it reveals what is usually hidden underneath the layers of rhetorical adornment. Tristram's ability to see beneath the surface of properly pinned garments allows him to encounter his fellow outcasts. Speaking—on a plain—undresses; it undoes the decorum of mannerly discourse and appearance. But whether the simple plainness of beggars, pilgrims, fiddlers, and friars is in fact the naked truth or just another rhetorical ruse remains in doubt. Whatever lies beneath only appears to be simple. The possibility that this clarity is the result of a deceived and deceiving imagination cannot be ruled out. Whether simplicity is perceived as plain or as ornamental rests on faith and fancy. Emblematic of this ambiguity of seemingly plain, unveiling rhetoric is the young woman Nanette. "Sprightly frankness" manifests itself in a certain negligence of the dress that sparks Tristram's encounter with her. On the road between Nimes and Lunel he interrupts his journey to join a "Gascoigne roundelay": "A sun-burnt daughter of Labour rose up from the groupe to meet me as I advanced towards them; her hair, which was a dark chestnut, approaching rather to a black, was tied up in a knot, all but a single tress. We want a cavalier, said she, holding out both her hands, as if to offer them—And a cavalier ye shall have; said I, taking hold of both of them. Hadst thou, Nannette, been array'd like a dutchess!—But that cursed slit in thy petticoat! Nannette cared not for it" (485).

Not only does a slit in Nannette's petticoat reveal her as part of the lower classes—a "sun-burnt daughter of Labour"—but the carelessness regarding her appearance, her lack of proper decorum, initiates a "running at the ring of pleasure." Nannette's demeanor is highly ambiguous. Her hair is all tied up except for a single tress, which, just like the slit in her dress, is a small almost imperceptible breach of decorum, a loosening of the tight knots of moral rectitude. This ambiguity concerning her behavior and whether it accords with the norms of respectability and modesty also shows in the way she draws Tristram into the "carousal" of the dance: "We could not have done without you, said she, letting go one hand, with self-taught politeness, leading me up with another" (485). Simultaneously holding on and letting go, Nannette approaches and retreats, reveals and conceals. Her "sprightly frankness" consists in an irresolvable interplay of politeness and the "self-taught," of tied-up hair and slits in petticoats, of simplicity and ornament, of drawing up and letting loose. The temptation of Nannette threatens traditional models of morality, making Tristram curse the petticoat and wish it to be sewn up: "But that cursed slit in thy petticoat! . . . I would have given a crown to have it sew'd up—Nannette would not have given a sous" (485). During the Gascoigne festival—interrupting the straightforward journey by a ring of pleasure, carousal, roundelay—passions are exposed and emotions aroused. The dance creates a space between Tristram and Nanette, across which "transient sparks of amity shot." This affinity expresses itself in language and gesture: "Viva la Joia! was in her lips—Viva la joia! was in her eyes" (485). Passionate communication and community transcend the laws and rules of the "graver gentry," whose sense of propriety suppresses sympathetic feelings as well as expressions of excitement. Dancing the roundelay bends straight lines into a curved space, across which "sparks of amity" are shooting. Communication follows parabolic paths, warped by the weight of words, collapsing distances instituted by social conventions and different mother tongues. Tristram dances on "sportive plains, and under this genial sun, where at this instant all flesh is running out piping, fiddling, and dancing to the vintage, and every step that's taken, the judgment is surprised by the imagination" (489). Here, in plain, rural Languedoc, wit and imagination "make up pleasant Pictures, and agreeable Visions in the Fancy" that surprise and overwhelm judgment's ability to "to avoid being misled by Similitude, and by affinity to take one thing for another."[93] Plainness of style and manner, on the surface direct and frank in a "sprightly fashion," are threatening to mislead by similitude and affinity. What draws Tristram toward Nannette surprises and interrupts his judgment. He is unable to decide whether her petticoat reveals the bare and simple truth or just another layer of veiling, dissimulating rhetoric. Nannette's dance oscillates between "heavenly amity" on the one hand and "insidious capriciousness" on the other.

With judgment being overwhelmed by wit and imagination, traveling, conversing, and writing cannot proceed in a straight line. Tristram as a writer, introducing the narrative of Toby's amours, defies "the best cabbage planter . . . to go on coolly, critically, and canonically, planting his cabbages one by one, in straight lines, and stoical distances, especially if slits in petticoats are unsew'd up—without ever and anon straddling out, or sidling into some bastardly digression" (489). Like a slit in a petticoat, unsewn breaches of decorum divert straight lines and disturb stoical distances. Tristram's approach to writing is neither "cool," "critical," nor "canonical." It is digressive and delayed. No plain method can protect judgment from being overwhelmed by wit. No method can maintain the proper distance and separation between things, since they continuously and incessantly generate digressive associations, that is, ideas that are not fully judged and analyzed, leading away from the straight path of unequivocal knowledge and moral rectitude. In the chapter on story lines that closes volume 6, the straight line is directly connected to the realm of ethics, as Tristram quotes not only Christian dogma but also the Stoic rhetorician Cicero: "This right line,—the path-way for Christians to walk in! say divines—The emblem of moral rectitude! says Cicero" (426). Linearity and its relation to interruption, as suggested in this passage, must be not only read in poetological terms but also treated in its ethical dimension. How do the passions, aroused by wit and imagination, interfere with the *via recta*, the right path of life?

In *Tristram Shandy*, rhetoric, anthropology, and ethics coincide. Language becomes the medium to create an image of the *good life*, a means to "control the accidents of everyday existence."[94] Eloquence preserves good temper and "creates pleasure in excess of the painful occasion."[95] Sterne contrasts the grave and learned philosophers, arguing in straight lines and stoical distances, with the frankness of the nut-brown maids and cabbage planters of southern France. Grave philosophers fail to perceive the precariousness of reasoning in a straightforward fashion. They confuse the straight line with the "line of GRAVITATION." Sigurd Burckhardt has shown how the line of gravity must be understood as a form of indirect projection and deferred meaning: "If you want to project something over a gap, your line can never be straight, but must be indirect, parabolic, hyperbolic, cycloid. It is for this reason that scarcely a sentence in Tristram Shandy, far less a chapter or an episode, and least of all the book as a whole, ever runs straight. The novel is a vast system of indirections, circuitous approaches."[96] Rhetoric, understood as a method of "devising paths for [words], which will get them to their true destination," simultaneously progresses and digresses.[97] Like Tristram on the plain of Languedoc, it stops at every turn, delays and slows down. It "straddles out and sidles," turning what seems plain and simple into a "ring of pleasure," a product of wit and fancy. Learned philosophy mistakenly attempts to hit its target directly, to shoot straight without taking into account the weight of words and things. In Tristram's curved and warped world, however, every advancement and projection is affected by erring and eccentric tendencies. Tristram's wit, according to John Traugott, constitutes "a description of experience in terms of unlikely relations."[98] It simultaneously draws together and pulls apart, combines wittingly and separates judgingly. More than a *sermon cottidianus*, colloquial speech, this form of speech at once direct and indirect refuses to be ordered according to clean and tidy categories. At the same time high and low, progressive and digressive, ornate and plain, each word, sentence, or chapter stops and turns, allowing for new and unlikely relations. Meanings and their material carriers, *les mots et les choses*, are divided and split to create a variety of surprising fanciful imagining.

CHAPTER TWO

Annoying Bagatelles

Jean Paul and the Comedy of the Quotidian

> Laurence Sterne shows himself to the public completely undressed, completely naked; Jean Paul, however, only has holes in his trousers.
> —HEINRICH HEINE, "The Romantic School"

RECALCITRANT WRITING

In the fourth part of *Truth and Fiction (Dichtung und Wahrheit)*, Johann Wolfgang von Goethe discusses the relationship between inspiration and the process of writing:

> I therefore often wished, like one of my predecessors, to get me a leather jerkin made, and to accustom myself to write in the dark, so as to be able to fix down at once all such unpremeditated effusions. So frequently had it happened, that, after composing a little piece in my head, I could not recall it, that I would now hurry to the desk, and, at one standing, write off the poem from beginning to end; and, as I could not spare time to adjust my paper, however obliquely it might lie, the lines often crossed it diagonally. In such a mood I liked best to get hold of a lead-pencil, because I could write most readily with it; whereas the scratching and spluttering of the pen would sometimes wake me from my somnambular poetizing, confuse me, and stifle a little conception in its birth.[1]

For Goethe, writing resembles sleepwalking, a state of inspiration that has to be preserved and protected from interruption for the poet to be able to compose his thoughts. But the *scene of writing*, to use Rüdiger Campe's term, which is constituted by a combination of language, technology, and bodily gesture, is constantly under threat.[2] Anything can interrupt the recording of thought on paper. The precarious process of inscription depends on the reliability of the instruments the writer uses to preserve his song: the desk, sheets of paper, pencil, and quill. This chapter examines various disturbances of writing scenes in Jean Paul's novel *Siebenkäs;* it also discusses several (failing) aesthetic, philosophical, and psychological strategies employed by Siebenkäs and other figures from Jean Paul's novels to cope with the recalcitrance of the "imaginary materiality of writing."[3] The most prominent of these are models of Stoic self-government, psychosomatic treatments, and idyllic and humorous modes of representation in literary writing.

The priest Frohauf Süptitz in Jean Paul's last, unfinished novel, *Der Komet,* is an exemplary figure who cannot come to terms with the constant interruptions of his environment. Süptitz's attempt to write a love letter is hampered by a dysfunctional pen, rendering his handwriting virtually incomprehensible: "During the most joyful outpouring [Ergüsse] of my love for you, my writing quill sprang open half an inch, thereby holding neither a single drop of ink nor a single letter."[4] Writing, which in this instance is meant to be a joyful outpouring, if not ejaculation, of love, dries up; the flow of love and words is blocked. "Körperströme" and "Schriftverkehr," to use Albrecht Koschorke's terminology, instead of phantasmatically uniting in the act of writing love letters, remain disjunctive.[5] For the traveling Süptitz to turn his distant wife into a "participant" (Teilnehmerin), he must rely on the unreliable quill offered by the inn where he spends the night. Pouring himself into the act of writing, he is stopped short by the recalcitrant obtrusiveness of the materiality of the writing utensils. All attempts by Süptitz to enthusiastically blur the border between body and writing fail. If flows induce soul, to refer to Koschorke again, the immediate outpouring of the soul in the medium of writing is impeded.[6] Therefore, Süptitz must reopen the channels of communication and thereby allow his soul to pour into the letters. In other words, he must focus on the materiality of writing, sharpening the tip of the quill: "Therefore I took my scissors . . . and cut off the long beak of the quill. I shortened it yet again, but unfortunately into the wide beak of a spoonbill, which had to be shortened again with scissors; then the slit was once again too short, even though any new splitting was highly perilous. So with the wide spade of a quill and without further ado, I wrote and plowed through [ackerte] my joys to you until I was done" (1014). Cutting the tip of the quill, which is supposed to guarantee the unhindered act of writing, if not performed properly, adds to the disturbances and ruptures, threatening the immediate communication of the soul. Writing turns into plowing. The opening of the quill is either too wide or too narrow. Therefore, the streaming of Süptitz's soul either overflows or is reduced to a trickle. Writing, according to Koschorke, "is therefore never wholly transparent, but rather involves something like a specific balance, a medial obstinacy [medialen Eigensinn], that it introduces to the articulation of thought."[7] These difficulties of writing provoke Süptitz to reflect upon the relation of body and soul, the real and the ideal, matter and thought, in the act of writing: "Yes, once again this pure, spiritual thought itself: from how many bodily detours might it finally arrive to you, my dear! Must I, unfortunately, not dip my quill, scatter sand, seal the letter and send it via post (I am leaving out the hundreds of in-between details); and on your side pay the postage, break the seal, and read the page until you reach the intended spot [bis zum gedachten Punkt]?" (1015). The expression of emotions in the medium of writing is limited and partly determined by the materiality of the manifold details involved in the process of writing, sending, and reading letters. To communicate an affect, the subject must divert his or her attention away from the actual experience to the concrete material of communication. Seemingly secondary and extraneous aspects of writing, like pen and ink or the postal service, which supposedly serve to guarantee the smooth transfer of emotion, are in fact essential for the actual process of writing. Süptitz complains:

> By the by, let me reflect upon one thing regarding the occasion of expressing emotion [Gelegenheit der Rührung]: on the whole, it is deplorable how one depends on so many sub-sub-subdivisions of base means to arrive finally at the noble. For instance, the way I come to feel emotion [Rührung] in the church: how I have to put on boots, vest, and everything, walk down and then up stairs, step into the church gallery, look out, and hear many corporeal things [vieles Körperliche] until I finally receive the spirit in the soul, or what we call an emotion. (1015)

Süptitz suggests that to deliver a sermon on emotion he himself needs to be in an emotional state. Here, he follows the ancient rhetorical tradition of self-affection.

The persuasiveness of speech depends to a large extent on the ability to communicate passion, be it mourning, pity, or anger. The speaker needs to be in the state of emotion he wants to convey. Shaftesbury, in his *Letter concerning Enthusiasm*, states that "to be able to move others, we must first be moved ourselves or at least seem to be, upon some probable grounds."[8] Süptitz is unable to accomplish this. He cannot stir the necessary emotions because he is distracted by his cramped situation within the pulpit, which constantly reminds him of his corporeality. The means and rhetorical devices that are supposed to bring about (self-)affection interfere with the sermon instead of supplementing its purpose. Süptitz's sermon turns into a mechanical, artificial series of "sub-sub-sub-divisions," devoid of any emotion.

In the *School for Aesthetics*, Jean Paul criticizes this rationalist, calculated form of artificial enthusiasm in the ancient and modern tradition: "With self-satisfaction and vainglorious coldness, for example, the old pedagogue selects and moves the necessary muscles and tear glands (according to Peucer [sic!] and Morhof) in order to have a lacrimose mourning face for the benefit of the public when he looks down from the school window in making a threnody on the grave of his predecessor, while he complacently counts every drop with a rain gauge."[9] Süptitz's performance ridicules the possibility of self-affection if it is based solely on an abstract, rational method that lacks "the instinct of the unconscious" [Instinkt des Unbewußten] (38 [59]). To write poetry in a state of enthusiasm or to give a moving sermon, the subject must be able to move from the conscious application of rhetorical instructions to an instinctive, unconscious mode of self-affection. Only then is it possible to exclude the vexing interruptions that threaten poetic imagination.

Jean Paul's novel *Siebenkäs*, originally published in 1796–97 and republished with considerable revisions in 1818 under the baroque title *Blumen-, Frucht- und Dornenstücke oder Ehestand, Tod und Hochzeit des Armenadvokaten Firmian Stanislaus Siebenkäs (Flower, Fruit and Thorn Pieces: Or the Married Life, Death, and Wedding of the Advocate of the Poor, Firmian Stanislaus Siebenkäs)*, presents several scenes of writing in which the precarious relationship between body, technology, and writing is negotiated. The protagonist of the novel, Firmian Siebenkäs, is a lawyer and a writer who is unable to reconcile these two different spheres of his existence. The unhappy site of the competing demands of his marriage, his career, and his writing is the confines of his small apartment. To recall Jean Paul's famous definition, in his *School for Aesthetics*, of the idyll as "perfect happiness within limits" [Beschränkung im Vollglück] (186 [260]), the bourgeois household would constitute the idyllic space par excellence. But as the longwinded title of the novel indicates, life within a confined parlor is anything but happy. Rather, it resembles a "secularized Passion of Christ" composed not of flowers and fruit but of thorns.[10] The "crowding concreteness" of the cramped living situation contributes much to the sense that modern marriage might be akin to Christ's passion.[11] The parlor is a place of both living and writing where the spheres of domesticity and literature fatally collide. Siebenkäs wishes that instead of being married to the mundane housewife Lenette he could be with a woman who would not "bring up the subject of his stockings in the middle of his loftiest and fullest flights of enthusiasm," someone "for whom this universe shall be something higher than a nursery and a ball-room."[12] Lenette does not complement Siebenkäs, not only because she is apparently simple-minded or uneducated but also because she lacks his fire of inspiration and thereby effectively obstructs his flights of imagination. In her presence, the writer cannot transcend his narrow surroundings—he remains the pedestrian figure of a lawyer, an *advocate of the poor,* who is unable to move beyond the vexing realities of his life.

In *Conjectural Biography (Konjektural-Biographie),* written shortly after *Siebenkäs,* Jean Paul describes writing within the confines of a marriage in a decidedly idyllic tone:

> He [Jean Paul] sits in his study above, wearing freshly laundered clothes like Buffon, and continues to write his best work. So as not to disturb the husband, the hard-working soul in the white housecoat wants only to pass through. But he lays down the quill on top of the ink bottle, offers her a hand and pulls her to him, and she leans over, reading what he's been writing. Because she benefits from everything, from honor and the gratuity for the creation, he dives back into his work with greater fervor [mit größerem Feuer], thinking of dinner while writing the most beautiful scenes![13]

The wife's interruption of the scene of writing is in fact a moment of inspiration. Hermine Rosinette becomes the "ideal reader,"[14] holding the poet's hand, bending toward the text, and, in so doing, spurring him to write "with greater fervor."

Both the act of writing and a happy marriage originate in an experience of anticipation. In this scene, Jean Paul refers to what Albrecht Koschorke calls a "fundamental redefinition of human happiness" in the eighteenth-century Enlightenment: "While happiness traditionally belonged to the figure of perfection and was connected with the metaphysical triad of the good, the true and the beautiful, it slowly assumed via rational philosophy a movement toward intentionality. . . . Ambition, lack, happiness, and perfection all determine each other mutually in this construction. . . . Henceforth, every feeling of happiness is merely an incomplete, preliminary stage of an expected, greater happiness."[15] Jean Paul reduces the rationalistic and eudaimonistic belief in the perfectibility of the human to a mere eagerness for basic bodily satisfaction, the cheerful anticipation of the next meal. But a different form of anticipation characterizes the marriage of Siebenkäs and Lenette. Because of their poverty—caused in large measure by Siebenkäs's slow writing—many of their conversations, instead of happily anticipating the satisfaction of a fulfilled future, are anxious calculations concerning the bare necessities of economic survival. The thought of food is depicted, not as the "most cherished moment," but as a disruption of the harmony of matrimony and the foundation of literary productivity.

It is the financial ruin of the Siebenkäs household that renders fantasy impotent as a remedy against the vexations of everyday life.[16] Siebenkäs's life turns from a *flower and fruit piece* into a *thorn piece*. He is unhappy and eventually becomes sick: "The money went. But worse than that, poor Firmian had fretted, and laughed, himself into an illness. A man who has all his life, upon the upper wings of Fantasy and the lower wings of good spirits, skimmed lightly away over the tops of all the spread-net snares and the open pitfalls of life, does, if once he chances to get impaled upon the hard spines of the full-blown thistles (above the purple blossoms and the honey-vessels of which he used to hover) beat in a terrible way about him, hungry, bleeding, epileptically" (293 [300]).[17] Neither fantasy nor "good spirits" (Laune) allow Siebenkäs to avoid the thorny thistles of reality.[18] No flight of imagination can raise the human beyond the nets and traps of earthly life. In fact, it is his aspiration to be a writer that prevents him from furthering his career as a lawyer. But it is not only the lack of money that causes Siebenkäs's misery as a writer. The act of writing itself affects the writer's health: "He sat through almost entire nights, wore down many chairs, and rode upon his satirical bench. In this way he wrote himself into an affliction of the throat" (294 [300]). Excessive writing at night in a sitting position causes "a sudden pausing of the breath and of the action of the heart, succeeded by a blank disappearance of the spirit of life; and then by a throbbing rush of blood up to the brain" (294 [300]). Writing is unhealthy, creating disruptions in the breathing and blood circulation. Here Jean Paul presents Siebenkäs as the figure of the dangers of excessive scholarship, which were the subject of a significant scientific discourse of the day. Exemplary of this school of thought is Samuel Auguste David Tissot's *Treatise on the Health of Men of Letters*, which describes cases of hypochondria caused by the constricting effects of the sedentary life of a scholar: "Hypochondria must also include the affliction, which develops almost inevitably through the sedentary lifestyle of the scholar, that disrupts the blood circulation in the intestines of the lower abdomen and therein provokes the onset of constipation."[19] For Jean Paul, mental and physical health cannot be separated: "Health of body only runs parallel with health of mind; it turns aside and departs from erudition, from over-much imagination, and from great profundity. All these as little indicate health of mind as corpulence, a runner's feet, a wrestler's arms, indicate health of body" (295 [301]). It is the philosophical as well as the physiological problem of the *commercium mentis et corporis* that is at stake in this passage. Jean Paul, very much in the vein of the emerging field of anthropology at the time, argues against Descartes's theory of a strict separation of *res cogito* and *res extensa*. In the preface to his *Anthropology for Physicians and the Worldwise (Anthropologie für Aerzte und Weltweise)* (1772), Ernst Platner, the admired teacher of Jean Paul, calls for a revision of the distinction between sciences of the mind and sciences of the body. Scientists, philosophers, and physicians must not limit their field of investigation to either sphere; rather, they must examine the *commercium mentis et corporis*. Platner defines the new anthropology as follows: "It is finally possible to observe body and soul together in their reciprocal relations, their limitations and connections, and that is what I call anthropology."[20] Jean Paul's literary oeuvre can be seen as a translation of the insights of the new disciplines of anthropology and physiology as well as medicine into the realm of aesthetics.[21] What in the case of Siebenkäs fails is a "dietetics" (Koschorke) or "hygiene" (Müller) of imagination.[22] From the middle of the eighteenth century, the human faculty of imagination not only had become central to a new form of aesthetics replacing older doctrines of mimesis but had served as a therapeutic agent in contemporary medical doctrines. Wolfram Mauser summarizes this discourse on the powers of imagination: "According to the medical scholarship of the time, the imagination is part of a theory of stimulation [Reiztheorie] that derives from the emotions of the senses (i.e., the capacity of the affections), from the ability to store the experience of sensuous pleasures, and from the particular capacity of the soul, all of which produce conceptions of sensuous pleasure as a means of dietetic and therapeutic effect with specific preconditions."[23] The ability of the imagination to simultaneously affect the human body and soul is highly ambiguous. When used in a controlled, therapeutical context, fantasy can relieve the human subject from affliction. If, on the other hand, it is given free rein and liberated from the supervision of reason, it can exacerbate or even trigger mental and physical ailments.

Symptomatically, the story of Siebenkäs's failed marriage begins with a moment of anticipation that combines "pleasure ... with annoyance."[24] Siebenkäs looks out of the window of his apartment, awaiting the arrival of his bride. And although the wait causes Siebenkäs to "depose an oath (more than once) that it was the devil who invented *seeking*, and his grandmother who devised *waiting*" (20 [33]), he still is able to cope with the increasing anxiety by transforming pain into pleasure: "Siebenkäs's butterfly-proboscis, however, found plenty of open honey cells in every blue thistle blossom of his fate" (20 [34]). The image of sweet honey within the thorns of a thistle becomes the emblem of Jean Paul's theory of the idyll. "Perfect happiness within limits" is achieved by protecting oneself against the "thorn pieces" (Dornenstücke) of man's existence. The idyll is not free of pains and afflictions, but one must be able to find honey among the thorns. In the idyllic, limited space, self and world, inside and outside, nature and culture are not harmoniously merged. Rather, the thorns and their sting remain, and it is the task of the human being to find the soothing honey "in every blue thistle bloom of his fate." In *Life of Quintus Fixlein (Leben des Quintus Fixlein)*, one of Jean Paul's most famous idylls, the narrator states: "Trifles we should let, not plague us only, but also gratify us; we should seize not their poison-bags only, but their honey-bags also."[25] Paul Fleming comments: "Jean Paul freely admits the annoyances of the quotidian. He doesn't idealize the microcosm, but stresses the need to turn it into a source of happiness. The 'rules of life' consist, then, not in fighting the small, quotidian annoyances, but in embracing them and transforming them into pleasure mixed with annoyance."[26] In *Siebenkäs* the first scene showing a failure of anticipation as well as of imagination to protect the subject from the afflictions of the bourgeois household and to guarantee the smooth progress of writing is in the fifth chapter of the second volume under the subtitles: "The Broom and the Besom as Passion Implements—The Importance of a Bookwriter—Diplomatic Negotiations and Discussions on the Subject of Candle Snuffing—The Pewter: Cupboard—Domestic Hardships and Enjoyments" (139 [150]). While Siebenkäs sits at his desk trying to write his *Selection from the Devil's Papers (Auswahl aus den Papieren des Teufels)*, he is constantly interrupted by the sounds of Lenette's cleaning efforts in the next room:

> "Oh! I shall get on somehow or other," said Siebenkaes quite gleefully, as he set to work harder than ever at his writing, with the view of getting a considerable haul of money into the house, at the earliest moment possible, in the shape of payment for his "Selection from the Devil's Papers." But there was a fresh purgatorial fire now being stoked and blown, till it blazed hotter about him. I have refrained from saying anything about the fire in question till now, though he has been sitting roasting at it since the day before yesterday, Lenette being the cook, and his writing being the larkspit. During the few days when the wordless quarrel was going on, he had got into a habit of listening with the closest attention to what Lenette was doing, as he sat writing away his "Selection from the Devil's Papers": and this sent his ideas all astray. The softest step, the very slightest shake of anything affected him just as if he had hydrophobia, or the gout, and put one or two fine young ideas to death, as a louder noise kills young canaries, or silkworms. (141–42 [154])

The housewife's actions in the next room kill the writer's thoughts and ideas. It is not the sound of her cleaning itself that is disturbing for Siebenkäs but his oversensitive attentiveness toward even the most muted and gentle sounds.

Henri Bergson, in his seminal study *Laughter: An Essay on the Meaning of the Comic*, reverses Jean Paul's description of distracted attention. While Siebenkäs or Quintus Fixlein cannot stop anticipating what will happen, the absentminded figure pictured by Bergson cannot stop thinking about what has happened. For Henri Bergson, absentmindedness constitutes "one of the great natural watersheds of laughter."[27] Bergson imagines the absentminded person as follows: "Let us try to picture to ourselves a certain inborn lack of elasticity of both senses and intelligence, which brings it to pass that we continue to see what is no longer visible, to hear what is no longer visible, to hear what is no longer audible, to say what is no longer audible, to say what is no longer to the point: in short, to adapt ourselves to a past and therefore imaginary situation, when we ought to be shaping our conduct in accordance with the reality which is present."[28] For both Jean Paul and Bergson, temporal asynchronicity causes laughter, owing to a manifest incommensurablity between the imaginary and the real. Bergson's ridiculous character is focused on the "no longer," while Siebenkäs is focused on the "not yet." Both miss the present, their minds being inelastic, unable to adapt to the current situation.

Absentmindedness in this sense does not simply mean distraction, the inability to focus, but the difficulty of reconciling the concrete situation with the products of one's imagination.

This failure of the subject to adapt to the objective world brings to mind the Stoic theory of emotions, which also equates the origin of affects with a failure of the psyche to adapt to its environment. Maximilian Forschner summarizes the Stoic view as follows: "In all of this, the fundamental principle of the Stoic theory of the emotions becomes visible: the main cause . . . of an emotional state in humans is based, not on the quality of an external event or on its sudden, unexpected, or unfamiliar arrival, but rather on the composition of the subject in an *incorrect disposition* [verkehrte Sinnesart], from which result the pathological conditions and activities."[29] Affect-inducing disturbances do not necessarily have to be sudden, unexpected, or unusual. Since they are caused by a specific mental disposition of the subject, even the most everyday events—like sweeping the floor—can ignite anger and frustration. A plea to Lenette to be quieter, therefore, instead of erasing the disturbances, only increases Siebenkäs's painfully attentive and expectant listening:

> It was truly in a moment of one of these days that Siebenkaes made the request above mentioned; for he had laid upon himself the necessity of lying in wait [unter dem Denken aufzulauern] and watching to see what Lenette would do in consequence of it. She skimmed over the floor, and athwart the various webs of her household labours, with the tread of a spider. Siebenkaes had to keep his ears very much on the alert to hear what little noise she did make, either with her hands or her feet—but he was successful, and he did hear the greater part of it. Unless we are asleep we are more attentive to a slight noise than to a loud one: and our author listened to her wherever she went, his ear and attention fixed to her like a pedometer wherever she moved. (142–43 [154])

The fainter the sound, the more heightened the attention. Lenette's attempts not to disturb Siebenkäs and to sweep as gently as possible create the opposite effect. He becomes increasingly irritated. The broom, even when used lightly, "drives away the whole of my best ideas out of my head"(144 [154]), making Siebenkäs grumble. The final, most vexing, but also most comical turn in the ever-escalating battle between sweeping floors and writing satires takes place when Lenette stops making any noise at all. Siebenkäs protests: "It's exactly that which I complain of, that I can't hear you in the next room; I'm obliged to rack my brains to guess what you're at—and the only ideas left in my head are connected with brushing and scrubbing, so that all the brilliant notions which I might otherwise be putting down on paper are driven away" (145 [156]). In this passage, writing is prevented by imagination. Not only does Siebenkäs anticipate Lenette's next actions, but he actively imagines what she might do. Silence, which he had thought would be the condition for the possibility of his writing, turns out to render writing impossible. Writing *hört auf*. Throughout the scene Jean Paul plays with the semantic ambiguity of the verb *aufhören*, meaning both "ending" and "listening for." Listening for Lenette effectively ends Siebenkäs's literary production.[30] What he hears or imagines supplants the inspired flights of imagination and resists being written down. His thoughts are "totally led astray" (völlig irre im Denken; 141 [154]), and his writing becomes "merely exhausted" (bloß matter; 142 [154]), "without reason" (ohne Verstand; 156), until finally thoughts of cloth and brooms have completely replaced his literary aspirations. Goethe's fears in the aforementioned quote that his poems will be suffocated at birth become true for Siebenkäs. They are killed by the silent noise of bourgeois domesticity. For Goethe as well as Jean Paul, the poetic act can be successful only when the writing scene is shielded from intruding influences, so that the writer can listen to his inner voice. But whereas Goethe's rush to the desk makes writing possible, Siebenkäs's progress as a writer is delayed and disrupted. His literary production, if it ever gets finished, lacks the fire of inspiration.

Fantasy and imagination, which in Jean Paul's theory of the idyll guarantee the subject's happiness and ensure the *good life*, produce in his literary works disruptions, pain, and anger in the face of an antagonistic reality. The idyllic escape into the anticipation of pleasure fails. Instead of being a source of comfort and consolation, all that is imagined increases the vexations of the everyday. The writer's desk becomes a "larkspit" where he, as "scribbling martyr" (142 [155]), has to endure the "hellish ... torment" (144 [155]) of writing in the face of—or with an ear for—a "quiet noise" [leisen Lärm] (145 [158]) with which he cannot cope.

The limitations of complete happiness, to quote Jean Paul's definition of the idyllic again, become manifest as the walls of his office, which in the confined space of the Siebenkäs household also serves as the dining and living room. Ironically, these walls do not protect the writer Siebenkäs from the vexations of life; instead they provoke forms of fantasy and imagination that do not console but incite disagreeable passions. Siebenkäs's solution for dealing with the unbearable silent noise of the everyday consists in changing the time of writing from morning to evening. Sitting at the same table with Lenette—he writes while she is silently working on her stitching—becomes the vision of a restored idyllic environment where husband and wife become one: "The evening of nectar and ambrosia came duly on, and was quite without a rival among all evenings that had gone before it. A young married couple, sitting one on each side of a table [bei *einem* Lichte einander an *einem* Tische], working away quietly at their work, with a candle between them, have a considerable notion what happiness is. He was all happy thoughts [Einfälle] and kisses" (156 [167]). But it is the unity of *one* candle and *one* table that will cause this scene of domestic harmony to break up. To give the proper lighting at night, the candlewick needs to be trimmed regularly. Inevitably, Lenette's cutting the wick of the candle distracts Siebenkäs from his writing. Again, his thoughts and fantasies are replaced by the anticipation of Lenette's actions. He scolds her: "'Well, dear,' he continued, 'I'll proceed to point out to you that, on the grounds of psychology and mental science, it isn't that it matters a bit whether a person who is writing and thinking *sees* a little more or less distinctly or not, it's the snuffers and the snuff that he can't get out of his head, and they get behind his spiritual legs, trip up his ideas, and stop him, just as a log does a horse hobbled to it'" (159–60 [170]). His train of thoughts is held up and interrupted. As in the case of the silent noise in the morning, it is not the actual lack of light that interferes with his writing but his over-attentive mind, which consumes itself in the anticipation of the next disruption. Siebenkäs's speech to Lenette continues: "For even when you've only just snuffed the candle, and I'm in full enjoyment of the light, I begin to look out [Lauern] for the instant when you'll do it next. Now, this watching being in itself neither visible nor audible, can be nothing but a thought, or idea; and as every thought has the property of occupying the mind to the exclusion of all others, it follows that all an author's other and more valuable ideas are sent at once to the dogs" (160 [170]). In today's terminology one could say that Siebenkäs is incapable of multitasking. There can always be only one thought in his mind that excludes all others. In Johann Christoph Reil's theory of the mind, which was developed around the same time when Jean Paul wrote his satires of matrimonial strife, it is similarly impossible for the soul to focus on two different things simultaneously: "When the soul dedicates itself to a task, then it must relinquish all other remaining tasks. It must let go of that task if it chooses to examine a new object." Therefore, the soul is forced "to perform multiple activities successively rather than simultaneously."[31]

The writer Siebenkäs, being in a constant state of attention, misses the presence and actuality of writing. He cannot bridge the gap between anticipating fantasy and the actual act of writing because he is unable to perform several tasks simultaneously. Maurice Blanchot's statement that the writer is "a stoic: he is the man of the universe, which itself exists only on paper, and, a prisoner or a poor man, he endures his condition stoically because he can write and because the one minute of freedom in which he writes is enough to make him powerful and free"[32]—is put to the test by Siebenkäs when he must share his desk with his wife. He inhabits two worlds, that of literature and that of his marriage, in the confined space of a poverty-stricken household. Unable to simultaneously exist within both spheres, he cannot reconcile the Stoic equanimity of writing with the miseries and pains of anticipation. Being trapped, the writer cannot write; therefore he cannot bear his existence with equanimity. The subject suspended between the universes of writing and marriage lacks a "technology of the self" that would allow for the successful creation of a writing scene. Language, technology, and bodily gesture constantly interrupt each other. Anticipation, a mode that is supposed to alleviate and transform pain into pleasure, becomes the emotion that undoes writing. Instead of pleasure, Siebenkäs feels anger and rage. Lenette's reaction to her husband's scolding is typical for Jean Paul's depiction of matrimonial strife disrupting the writing scene. The next day "she *hardly ever left off snuffing*" [ordentlich ohne Aufzuhören] (16 [171]), thereby again disrupting and angering Siebenkäs and triggering another criticism: "'Don't snuff *too* often, darling,' he said, at length, but very, very kindly. 'If you attempt *too* fine sub-sub-sub-divisions (fractions of fractions of fractions of fractions) of the wick, it'll be almost as bad as ever—a candle snuffed too short gives as little light as one with an overgrown wick. . . . It's only for a short while *before* and *after* the snuffing, *entre chien et loup* as it were, that that delicious middle-age of the soul [die schöne mittlere Zeit der Seele] prevails when it can see the perfection'" (160–61 [171]). The time of uninterrupted writing is situated between *too early* and *too late*, keeping the balance between before and after, "before and after the snuffing." It is the middle and mean time when the writer is not preoccupied with the medium and materiality of writing—when the light and time are just right. But this time of beautiful harmony is constantly threatened by the preoccupation of Siebenkäs's lurking anticipation. "*Entre chien et loup,*" between dog and wolf, the happiness of writing as well as that of marriage is reduced to the mere difference between pre- and post-, before and after: Siebenkäs *hört nicht auf aufzuhören.*[33]

In an addendum to the sixth chapter of the second volume of *Siebenkäs* entitled "Extra Leaflet on Consolation" (Extrablättchen über den Trost), Jean Paul again stresses the importance of fantasy in the creation of vexations:

> It is only through the imagination, as from an electric condenser, that even physical pain emits its sparks upon us. We would bear the severest physical pains without a wince if they were not of longer duration than a sixtieth part of a second; but we never really do have an hour of pain to endure, but only a succession of sixtieth parts of a second of pain, the sixty separate rays of which are concentrated into the focus and burning-point of a second, and directed upon our nerves by the imagination alone. The most painful part of corporeal pain is the incorporeal part of it, that is to say, our own impatience, and our delusive conviction that it will last for ever. (187–88 [197])

As in the case of the silent noise, it is not only the actual, physical irritation that causes pain but the subject's fantasy and imagination, which cannot separate itself from the possibility of disturbance. Impatience, like the anticipation of Lenette's cutting of the wick, is worse than the actual lack of light. Here Jean Paul cites a classic argument of Stoic doctrine. For the Stoic, only the present matters, since both past and future are beyond his or her will: that is, they are independent of the subject's intentions. Marcus Aurelius, for example, prescribes that "if you separate from yourself the future and the past, and apply yourself exclusively to living the life you are living—that is to say, the present—you can live all the time that remains to you until your death, in calm, benevolence, and serenity."[34] This focus on the present as a prerequisite to achieve happiness is based on the idea that one must learn, as part of one's cultivation and formation, to distinguish between those things for which one is responsible and those for which one is not. The very first entry in Epictetus's *Enchiridion* states this basic tenet of Stoicism clearly: "We are responsible for some things, while there are others for which we cannot be held responsible. The former include our judgment, our impulse, our desire, aversion and our mental faculties in general; the latter include the body, material possessions, our reputation, status, anything not in our power to control."[35] The past and the future are beyond our power to control; hence it is unreasonable, according to Epictetus, to attach any emotions to them. This extirpation of all temporal affects extends even to a seemingly "positive" sentiment like hope. The idyllic anticipation of future happiness is as unreasonable and therefore as unacceptable as, for example, the fear of death. Jean Paul's reception and discussion of Stoic and neo-Stoic doctrines of practical wisdom changes significantly between "On the Natural Magic of Imagination" (Über die natürliche Magie der Einbildungskraft) from 1796 and the fragmentary "Little Book of Joy or *Ars Semper Gaudendi*" (Freuden-Büchlein oder Ars Semper Gaudendi)—a revision and continuation of the tract *Ars Semper Gaudendi* by the seventeenth-century Spanish neo-Stoic Alfons Anton de Sarasa—from 1811/13. While in "On the Natural Magic of Imagination" hope, as a certain mode of anticipation, allows one to cope with the afflictions of everyday life, in the "Little Book of Joy" imagination and anticipatory fantasy are denounced as empty and misleading. In the tradition of Marcus Aurelius, Epictetus, and Sarasa, *ataraxia*, the freedom from *all* expectations, becomes the goal of Jean Paul's technologies of the self.[36]

Siebenkäs is caught in a disjunctive mode of anticipation. The temporality arising from his anticipation of interruption destroys the idyll promised by the idealized scene of writing. In the "Extra Leaflet on Consolation," affective expectations such as hope, resembling madness, have their own time, independent of any "objective" or chronological order: "The reason is that every sentiment and every passion is a mad thing, demanding, or building, a complete world of its own. We are capable of being vexed because it's past twelve o'clock, or because it's *not* past, but only *just* twelve o'clock. What nonsense! The passion wants besides a personality of its own [sein eigenes Ich] and a world of its own, —a time of its own as well" (188 [197–98]). The time of affect is in principle infinite, as Jean Paul asserts in the "On the Natural Magic of Imagination": "All our affects carry with them an indelible feeling of eternity and exuberance [unvertilgbares Gefühl ihrer Ewigkeit und Überschwenglichkeit]—love, hate, pain, and joy are all experienced as eternal and infinite."[37] When humans love or hate, they dissociate themselves from chronological measures of time and in so doing miss the present time of Stoic apathy. Suffering from an affect like anger resembles madness. Both create a world of imaginings that can either have a therapeutic influence or increase the subject's suffering. Again, Jean Paul addresses the ambivalence of imagination, oscillating between poison and remedy. To see through the fantastic world created by mad affects, Jean Paul suggests the traditional Stoic therapy of self-reflection: "I ask each one to let his affects for once completely express themselves internally, to reflect upon them and ask them what they actually want: he will be shocked by the monstrosity of their wishes, which until then were only partly articulated."[38] Pierre Hadot calls these modes of listening and questioning, following Stoic paradigms, "spiritual exercises."[39] One of the most prominent elements of these exercises, understood as a method to form the self and overcome pathogenic affects, is regular self-examination.[40] The cultivation of mental health, for Jean Paul, consists in a form of self-analysis to attain a proper sense of temporality, which includes the extirpation of such affects as impatience or nostalgia. Seneca in *On Anger* 2.26, in a section entitled "Examine Your Conscience Every Day," proposes: "I make use of this opportunity [of self-reflection], daily pleading my case at my own court. When the light has been taken away and my wife has fallen silent, aware as she is of my habit, I examine my entire day, going through what I have done and said. I conceal nothing from myself, I pass nothing by."[41] The habit of silently reflecting upon one's actions, affects, and thoughts in the court of reason allows the subject to recognize the nature of those causes that affected him over the course of the day. At this time, the subject habitually reflects upon his or her actions and whether he or she has "the right idea about what really belongs to [the subject] and what does not."[42]

The mind, that is, reason, if undisturbed, can create a form of timelessness by focusing on the present moment. The more the writer stays within the moment, the more intensely he or she focuses on the act of writing, and the more he or she forgets time. Writing happens in a realm where the writer is not afflicted by the corporeality of the body existing in time. As in the case of the apathetic Stoic who lives only in the present, hope and memory, impatience and melancholy, are forgotten and leave the writer without affect. The Stoic can "delimit the present," which Hadot describes as turning "one's attention away from the past and the future, in order to concentrate it upon what one is in the process of doing."[43] This form of happiness in the moment differs categorically from the idyllic model of Quintus Fixlein, where cheerfulness and pleasure result from the anticipation of a happy future or the remembrance of a joyful past. In opposition to the timelessness of a delimited present, Siebenkäs's time is always out of joint. He can neither successfully anticipate or remember joyful moments nor focus his attention on the present. His mind is always ahead of his or Lenette's actions, and he is unable to synchronize the infinity of reason with the finitude of action. This asynchronicity becomes evident in the ever-intensifying argument between husband and wife regarding the proper time for brewing the morning coffee. Early in the morning in bed before rising, Siebenkäs the writer is able to escape the household's restrictions and produce his best thoughts. Lenette's call for Siebenkäs to get up because the coffee is ready hurries his thoughts, as he has to finish his reflections before the coffee gets cold or, worse still, before she calls him again. Lenette, noticing her husband's delay in getting up, takes up calling him at the moment the coffee water starts to boil: "The notonectic satirist [Siebenkäs], for his part, had observed the law which governed this precession of the equinoxes, and lay quietly among the feathers breeding his ideas happy and undisturbed when it was only once that she had summoned him, merely answering, 'This very moment!' and availing himself of the double usance prescribed by law. This obliged his wife, for her part, to go farther back, and when the coffee was made and standing by the fire, to cry 'Come, dear, it's getting quite cold'" (277 [284]). This interaction between husband and wife, their respective anticipation of each other's actions, ultimately ensures the frustration of both: his thoughts are rushed and incomplete, and the right moment for drinking the morning coffee is missed. The writer's desperate attempts to create a grace period of writing before he has to enter the household are counteracted and negated by the wife's attempts to serve him coffee while it is hot. For him, she acts too early, while for her, he acts too late. This reciprocal anticipation keeps escalating: "Now, on this system, of getting earlier on one side and later on the other, matters became more and more critical every day, with nowhere a prospect of extrication from the difficulty; in fact, what was natural to be expected was an escalation [Steigerung] of things in which Lenette would end by calling him to get up a whole day too soon" (277 [284–85]). Between too early and too late both the act of writing and the marital habit of a common breakfast fail.[44] It is again impossible to synchronize the time of writing with the time of the marriage, the realm of the imaginary with that of the real. The last section of the "Little Book of Joy," possibly Jean Paul's most explicit discussion of Stoic thought, explains the futility of anger in terms of its atemporality, that is, as a way of being either too early or too late: "There is no span of time [Zeitzwischenraum] to be annoyed with a person. If he has already done something, it is useless; if he is about to do something, it is too early."[45] To become angry at a past event is pointless because the subject has no power over the past, while getting angry in anticipation of a future event always comes too early. The following section will discuss in detail the close connection of Stoic and aesthetic (in the form of the idyllic) models of anger management as they both relate to the development of new therapies in the emerging fields of anthropology and clinical psychology.

THE IDYLL AS STOIC REMEDY

In one of the four addenda to *Life of Quintus Fixlein*, entitled "The Libel of Bailiff Josuah Freudel against His Accursed Demons" (Des Amts-Vogts Josuah Freudel Klaglibell gegen seinen verfluchten Dämon), Jean Paul humorously depicts the belief that the vexations of everyday life are caused by malicious spirits constantly assailing human beings. The protagonist of the addendum, Josuah Freudel, who happens to be locked into a church, complains about the persistence of pain and suffering in his life. These vexations he attributes, as already indicated in the title, to a spiteful demon: "Nothing is more certain than a spiteful demon [tückischer Dämon] that hounds certain people and throws a monkey wrench into their lives, precisely when everything is going well and even seems to turn out for the best" (206).[46] As in the case of Frohauf Süptitz, the name Freudel is a telling one, insofar as Josuah Freudel, whenever he feels joy (Freude), is at the same time bothered by what he believes to be a demonic force. His predicament consists not so much in being constantly unhappy, as was the case with Frohauf Süptitz, as in being disturbed in moments of joy and happiness: "It is precisely when I have feelings of (sometimes very) great pleasure, acclaim, or poignant impressions that I can count on the demon to notice it all and for him to bless me afterwards. In this way he loves to spoil my beautiful flights of fancy with a domestic quarrel, and a triumphal arch [Ehrenbogen] becomes for me a rainbow [Regenbogen] that signals three days of misery" (206–7).

The greater the joy, the sooner the demon interrupts and destroys Freudel's happiness. Therefore, he is not able to enjoy himself for long. In his life, happiness and unhappiness are "separately packed on top of and next to each other" [mutschierungsweise neben und auf einander verpackt] (206). Although separated—the anachronistic judicial term *mutschieren* refers to the legal separation of property—fortune and misfortune are packed on top of each other. The ethical project of living a good and happy life is undermined by the jests of an evil demon. Jean Paul contrasts Freudel, who cannot enjoy his life, with the protagonist of the idyll *Life of Quintus Fixlein*, a parson who is healed from an obsession with his own death by the narrator through the "elementary principles of the Science of Happiness" [Elementarkenntnisse der Glückseligkeitslehre] (299 [185]). This knowledge the narrator condenses into several maxims, the second of which states: "Trifles we should let, not plague us only, but also gratify us; we should seize not their poison-bags only, but their honey-bags also: and if flies often buzz about our room, we should, like Domitian, amuse ourselves with flies, or, like a certain still living Elector, feed them" (300 [185]). Rather than dwell upon the small vexations of everyday life, human beings should find pleasure in them. Trivialities are something to rejoice in as a "form of microscopic amusement."[47] Freudel is unable to live according to the basic maxims of the doctrine of happiness expounded by the narrator of *Life of Quintus Fixlein*. Although his life also appears to be a mixture of pleasure and annoyance, he cannot properly separate or satisfactorily merge the two passions. Freudel lacks Fixlein's ability to enjoy the fleeting moments of happiness by looking at life as something artificial in the way that another of the narrator's maxims from *Quintus Fixlein* stipulates: "For *civic* life and its micrologies, for which the Parson has a natural taste, we must acquire an artificial one; must learn to love without esteeming it; learn, far as it ranks beneath *human* life, to enjoy it like another twig of this human life, as poetically as we do the pictures of it in romances" (300 [185]). Successfully coping with the minor vexations of the everyday involves transforming reality into fiction. Ethics relies on aesthetics. Enjoying one's life as if it were a novel guarantees a way of dealing with its annoyances and pains. Aesthetic pleasure, as it is exemplified by reading a book, installs a form of distance. One loves the characters without giving them any esteem or regard. Therefore, love without esteem, as a mode of aesthetics and ethics, does not shy away from what seems to be small, lowly, or mundane, since everything is a "twig" (Verästung) of the human. The most sublime and the most debased are branches of the same human essence. Both are representations of "the *same sort* of things" [einerlei Dinge] (300 [185]). In this perspective, the lives of a bourgeois, a priest, and a nobleman are all related to the same idea of humanity. The abstract idea of man, which Jean Paul puts in italics (*"human* life" [dem *menschlichen*]), once it is perceived poetically, coincides with all concrete representations of the ideal, which Jean Paul does not italicize: "human life" (des menschlichen).

In 1813, the journal *Museum* published a small collection of Jean Paul's aphorisms under the title "The Art of Being Constantly Cheerful" (Kunst, stets heiter zu sein). It contains fragments and reflections, written and compiled in May and June of 1811, in reaction to the German publication of James Beresford's *The Miseries of Human Life, or, The Groans of Samuel Sensitive, and Timothy Testy*. The two protagonists, Samuel Sensitive and Timothy Testy, list and discuss at length the many and often miniscule afflictions and miseries that threaten the happiness of man. Many of these instances can be read as direct precursors to what Friedrich Theodor Vischer calls malicious objects. The chapter "Domestic Miseries," for example, mentions a malfunctioning door, an object that, from Sterne's *Tristram Shandy* to Jean Paul's *Siebenkäs* and Latour's *Recalcitrant Objects*, figures prominently as an embodiment of dysfunctionality. Samuel Sensitive's complaint No. 17 reads as follows: "A door so tight at the bottom, that it calls for your shoulders, as well as hands, as often as you enter or leave the room—and even when you have forced it to move, insists upon the company of the carpet every inch of the way."[48] The especially choleric Timothy Testy relentlessly piles one misery on top of the other to convince the more stoic Samuel Sensitive of the shortcomings of any doctrine of happiness. While Sensitive has found happiness on a recent trip to Europe, Testy characterizes his own situation as "continually shifting from the frying-pan to the fire, and from the fire back to the frying-pan."[49] Jean Paul replies to Beresford's tragicomic compendium by drafting about two hundred notes, giving them the title "Little Book of Joy or *Ars Semper Gaudendi*" (Freuden-Büchlein oder Ars Semper Gaudendi),[50] and these serve as the blueprint for the aforementioned *Museum* article, "The Art of Being Constantly Cheerful."

Next to Beresford, the other influence on Jean Paul's reflections was Alfons Anton de Sarasa's *Ars Semper Gaudendi ex Sola Consideratione Divinae Providentiae et per Adventuales Conciones Exposita*, published in Antwerp in 1664. Sarasa's neo-Stoicism is based in his Christian belief in God's providence, which he combines in his sermons—from which *Ars Semper Gaudendi* was drawn—with an interpretation of ancient Stoics, in particular Seneca and Epictetus. According to Götz Müller, it was especially Epictetus's maxim "We are tormented with the opinions we have of things, and not by things themselves" from the *Enchiridion* that influenced Sarasa's philosophy.[51] It is no coincidence that the same maxim functions as the motto to Lawrence Sterne's *Tristram Shandy*.[52] Jean Paul considered his "Little Book of Joy" not as an "imitation" but as a "continuation" of and addition to Sarasa's treatise, as he states in a letter from June 10, 1811: "This book can only be completed in several years; it is not an imitation but a continuation of and addition to Alfonso de Sarasa's *Ars Semper Gaudendi*"[53] The incomplete status of the text is evident in aphorism 68, which lists possible titles for the project without coming to a definite conclusion: "Title: system of cheerfulness—order of salvation—actually book of healing—sunny side of life—dispensations—anti-hypochondriacus—Ars semper gaudendi—painted winter landscape—eternal spring—knight of happy countenance—quarter-mourning—libri tristium—winter quarters—pharmaceutics—mineral spring—medicine chest—rescue ladder—sine-cure-place—new year's singing—musical circle."[54] While for Sarasa the ability to remain calm and cheerful in the face of life's many afflictions is rooted in divine providence, for Jean Paul it lies in the subject's own capacity.

Earlier, in "On the Natural Magic of Imagination" (1796), Jean Paul had been a proponent of the transformation of negative affects with the aid of the imagination. But in 1811 and 1813, he instead called for composure guided by reason: "Clarity of thought about every event—however strong its sensation [Empfindung]. Continue in this manner and you will become an Epictetus."[55] He replaced his initial praise for the metaphoric powers of imagination, which would soothe and cover the miseries of everyday life by creating dreamlike images, with the sober demands of reason, which is assigned to defend itself against all kinds of affect, whether painful or pleasurable. By repeatedly reflecting upon every event, be it positive or negative, everyone can become like Epictetus and reach a state of rigid self-control and self-containment, unfazed by the pains and sufferings of life. *Ataraxia* is a form of self-command and self-government, the rule of reason over affect. Despite this apparent turn to Stoic *ataraxia* and a rationalistic discourse that would rigorously separate the opinions we have of things from the things themselves, there are moments in the "Little Book of Joy" that seem to return to Jean Paul's older sympathies for the magical healing powers of the imagination. The most famous figure in the works of Jean Paul, one that happens to incarnate this therapeutical concept of fantasy, is the cheerful little schoolmaster Wutz, "who has it good, despite everything."[56] In the *School for Aesthetics*, Jean Paul lists *Life of Quintus Fixlein*, *Life of the Cheerful Schoolmaster Wutz*, and *Life of Fibel* as representatives of the genre of the idyll. The idyll is defined in *School for Aesthetics* as an epic form, representing full happiness in limitation: "We have at least a small epic version of it in the idyll. This is the epic representation of *perfect happiness within limits*" (186 [258]). While the conventional theory of the idyll, as represented by Fontenelle, Gottsched, and Gessner, mourns the loss of an Arcadian golden age, Jean Paul, influenced by Herder and Voß, claims the possibility of establishing the idyll in the midst of modernity. Instead of depicting an ideal world beyond the concrete realities of the everyday, Jean Paul calls for a representation of contemporary issues and "natural" life. Among such moments are those that rejoice and take pleasure without work, countering the economic pressures of the petit bourgeois: "Thus the vacation of an oppressed school teacher, the blue Monday of an artisan, the baptism of the first child, even the first day when a noble bride agitated and weak from the court feasting finally escapes alone with her prince (the attendants follow much later) to a full, blooming hermitage—in short any of these days can become idylls and can sing, 'We too were in Arcadia'" (187 [259]). Happiness is limited, insofar as it does not simply negate or overcome suffering but is itself interspersed with moments of pain and anguish. In the idyll, the subject never completely breaks free from the constraints of his or her surroundings. Instead one creates interruptions, like holidays and "blue Mondays," within one's limitations. Jean Paul explicitly defines these limits in sociopolitical terms: "The limitation of the idyll can apply to possessions, ideas, social rank, or to all at once" (186 [258]). While the traditional idyll in the tradition of Geßner is situated in a location that is typically characterized as simple, rural, and natural, Jean Paul redefines such secluded limitation within the economic, social, and intellectual conditions of his time. Not only shepherds or farmers can appear in an idyllic setting but also the petit bourgeois of the late eighteenth and early nineteenth centuries. His idyll is not constrained by any traditionally defined boundaries; it could take place in "alps, pasture, Tahiti, a parson's study, or a fisherman's skiff" (188 [261]). The idyll is created by the act of separating oneself from one's environment; it is an active retreat and renunciation, rather than a passive acceptance. Wutz, for example, takes pleasure in closing the window shades, thereby establishing a protective barrier against the intrusions of an antagonistic world. Such acts of separating oneself become the source of joy and cheerfulness. They generate a space and time in which the pleasures of fantasy can be experienced. *School for Aesthetics* argues that separating and limiting oneself opens the "blue heaven of fantasy" (188 [261]) within the subject, enabling a poetical perception of the world.

In "On the Natural Magic of Imagination," the idyll becomes the paradigmatic genre of idealization. In Geßner's idylls, according to Jean Paul, real farmers turn into personified idyllic ideals, while these farmers reciprocally idealize their readers into literary figures: "Learned girls who travel to the countryside in the summer transform the rural population into walking ideals of the idyll in Geßner's sense. Reciprocally, the rural population idealizes these girls as princesses that can be found in the marionette theater or in history books" (199). While in this passage, Jean Paul repeats in a satirical fashion his criticism of traditional concepts of the idyll, he affirmatively takes up the mode of fantastic idealization to describe the life of Quintus Fixlein: "And in the same vein in chapter 13 I praised the otherwise abhorred dungeon and debtors' prison [Zwinger und Schuldturm] of bourgeois life, because in it and its holding pen [Notstall] I already recognized the biographical and ideal glow of the moon [den biographischen und idealischen Mondschein]" (199). In chapter 13 of *Quintus Fixlein*, the narrator describes the protagonist's baptism. His description focuses on full happiness in limitation, thereby fulfilling Jean Paul's definition of the idyll in the *School for Aesthetics*, but it does not overlook or negate moments of anxiety, anguish, and death. That which threatens to interrupt or destroy the idyll is always implicated in it.[57] Concluding chapter 13, the narrator reflects upon the affliction that will soon befall young Quintus: "For I remembered that his father might perhaps this very day grow pale and cold before a suddenly arising mask of Death; I thought how the poor little one had only changed his bent posture in the womb with a freer one, to bend and cramp himself here ere long more harshly in the strait arena of life; I thought of his inevitable follies, and errors, and sins; of these soiled steps to the Grecian Temple of our Perfection" (288 [177]). The life of the subject, released from the enclosure of the mother's womb, far from being free, is even more constrained than before. Death and destruction inhabit Quintus Fixlein's idyll. The theological interpretation of the sinfulness of the world that can be overcome only in the transcendence of the afterlife is opposed by the highly concrete descriptions of the decaying body. Wutz's grave, for example, becomes a "pleasure ground for tunneling earthworms, sluggish snails, teeming ants, and nibbling caterpillars."[58] Consolation derives from the knowledge of having lived *this* life happily, not from the Christian belief in the eternal life of the soul, transcending the materiality of the decaying body. Therefore, the narrator ends his biography of Wutz with the statement: "While he had life he enjoyed it more merrily than we all" (114 [461]). Happiness derives from the ability to enjoy life, not from the hope of an afterlife. It is an ability to cheerfully cope with the "drilling," "spinning," and "gnawing" of everyday life in all its physical reality. Against an idealizing interpretation of the idyll in the eighteenth century, Erwin Panofsky revived an elegiac reading of the emblematic inscription *Et in Arcadia ego* that focuses on the significance of mortality in pastoral settings. Panofsky quotes Poussin's friend and biographer G. P. Bellori, who, according to Panofsky, correctly grasped the inscription's meaning: "'Et in Arcadia ego' means that the grave is to be found even in Arcadia and that death holds sway in the very midst of delight."[59] The line "We Too Were in Arcadia" (Auch wir waren in Arkadien)—Jean Paul's variation of Goethe's "I too in Arcadia" (Auch ich in Arkadien)—therefore should not be misunderstood as a flight into a transcendent golden age that would eliminate experiences of death or pain but as an embrace of the possibility of an idyll in the concrete *hic et nunc*. The "we" who are singing includes shepherds but also craftsmen, schoolteachers, village parsons, and so on.

In the preface to *Life of Quintus Fixlein*, Jean Paul mentions three paths by which human beings can achieve a happier life. The first path, moving up and beyond the realm of human quandaries, leads to an elevated, absolute position from which life appears small, thereby losing its threat of pain and death: "Of ways for becoming happier (not happy) I could never inquire out more than three. The first, rather an elevated road, is this: To soar away so far above the clouds of life, that you see the whole external world, with its wolf-dens, charnel-houses, and thunder-rods, lying far down beneath you, shrunk into a little child's garden" (116 [10]). As Jean Paul, discussing "The Annihilating or Infinite Idea of Humor," states in the *School for Aesthetics*: "When man looks down . . . from the supernatural world to the earthly world, it seems small and vain in the distance" (92 [127–28]). In the preface to *Life of Quintus Fixlein,* while this "skyward track" [Himmelfahrt] (117 [11]) minimizes terrestrial life's pains and miseries, in a manner similar to the humorist's laughter, it also contains the danger of insanity. Both madman and genius enthusiastically reject reality by creating an imaginary world of the beyond, separating themselves from the "bed and board of this earth"(116–17 [11]). They are governed by an idée fixe, lifting them above the mundane world and protecting them from the catastrophes of everyday life:

> The Hero, the Reformer, your Brutus, your Howard, your Republican, he whom civic storm, or genius poetic storm, impels; in short, every mortal with a great Purpose, or even a perennial Passion (were it but that of writing the largest folios), all these men fence themselves in by their internal world against the frosts and heats of the external, as the madman in a worse sense does: every *fixed* idea, such as rules every genius, every enthusiast, at least periodically, separates and elevates a man above the bed and board of this Earth, above its Dog's-grottos, buckthorns and Devil's walls; like the Bird of Paradise, he slumbers flying; and on his outspread pinions, oversleeps unconsciously the earthquakes and conflagrations of Life, in his long fair dream of his ideal Mother-land. (116–17 [11])

By flying high above the terrestrial realm, madman and genius enter an upper sphere of ideals and dreams. They become insensitive to the lower regions of physical materiality, symbolized by "Dog's-grottos, buckthorns and Devil's walls," literally sleeping off their stings. Living life like a long, beautiful dream creates indifference toward reality. In these sublime states of heightened enthusiasm and blinding visions, the subject finds solace and calm. Man as genius separates himself from the world by building an inner world, similar to an idée fixe. In *Discourse Networks: 1800/1900,* Friedrich Kittler discusses the function of the idée fixe as the term that connects poetics to the newly developing sciences of man: "The new human sciences, with their medico-psychological investigations of insanity, discovered around 1800 among the countless manifestations of unreason a distinguished form that revealed the very nature of unreason. This was the *idée fixe*.... The fixed idea became the sole form of unreason to be accorded the rank of poetic dignity."[60] It is therefore no coincidence, according to Kittler, that "a writer who cultivates the *idée fixe* in miniature can only be called Fixlein."[61] To deal with the recalcitrance of the real, one must become a *little fixer.* What differentiates the genius from a madman is the temporary character of his flights of fantasy. While the insane person is permanently under the power of his inner visions, which not only protect him from but also blind him to reality, the enthusiastic artist is under the reign of his idée fixe only periodically. Quintus Fixlein's fixed idea consists in the belief that he will die, like his ancestors, in his thirty-second year. Shortly before the anticipated time of his demise, this superstition causes a delirious fever. The fantasy in this case does not transport the subject to an "ideal Mother-land" that facilitates coping with reality but on the contrary increases and intensifies the subject's anxieties. The narrator states: "Nothing afflicts one more than to see a reasonable moderate man, who has been so even in his passions, raving in the poetic madness of fever [poetischen Unsinn des Fiebers]" (293 [180]). Imagination, in this passage, is not a *tonicum* but a poison—it stirs up passions and so works against the quasi-Stoical task of reaching a state of calm, measure, and reason. Jean Paul shares this implicit critique of passion as a path to madness with other contemporary critics of poetic enthusiasm and romantic rhapsodizing, such as Shaftesbury in his *Letter concerning Enthusiasm*. In such discourses of therapy, "the fixed idea moved in to the center of nosological categories, etiological explanations, and psychic cures, which were directed above all toward distraction."[62]

As a remedy to overcome the feverish visions and superstitions of Quintus Fixlein's imagination, Jean Paul, as a figure within the novel, acts as a "philosophical physician." In the novel *The Comet* he similarly appears in the narration, counterbalancing Süptitz's enraged jeremiads on malicious objects and accidents. Jean Paul's method of healing Fixlein's madness consists of replacing one form of fantastic imagination with another. He transfers Boerhaave's physiological treatment of bodily diseases to psychology and attempts to heal illusion with illusion: "It first occurred to me, that as Boerhaave used to remedy convulsions by convulsions, one fancy [Einbildung] might in my gossip's case be remedied by another" (294–95 [181–82]). Jean Paul's treatment of replacing one illusion with another was a popular method used in psychotherapy at the end of the eighteenth century. Michel Foucault in *Madness and Society* calls it "theatrical representation": "Insofar as it is of the essence of the image to be taken for reality, it is reciprocally characteristic of reality that it can mime the image, pretend to the same substance, the same significance. . . . If illusion can appear as true as perception, perception in its turn can become the visible, unchallengeable truth of illusion. Such is the first step of the cure by 'theatrical representation': to integrate the unreality of the image into perceived truth, without the latter seeming to contradict or even contest the former."[63] During the late eighteenth century, treatment from within, in which "the therapeutic operation functions entirely in the space of the imagination, . . . must play its own game, voluntarily propose new images, espouse delirium for delirium's sake, and without opposition or confrontation, without even a visible dialectic, must, paradoxically, cure."[64] Treating delusion by delusion, as proposed by Jean Paul, combines the old method of "waking" with the newer doctrines of theatrical representation.[65] The isopathic treatment of anger by cursing, discharging the devil by evoking him, repeats itself on the imaginary level. Illusion is opposed not by reality, as poison would be by a remedy, but by another illusion, by another poison that functions as an antidote. The first step in Quintus Fixlein's treatment consists in creating the illusion that he is not thirty-two but rather eight years old. By returning the patient to his childhood, Jean Paul relocates Fixlein in a "heavenly time, which none of us forgets, which we love for ever, and look back to even from the grave" (296 [182–83]). This return is achieved by presenting Fixlein with an array of objects from his childhood: "First of all his copy-book, where Egidius in his eighth year had put down his name, which he necessarily recognized as his own hand-writing; then the black velvet *fall-hat* or roller-cap; then the red and white leading-strings; his knife-case, with a little pamphlet of tin-leaves; his green hussar-cloak, with its stiff facings; and a whole *orbis pictus* or *fictus* of Nürnberg puppets" (295–96 [182]). The medium of artificial recollection equals a collection of objects such as toys and trinkets. Through these objects associated with a happier time, Jean Paul installs—as a therapeutic measure—a different memory in Fixlein's mind.[66] He substitutes the false belief of dying in one's thirty-second year with another false belief: that of being a child surrounded by its toys. It is a staged, artificially reproduced childhood—the room becomes a theater in which different animate actors (Jean Paul, Fixlein's mother, the butcher) and inanimate actors (toys) perform.[67] The toys function as a *memento mori* in reverse. They turn the anticipation of death into the remembrance of a forgotten life. This memory is not necessarily a purely happy one, but it mixes life and death, happiness and melancholy: "The sick man recognized in a moment these projecting peaks [vorragende Spitzen] of a spring-world sunk in the stream of Time" (296 [182]). Objects protrude from the past into the present, carrying the subject back to happier days. In an instant, Fixlein experiences the past as it pierces the present. Its recollection is established as a form of memory that is not a memory of objects themselves but an experience of interruptive emotions. Childhood can never return as such; it only reappears in sudden, piercing moments.

One of the dangers Jean Paul associates with this attempt to overcome the pains of man's terrestrial existence through memory, which for Jean Paul is structurally analogous to fantasy, is connected to a false sense of individuality. Retreating into the private realm of memory and imagination threatens to undermine the subject's position within society. Wutz and Fixlein are perceived as fools, oddballs, and outsiders. Max Kommerell traces a typically German tradition of the *Kauz* (eccentric) in the works of Jean Paul and contrasts him with the figure of the eccentric Englishman. While the English eccentric shows his spleen in only a few minor aberrations, the German eccentric "becomes addicted to the compulsion of eccentricity in his whole being and, as a figure, . . . emulates in miniature the inarticulated, askew, and almost crotchety relationship that the great Spirit in Germany used to have with real things."[68] The relationship between object and subject, reality and fantasy, spirit and matter is in disarray; therefore the fool cannot develop a balanced approach to dealing with "real things." It is the "most inner dissonance" between "spirit" and "earth" that is given form in the figure of the fool.[69]

In "On the Natural Magic of Imagination" (1796), discussing the Stoic doctrine of treating the world like a theater, Jean Paul still believes in the powers of imagination, creating steadfastness that is stronger than Stoic apathy. All humans should think and act like "the poet and he, for whom the external (i.e., civil and physical) life is more than just a role: such a man is a child of comedy, who confuses his role with his life and who begins to weep in the theater. From this point of view, which seems more metaphorical than it really is, one achieves a steadfastness that is more sublime, more rare, and sweeter than Stoic apathy, and that allows us to feel everything in joy, except its loss" (198–99). The poet resembles a "child of comedy," confusing life and stage. Whereas Epictetus offers the doctrine "Remember that you are an actor in a play" as a remedy to cope with the miseries of everyday life, Jean Paul radicalizes the Stoic posture to the point of making no distinction between imagination and reality.[70] The Stoic in Epictetus's sense uses the idea of life metaphorically, retaining the distinction between actor and audience, but Jean Paul's concept only appears metaphorical, while in fact it asserts the identity of life and literature.

Johann Christoph Reil, in an essay entitled "The Collapse of Our Corporeal Unity in Self-Consciousness" (Das Zerfallen der Einheit unseres Körpers im Selbstbewußtseyn), describes dreams and madness analogously in theatrical terms: "The Ego dismantles itself in madness and dreams, dramatizing its faculties. It is simultaneously actor and audience."[71] According to Reil, the Stoic identification of life and stage as a means of dealing with the miseries of life contains the danger of turning into insanity. Even more pathological, according to Reil, is the inability to differentiate between life and stage, as prescribed by Jean Paul. It is in such modes of heightened imagination as dreaming or madness that the self loses the ability to differentiate between fiction and reality, subject and object. The subject disintegrates into a plurality of separate souls.

MEDICINAL CURSES

For the young Jean Paul it is Immanuel Kant who improves and fulfills the basic tenets of Stoic doctrine in the realm of moral philosophy and ethics: "In the past six thousand years, no other has propelled the improvement and continuation of this Stoic response with such acumen as Kant."[72] In the late *Anthropology from a Pragmatic Point of View* (1798), Kant offers a model of affects, understood as a form of energetic discharge, breaking through mental as well as physiological blockages within the human body. He narrates an incident of stubbing one's big toe on a rock that ignites not only physical pain but also an angry outburst: "He who *cries out* under the surgeon's knife or under the pain of gout or stone is therefore not cowardly or weak in his condition; his cry is like cursing when one is walking out and bumps against a loose cobblestone (with one's big toe, from which the word *hallucinari* is derived)—it is rather an outburst of anger in which nature endeavours to break up the constriction of blood in the heart through cries."[73] The angry outcry or curse has the effect of loosening the blockage of the blood flow near the heart. This focus on the loosening of the human body's and soul's constrictions is central to most medical and physiological theories of the emotions of the day. According to Albrecht Koschorke, "Bourgeois disciplinary actions expose people to a pathogenic, rigid internal pressure" that needs to be released.[74] The social pressure from living within a highly stratified and rigid society is transformed into an internal pressure, threatening the physiological and the moral equilibrium of the individual. Treatment of physical, mental, or behavioral problems consists in the proper and controlled discharge of liquids as well as affects. Through Reil's therapy, for example, "we are in a position of reestablishing the balance and accepted relative strength of the different driving mechanisms of the soul, the unison and correct relations [rapport] of each to another, and thereby the harmony of the internal and external senses, the proper intensity of fantasy, the internal and external prudence [Besonnenheit], subordinating the correct correlation of ideas to the functions of willpower."[75] In the *Anthropology* Kant's treatment of passions and affects, despite his affirmation of Stoicism's principle of *ataraxia*, moves, especially in discussing anger, toward physiological concepts of ventilationism.[76] For Kant, cursing as an expression of vexation is a "natural" release, a therapeutic utterance, that serves to unblock the blood's circulation. Kant's pseudoetymological explanation of the word *hallucinari* explicitly rejects the possibility of any purely psychological determination of anger. Consequently, the moral management of rage should not attempt to control or suppress anger but rather allow for a discharge of psychic energies. Reil concurs: "We must therefore give enough leeway to the strained excitability so that it may express itself in its most natural way. The accruing attack, through its excess of agitation, destroys the congestions of the vital principle [Lebensprincip] in the organ of the soul [Seelenorgan], just as an epileptic paroxysm brings about its conclusion through its convulsions."[77] In the case of an angry outburst, all the physician should do is provide a safe context for the angry patient to release his or her energies and remove all possible causes of further irritation. Reil is in this respect in agreement with most of the contemporary psychiatrists of the time, like Pinel, Esquirol, and Hayner, who claim that "drive and power [Trieb und Kraft], when restrained by external forces, are redirected inwards, making the passions more violent and fantasy's manifestations more powerful and destructive."[78] Kant allows for the expression of anger, understood as a form of venting since its function is quite literally to release pressure. Letting off steam is healthy as long as the cathartic outburst happens suddenly and within a controlled environment.[79] Holding back rage can turn it into a permanent condition, which Kant calls "rancor" (Groll): "Neither affect [neither anger nor shame] is detrimental to health if people are able to give vent to anger through the quick composure of the mind; but where this is not possible, then in part they are dangerous to life itself or, when their outbreak is restrained, in part they bequeath a rancor, that is, a mortification at not having responded in the proper way to an insult. Such rancor, however, is avoided if people can only have a chance to express themselves in words."[80] Cursing, for example, is a "natural" and therefore healthy release of affects. Cursing in anger releases the subject's paralysis, which has been brought about by a specific type of shock. Shock and anger are both related to fright, "a suddenly aroused fear that disconcerts the mind."[81] But while in shock the human being is paralyzed, its vital spirits blocked. Anger, on the contrary, "is fright that at the same time quickly stirs up powers to resist ill."[82] Cursing, like laughing and crying, frees the movement of the vital spirits from any obstructions: curses "are liberations from a hindrance to the vital force through their effusions."[83] As early as 1708, Georg Ernst Stahl, in his *Theory of Medical Science (Theorie der Heilkunde)*, first published under the title *Theoria Medica Vera*, asserts the medical necessity not to suppress anger but to express it: "It is important to recognize the common observation that, when rage [Zorn] is satisfied and no remorse [Reue] is left behind, there is also no harm done to the body. On the other hand, when it is suppressed, a persistent displeasure and rancor [Unmuth und Groll] in the body's disposition remain. Disorder of digestion and nourishment follows, along with weakness and a cumulative exhaustion of vital functions, or incoherent speech [Iurreden] or spasms present themselves concurrently."[84] For Stahl, the physiological symptoms of rage are similar to the subject's attempts to suppress and control these symptoms. To control anger, the human being must become angry. If rage is not allowed to express itself, it causes physical irritations. In principle, there is no difference between the involuntary motions of affect and the voluntary means to control them:

> Let us observe more closely the outward effects of the passions [Leidenschaften] on our life activity, especially those that seem to have no immediate connection to the endeavors and tendencies of the will. In doing so, we will be easily convinced that the peculiar and unfamiliar changes in our life activity are caused by arbitrariness and a clear and calculated intention. For what else is meant by rage [Zorn]—that copious allocation of blood at the body's surface and in its muscles, or the heightened tonus that palpitates with ever-tightening strain—other than a preparation of the body for the most extreme development of energy through the most impetuous and

intensely haphazard movements? All convulsions are closely related to the violent struggles with which the infuriated defend themselves against those who want to suppress them and wish to keep their impetuousness [Ungestüm] at bay.[85]

The insight that anger and its control are related influences Stahl's therapeutic theory and practice insofar as it is not based on the treatment of anger's symptoms and instead—very much in the ancient Stoic tradition—focuses on the human being's mental as well as physical constitution. The human being's physiology, according to Stahl, is the "immediate tool" (unmittelbare Werkzeug) of the soul.[86] In the 1812 essay entitled "On the Question concerning the Origin of the First Plants, Animals, and Humans" (Frage über das Entstehen der ersten Pflanzen, Tiere und Menschen), Jean Paul characterizes Stahl's concept of the "body-building soul" (körperbauende Seele) as the "master builder and physician of the body" (Baumeisterin und Ärztin des Körpers).[87] Hence, according to Jean Paul, healing mental as well as physical diseases must begin with the treatment of the soul. What is called for is a "psychic healing method" (psychische Curmethode) as developed by Reil. In this conception, mental illnesses do not merely originate in physiological or anatomical disturbances but require a treatment of the patient's psyche. Body and soul are so tightly connected that only a holistic approach, encompassing both, can succeed. Psychotherapy differentiates itself from the Galenic model of bodily humors, as well as from purely mechanical models in the tradition of Descartes and la Mettrie, in that it perceives the human as defined by an interaction between mental and physical processes. It looks at the patient from the standpoint of an "anthropological physician," who treats the whole human being.[88] Hans Jürgen Schings calls the representatives of this theory, uniting philosophy, physiology, and medicine, "philosophical physicians."[89] For these doctors, only the combination of physiological and psychological knowledge provides the means for a proper diagnosis and successful treatment of mental as well as physical diseases.

In this context, Kant's description of shock and anger can be traced back to Johann Friedrich Zückert's *Medical and Moral Treatise on the Passions (Medicinisch-moralische Abhandlung von den Leidenschaften)*, a popular medical treatise first published in 1764.[90] Zückert characterizes anger as a shock caused by the experience of an injustice: "Rage [Zorn] is a shock from an endured injustice and begins with all the signs of shock and terror."[91] Shock is a bodily form of implosion, inhibiting life's vital forces, combined with a paralysis of the brain:

> The whole system of fixed parts is drawn together unexpectedly, and the person collapses in upon himself. The stifled sweat glands immediately inhibit transpiration. With acute force, all blood is driven inward. The veins under the skin break down, the face grows pallid, the lips pale, and the eyes become glassy and motionless. The heart beats, attempting to overcome the blood's resistance. The patient takes quick and short breaths. Even the brain is constrained by the blood: hence the patient grows stupid [dumm] and can no longer make any decisions. Any discharge of the vital spirits is curbed, and along with the muscles' strength and movement being diminished, so too the tongue becomes paralyzed.[92]

But while the person in shock remains in this state of paralysis, the angry one immediately reverses the blockage of all vital forces. After the initial shock "the strength of the heart and the vessels is greatly increased. With unbelievable force, the blood is pumped to all parts of the body, especially to its outer extremities."[93] Zückert, although still quoting Aristotle's definition of anger as the desire to avenge a slight, develops a dynamic medical theory of anger. Rage can be described as a form of discharge, a release of energy. These violent paroxysms require therapy because they are socially—Zückert describes in detail the antisocial behavior of the angry person—as well as physiologically destructive. The body is affected by the constant oscillation between shocking paralysis and angry outburst, between contraction and expansion. It is the curse, as the transformation of angry energies into a speech act—that paradigmatically manifests this entanglement of body and soul, physis and psyche.

In *Siebenkäs*, Jean Paul satirizes the use of curses as a way to release and channel the destructive energies of rage. Uttering the curse "Devil!" soothes angry inflammations: "I have observed, for my part, that the spotted, malignant fever of wrath, so readily diagnosed by the raving delirium of the patient, is instantly relieved, dispersed, and mitigated, by invoking the name of the devil. . . . As regards the inflammatory fever of anger, however, the greater the quantity of morbid matter which has to be ejected from the system through the secretions of the mouth, the greater is the number of devils necessary to make mention of" (223 [231]). "Morbid matter," or *materia peccans* in the medical tradition of Hippocrates and Galen—founders of the humoral theory of man—names the substance that causes illness and disease. Therapy, in this context, thus consists in purifying and cleansing the body by draining the spoiled humors, namely the *materia peccans*. Removing poisonous material from the body reestablishes a balance between the different humors and leads to physical and mental health. The curse, in Jean Paul's ironic narrative, functions as such a discharge. The angry subject uses the malediction "Devil!" to purge the body of the pathogenic substances that cause inflammatory rage. The efficacy of this treatment is considered to be in direct relation to the intensity of rage. The angrier the subject, the stronger and more vivid the expletive: "For a mere trifling irritation—a mild case of simple anger— 'the devil,' or perhaps 'hell and the devil,' will generally be found sufficient; but for the pleuritic fever of rage I should be disposed to prescribe 'the devil and his infernal grandmother'; strengthening the dose, moreover, with a *'Donnerwetter'* or two, and a few *'sacramenta,'* as the curative powers of the electric fluid are now so generally recognized" (223–24 [231]).The direct link between the intensity of anger and the discharging curse originates in the medicinal character of the expletive. The devil is the one who causes anger, hence the uttering of his name functions like an antidote: "But what I would fain render clear is that, in all these remedies, the real *specific* is the devil; for as it is his sting which is the cause of our malady, he himself has got to be employed as the remedy, just as the stings of scorpions are cured by the application of scorpions in powder" (224 [231]). Poison can be cured only by another poison. Cursing promotes health. Already Paracelsus and before him Hippocrates had declared that whatever makes man ill will also cure him. Consequently, by evoking the devil as the source of all evil, man can rid himself from anger caused by the afflictions and vexations of everyday life. In this passage from *Siebenkäs*, Jean Paul develops a quasi-medical theory of anger treatment that is not based on forms of self-control but instead instrumentalizes the speech act of the curse to purge the human body and psyche of its raging energies. This model of an energetic discharge stands in direct opposition to the stoic doctrine of *ataraxia*. "Seneca," writes Jean Paul, "has omitted the simplest of all [remedies against anger], the devil" (223 [231]). To overcome rage, the subject, rather than suppressing it, needs to find a way to release the anger-inducing *materia peccans*.

BESONNENHEIT AND LAUGHTER AS RESPONSES TO THE RECALCITRANCE OF REALITY

Jean Paul's novel *The Comet* ends with two addenda to the main text. The first of these, which Jean Paul compares to the "tail of a comet" [Kometenschweifanhängsel] (6,1007), is entitled "A Few Accounts of the Travel-Weary Court and Prison Clergyman, Fohauf Süptitz, Excerpted from His Diary by a Sincere Admirer and Roommate of His" (Einige Reiseleiden des Hof- und Zuchthauspredigers Frohauf Süptitz; aus dessen Tagebuch entnommen von einem aufrichtigen Verehrer und Stubenkameraden desselben).[94] It narrates in minute and highly comical detail the sufferings and afflictions of Frohauf Süptitz, a prison priest who is angered by malicious objects that interrupt his daily routines. This short piece contains a letter in which Süptitz describes his difficulties with the mundane task of putting on stockings: "Freshly laundered, tight stockings (first linen, then silken), both put on exactly the same (first over and then under each other): this had always been my true work on the Sabbath at home. But outside the home, without any assistance and with ten abjectly thick fingers, the pulling—yanking—plucking—smoothing—stretching—and bending over—my dear, no: I would not lend my hand to that this time" (1018). Away from home, Süptitz is traveling with the protagonist of *The Comet*, Nikolaus Marggraf, a pharmacist who falsely believes himself to be of noble descent. On the road the already difficult task of taming unruly stockings, which are freshly washed and therefore too tight, becomes impossible. Whatever Süpitz does to relieve his discomfort is of no use: his efforts are nothing more than a desperate sequence of pulling, yanking, plucking, smoothing, stretching, and bending. As the dashes between the verbs indicate, these actions do not follow an ordered method but proceed rapidly and irregularly, effectively canceling each other out. After giving up the idea of wearing stockings, Süptitz continues dressing by moving on to a pair of boots, which also resist being put on without a struggle: "After I successfully, albeit laboriously [glücklich-mühsam], put the right one on, I sought, by driving my unfortunately footlong heel into the left one, to somewhat relax. I held by my fingers both leather boot straps [Ziehleder] (the locals call them straps [Strupfen]), and it suddenly occurred to me how long I could just keep on thinking in this peaceful repose, and how I would finally be able to simply stop. Heavens!" (1018). In an earlier passage, Süptitz blames moments of "unaccustomed" reasoning for disrupting the procedure of putting on one's clothes promptly and properly.[95] In this incident, it is not the shoes or stockings but a shirt that resists:

> I mention it not actually as the misfortune of the festival—whether the event itself helped me to be late or not—but rather as the simple consequence of my unaccustomed reflection: I got out of bed later because I wanted to pay attention for the first time to my shirt, which I've beforehand mechanically and without thought [ohne Nachdenken] put on a thousand times, to find out how I have hitherto done so. But nothing came of it: not once under careful scrutiny [Achtgeben] was the shirt revealed, nor did I even know which arm should go in which sleeve first. After much work, I finally bequeathed myself blindly to the old mechanics and without any further reflection put on the fresh shirt—so it was, and the art of the instinct showed me the way again. (1017)

It is neither an objective quality of the piece of clothing—being freshly washed and too tight—nor a physical impediment—ten abjectly fat fingers—that hinders and obstructs his progress. Süptitz himself is the cause of such failures. Uwe Schweikert notes correctly: "Süptitz is tormented by the objects' malice [Süptitz wird von der Tücke des Objekts geplagt], or more precisely, he thinks too much about their being malicious. His mistake is less the consequences of their malice than the consequences of his reflections upon that malice."[96] What appears to be caused by the malice of the object proves to be caused by the incompetence of the reasoning subject. In paying attention to one's actions too closely, one loses one's habitual abilities to cope with the small tasks of everyday life. Success is blind, while the light of reflection renders accomplishment virtually impossible. To put on the shirt, Süptitz finally lets his body act of its own volition, as if it were a machine. What characterizes man as opposed to things and animals, his ability to reflect, chronically slows down and blocks his actions. The following section will discuss a specific form of reflection that the German theologian and philosopher Johann Gottfried Herder termed *Besonnenheit*. It distinguishes man from animal, marking the autonomy of the sovereign subject, but if not applied properly can cause pathological dispositions like madness.

From Herder's *Essay on the Origin of Language (Abhandlung über den Ursprung der Sprache),* published in 1772, Jean Paul appropriated the distinction between the purely instinctual animal and the free and reflexive human, whose *"Besonnenheit"* transcends his instinctual sensuality and create language.[97] For Herder, *Besonnenheit* is closely connected to attention:

> Man manifests (*Besonnenheit*) reflection when the force of his soul acts in such freedom that, in the vast ocean of sensations which permeates it through all the channels of the senses, it can, if I may say so, single out one wave, arrest it, concentrate its attention on it, and be conscious of being attentive. He manifests reflection (*Besonnenheit*) when, confronted with the vast hovering dream of images which pass by his senses, he can collect himself into a moment of wakefulness and dwell at will on one image, can observe it clearly and more calmly, and can select in it distinguishing marks for himself so that he will know that this object is this and not another.[98]

The attentiveness of *Besonnenheit* is able to arrest the waves of free-flowing impressions and perceptions into one image. Out of the surging ocean of sensations stable objects appear.

For Jean Paul in the *School for Aesthetics*, it is the faculty of *Besonnenheit* that demands an "equilibrium between inner and outer worlds. In the animal the external world swallows up the inner; in the man moved by passion, often the inner swallows up the external world" (36 [57]). While the *Besonnenheit* of the average human being is always directed outward toward the world, the *Besonnenheit* of the genius, according to Jean Paul, is directed both outward and inward: it is characterized by the simultaneity of the consciousness of reality and of self-consciousness. This differentiation between inner and outer *Besonnenheit* can also be found in Johann Christoph Reil's *Rhapsodies on the Application of Psychic Treatment to Mental Disturbances (Rhapsodieen über die Anwendung der psychischen Curmethode auf Geisteszerrüttungen),* which is considered to be "the most influential work in the shaping of German psychiatry before Freud."[99] For Reil, the mental health of a human being depends on the balanced reciprocity between consciousness, attentiveness, and *Besonnenheit,* of which there are two types: "*Besonnenheit* has both an external and internal dimension. The latter corresponds to the perception of the internal sense's reproductions, while the former relates to the perception of impressions of the external sense."[100] According to Reil, numerous pathologies are caused by a dissonance between inner and outer *Besonnenheit:* "It is possible for *Besonnenheit* to deviate from the norm in numerous ways. If the sensitivity of the soul is too lethargic, then faint impressions glide over it imperceptibly. If it is too delicate, a certain flightiness ensues so that we are enthralled by trifles rather than serious matters."[101] *Besonnenheit* is constantly threatened by either its dissolution into distraction or a pathological intensification: "*Besonnenheit* thus falls between distraction and total absorption.... The farther one strays from the normal, central position, the more he is either engrossed in one extreme or distracted in the other. Furthermore, both extremes lead to madness [Verrückung]: in distraction, one wanders through a multitude of items [Gegenstände] without fixing upon any one, while the fully engrossed person cannot tear himself away from the object [Objekt] that currently fascinates him. Both thus misconceive the impressions [Eindrücke] that they should otherwise notice in their present circumstance."[102] One example of a pathological deepening of *Besonnenheit* that Reil mentions is the case of the German theologian Johann Salomo Semler, who continued his meditations while his house was burning down, and Archimedes, who did not interrupt his studies during the invasion of his city by an enemy army. In Jean Paul's *Siebenkäs*, the protagonist's friend and rival Stiefel brings up the case of Archimedes while defending Siebenkäs against his wife:

> Is it any wonder, then, that great writers, in the terrible strain and absorption of all their ideas, have often scarcely known where they were, what they were doing, or what they would be at; that they were blind and dumb, and insensible to everything but what was perceived by the five interior spiritual senses, like blind people, who see beautifully in their dreams, but in their waking state are, as we have said, blind! This state of absorbedness and strain it is which I consider to explain how it was that Socrates and Archimedes could stand and be completely unconscious of the storm and turmoil going on around them. (169 [179])

While Reil identifies deep *Besonnenheit* as a potentially pathological mental disorder, for Stiefel it represents the condition for the possibility of writing. To write, one has to be blind and deaf to one's surroundings—a state of *Besonnenheit* that Siebenkäs is unable to establish.[103] In *School for Aesthetics*, discussing the figure of the genius, Jean Paul further reflects upon forms of increased *Besonnenheit*: "The reflectiveness [Besonnenheit] of genius differs so much from the other kind that it often appears as its very opposite. Like a burial lamp, this eternally burning lamp within is extinguished, if *outside* air and world touch it" (36 [57]). Intensified *Besonnenheit* can appear as its opposite, distraction, when viewed in its relationship to the outer world. The more focused the inner, the less focused the outer *Besonnenheit*. This lack of outer *Besonnenheit* is exemplified for Jean Paul by La Bruyère's character of Ménalque, who "comes down the stairs, opens the door to go out, and shuts it again, for he perceives that he is in his night-cap. On examining himself closer, he finds that he has only half shaved; that his sword hangs on his right; and his stockings are turned down over his heels."[104] The distracted character Ménalque resembles Süptitz insofar as both are afflicted by a derangement of their outer appearance. Both lack *Besonnenheit*. But while Süptitz lacks inner *Besonnenheit*—by desperately trying to fix his clothes he loses sight of his intentions and hence is unable to function in society—Ménalque lacks outer *Besonnenheit*. In his distracted state of mind, he simply forgets to keep up appearances: to dress properly, shave, and so on. Ménalque is too distracted, while Süptitz is too attentive. In a footnote to the aforementioned quote, Jean Paul continues to elaborate on the distinction between inner and outer *Besonnenheit*, between attentiveness and distraction: "For the unreflectiveness in action, i.e., the forgetting of personal relations, agrees so well with poetic and philosophic reflectiveness, that reflection and writing poetry often occur in dream and in madness, where such a forgetfulness governs most strongly. The genius is in more than one sense a somnambulist: In his bright dream he can do more than he who is awake, and he climbs every dark height of reality. But rob him of the world of dream, and he tumbles in the real world" (36 [57]). The actions of the genius may appear to the world as *unbesonnen*, since his deepened inner *Besonnenheit* makes him forget outer reality. Dreams and madness represent such states, which produce reflection and poetry but are dissociated from perception of the subject's environment. Writing requires a forgetting of the "personal relations" of the writer. In such a state, he or she resembles a sleepwalker, who acts undisturbed by any external influences in his internal world of dreams and imaginations. J. A. Bergk's *The Art of Reading Books (Die Kunst, Bücher zu lesen)* (1799) points to a similar form of heightened attentiveness in the act of reading:

> Our body is tortured with a most terrible pain, and our Spirit sinks powerlessly under the weight of the destiny with which we are burdened. We think only of our suffering, to which we become wholly attentive [ganze Aufmerksamkeit] and which in the process becomes ever greater. We are plagued by phantoms and fancies, and our life becomes an endless collection of self-wrought torments. Are there ways that would still our pain and dispel the afflicted spirits [Quälgeister] from our disposition? Let us flee into the pages of a book,

one that invites our most difficult thoughts, is rich with ideas, and attracts us with its new opinions that are refreshing to the heart. We bury our sorrows in nonconsciousness [Nichtbewußtsein], making them disappear. By not being attentive [Nichtaufmerksamkeit] to their existence, we destroy the pain and calm our disposition.[105]

Reading, in Bergk's pedagogical treatise, functions in the mode of a deep inner *Besonnenheit* that buries pains and vexations in "nonconsciousness." The soul gains control over the body by forgetting it, freeing itself from "the slavery of its animalistic desires and passions"[106] Analogously, for Jean Paul in *Life of Quintus Fixlein*, "Every mortal with a great Purpose, or even a perennial Passion (were it but that of writing the largest folios)" (116 [10–11]) builds within him- or herself an "internal world against the frosts and heats of the external" (116 [10]). In literary imagination, creating a protected inner world, the opposition between body and mind, fantasy and reality, is dissolved. The reader (in Bergk), as well the writer (in Jean Paul), lives, as Reil writes, "happily in his dreams."[107]

Besonnenheit as a form of "inner freedom" (Herder) also involves, according to Jean Paul, who relates it to the Platonic concept of *sophrosyne*, an ethical element.[108] Again, it is the idea of a medium between profundity and distraction that marks the proper place of *Besonnenheit*. In dealing with the objects of everyday life, the subject, to equilibrate between inner and outer world, requires a form of prudence and moderation. In Plato's dialogue *Charmides*, Socrates calls for abstinence from any kind of excess in order to live a happy and ethical life. Temperance is a form of practical wisdom, achieving *harmonia*, an orderly and structured state of the world. This form of practical wisdom is the epitome of self-knowledge, as expressed in the Delphic motto *Gnothi seauton* (Know thyself). Knowledge is not abstract, theoretical reasoning; it is based in the concrete lifeworld of the individual. Süptitz's reflections lack this practical and ethical element; they lack a form of habitual knowledge balancing inside and outside, subject and object, theory and praxis. Once he acts not mechanically but consciously, he loses the blind dexterity of the sleepwalker and therefore is unable to live happily in his dreamworld.

The desire to reflect is an urge that is beyond the parson's power. It is impossible for him not to reason. "Oh, my dearest, most worthy wife!" Süptitz in *The Comet* addresses his wife, "would that you had been given a husband who reasoned ten times less—But it is not within my power, I reason a lot" (1021). The less the subject thinks, the fewer disruptions of a straightforward progress there are. Süptitz is stuck in an ever-intensifying circle of reflection that increasingly hinders concrete actions. His own urge to reflect, which is beyond his control, is as disturbing as the interruptions of his intentions caused by a recalcitrant environment. A parody of a German idealist philosopher, Süptitz can function as a member of society only when he delivers himself over to the blind mechanism of his body. The dissonance between mind and body, spirit and matter, characterizes, according to Max Kommerell's study, the core of Jean Paul's writings.[109] In *The Comet* this chasm between an unconditional I and the contingent body can be experienced as painful and perturbing, as in the case of Süptitz, or it may become the source of a humorous attitude. Kommerell states: "The beginning of all humor is the laughter of the unconditional I about his conditional form."[110]

The humorist Schoppe in Jean Paul's novel *Titan* notes of the dissociation between *res cogitans* and *res extensa* that "one sees this best on journeys, when one looks at one's legs, and sees them stride along, and then asks, Who in the world is that marching along so with me down below there?"[111] A part of the body, in this case the legs, becomes a quasi-object for the subject that acts of its own accord. Who or what governs the movement of the legs? Schoppe differentiates between the upper regions of the spirit and the lower regions of the corporeal. Conceiving of the body as a machine, as it was described by Descartes and then radicalized by the French materialists of the eighteenth century, poses the question of how the mind is able to influence the body and furthermore opens the disturbing possibility that the whole human being might be nothing more than a machine.[112] Embracing Fichte's solipsistic idealism, for which the body is nothing more than a positing of the ego, is one way of dealing with this unsettling thought of an essential rift between subject and object. In *Titan*, Schoppe, a student of Fichte, claims that Fichte's philosophy allows the human to be "undisturbed and alone, is the reigning house in the shadow-realm . . . of ideas, and . . . just as a philosopher, makes everything that he thinks,—he also draws his body out of the waves and surges of the external world."[113] The life of the self appears to be without disturbances if one claims, as Fichte does, that all impressions, whether pleasurable or painful, are nothing but productions of the I. Everything is *made* by the self; it is the ruler in its own house. It becomes clear that Jean Paul's interest in the transcendental idealism of Fichte goes beyond its main epistemological framework by introducing ethical questions regarding the possibility of living the good life. Can Fichte's solipsistic philosophy provide a practical theory that can guide man through the vicissitudes of a reality that is experienced as torn and dissociated? Is it possible to utilize the autonomous act of self-positing for a method of self-government? While the solipsistic position reduces reality to a product of the mind, this ridiculous figure of a systematic philosopher is unable to cope with the contingencies of everyday life. He cannot remove his inner self from the *surging outer world* and remains entangled by a "thousand . . . accidents and coincidences" (851). Süptitz has lost control not only over the objects of his environment but, more importantly, over his impulses and affects.

Stoic doctrine differentiates between sustaining and auxiliary causes:

> The "sustaining" . . . or "complete" . . . cause of this action lies within the soul, viz. the (persisting) decision to walk. In general, any event lasts as long as the sustaining cause is present. Hence the soul is the locus of moral responsibility. The related image of the runners might seem to introduce what the Stoics call an auxiliary cause, viz. the slope of the hill. Auxiliary causes typically *intensify* an effect, which would occur anyway (e.g., walking). The point of comparison between the running and the soul's emotional response lies precisely in the aspect of intensification or excess and the consequent loss of control.[114]

Many of Jean Paul's stories about ridiculous figures struggling with the vexations of everyday life can in a similar fashion be interpreted as narratives of intensification and excess. Süptitz acts like a runner on a slope who accelerates uncontrollably until he finally tumbles. The sustaining cause of action, dressing properly for a festive occasion, is brought into disarray by the auxiliary causes of a recalcitrant environment. To avoid the consequences of excessive intensifications like stumbling and falling, Jean Paul's advice, by ridiculing the philosophizing theologian, Süptitz, is to let the body move along its own path, remain blind to its inner workings, and follow the *art of the instinct*. Jean Paul's focus on the act of walking ironically cites the Stoic ethics of Chrysippus, for whom undisturbed walking, as in a stroll, is taken as indicative of the unperturbed, self-assured subject, while the one running and thereby missing his destination supposedly exhibits an excess of affect.[115]

While the Stoic philosopher reasons (i.e., attempts to separate sustaining from auxiliary causes), Jean Paul—at least in this depiction of Süptitz—rejects the idea of a purely rational method of controlling one's affects that would reconcile subject and object. Süptitz exemplifies the danger and futility of relying on rationality as the sole mode of dealing with the recalcitrance of the world. By paying too much attention to the mechanics of the body and reflecting upon its workings, the mind is unable to carry out its intentions without disruption. The aforementioned attempt to put on a pair of boots continues:

> Good heavens! There I sat, thought, and saw no end to it until, once and for all, I ended it suddenly with a swift resolve and a rough pull on the boot and—with that ripped a stocking. But, dear wife! How I pulled on a single boot strap now, so I could depart—how the other straps firmly gripped and tugged at the flush boot leg—like a living bootjack [als lebendiger Stiefelknecht], oh how I was worn out by this loss of time, and merely through the act of dressing, as it is with high jackboots [wie an einem Pumpenstiefel]. (1019)

Not only does Süptitz, in a sudden rush to action, damage the boots, but he also turns into a living bootjack. He becomes himself an animated object. The German word *Stiefelknecht*, usually translated as "bootjack," has its etymological roots in the figure of a human servant helping his master to put on or take off his boots. This relation of dominance and subservience reappears in Süptitz's vain attempts to master malicious articles of clothing. The subject serves the object, losing mastery and autonomy. Süptitz literally turns into the servant of his boot. Around 1800, *Stiefelknecht* also could be used as a curse word. Herder, one of Jean Paul's early influences, uses it in connection with the terms *creep* (Kriecher) and *sycophant* (Schmeichler).[116]

In Jean Paul's first proper novel, *The Invisible Lodge (Die Unsichtbare Loge)* (1793), the narrator complains about the miseries of writing: "Must I not, when I thus come within the electric range of death, jump up, circulate through my chamber, and in the midst of the tenderest or sublimest passages break off and black the boots on my feet or brush my hat and breeches, merely that it may not take my breath away, and yet go at it again, and in this cursed style alternate between emotion and boot-blacking?—A curse upon you critics in a body!"?[117] As in the case of Siebenkäs, it is the everyday that interrupts the act of writing. The writer resembles a *Stiefelknecht* who has to polish his boots or brush his clothes whenever he is ready to write the most tender and sublime passages. The focus of the narrator's attention alternates between the sensitivity of sublime literature and the recalcitrant obtrusiveness of his clothing. Writing is a cursed practice, torn between sensibility and the task of polishing boots. But Stiefelknecht Süptitz's travails do not end with the boots. After wasting time tightening a loose knot, and thereby increasing his delay, he arrives at the house of court chaplain Hasert, a high-ranking clergyman, with a button on his vest that is about to come off. The loose button threatens to open a hole in Süptitz's outfit, unraveling his show of gravity and solemnity: "The lowest button on my vest had torn (as I did not immediately notice) from all but one thread, so that it hung like a padlock in front of the distant buttonhole" (1020). The appearance of Süptitz, and indeed his good standing with the members of the court, are hanging by a thread. His predicament consists in being able neither to close the button by refastening it, since Hasert's guests would perceive such an action as a breach of decorum, nor loosening the button completely: "Because all the guests would surely see me, I couldn't sew the button in the open street. Given also that, had I turned around or hid behind a tree in order to affix the button (I always carry with me needle and thread), I would have been falsely interpreted by those at the country house. The button could, however, not remain hanging like a signet; just below it the vest yawned open in a ridiculous, triangular gap, not unlike the vests of those country aristocrats, left unbuttoned for decoration [aufgeknöpft zur Zier]" (1020). Whatever path of action Süptitz chooses, he will be rendered ridiculous. Not only does the malicious object in this incident interrupt or delay the subject's intentions, it also effectively traps Süptitz in an inescapable predicament, leaving him at an impasse. Paul Fleming, discussing Jean Paul's humor, asserts: "In Jean Paul, one never feels quite at home in the clothes of finitude; the body (and, by extension, all of finitude) is always a bit baggy, a bit saggy, or oppressively tight."[118] For Max Kommerell, the always-ill-fitting clothes represent the "false embodiment,"[119] exemplary of Jean Paul's humor. Laughing, for Kommerell, is caused by a certain "sensible nonsense": "Abiding by the concept of living in spirit [im Geist zu wohnen] while being susceptible to the comforts and discomforts of a thousand nerve fibers, or to say 'I' while having to give in to the skin that is stretched over this I: such sensible nonsense causes laughter."[120] The laughing one, in Kommerell's view, is he or she who, observing the antagonism of mind and matter, accepts it, unlike those heroes and rulers who rail against matter's resistance:

> Every laugh is a renouncing of will, the repetition of which would weaken the agent [den Handelnden], while making the observer all the more free. He who laughs recognizes the rift between idea and world, while the agent uses the world as material to accomplish his goal; he models and remodels, just as the hero, creator, or even philosopher and poet do, insofar as they too are leaders in their field. As a humorist, Jean Paul is no leader. Obviously, every agent experiences the moment in which the material becomes tougher than the will that works against it: the evil grinding [böse Knirschen] of will against matter, before it abates, can be heard in the glosses and remarks of a Napoleon, a Friedrich, or another such figure. Such discord sets the rage of their objectivity [Ingrimm ihrer Sachlichkeit] radically apart from the more tolerant remarks of the observer.[121]

The laughing observer does not act but is nevertheless freed from the restraints of his or her environment. Such observation involves an element of relinquishing one's will. The one who laughs does not get involved: he or she refrains from taking charge and becoming a "leader" who actively intervenes in reality.[122] Through such passivity the laughing observer can recognize the rift between idea and reality. Furthermore, this response provides a specific form of acquiescence and tolerance in dealing with the recalcitrance of reality that differs from the anger and rage experienced by those who actively attempt to overcome it.

PROJECTIVE HUMOR

For Süptitz, the acts of tightening or loosening the waistcoat have only one result: looking ridiculous. There is no loophole by which Süptitz could avoid mockery and humiliation. His attempt to repair his outfit underneath the stairs in Hasert's mansion, although successful, leads to more ridicule at the hands of the servants: "But luckily I wasn't noticed by anyone except one of the servants passing overhead, who, in peering over the handrail, whispered to another servant: 'Blimey! The fat one down there is patching himself up" (1020). This section deals with Jean Paul's theory of humor as the paradigmatic strategy of coping with the ridiculousness of human existence in a world where nothing fits properly. Like Süptitz, whose desperate attempts to fix his outfit cannot be concealed, humor and laughter in Jean Paul always imply uncertainty regarding the relation of perception and projection, reality and imagination. The sixth program of *School for Aesthetics* defines the ridiculous as a foolishness perceived by means of the senses: "But in order to evoke any feeling this folly must be perceived sensuously in an action or situation; and that is possible only when the action both represents and belies the rational intention of the understanding as the wrong means to an end, or when the situation both presents and contradicts a certain interpretation of the situation" (76 [109]). Jean Paul exemplifies the gap between "situation" (Lage) and "effort" (Bestreben) with an alleged episode from *Don Quixote* that curiously cannot be found in Cervantes' text itself.[123] For a whole night that emblem of good-humored wit, Sancho Panza, hangs above a shallow ditch that he believes to be a gaping abyss. Jean Paul asks why one laughs even though, given the premises, Sancho Panza's actions seem perfectly reasonable. His answer is that "we lend *our* insight and perspective [leihen seinem Bestreben unsere Einsicht und Ansicht] to *his* effort and produce through this contradiction the infinite absurdity" (77 [110]).

The ridiculous is not objective; it "resides in the perceiving subject, not in the object."[124] What creates laughter is the reader's application of his or her knowledge to the rift between situation and assumption. It is the reader (or observer; ridiculous situations arise in real life as well as in literature)[125] who produces the contradiction of an infinite inconsistency between two finite entities. Reading the ridiculous means imposing one's own insight on the scene. The faculty of imagination, triggered by the manifestation of the contradiction, performs this transference: "Our imagination, which here as in the sublime is the mediator between inner and outer realms, is enabled to make this transfer [Übertragung] as in the sublime, only by sensuous clarity, in this case, that of the error" (77 [110]). Perceiving someone as ridiculous is a fantastic projection of the observer onto the observed. When watching a funny scene, like Sancho Panza hovering over a ditch as if it were an abyss, the observer projects his or her own insight onto the actor and his actions within the scene. Sancho Panza is funny only because the observer with all his or her insight takes the place of the actor. "Infinite absurdity," as the source of the comical, derives from an act of projection, conflating subjective and objective maxims. It is produced by the fact "that the reader goes about as if the agent [Handelnde] *knew* that his actions were unsound or even insane, and *nevertheless* brought them to fruition."[126]

The comical is not the complete lack of reason. Objects that are not anthropomorphized (which is to say endowed with a certain reason) and unreasonable, completely mad subjects cannot appear ridiculous. Only the contrast of the sensual and the spiritual, of matter and spirit, of reason and unreason, can create the comical effect of the ridiculous: "The simply physical cannot be ridiculous, nor the inanimate, except through personification, nor the simply mental, either pure error nor pure folly" (76 [109]).Therefore, Jean Paul explains in a footnote, Parisian puppets cannot be ridiculous, since they lack subjectivity. Süptitz's desperate attempts to cope with his boots or necktie are not funny in themselves, nor does the humor lie in the mere contrast between means and end. Instead, what is funny is an "illusion of the comic" [Täuschung des Komischen] (77, [111]). Although Süptitz might act automatically, almost without any room to free himself from the vexations of everyday life—this would be a Bergsonian interpretation—the reader ascribes the "appearance of freedom" to his actions: "Hence the usual definitions are false because they suppose only a simple, real contrast, instead of the second, apparent one. The ridiculous being and its deficiency must at least have the appearance of freedom. We laugh only at the more *intelligent* animals which make a personifying, anthropomorphic projection possible" (79 [113]). Laughing is tied to a personifying and anthropomorphizing projection. For the same reason, madmen and their actions are excluded from the realm of the comical, since they do not allow the ascription of even a minimal element of reason.

Jean Paul discusses the proximity of personification and metaphor in the section of *School for Aesthetics* entitled "Figurative Wit." Figurative wit is double, as already indicated in the section's title "Two Forms of Figurative Wit," in that it "can either *animate* the body or *embody* the spirit" (131 [184]). In other words, it functions either as a personification or as a metaphor. Jean Paul imagines, in the tradition of Rousseau and Herder, a time in the history of mankind when metaphor and personification were not yet dissociated. Tropes were "metaphors, like those of children, . . . only involuntary synonyms of the body and spirit" (131 [184]). In this childlike state of nature, I and world, subject and object were one; hence there was no difference between personification and metaphorization. This age of tropical speaking precedes, as Jean Paul points out by indirectly quoting Herder's *On Recent German Literature: Fragments (Fragmente über die neuere deutsche Literatur)*, any type of conceptual, nontropical language. After this undifferentiated unity broke up, man had to invent artificial devices to bridge the gap between body and spirit: "As man distinguishes himself from the world and invisibility from visibility, his wit must *animate*, although not yet *embody*. He lends his self to the universe and his life to the matter about him" (131 [184–85]). It is the self that projects—understood as a form of lending—itself onto the universe. It animates inanimate matter; it personifies the world.

Jean Paul is careful to point out that personification and metaphor are not to be misunderstood as artificial rhetorical devices. He mentions Johann Christoph Adelung and Charles Batteux, stressing the immediate, affective force of tropical language. The primitive usage of personification is not one rhetorical device employed among others to stylize or embellish spoken or written discourse: "But with neither trope [personification and metaphor] does he wish to appear as if he were adopting a special style according to Adelung and Batteux any more than an angry man cites his curse as exclamation point or a lover his kiss as a dash" (131 [185]). In this passage, Jean Paul not only stresses the linguistic and epistemological aspects of personification but, by mentioning the curse and the kiss, focuses on its affective qualities. Personification is not a mere ornament or an empty, mechanical abstraction, as in the classicist doctrines of Adelung and Batteux, but the immediate, spontaneous expression of an affect. Anthropomorphism originates in an affectual interjection. Here Jean Paul is in agreement with the extensive discussion of personification in eighteenth-century England. Hugh Blair, in his *Lectures on Rhetoric and Belles Lettres* (1785), for example, states that personification "is plainly the boldest of all rhetorical figures; it is the style of strong passion only; and, therefore, never to be attempted, unless when the mind is considerably heated and agitated."[127] Rhetorical devices in this tradition "were not considered merely mechanically contrived ornaments, but rather . . . the natural means of expression."[128] The angry person does not use the curse to emphasize his pain. The curse is a passionate figure of speech that embodies, and does not represent, violent affect. Hence the angry, cursing person, much like the loving, kissing one, resembles a child or a primitive for whom word and action are not yet separated. The proximity of personification to primitive animism is by now a commonplace, but it also connects to Herder's theory of the origin of language. For Herder and other theoreticians of the eighteenth century, the origin of human speech had to be found in immediate expressions of the passions such as interjections and cries. The function of personification and anthropomorphism then "seem[s] to be the illusionary resuscitation of the natural breath of language, frozen into stone by the semantic power of the trope."[129] For Herder, it is again *Besonnenheit* that separates human language from animal cries, turning the immediate expressions of affect into language. In the early, primitive stages of the development of language, this process relies on the rhetorical tropes of personification and anthropomorphism. For the primitive, "nothing is more natural to a sensuous human being than to think that it [nature] lives, that it speaks, that it acts."[130] The human being projects his or her own constitution onto nature, which thus appears as "a realm of animated, of acting beings!"[131] For Jean Paul, this primitive, anthropomorphic structure of language constitutes an anthropological a priori of human existence. Human beings are incapable of not projecting themselves onto animate and inanimate objects. In "On the Natural Magic of Imagination," Jean Paul asserts that nature "compels us to believe in foreign I's [zwingt uns an fremde Ichs zu glauben] next to our own, so that we forever see ourselves as mere bodies and transmit our soul via foreign eyes, nose, and lips. In short, we animate [beseelen] first all flesh [Leiber] via physiognomy and pathognomy, and later all disorganized bodies [Körper]. We assign a distant human character to the tree, church steeple, or milk jar and with them, spirit" (203–4). Turning church steeples and milk jars into humanlike figures stems from the incapacity of humans to perceive anything other than bodies. To believe that another human is actually alive requires a projection of one's own subjectivity onto the other's body. In this way, it resembles physiognomy and pathognomy, pseudosciences that claim to interpret the inner essence of a human being by assessing his or her outer appearance. For the physiognomist, the body, and in particular the face, function as signs that can be deciphered. Jean Paul defines this idea of a relationship between essence and appearance in terms of a transference. Objects appear to be both humanlike and beautiful because of the human subject's perpetual disposition to personify: "Our incapacity to think of something lifeless as actually existing, i.e., as living, coupled with our custom of eternally personifying all of creation is what makes us conceive of a beautiful region as a painterly and poetic thought [Gedanke]" (204). The beautiful and the sublime are the result of an inherent necessity to animate and personify. This impossibility of perceiving things as lifeless sheds light on the notion of malicious objects. Karlheinz Stierle's theory of the comical, which draws heavily on Jean Paul's *School for Aesthetics*, lays out the logical structure of malicious objects as follows:

> A subject has at its disposal an object, the instrument of action, through which the action should itself materialize. The action may very well fail comically when the object turns out unexpectedly and suddenly to be resistant. The object reacts in such a way that the plan of action not only fails but proceeds as a mistake [in einer Unhandlung], giving the impression that it is acting contrary to the originally intended act. Through the arrangement of coincidences, the object becomes a quasi-subject that appears to have at its command the acting subject, which is itself turned into a quasi-object.[132]

Not only does an object—such as, in the case of Süptitz, the boot—seem to gain agency, as if inhabited by spiteful demons, but the subject appears to become more and more like an object. Stierle refers to this sudden reversal between the position of the subject and that of the object as one of the most powerful forms of the comical.[133] The actions of the subject seem to be determined by an uncontrollable nonhuman agency. This irruption of contingency, something that is beyond one's power, manifests itself in a personified and anthropomorphized form. Malicious objects as quasi-subjects appear not only in "sudden changes," in "autonomous situational movements," or as a "concise structure of repetition"—these are all terms used by Stierle[134]—but as agents endowed with intentions and the power to act upon them. According to Jean Paul, the reversal between subject and object is not sufficient to create laughter. It requires the addition of the observer's projection of his or her contrasting insights onto the agents involved in the comic situation. Friedrich Theodor Vischer, who coined the phrase of the "object's malice" (Tücke des Objekts) in the novel *Another One*, criticizes Jean Paul precisely for this focus on subjective intervention and human action. In his early essay on the relation of the comical to the sublime, "On the Sublime and the Comical" (Über das Erhabene und das Komische) (1837), Vischer states: "Jean Paul's sentence is insufficient because it is applied merely to the comical in human activities. . . . The comical conflict is of a universal nature and must be traced, above all, back to its metaphysical foundation [Urgrund]: the being-within-each-other [Ineinandersein] of the finite and the infinite."[135] What for Vischer appears to be a limitation of Jean Paul's theory is in fact the condition of its possibility. For Jean Paul, the comical, like the sublime, "resides within the subject";

it is the projection of a privileged subjective insight onto an objective situation. In chapter 14 of *The Comet*, Süptitz, after being denied the chance to participate in a theoretical discussion of the weather because of his difficulty chewing a piece of tough ham, starts a diatribe about the accidents that disrupt his daily life: "He thus began with serenity [Gelassenheit], but emphatically [mit Nachdruck], to protest: a thousand similar misfortunes and accidents, like this pathetic one that disturbed him in the process of answering, would meet him daily and were his daily bread. There was a system to it, which he had figured out. For instance, on the day before yesterday, when he looked at the weathervane in anticipation of travel, he could bet that its pointer would stare straight back at him, so that the sharpest eye wouldn't be able to tell whether it was pointing north or south" (851). The prison chaplain suffers from thousands of little accidents. For him, these incidents—random and chaotic at first glance—are part of a system. Failures, misfires, and miscarriages systematically undermine Süptitz's life. It is not surprising that in the context of his diatribe Süptitz returns to the aforementioned episode about the difficulties of putting on his clothes properly:

> So accustomed to failures of every sort, not the less so because they were small, he therefore reacted much as he had when it had once already happened to him: when, in circumstances that made the most polite urgency and the calmest dressing otherwise imperative [unerlaßbar], a button or a hole was skipped during the buttoning of his vest. To keep the vest's neckline from sticking in an unruly fashion around the neck, he once again had to pull down and thread everything through with his fingertips (unfortunately they were the most delicate buttonholes and buttons), the end result being that, by the time he entered the consistorial councilor's dining room, the councilor was already sitting at table. (852)[136]

A small failure, like missing a button, can have great consequences, such as the breaching of decorum by a too-late arrival. One accident leads to another, entangling the subject in a chain reaction of events that leaves him helpless. It is one of the characteristics of a subject caught in a web of recalcitrant objects that remedies, instead of bringing about a resolution, worsen and intensify the entanglement. Süptitz is trapped in an escalation of accidents caused to a large degree by his own attempts to reinstall order and control over the situation.

Frohauf Süptitz, as a systematic theologian and philosopher, performs acts of projection. For a highly irritable mind like his, the little vexations of everyday life that interrupt his intentions and plans are caused by malicious spirits that possess physical objects: "Es ist bekannt genug, daß der Hof- und Zuchthausprediger ein ordentliches Lehrgebäude hatte, worin er den Satz festgestellt, daß der Arihman oder der Teufel, d.h. nämlich Teufelchen oder boshafte Geschöpfe den Menschen mit mikroskopischen Wunden, mit elenden Kleinigkeiten hetzen, deren ein guter Engel von Verstand sich in die Seele hinein schämen würde" (1008). According to Süptitz's philosophy, accidents and disruptions do not happen randomly; they result from the interventions of malevolent devils, moving and manipulating objects in such a way that they disrupt his objectives in life. The devil is a malicious jester, ridiculing human beings: "He probably even enjoys it. . . . Such a fallen angel would rather jest than rest and, being prevented to make grand interventions from above [von oben], he at least snatches at small ones and executes merry pranks" (1009). The devil lacks the power to directly attack human beings—being denied this ability "from above," and must therefore resort to indirect means. If evil spirits had an immediate influence on matter, natural laws would lose their explanatory value and life would become completely unpredictable: "'But never presume,' he continued, 'that I am lending Beelzebub physical strength, giving him power over the movements of bodies, machines, books, or the like—truly, how could we then rely on the hands of a clock, a weathervane, or a piece of gold in a safe?" (1008). If the devil were all-powerful, life on earth would become unreliable, lacking orientation and structure. (Un)fortunately, the devil is reduced to baiting and hunting humans with microscopic injuries and minor trifles.[137] Man is defeated, not in the realm of sublime ethics or morality, but in the microcosm of small vexations and irritations. The devil lacks any direct, physical force. Hence he affects the human and material world by a form of magnetic energy: "Rather, I am only admitting that this god of the flies—who may not even be as physically powerful as a fly, so that he could be carried away simply by a spider's web or even another fly—can nevertheless bring every human soul into a magnetic connection with his organic shell [organische Hülle] (every spirit must have one protecting itself) and, like a *magnetiseur* to the clairvoyant, convey his thoughts and thereby achieve anything he wants [und dadurch alles durchsetzen]" (1009). It was especially F. A. Mesmer's discovery of "animal magnetism" that triggered Jean Paul's interest in phenomena like magnetism, animism, and clairvoyance. Mesmer combined old ideas of a *magia naturalis* with contemporary discoveries in magnetism and its relationship to electricity. According to Mesmer's writings, the *magnetiseur* can impart a cosmic influence, imperceptible to the common senses, to humans, animals, and objects. This magnetic force "can be communicated through all organized substances: animals, trees, plants, stones, sand, water, and all other fluid and concrete substances, at any distance and any size, even the sun and the moon, etc."[138] Such influence is characterized by a disproportionate relationship between physical activity and spiritual effect. Eberhard Gmelin, a medical doctor in Heilbronn, whose *On Animal Magnetism (Ueber Thierischen Magnetismus)* from 1787 Jean Paul read attentively, describes a "effect that is completely out of proportion with the smallest muscular movements causing them."[139] Just a very small initial muscular movement can have physical and spiritual results that go beyond a simple, mechanical relation of cause and effect. The moment of transference ignites a sudden change—a crisis—that eventually leads to a restitution of harmony.

While in Mesmer's and Gmelin's systems the *magnetiseur*, by focusing (i.e., projecting) the cosmic influence onto a human, tries to heal diseases, the devil, according to Süptitz, influences bodies in order to injure and hurt. The evil spirits harassing Süptitz "achieve anything [they] want" (alles durchsetzen), in the same fashion as a medical doctor would apply magnetism as therapy. *Durchsetzen* can be translated as "enforcing" or "asserting," but it literally also indicates an act of permeation and even penetration. Following Süptitz's theory, the devil can "alles durchsetzen": he is able to assert himself in the physical world by penetrating and perforating it. Natural laws and the devil's malevolent intentions are interwoven. This penetration of the physical world by metaphysical demonic influences also appears in "The Libel of Bailiff Josuah Freudel against His Accursed Demons." To exemplify his affliction by satanical influences, Josuah Freudel narrates an episode from his past as a young theology student attempting to give a sermon in the church of his hometown. After he has mixed up the different parts of his sermon, his wig, under and behind which he hides, makes it impossible for him to read his prepared text. Freudel orders the congregation to sing a hymn while he tries to regather his composure and reorder his sermon. This decision turns out to increase his calamity: "So I searched among the papers on the lectern for the beginning of the part which

I wanted to conclude, in order to revise the moral of my sermon. I was thrown from one section to another. I had stumbled around my thoughts [unter meine Gedanken verstiegen] like a sleepwalker when suddenly I froze, realizing that no one had been singing for a while now and that I had been deliberating while the whole congregation was waiting for me [auflauerte]" (208). The longer Freudel remains in the extravagant state of "Verstiegenheit," the more difficult it becomes for him to regain orientation, so that he can bring the sermon to a meaningful close and keep his sense of honor and decorum intact.[140] The only solution is to interrupt the situation: Freudel sneaks out from under his wig and, hidden from public sight, climbs down from the pulpit and escapes:

> Since the pulpit's hourglass was running out, now even more time had elapsed. The exceptional lull over the congregation lay heavily on my breast. The whole thing in the end appeared so ridiculous to me: the way the Church mass [Kirchenhaufe] was heedful with ear and foot, and so sure I was hiding behind my prickly helmet of hair. Yet I easily perceived that I could neither remain forever so concealed [niedergestülpet] nor with honor raise myself. I therefore deemed it the most decent to moult [mich zu haaren], which meant slowly sliding my head out of the wig as if it were an egg coming out of its shell and, with naked head, surreptitiously making my way down the pulpit staircase and into the adjacent sacristy. (208)

Freudel leaves the stage of the pulpit by sliding out of the wig. He dissociates himself from this mark of decorum, regaining a form of freedom. Ironically, it is precisely the wig, worn to convey Freudel's sense of *gravitas,* that leads to the breach of decorum. What is left is an empty shell, a form without content. The wig is "robbed of all its content [Inlage]" (208). The sermon remains unfinished; the congregation awaits its edification in vain.

This story about extravagantly being stuck in the pulpit serves Freudel as proof for his theory of the existence of a malicious demon interrupting and frustrating his plans and projects: "Precisely this story, narrated in such an excessive way, serves more than any other to prove the existence of that demon who, like a rat, shoots between the feet of those people who are full of the best ideas" (209). He can make sense of the situation only as the projection of an evil spirit onto the recalcitrant objects of his environment. The pains and miseries of everyday life, instead of being unpredictable coincidences, gain an underlying meaning, a meaning that is, in Jean Paul's words, "foisted upon" (unterlegt), "attached" (beigelegt), or "lent" (geliehen). The structure of projection and transference that characterizes the comical not only is a function of the observer's reaction to a subject caught in an irresolvable predicament but appears also to be a coping strategy of the cornered subject himself.

CHAPTER THREE

Malicious Objects

*Friedrich Theodor Vischer and the
(Non)Functionality of Things*

BEING CORNERED

On November 29, 1879, the British satirical magazine *Punch* reported on a recently published article by the German philosopher and poet Friedrich Theodor Vischer. Earlier that month "Herr Vischer, an eminent authority on Art and Aesthetics," appalled by the obnoxious behavior of a fellow traveler on a recent train ride, had been "emptying the vials of his wrath ... over rude people who lay their dirty foot-coverings on railway cushions in front of him."[1] What exactly was the cause of Vischer's rage, which he had meticulously documented in an essay for a Stuttgart newspaper under the title "Podo-Booetism [Podoböotismus], or Impertinence of the Foot"? Vischer describes the nasty habit of a fellow traveler who put his feet up on the seat next to him as follows: "This face says silently: 'I'd like to see someone shameless enough to challenge me while I scuff my dirty boots on this uppolstered seat.' Boot, sole, heel actually stare right out his face, a certain dirty leatheriness, shoe-studdedness, occupies the forehead, nose, mouth, and chin."[2] Vischer's description of the impertinent traveler focuses on his appearance in a way that brings to mind Bergson's definition of the comic as "something mechanical encrusted on the living."[3] His boot is not just one piece of clothing among others worn by the traveler but seems to merge with the wearer's body. Boot, sole, and heel are part of the face; leather and shoe nails "stare right out of his face." Subject and object, man and boot become one, creating an overall impression of impertinence. Whether the pronoun *er*, the grammatical subject of the following sentence, refers to the traveler or his shoe remains unclear: "He/it [er] sits—right opposite me—the place next to me is free—so he/it [er] has an open field—a foot-romping-ground [Fußtummelplatz]—what a pain!"[4] The cause of anger—the "impertinence of the foot"—is not so much a rude human being as the effect of a certain insistency of the part over the whole, the accidental over the essential, the mechanical over the living. Feet and shoes, mixing *physis* and *techne*, take on agency, undermining the will of the sovereign subject. Something acts within the body of the young man: "We've been traveling a few minutes and so it starts already, step by step. An impatience, a titillation, an impulse to indulge in the childish bad habit tingles in the legs, they fidget, they won't settle. Now he throws one leg over the other."[5] The traveler's limbs seem to be endowed with their own intentions. Vischer perceives the force that rules the actions of the young man as impertinent, since it threatens to disrupt the fragile spatial order within the confined space of the train compartment. The empty space next to Vischer will be occupied by feet: "The place next to me is free—so he has an open field—a foot-romping-ground."[6] With the arrival of the young man, the habitual arrangement of the cabin is disturbed. Its already cramped conditions are intensified by Vischer's fear of making contact with the protruding boot: "Where people sit next to and across from one another—really close together, as in a railway carriage—there, this cannot go on, it is not permitted. And this because at any moment the raised, hovering sole threatens to touch a neighbor's knee."[7] In the cramped conditions of the train compartment, humans are reduced to bodies that have the tendency to mechanically act on their own, interrupting the precarious social order. The physical acts with disruptive impertinence, showing a lack of respect for the intentions and needs of other humans. Vischer defines this condition by the dialectic of the need for distance, a spatial order, and the feeling of being crowded not only by humans but also by inanimate objects. Vischer suffers from a form of *claustrofuror*. Humans as well as objects that impose limits on his ability to freely make use of his personal space enrage him. This chapter analyzes several scenes from Vischer's novel *Another One: A Traveling Acquaintance (Auch Einer: Eine Reisebekanntschaft)* in relation to his aesthetic, philosophical, and autobiographical writings. They all try to come to terms with the individual's existence in the age of industrialization, radically altering the lifeworld of human beings threatened by processes of alienation and reification. The German word for reification, *Verdinglichung*, literally translates as "turning something into a thing." In Vischer, this specifically modern condition of human estrangement manifests itself in the grotesque idea of malicious objects.

Michel de Certeau in *The Practice of Everyday Life* maintains that traveling in the confined space of a train compartment controls and disciplines the body of the traveling subject: "TRAVELLING INCARCERATION. Immobile inside the train, seeing immobile things slip by. What is happening? Nothing is moving inside or outside the train. The unchanging traveler is pigeonholed, numbered, and regulated in the grid of the railway car, which is the perfect actualization of the rational utopia."[8] A.E., the protagonist of *Another One*, which was published roughly one year before the "Podo-Booetism" article, narrates a similar experience of "travelling incarceration": "They crouched again in the cabin, which stank of leather, and in which there was not even space to spit."[9] Again, the infuriating behavior of a young arrogant businessman, with whom A.E. has to share a ferry and a carriage, leads to a bizarre fit of rage. This outburst initiates A.E.'s dramatic exit from the moving vehicle: "Here, in the midst of the course, momentum, and forceful intonation of his speech, he was suddenly overcome by a spasmodic need to cough, his voice cracking in ridiculous fistula-tones. Gnashing in fury he rose up, threw the carriage door open, leapt out, got caught on the step and fell down into the thick dust of the road" (11). The experience of sudden unconquerable confinement generates an ineffable rage. A.E. feels cornered and trapped, unable to express his emotions in language. Communication breaks down as his voice turns into a sequence of ridiculous high-pitched sounds. A sudden, spontaneous physiological reaction, a squeaking sound, replaces speech. Instead of words he utters mere interjections. He feels compelled to free himself from his situation of confinement by the only means apparently left to him, jumping out of the carriage. But not only his voice but his body fails him, and his attempted escape turns into an accident: he falls and ends up a ridiculous figure in the dirt.

In one of A.E.'s autobiographical fragments, Vischer interprets the tragic figure of Hamlet in similar terms of confinement signified by a certain breathlessness: "Hamlet goes around like a person whose shoes are too tight and who can't take them off. All his blood, therefore, shoots to his heart and brain such that his skin can barely hold out.... The monologue 'To be or not to be' is greatly overestimated with regard to its thought content. Its worth lies in the depth of feeling: the expression of brooding that knows no way out of its state of breathless confinement and constriction is unattainable" (518).[10] For A.E., the sublime speech of Hamlet originates in the physical fact of having to wear shoes that are too tight. Hamlet's mood of melancholia has physiological causes: his blood is pressed into the heart and brain, making it impossible for him to breathe freely. Like a shoe that is too tight, the environment—mainly made up of inanimate objects—oppresses the subject, limiting his ability to move and act. In a similar fashion, the fellow traveler's feet occupying the empty seat in the train compartment limit A.E.'s legroom and breathing space. Things put stressful demands on the subject's space, time, and energy, their material resistance affecting thoughts, behavior, and emotions. An increasingly antagonistic environment traps the subject, amplifying his mad but futile desire to break out of his confinement. For Hamlet and A.E. the world turns into a tightly restricted space, fully enclosed, causing emotions like melancholia (Hamlet) or rage (A.E.). In a letter to his friend, the philosopher and theologian David Friedrich Strauß, Vischer again refers to the problem of tight shoes: "I always ask for broad boots of the following *façon*: ... for such is the form of the human foot, but I always get some such as these."[11] Vischer calls for loose boots because his feet do not match the mold of the average shoe. Those that cobblers produce do not, he claims, fit the needs of the walking man. The size and shape of shoes do not facilitate and support the act of walking but become instead an obstacle to it, which is to say, a source of pain and anguish. Hermann Lang, another friend of Vischer, remembers his attempts to improve the fitting of his shoes: "The reason for the little hole in the shoe was as follows: the Professor had himself cut into and bored it out with a sharp penknife, not long, a few days, before he arrived with us, near Wiesensteige or somewhere in any case at the foot of the Alb, all because of a corn. He then told Father with some satisfaction that every once in a while he manages to turn a cove of a cobbler or a cretin of a tailor into a halfway human craftsman."[12] To avoid physical and eventually psychological torment, Vischer has to modify and essentially destroy the fabric of his shoes. Cobblers and tailors are incapable of producing clothing that makes life more comfortable. Therefore it is necessary to "improve" their products, making them "human," properly rendering the *façon* of the foot and the footwear. Such adjustment, understood as a form of humanization, involves a certain violence against the object—its obstinate structure needs to be altered and loosened.[13] Another memoir, by Moritz Lazarus, also describes a hole in Vischer's attire: "He [Vischer] was wearing a long plaid nightgown, in which at its most worn-out spot a large hole could be seen. I was immediately reminded of his recently published book *Fashion and Garb [Mode und Trachten]*, in which he polemicized virulently against the tastelessness of women and men's clothing and in particular made fun, in his fiercely scolding manner, of plaid textiles. Jokingly I suggested that at least with the negative hole [negative Lochstelle] of his own dress he followed his own theory in practice."[14] Vischer is oblivious to a hole in his nightgown. A "negative Lochstelle," created by habitual usage, marks the usability of the sleeping gown. Indeed, only in its worn-out state is it finally ready to be worn. Making equipment comfortable and useful for the human being means altering it, dissolving the particular texture of the textile and letting it develop holes. The physical structure of clothes, shoes, and garments, if unaltered, takes hold of the one who wears them. It is oppressive, causing pain and anger. Only when the object begins to lose its structure, to fade, wear out, and even disintegrate, does the wearer finally enjoy it as something ready-to-hand. Only at the end of its use does it lose its character of recalcitrance and unhandiness. Its functionality relies on a "negative Lochstelle," a hole in the garment without resistance. This hole produces an open space that no longer binds, restrains, or inhibits the human condition.

Vischer, in *Another One*, traces back the incompatibility of subject and object, of bodies and clothing, to the inability of craftsmen—in times of industrialized, standardized production—to create genuinely functional devices:

> In any case, he [A.E.] added, such a product is the true image of our German industry, whose principal aspiration is indeed to make everything adverse to its purpose [zweckwidrig]. One would think, he said, that a specialist would know what he is doing—oh certainly; it's quite the opposite! The tailor precisely cannot tailor, the upholsterer cannot upholster, the carpenter certainly cannot make a chair! The first cuts a box rather than a coat, the second stuffs mattresses in such a way that you cannot lie on them, and the third builds a chair such that you have hold fast with your feet in order not to slip under the table. (84–85)

Craftsmen have lost their craft. They are no longer capable of making properly functioning products; these instead appear to take on

Malicious Objects

a life of their own. Such products do not ease everyday life and merge into the inconspicuousness of ready-to-hand equipment but are marked by flaws that impede their application, indeed in such a way that they appear to positively obstruct the purpose for which they are employed. Modernity for A.E. is characterized by the loss of a measure that would allow objects and humans to coexist, each having been assigned a determinable position within the *Lebenswelt*. The walker cannot walk properly, nor can he sit or lie down. Human beings are constantly fighting the objects that surround them, losing themselves in an obstinate environment. Subjects and objects do not match or fit into the same space, creating a world of misfits, collisions, and accidents.[15] A.E. is a misfit in the double sense that he as an eccentric not only rejects certain demands of social decorum but literally does not fit into his clothes. Tools and devices are not ready or suitable for the tasks, functions, or purposes they were designed for. Life turns into a constant struggle to regain space, to undo and repair dysfunctional devices and gadgets, to muster the resolve necessary to accomplish intended goals. The feeling of being bound, unable to breathe, within a world of things incommensurate with one's practices and intentions expresses itself in fits of rage.

In his essay "The Origin of the Work of Art," Martin Heidegger famously uses "a pair of peasant shoes," as they are depicted in one of van Gogh's paintings, as the primary example of "a common sort of equipment."[16] The character of the shoe as equipment (Zeug) is its service and reliability. These traits tend to escape perception in daily usage. If tools function properly, the user does not perceive them as such. The less the farm woman looks at her shoes or thinks of them, the more tool-like they are: "The peasant woman wears her shoes in the field. Only here are they what they are. They are all the more genuinely so, the less the peasant woman thinks about the shoes while she is at work, or looks at them at all, or is even aware of them."[17] The truth of equipment, its ready-to-hand quality (Zuhandenheit) consists in a certain absence: equipment retreats into unobtrusiveness. Equipment is discreet and inconspicuous, its essence constantly disappearing in its use: "To be sure, 'that' it is made is a property also of all equipment that is available and in use. But this 'that' does not become prominent in the equipment; it disappears in usefulness. The more handy a piece of equipment is, the more inconspicuous it remains that, for example, such a hammer is and the more exclusively does the equipment keep itself in its equipmentality."[18] The tool, during its proper usage, is nonapparent. But what happens when equipment becomes obstinate and unreliable? When the shoe does not fulfill the function it is meant for? What if the shoes—following Vischer—do not fit, are too tight or loose and cause corns? What if the shoes—following Jacques Derrida—do not constitute a useful pair?

Derrida, in an essay entitled "Restitutions," points out the uncanniness of two shoes in van Gogh's painting *Old Shoes with Laces,* which Heidegger refers to in his essay, that do not seem to form a pair: "Yes, let us suppose for example two [laced] right shoes or two left shoes. They no longer form a pair, but the whole thing squints or limps, I don't know, in strange, worrying, perhaps threatening and slightly diabolical fashion."[19] Derrida and Vischer stress the alienating, diabolical tendencies of objects. As elements that disrupt instead of facilitating the routines of everyday life, such shoes create moments of anxiety. For Derrida, the diabolical that appears in van Gogh's shoes cannot be reduced to their semantic ambivalence—whether they are the shoes of a farmer (Heidegger) or those of a city dweller (Meyer Schapiro)—but must be found in their possible impractibility:[20] "The diabolical is perhaps already caught, a supplementary bait, in the limping of these two shifty shoes which, if the double doesn't make a pair, nonetheless trap those who want to put their feet back into them, precisely because one cannot—must not—put one's feet in them and because that would be the strange trap."[21] Van Gogh's ambiguous shoes constitute a demonic trap, making every interpretation limp, enticing false identifications and generalizations with the aim of creating a pair of usable shoes on which a philosophy of the thing could be based.

The uncertainty concerning the origin of van Gogh's shoes is echoed in Vischer's article about *Podoböotismus* when he states that the observed impoliteness of the fellow traveler introduces an element of the primitive and rural culture of the lower classes into the sphere of the bourgeoisie: "It [putting feet up on railway seats] is the uncouthness of the cultivated, the poor manners of those who are well-bred, the backwardness of the educated, the crassness and crudity of the refined, it is *Booetisms* in the Attic country (*si parva licet*—)."[22] For Vischer, *Podoböotismus* is the intrusion of unrefined, primitive tendencies into the sphere of culture and society. Regression becomes a symptom of enculturation. The city dweller regresses to being a farmer, the Attic citizen turns into a stupid peasant from Boeotia.[23] Vischer remembers an Englishmen—combining the most refined and most coarse manners—who once put his feet on the seat next to him: "In Munich an elderly gentlemen boarded after me. He was smartly dressed to the point of wearing glacé gloves, which he did not remove for the duration of the journey. He was English, to judge from his face, and might have been a parson, his traits smooth and velvet, as if ironed. Hardly had the gentleman sat down when a foot was on the empty seat opposite, and this foot was by no means in glacé gloves but in a sturdy, thick-soled, heavily studded, filthy hiking boot."[24] The "greatest conceivable opposition" (denkbar vollster Gegensatz) appears between gloves and shoes, glacé and leather, cleanliness and dirt.[25] Impossible to clearly define as either town or country, the character of the Englishman consists in this "greatest conceivable opposition" that cannot simply fit into the category of peasant or bourgeois.

By hastening to identify the shoes in the van Gogh painting and interpreting them in a determinate context, as Heidegger does when he claims they belong to a peasant woman and Schapiro does when he makes their wearer a city dweller, both interpreters, according to Derrida, step into the trap of assuming and so obfuscating the specific equipmentality of the shoes. They ignore the possible uselessness of the shoes, being instead too quick to assign them functions and project meaning. What if the shoes—"sturdy, thick-soled, heavily studded, filthy"—are those of a British gentleman taking a walk in the picturesque landscape of the Low Countries? Vischer, in his call for a law to punish the "impertinence of the foot," grudgingly admits the impossibility of clearly separating proper from improper use of shoes in train compartments: "The borderline between proper and decent and improper and indecent" is fluid and therefore needs to be strictly enforced.[26] The necessity for a law and its vigorous, even violent enforcement corresponds to Heidegger's and Schapiro's interpretations of van Gogh's shoes, which similarly attempt to define and ascribe a particular, unequivocal meaning to a "greatest conceivable opposition."

Vischer, in relating his various disturbing experiences with footwear, shows how equipment can be disruptive and recalcitrant. It resists and does not retreat into the invisibility of reliable use. Shoes apply pressure, squeeze, and distort the human body in uncomfortable ways or threaten in uncomfortable and often painful ways. Whoever tries to slip his feet into Vischer's or van Gogh's shoes starts to limp, is caught in the ambiguity of two unsuitable shoes that do not match. And yet something appears in this moment of painful irritation.[27] In the moment of frustration and exasperation, when the proper use of the tool breaks down, the truth of equipment shows itself. Truth appears in limping, squinting, strange, disquieting, maybe diabolical ways. This differs from the theoretical attitude of the ready-to-hand, which systematically attempts to exclude all forms of failure, irregularity, and dysfunction.

Another way to experience the essence of equipment suggested by Heidegger is to decontextualize it. Shoes need to be cut out of their context, removed from their surroundings. The most prominent such decontextualization happens for Heidegger in the work of art. Heidegger states:

> As long as we only imagine a pair of shoes in general, or simply look at the empty, unused shoes as they merely stand there in the picture, we shall never discover what the equipmental being of the equipment in truth is. From Van Gogh's painting we cannot even tell where these shoes stand. There is nothing surrounding this pair of peasant shoes in or to which they belong—only an undefined space. There are not even clods of soil from the field or the field-path sticking to them, which would at least hint at their use. A pair of peasant shoes and nothing more. And yet—[28]

Nothing in the picture defines the shoes' environment. They are without use, severed from their context. Despite this claim of complete separation, Heidegger in the following passage continues to characterize shoes in terms of a certain connection between *Zeug* and *Erde*, equipment and earth, forcing Schapiro's and Derrida's intervention regarding Heidegger's rash identification and definition of the depicted shoes as those of a farmer:

> From the dark opening of the worn insides of the shoes the toilsome tread of the worker stares forth. In the stiffly rugged heaviness of the shoes there is the accumulated tenacity of her slow trudge through the far-spreading and ever-uniform furrows of the field swept by a raw wind. On the leather lie the dampness and richness of the soil. Under the soles slides the loneliness of the field-path as evening falls. In the shoes vibrates the silent call of the earth, its quiet gift of the ripening grain and its unexplained self-refusal in the fallow desolation of the wintry field.[29]

In this passage characterizing the shoe-equipment, a passage that Derrida calls a "pathetic tirade," the opening verb "to stare" (starren) oscillates undecidably between staring and stiffening, between activity and passivity.[30] It is as if the object stared back at the observer and simultaneously incarnated the essence of equipment in its "worn insides" (ausgetretene Inwendigen). This phrase, possibly playing on Hegel's analysis of *Auswendigkeit*, formulates the possibility of an opening in which the being of equipment can appear as the result of its use. The phrase "worn insides" can be read either as a form of comfort—the shoes, through long usage, have lost their stiffness, so that they finally fit the shape of the human foot—or as a sign of the possible loss of their usefulness, a fading and wasting of reliability. Is the "form of the shoe still in-formed by the foot"?[31] Being worn out and having lost their shape, van Gogh's shoes are *ausgetreten*, stepped out, formless. The inside appears on the outside through a lack when the usefulness of the equipment starts to fade. Being reveals itself in the mode of stepping out, opening, making the darkness of the inside visible. It is the mode of *Ausgetretenheit*, of being worn out, that guarantees what Heidegger calls an "occurring, a happening of truth at work."[32] The verb *austreten*, in this context, needs to be read in all of its ambiguity. It can refer either to a process of widening or to an act of destructive stomping. The act of *austreten*, that which guarantees the connection of equipment and earth, human beings and their environment, oscillates between serviceability and violence. In light of this discussion, it is no coincidence that Heidegger conceptualizes *Ausgetretenheit* in terms of positioning and standing: "In the work of art the truth of an entity has set itself to work. 'To set' means here: to bring to a stand. Some particular entity, a pair of peasant shoes, comes in the work to stand in the light of its being. The being of the being comes into the steadiness of its shining."[33] The pair of peasant shoes comes to a stand, it *starrs*, connected with the earth, appearing in the light of its being. It exhibits what Heidegger calls in his *Introduction to Metaphysics (Einführung in die Metaphysik)* "our roots in being [Bodenständigkeit]."[34] Standing on firm ground becomes the premise—*Voraussetzung*—for the truth of the shoes to appear. In this context, Vischer's plea to Strauß for better-fitting shoes gains urgency insofar as his demand for a wider, more comfortable shoe allows for a broader footing, a more secure connection with the ground. Modern footwear, for Vischer, with its slim fit, reduced almost to a straight line, not only causes pain but also threatens the loss of grounding. Heidegger identifies this deficient foundation as the "rootlessness of Western thought."[35] How is this grounding and positioning of equipment to be understood, since Heidegger, in introducing van Gogh's painting, claims that "as long as we only imagine a pair of shoes in general, or simply look at the empty, unused shoes as they merely stand there in the picture, we shall never discover what the equipmental being of the equipment in truth is"?[36] Isn't van Gogh's painting an example of the rootlessness of Occidental thought, since, as Heidegger posits, "There is nothing surrounding this pair of peasant shoes in or to which they might belong—only an undefined space"?[37] In van Gogh, shoes are situated in an "undetermined space" (unbestimmter Raum). This indeterminacy is doubled by the status of a painting as a material object that circulates between exhibitions and museums, constantly moving between places without a proper home: "A painting, e.g., the one by Van Gogh that represents a pair of peasant shoes, travels from one exhibition to another. Works of art are shipped like coal from the Ruhr and logs from the Black Forest."[38] Art as commodity enters the realm of exchange and circulation, devoid of its originary character.

In the 1960 edition of "The Origin of the Work of Art," Heidegger adds to the sentence "From Van Gogh's painting we cannot even tell where these shoes stand," the words "and to whom they belong."[39] This addition questions the possibility of assigning a proper owner—be it a peasant or a city dweller—to the depicted pair of shoes. The act of determining who possesses the equipment cannot be guaranteed and founded by a work of art. The equipment in the painting, if merely looked at, remains unused, empty, and *ausgetreten*. It belongs to no one and nothing. If the shoes are contemplated in this detached fashion and not used, they simply "stand there"—within a space of indeterminacy—without their inherent emptiness being *ausgetreten*. They are "represented" (dargestellt), but one does not know where they "stand" (stand).[40] The peasant, in contradistinction, by walking in them, wears them out (tritt sie aus), turning emptiness into a dark opening where truth can appear. *Hervortreten* is the result of *Austreten*.

Shoes are hollow.[41] In Heidegger's interpretation of van Gogh's shoes, equipment appears in the work of art as the limit between two forms of nothing, manifesting itself between the indeterminate space of its surroundings and the empty, gaping hole within. It is the phenomenalization of the border between two absences. In *Introduction to Metaphysics*, Heidegger, discussing the words *being* and *nothing*, returns to van Gogh's painting and plainly states: "A painting by Van Gogh. A pair of rough peasant shoes, nothing else. Actually the painting represents nothing [Das Bild stellt eigentlich nichts dar]."[42] Van Gogh's painting represents—actually (eigentlich)—nothing. How is the modifier *eigentlich* to be read? What is *actually* a representation of *nothing*? *Eigentlich* can be read as "the proper," in the linguistic sense, as the opposite of metaphorical.[43] The truth of van Gogh's painting cannot be rendered as a symbolization or representation, in which the shoes stand for something else. They are not a mere representation of truth. Van Gogh's shoes do not represent in a traditional way, they *stellen eigentlich nichts dar*. Does the painting represent that nothing of the first sentence—"a pair of rough peasant shoes"? Such a reading would imply that it is actually the nothing, enclosing the shoes, that is being represented rather than a definite, observable thing or piece of equipment. What is of interest for Heidegger is the empty space enveloping the shoes—the truth of the painting appears as empty space, framing the borders between nothingness and the thing. Being in proximity to the artwork suddenly transforms the ordinary position of the observer. Art disrupts the everyday, transforming man's place in and relation to the world. While equipment requires a forceful interruption of its habitual use in order to be perceived as such, the work of art in a similar fashion transforms the invisibility of the ready-to-hand, characteristic of the ordinary, into something extraordinary: "In general, of everything present to us, we can note that is *is*; but this also, if it is noted at all, is noted only soon to fall into oblivion, as is the wont of everything commonplace. And what is more commonplace than this, that a being is? In a work, by contrast, this fact, that it *is* as a work, is just what is unusual."[44] The extraordinariness of the artwork, turning being into something outstanding, is related to an open *Stelle*, in which the interplay of concealment and unconcealment, of *Darstellung* and *Verstellung*, takes place. This opening is "the open place in the midst of beings" (offene Stelle inmitten des Seienden).[45]

The space of the opening is not fixed (starr) but ever-changing, giving things a site where they can appear. Things take place and thereby "gain their lingering and hastening, their remoteness and nearness, their scope and limits."[46] In paragraph 6 of *Introduction to Metaphysics*, Heidegger points to the activities of poets and thinkers, who create spaces around things, rendering them extraordinary: "Poetry, like the thinking of the philosopher, has always so much world space to spare that in it each thing—a tree, a mountain, a house, the cry of a bird—loses all indifference and commonplaceness."[47] Poetry and thinking allow for an open space surrounding and enfolding the thing, in which the seemingly ordinary and indifferent steps into the realm of the extraordinary and unusual, where the familiarity of the everyday is disrupted. This blank, empty space is formed by the artist or thinker through a quasi-passive mode of *aussparen*, leaving out and allowing breathing space, setting the thing apart from its environment, cutting it off from its ordinary context. If this space, in which the thing comes to a stand—simultaneously grounded and separated, down-to-earth and outstanding, *bodenständig* and *außerordentlich*—is not given, the thing's being degenerates and it becomes merely one among many identical objects within an undistinguished crowd.

SHIFTING OBJECTS

In *Another One*, A.E. demonstrates the problematic relation of *Ding und Raum*,[48] as discussed in the preceeding section, by shifting pieces of tableware to create an open *Stelle:* "For what is space other than the obscene arranging, by means of which I, in order to place the body A here—he pointed to the cups, pots, baskets, bottles, glasses, that stood bunched together on the table—have first to shift B to there, but in order to make space for B must in turn place C over there and so on, with grace ad infinitum?" (32). The surface of the table, covered with different items of tableware, becomes the site for discussing a specific concept of space. This space is characterized by being fully occupied; it is covered with solid bodies. There is no open space or empty place onto which a body could be placed. To move one thing one has to move another because, as Freud puts it, "The same space cannot have two different contents."[49] Since the surface of the table does not provide empty space to place the body, A.E. must move another body to make space. This simple motion from position A to position B creates a possibly infinite shifting of bodies, equaling A.E.'s troubles with positioning himself in a world of recalcitrant objects. Life, for A.E., is reduced to the permanent creation and occupation of vacant places, in which things can come to a stand. As such, it is subject to the vicissitudes, anxieties, and frustrations of the sort Vischer himself experiences when attempting to keep the seat next to him on the train empty. Vischer's fury, which is occasioned by the bad manners of his fellow traveler, relates at a fundamental level to a particular perception of space. The cause of his rage is the *impertinent constitution* of space, of the sort that Vischer derives from an idiosyncratic interpretation of Kant's categories: "What is going on with that thing there is a matter of generally the same sort as the two things

Malicious Objects

that Kant called pure a priori forms of intuition" (32). Because of the cramped nature of space, things can appear only in the process of being shifted around. In Vischer's crowded universe, every attempt at representation (Darstellung) only leads to another displacement (Verstellung), another form of occupying an empty place, restricting and confining, hampering and obstructing. Things lack openings. Space is *verstellt* in the double sense of the German verb *verstellen* as displacing and obstructing.

In another passage from *Another One*, Vischer describes more precisely the creation of empty space that leads to constant shifting of things from one place to another, "with grace ad infinitum." Again, the protagonist A.E., this time in order to unfold a map, tries to clear the table in front of him, only to find that all attempts at clearing and ordering are futile:

> At this point he took out his map to show me his itinerary. There was not room enough on the table to spread it out: having brought the map out, he opened it at first to the extent that there was room on the table, but tracing the journey required that more and more parts of the map be unfolded, and so began a reorganization and tidying up of the various objects that covered the surface. The innkeeper appeared keen to show that he owned a comprehensive and well-adorned dinner service and so had not cleared away some of the vessels that were no longer needed; all over a second table and a commode stood flower vases, cups, and more, all in the same style adorned with gold rims and colorful patterns. If we wanted to clear the dining table, it was necessary first to undertake the same work on one of the other pieces of furniture, for which, however, the dining table, which one actually wanted to clear, provided the only space. And so began a circular activity of the most confusing and exhausting sort, which finally turned into a whirling back and forth and threatened never to end. (85)

Equipment is always in the way, not providing enough room for A.E. to unfold the map, effectively obstructing its utilization. The table lacks space, and space is always lacking, despite A.E. and his companion's frenzied attempts to clear the crowded surface. Things move back and forth within a closed circuit of infinitely exchanging positions. Moving an object from one position to another does not create more space but only relocates the problem of crowding. What Vischer describes here is a concept of space and movement that categorically distinguishes between a place and the thing occupying this place. In the lecture "What is a Thing" (Die Frage nach dem

Ding), Heidegger identifies this concept of space in Newton's *law of inertia* and Kant's transfer of this law of the relation of space and movement into his philosophy of transcendental categories.[50] Newton introduced a new concept of space, in opposition to older Aristotelian theories. Heidegger summarizes: "The concept of site [Begriff des Ortes] itself becomes something different. Site is no longer the place [Platz] in which a body belongs according to its inner nature, but a location [Lage], which is always relational, given in relation to any other such locations."[51] Movement does not stem from an inner principle but is the mere change of positions, relative to each other, a measurable "change of location" (Lageänderung).[52] This new theory of nature replaces qualitative with quantitative explanations. In this sense, the movement of tableware—initiated by A.E.'s attempt to create space for his map—could be read as an ironic exemplification of Newton's law of conservation of linear movement. Once a body is set into motion, its momentum will remain constant until a different force affects it.

Paradoxically, this constant movement of objects Heidegger calls *Bestand*. Samuel Weber, commenting on Heidegger's concept of *Gestell* and translating it as "emplacement," points out this tension between moving and standing: "The notion of emplacement, then, collects and assembles the various ways in which everything, human beings included, is 'cornered' (gestellt) and set in place. But since the places thus set up are the result of emplacement, they can never simply be taken for granted. Places must continually be established, orders continually placed. As emplacement, the goings-on of modern technics thus display a markedly ambivalent character: they arrest, bring to a halt, by setting in place; but this placement itself gives way to other settings, to the incessant re-placing of orders through which new places are set up and upset."[53] In the mode of emplacement, things have no determined bond to the place they occupy; therefore they can easily be moved back and forth without ever reaching a point where the incessant oscillation between placing and displacing would come to a standstill. It is this permanent vacillation that, for Vischer, exemplifies the impertinent installation/emplacement of space.[54] Things are simultaneously cornered and cornering, effectively causing human beings' inability to control or limit their and his movement, upsetting his or her habitual handling of equipment. The "circulation of objects" [Kreisen der Objekte] (86) within space is potentially infinite: the back and forth of tableware threatens to have no end, and the acting participants—human beings as well as things—lack the means to break out of the ever-accelerating circle. Both are cornered; their ability to move is limited to setting and keeping in motion the arrangement of places, never arriving at a stable state in which A.E. would be able to unfold and read the map and continue his journey to Italy. He is forced to constantly create space, a process that ultimately blinds him to the specificity of the things themselves disappearing into the ever-circulating context of placement and displacement: "A god seems to have struck us with blindness" (86–86). Empty positions appear and immediately disappear in front of A.E.'s eyes, blinding him with rage.

MOVING THROUGH THINGS

The instances of fury that Vischer's stories depict, generated from the sense of being cornered, or having lost one's legroom, or being deprived of breathing space by the objects among which one lives, are analogous to the experience of being caught in a crowd. In this regard, A.E. is once again exemplary—he could be considered as the choleric brother of Poe's or Baudelaire's *man of the crowd* who turns *flanerie* into an "uncomfortable walking-in-the-way" [unbequemes Indenweglaufen] (345):[55]

> In the crowd of people, it was not possible to hurry directly toward one's destination. . . . He took the crowd into consideration: in a flash determining with his sharp senses the image of the space in which the people were moving and immediately drawing in his mind a line along which he intended to shoot like an arrow through the holes. In the course of this linear calculation he forgot only that contingency is even faster than our strategy and that in an instant new walkers will be sure to wander into such narrow passageways. When this happened, he would become downright furious. (345)

The walker is obstructed in his straightforward progress in at least two ways. On the one hand, the "walking-in-the-way" is experienced as a physical shock, where the body of the walker lacks space and is under the threat of touching and being touched by others. Walking in the modern city almost inevitably leads to bumping into others. On the other hand, it is experienced as a mental shock, as the image of the space in the walker's mind is persistently threatened by the flux of the crowd. The observation of space as an empty and neutral field in which things move in a calculable course is assaulted by the violent incursion of contingency. Bodies of fellow walkers, shoved into A.E.'s path by chance, make it impossible to perceive space as an image, as a "space-image" [Raumbild] (344). Moving in the crowded space of the city resists being arrested, brought to a stand in an image, a *"dessin"* (344). The narrator, using the French term for "sketch" or "drawing," refers to the game of billiards, the paradigmatic exemplification for mechanistic concepts of space and movement:[56] "Do you play billiards? . . . Well, then, you know what is referred to as the *dessin*, to play with or without *dessin*. . . . I need only the word *dessin*.—We can translate it as *Vordenken*" (344). *Vordenken,* translated as "projecting, thinking in advance," relies on a continuous linear idea of movement that makes the walker unable to cope with the accidental shocks of an urban environment. It relies on an *Umriß*,[57] unsuccessfully planning progress along preconceived, stable paths through the thicket of things and human beings. Crowded spaces impede the possibility to project one's future movement. The gaps that open within the crowd, allowing the walker to move forward, appear and disappear according to laws that are beyond A.E.'s comprehension. Sudden, random occurrences disrupt any strategy based on linear calculation.

A.E.'s rage flares up in the moment when he feels cornered; his *sharp senses*, linear calculation, and strategy fail him, and coincidence and randomness begin to act against him. It is not that other walkers intend to disrupt his stroll and are acting against him; rather, chance—as an active agent—pushes these bodies into his envisioned route, blocking his way. Michel de Certeau mentions the walker in the city as being accustomed to the invisibility of urban space: "These practitioners make use of spaces that cannot be seen; their knowledge of them is as blind as that of lovers in each other's arms. . . . It is as though the practices organizing a bustling city were characterized by their blindness."[58] Walking—as a way of experiencing the city—is related to a form of blindness as sightless familiarity. Paths through the city are not seen but playfully perambulated. For A.E., walking is not characterized by such blind trust in the physical, intimate bustle of the city; rather, it is a rational, calculated method for traversing space. But such a projective procedure is inevitably frustrated as one's progress is constantly obstructed and diverted from the path and destination one imagines. A.E.'s plans break down in the face of the contingent reality of the crowd. The narrator characterizes these interruptions as a "Durchkreuztwerden im Gehen." The verb *durchkreuzen* should be translated not only as "to foil" or "to thwart" but also as "to cross out" and "to frustrate." The strategic plan on how to reach a specific goal is blocked, crossed out, voided. New intersections and turns interrupt A.E.'s progress, creating a "chaos of crossings" (Chaos der Durchkreuzungen).[59] It becomes impossible for him to represent this chaos in an image or a map. The success of a quick, linear, straightforward motion—like an arrow—relies on the perception of empty spaces in the crowd through which the walker can pass. The gap in the crowd that would allow the walker to proceed is fleeting, defying its permanent arrest. One cannot plan the movement from one position to another by projecting a line, making the linear progress that characterizes A.E.'s movement through the crowd of the city street: "Indeed, it seemed to me that, always moving in a straight line, he was simply incapable of strolling. I noticed that he, wherever possible, ignored the path's bends and moved ahead along the line of a bowstring" (345).

A.E. cannot stroll; his walking is always aimed toward a destination, directed—without detours or delays—by a definite goal. This sense of rigid calculability and purpose makes him unable to cope with the inconvenient "walking-in-the-way" of the other walkers. And although the open spaces within the crowd can be observed, A.E.'s attentiveness simultaneously heightens his sense of helplessness: "Those who by nature think ahead always have it worse than the happily blind, who simply fumble about—for them life becomes so difficult because their sense of the obstinate [Gefühl des Zweckwidrigen] must be just as sharp as their sense of the purposive [Gefühl des Zweckmäßigen]" (346). A.E.'s calculating nature displays a heightened, sharpened attentiveness, which, however, precisely prevents him from making his way effectively through the crowded streets. He is overwhelmed by the potentially infinite calculation of his progress, not by the structural impossibility of it. The projection of calculations impedes life instead of facilitating it. Those who are blind to the disturbances of the street, who do not experience them as a distraction, move with wondrous ease and grace. A.E. lacks the playful *arts de faire* that de Certeau examines, so he is unable to find openings and utilize them for his progress.

Vischer analyzes the difference between the necessity of the ideal and the randomness of the concrete, of "Nature, out of whose blind womb raw collisions of chance come to us."[60] He describes two lines crossing each other. The first one represents a "rational and progressive [line], which precisely grounds Hegel's logic, and a second, which cuts through the first, the line namely of chance, grounded in the collision of the different stages, the active movement of which takes place in One space and One time."[61] The stress in this passage should be put on "One space" and "One time," both capitalized by Vischer, marking the temporal-spatial position where linearity and deflection, ideality and reality, necessity and contingency collide. It is precisely this collision that constitutes the inner unity and contradiction of things. It allows a glimpse of "the inner unity of the thing and the contradiction in this unity."[62] In the early *Aesthetics*, the collision between contingency and necessity is sublated into a higher unity, following the model of Hegel's dialectics. The novel *Another One*, in contrast, shows the late Vischer's skepticism regarding the possibility of any such dialectical reconciliation. In a parody of Hegel, A.E.'s "gaze of the thinker" (Denkerblick) attempts to organize and classify the multitude of little evils and annoyances that manifest themselves in seemingly malicious objects of everyday life.[63] His scientific approach, following a strictly rational methodology, fails. Once again, the right path—the Greek *methodos*—leads to disorder and confusion.

A paradigmatic instance of this inevitable methodological *aporia*—getting stuck and entangled in the discrepancy between a structured, organized plan and chaotic reality—is A.E.'s "system of universal harmony" [System des harmonischen Weltalls] (322). Aiming to create a systematic diagram of all demonic evils in the world, A.E. is forced to continuously complicate his chart until it becomes utterly indecipherable. The narrator reports:

> At first, among the pages of normal format, I was struck by two sheets of thick drawing paper of unusual dimensions folded together. I unfolded them and a chaos of lines and colors appeared before my eyes on the one sheet, and an even greater chaos of lines and colors on the other. In the fields of these tangled nets stood writing going in different directions such as was available between the dividing lines: vertical, horizontal, and crisscrossed in diagonals. Both laborious artworks were incomplete; one saw a filled-out part and next to it, on the same surface, attempts to draw other dividing lines, which became more and more confused and finally made clear that the artist no longer knew how to proceed, stalled, and gave up. (322)

The graphic representation of a harmonious universe fails; the designer, as Vischer describes A.E. in this passage, is unable to reach the goal of a clear and structured layout of the different elements, which causes frustration. It is, after all, impossible to calculate "crisscrosses"

Malicious Objects 141

[Durchkreuzungen] (333), since they are essentially accidental: "I cannot calculate or order them, they come and go on all sides and are purely indeterminate; . . . there is no plan for the planless, no system for the systemless" (333). Beyond the inherently chaotic character of demonic nature that resists representation, there is a further obstacle for the "ordered image of the unordered" (333). Within the limited space of a piece of paper it is impossible to organize space in such a way that all "crisscrosses"—places where two elements randomly try to occupy the same position—can be perceived. Each attempt at clearing up, ordering, and rearranging—resembling the desperate back and forth of the tableware—leads to a further complication and intensification of the problem. The crisscrossing of lines and colors blurs the classifying diagram as a clearly structured space of vacant positions that can be filled. The more comprehensive, the less comprehensible the image: "But now, since all the fields and their contents coincided, all these colors permeated one another to produce a blurred messy image [Schmutzbild], underneath the smears of which one could hardly read the writing. . . . In spite of everything, the tangles and splodges grew and grew" (332).

The "Raumbild" turns into a "Schmutzbild." Instead of providing a clear design, the graphic representation of the crisscrossing of contingency and necessity dissolves into an unreadable blur of colors and lines.[64] Vischer in his theoretical writings sternly rejects chaotic, dissonant forms like A.E.'s failed system of a harmonious universe. It is the function of art to give order, harmonize dissonances, and transfigure the random shocks of everyday life: "When art is no longer capable of dissolving what is deeply felt, of harmonizing sharp dissonances, . . . then it is weak, its potency is wanting. When art is not able to bring its eye to the microscope, when one does not believe that it is capable of raising in transfiguration even that smallest thing when it is seen with the greatest accuracy, then good night! Then it is not capable of doing anything right."[65] "Crisscrosses" in their randomness have to be transfigured; the universe needs to be structured into a grid of empty, determinable positions that allows for the sublation of dissonances. But all of A.E.'s attempts at harmonization fail. In his *dessin*, colors and places overlap, lines crisscross, leaving no space.

"Mein Lebensgang"—an autobiographical sketch by Vischer from 1874—directs attention to another explanation for A.E.'s inability to design a harmonious system out of the unsystematic and dissonant:

Vischer's own position oscillating between literature and philosophy, reason and imagination. Because of this hybridity he, like A.E., is unable to excel in either genre, since the one is always interrupted by the other: "And from this, out of the coexistence of these opposing forces, a further, special source of unhappiness has to show itself: the man is at war not only with the object but also with himself. The talent for thought and that for fantasy disrupt each other's trajectories; he knows it, and this introduces a tragic trait into his life."[66] Imagination and reason cross each other's path, impeding the conclusion to any of Vischer's projects. This becomes especially clear in Vischer's attempts to finish his *Aesthetics*, during which he increasingly realizes the impossibility of reconciling the singular and the universal in a Hegelian fashion. The difficulties in applying Hegel's model of dialectical sublation are already apparent in Vischer's first theoretical text. Discussing the transition from the sublime to the comical in *On the Sublime and the Comical (*Über das Erhabene und das Komische) from 1837, Vischer points toward the disruptive power of the small, material thing. The comical is triggered "by the bagatelle, a thing that merely belongs in the lower world of appearances, which, having been hidden, appears all of a sudden between the legs of the sublime and trips it up."[67] It could be a pair of ill-fitting shoes causing one to stumble and disrupting the walker's straightforward, ideal progress. The bagatelle—a concrete, material thing—interferes with the abstract idea of the concept, effectively bringing about its fall. It is a moment of interruption resisting conventional forms of representation that makes the perception of the sublime possible. The interruption accomplished by the comical bagatelle reveals the sublime as such: "One might also say, and this opens an interesting perspective: the comical is the articulation [deutlich gemachtes] of the sublime."[68] The move from the sublime to the comical is provoked by the sudden appearance of a small detail tripping up the ideal: "der Idee ein Bein stellen."[69] The humorous revelation of the sublime results from stumbling and tripping over the materiality of the thing or the defectiveness of equipment. In each case the eruption of sheer materiality solicits a revelatory insight. Interruption is the mode of the comic and of cognition. It is not the systematic philosopher but the angry civil servant and unsuccessful writer A.E. who, in his failures and frustrations, becomes a model for approaching the truth of things. It is a twofold cognition that A.E. describes as "see[ing] the world with calluses" (die Welt mit Hühneraugen an[zu]sehen).[70] What does it mean to see the world with calluses? The German word for "foot corn" or "callus," *Hühnerauge,* retains an allusion to the eye, "das Auge." Calluses, as Vischer stresses in his reading of *Hamlet,* are usually the symptom of shoes being too tight. Sublime tragedy and grotesque comedy are closely connected to instances of aching and soreness. Both deal not only with abstract ideas but also with acutely unpleasant physical discomforts. The grotesque makes visible; seeing with *Hühneraugen* uses pain to perceive what escapes common means of representation. It takes only one step to cross the threshold between the sublime and the ridiculous. Anger and laughter, caused by areas of callous skin on the foot or by a stumbling misstep, become the moods through which the world reveals itself. They function as modes of cognition of the "inexpedient" (Unzweckmäßige), the "insubordinate" (Unbotmäßige), the "individual" (Individuelle), and the "deficient" (Defizitäre).[71]

MALICIOUS OBJECTS AND THE CUNNING OF REASON

Objects behaving in *inexpedient, insubordinate, individual,* and *deficient* ways interrupt daily routines and with it the idea of man's dominance over nature in general and his equipment in particular. Vischer coined the by-now proverbial phrase *die Tücke des Objekts* to render the contingent, interruptive force incarnated in malicious objects. Ingrid Oesterle explains: "With the degeneration of an ontologically understood aesthetic world harmony, chance is exacerbated to become a direct, even physiological, ill."[72] In his theory of the comical, as laid out in *On the Sublime and the Comical* and *Aesthetics,* Vischer, in discussing the sublime under the rubrics of the mathematical, the dynamic, and the moral, introduces a moment when the conflict between the sublime and its opposite is perceived as a comical rupture: "The sublime breaks down upon its opposite [Das Erhabene bricht sich an seinem Gegenteil]. Given that the former is infinitely large, the latter must be infinitely small."[73] Only the infinitely small can create a powerful antagonistic opposition, a "foreign power" (fremde Macht), that can contrast the mathematical sublime with reality's contingency.[74] In accordance with the infinitely small being that is opposed to the infinitely large of the mathematical sublime, Vischer examines the purely random mechanical blow as the opposite of the dynamic sublime and purposelessness as the opposite of the moral sublime. The stronger and more sudden the contrast between the ideal and the real, the more comical the effect of the disruption. The most sublime activity, preaching, becomes funny the moment it is interrupted by something banal, common, and low: "Even the most spiritual activity can be interrupted by so lowly an opposite as a sneeze, a slip, and the like."[75]

Vischer differentiates two different types of forces that are capable of disrupting and eventually overthrowing the sublime. One originates in the outside world of objects, while the other is located within the subject: "The base and the lowly can break through at two different points in order to bring down the sublime: either as external chance in the form of an incident that the sublime subject could not have foreseen or from within by means of a real lack of consciousness on the part of the subject."[76] Both external and internal randomness strike suddenly. Instantaneously, without calculation or plan, the contrast between the ideal and the real appears. A mere opposition does not suffice to create the comical—it requires a sudden movement, a tearing of the bond between the idea and physical reality. In the experience of the sublime, the tearing of the connection is never really fully enacted, remaining in the realm of illusion. The comical, however, tears apart the illusionary and allows for a sudden experience of a disjuncture:

> The sudden is a questionable moment in the sublime. One always feels as though the bond, which holds the idea and its sensible container together, were about to rip; but it does not necessarily come to a real rupture. On the contrary, precisely this semblance of ripping rips suddenly within the comical. Just when it looks as if the idea would suddenly outgrow and transcend the finite, it comes to a sudden end: a feeling like that when one imagines in climbing a stair that there is still a step before one and the raised foot falls back down to level ground.[77]

A movement suddenly stops, as if the ground on which one walked were pulled away underneath one's feet. Progress buckles and cracks; the lifted foot finds no ground to step on. The subject, losing his or her footing, experiences a loss of ground. Vischer describes this comic experience as one of self-sublation: "The comical is the movement of self-sublation that at once leads toward the goal and away from it."[78] "The self-sublating movement that the comical here presents resembles the progress one makes on a wheel or that of a walk on a ship against its course."[79] Being comical is analogous to walking toward a destination without ever reaching it; it is the simultaneity of aiming and erring, moving forward and backwards, up and down.

In *Another One* Vischer not only develops this contrast in terms of comedy but extends it to the realm of the tragic. Tragedy, according to Vischer, takes up the concept of the sublime and shows the constant struggle of high ideals with common, low disturbances and little evils. The truly tragic resides, according to Vischer, in the conflict between human beings and the disturbing evil spirits that possess the objects of everyday life: it is "the war of people with the spirits in which the truly sublime blows and wounds are struck, in which the terrible defeats occur, the shudder from which gives rise to the fundamental tragic feeling, that is to say, the whole feeling of our finitude" (40). The tenuous distinction between the tragic and the comic is captured by reference to the legend of Wilhelm Tell and his literary representation in Schiller's famous drama of the same name. A.E. rewrites Schiller's account of the "Rütlisprung," turning the sublime moment of Switzerland's constitution as a nation-state into a comical slapstick act. Tell's leap into freedom fails as he slips and tumbles into the water of Lake Lucerne. The sublime-tragic failure ends with Tell, after being saved from drowning, receiving a spanking from the enemy: "So: Tell leaps, slips, and falls in the water. He's pulled out and, despite all his resistance, dragged into the boat. Gessler shouts in a demonic tone: 'Now give his bottom a right proper beating!' It takes place, and all the more effectively given that Tell's trousers were already stretched tight from the water" (41). Tragicomedy, in sharp contrast to the historical and symbolical significance of the scene, results from a misstep and ends with a humiliating punishment. Switzerland's national hero is spanked like an unruly child. Such accounts, which take into account vagaries and coincidental accidents, are instances of what A.E. calls realism: "This realism, which is actually itself the only authentic idealism, must of course apply to the whole; these shepherds are portrayed in a too universal, too Greek way; they are merely well-trained speakers and achieve the good and the courageous only in this way, as if there were no goblins" (40–41). For A.E., true idealism equals realism because it does not deny the existence of demonic goblins interfering with pastoral idylls. Hence Schiller's and other idealists' depictions of a lost harmony between man and nature, *physis* and *thesis*, in Greek antiquity are false. For A.E., all idylls are constitutively disturbed.[80]

In a similar fashion A.E. criticizes historians for not properly recording random, physical accidents, which he ironically describes in medical terms as a catarrh: "He reproached history writing for failing in its duty, since it is incapable of understanding and doing justice to what is great and small in the course of world history without thoroughly acquainting itself with the accompanying catarrh that played a role in its essence, development, and individuality" (43). A.E.'s farcical rewriting of the Tell legend continues with a depiction of the failure of Tell to assassinate Gessler: "For no arrow has struck him [Gessler]; rather one hears only the twang of a bow and at the same time an extraordinarily powerful sneezing in a bush and the words: 'Damned chance, hell's cunning and deceit!' This cannot be misunderstood. Tell has of course caught a cold and sneezed his shot; Gessler shouts: 'That is Tell's sneezing, chase him'" (42). In A.E.'s "ideal project for a better tragedy Wilhelm Tell" (43) the arrow misses its aim and the killing of the tyrant fails. A chance sneeze interrupts Tell's mission to bring down Austrian rule and liberate the people of Switzerland. A.E. ironically translates Hegel's phrase "the cunning of reason" (List der Vernunft) into "the cunning of hell" [List der Hölle] (42). It represents an "authentic, higher irony of fate" (42). The world, according to A.E., resembles a "common cold of the Absolute" (59).[81] God himself is "ein alter Rotzler—Triefnase," an old "Rotzler"—runny-nose—who is responsible for the catarrh in the world: "And God said: let it be! And there was catarrh" (59).[82] Tell's true fate realizes itself in A.E.'s account in the form of an escape to Vienna, where he becomes a carpenter and enters into an idyllic, petit-bourgeois family life: "The closing-scene would offer a wonderful, heart-warming tableau: Tell, saved, in wistful contentment with wife and child in his workshop" (42). Private happiness stems from the abandonment and essential failure of political action. Tell gives up his heroic vocation and proceeds to live in Vienna, the capital of the occupying force, while Switzerland succeeds in its liberation through a rebellion of the masses, not the mediation of a heroic individual.

While for Hegel, and for the early Vischer during the writing of the *Aesthetics* and his essay on the sublime and comical, cunning reason can, via a dialectical historical process, integrate the accidental, in Vischer's late texts there is no possible reconciliation or sublation. The truly tragic equals the truly realistic; it is simultaneously sublime and comical. Killing a tyrant fails because of a random sneeze.[83] Accidents resist their integration into a universal, progressive development. In *Another One* they are described as "Hustenanfälle erhabener Art," fits of coughing of the sublime variety (75). Another literary example of the interruptive power of sneezing and coughing is Shakespeare's *Othello*, which, according to A.E., depicts the "conflict of conflicts," the "tragedy of all tragedies": man's struggle with the cunning of demonic forces. Othello is the tragedy par excellence, since it has "distilled the pure essence of man's being."[84] A.E. develops an idiosyncratic interpretation of Shakespeare's drama that relates every major turn of the play to a physiological condition. Essentially, Othello's suffering and rage stem from having a cold. The scratching, itching, and gurgling of the catarrh infuriate him. A "hellish flu," characterized by "harrumphing, coughing, endless nose-blowing" (75), accompanies Othello's every step. Shakespeare's description of Othello's sufferings, A.E. reminds the reader, should be understood not as a bare, common naturalism but as an expression of the highest, most sublime style: "Othello is now at the height of his suffering; not in a petty naturalist sense, no, this extreme point of the tragic condition is entirely presented in a terribly high style: in fits of coughing of the sublime variety" (75). The decision to choke Desdemona stems from his own suffocation: "He is on the point of asphyxiation, and so, in the fury of this struggle for life, this frantic seething of the brain, he becomes a devil: *I shall suffocate, so then should you*" (75).

To abreact his rage and turn it against another human being requires the intrusion of an object: the missing handkerchief. Lacking a handkerchief to ease his agony pushes Othello over the edge: "The handkerchief! The handkerchief! This cry—he has obviously mislaid his own—shows which object has become the sole concern of his increasingly deranged imagination—he chokes Desdemona" (75). Othello is unable to control his fantasy, which is subject to the demonic incursions of external objects and chance happenings. The world appears to him "Besinnungslos," (senseless) populated by antagonistic demons.

The absent handkerchief that causes Othello's murderous rage exemplifies how a missing piece of equipment can be perceived as malicious. Searching for a lost object constitutes one of the major sources of anger in *Another One*. Indeed, life, for A.E., is a permanent, unfinished search. The moment one thing is found, another is found to be missing, reigniting another desperate rummaging: "I had to waste my poor precious time in such doglike searching! Searching, searching, and more searching! One should not say: A. or B. lived for such and such a period of time, no: they searched!" (24–25). Living equals searching—not for metaphysical solace but for the missing objects of everyday life: "pencil, quill, ink well, paper, cigar, glass, lamp" (30). Things are not where they are supposed to be, they interrupt life, delaying the habits and routines of the everyday. Life as an infinite search, wasting precious time, functions as an example of a broken, disrupted teleology,[85] as does A.E.'s career as a writer and as a civil servant. Given the way his daily routines are persistently interrupted by the search for missing tools, his life refutes any idea of a progressive development leading to the goal of a harmonious unity of body and mind, self and society. In this sense, *Another One* reflects the failure of writing a Bildungsroman. Life and literature lose their telos, their development is delayed by a demonic temporality of constant postponement and delay as well as deflection and diversion.

THE BEING AND TIME OF MALICIOUS OBJECTS

In paragraph 16 of *Being and Time,* Heidegger, while analyzing the concept of being-in-the-world, discusses the essential inconspicuousness of equipment. What is ready-to-hand in everyday "circumspection" is in a certain sense imperceptible: "Being-in-the-world, according to our Interpretation hitherto, amounts to a non-thematic circumspective absorption in references or assignments constitutive for the readiness-to-hand of a totality of equipment."[86] Equipment disappears in the familiarity of the network of "references" (Verweisungen) that constitute the world. The ready-to-hand holds itself back; it cannot be thematized, made into an object of investigation. It appears only in its customary usage. Equipment is implicitly ready-to-hand, but not explicitly present-at-hand. It is *there,* prior to any direct observation. A disruption must occur to make manifest the tool and the network of references of which it (normally) functions as a part: "When equipment cannot be used, this implies that the constitutive assignment of the 'in-order-to' to a 'towards-this' has been disturbed. The assignments themselves are not observed; they are rather 'there' when we concernfully submit ourselves to them [Sichstellen unter sie]. But when an assignment has been disturbed—when something is unusable for some purpose—then the assignment becomes explicit" (105). Hence the perception of equipment as equipment cannot consist in an active, focusing thematization. Instead, an "ontological interpretation" (102) must rely on a disturbance in its use:

Malicious Objects

"When we concern ourselves with something, the entities which are most closely ready-to-hand may be met as something unusable, not properly adapted for the use we have decided upon. The tool turns out to be damaged, or the material unsuitable. In each of these cases *equipment* is here, ready-to-hand. We discover its unusability, however, not by looking at it and establishing its properties, but rather by the circumspection of the dealings in which we use it. When its unusability is thus discovered, equipment becomes conspicuous. This *conspicuousness* presents the ready-to-hand equipment in a certain un-readiness-to-hand" (102–3). The unreadiness of equipment manifests itself in "modes of conspicuousness, obtrusiveness, and obstinacy" (104).

The life of A.E., the protagonist of Vischer's *Another One,* could be described in these Heideggerian terms as a continuous struggle against equipment that appears as conspicuous, obstinate, and intrusive. At one point, A.E. commands his companion, who is also the narrator of the novel, to look at a dysfunctional cigarette lighter: "'There, you see: isn't that absolutely infuriating!' He showed me that the device was missing the flat little leaf on the handle where you have to put your thumb in order to hold it securely. The metal was bent round at this point and so did not offer much grip; it threatened to slip out at any moment" (84). The function of the instrument, to safely light a cigarette, is impaired. The lighter as equipment is being noticed, moves out of the circumspection of ready-to-hand into the thematic presence-at-hand: "There, you see." Dysfunctional tools, for A.E., are symptoms of the general state of German industry in the second half of the nineteenth century. Vischer's criticism of impractical and inefficient tools goes beyond a mere anti-industrial resentment, nostalgically yearning for a lost time of artisan craftsmanship, since even the craft of the tailor, the saddler, and the cabinetmaker is affected. What they produce are ill-fitting, impractical artifacts that do not accommodate man's needs. Everyday life is not facilitated but aggravated, not improved but impeded: A.E. complains that "the first [craftsman] cuts a box rather than a coat, the second stuffs mattresses in such a way that you cannot lie on them, and the third builds a chair such that you have hold fast with your feet in order not to slip under the table" (84–85). Not surprisingly, all of the listed examples affect the human body and its spatial position within the *Lebenswelt* of the individual. As Heidegger puts it, the thing "becomes 'equipment' in the sense of something which one would like to shove out of the way"

(104). Equipment materializes as a resistance, constricting one's ability to situate oneself. If things are too close, leaving no space between subject and object, they become obtrusive, creating emotions of indignation and outrage.

One mode in which the *Verweisungszusammenhang* of equipment is broken Heidegger calls "obtrusiveness" (Aufdringlichkeit). The function of equipment becomes visible when the tool is not in place to serve its user. As long as a tool is at hand, located in the user's proximity, ready for habitual use, it remains unnoticed. While ready-to-hand, equipment cannot be separated from its position within space, its inconspicuous connectedness with the surrounding environment. Emptiness introduces a break within the environment's coherence: "Our circumspection comes up against emptiness, and now sees for the first time *what* the missing article was ready-to-hand *with*, and *what* it was ready-to-hand *for*" (105). Obtrusive equipment is experienced as lacking. This lack again confines and limits man's ability to move freely: "The more urgently [Je dringender] we need what is missing, and the more authentically it is encountered in its un-readiness-to-hand, all the more obtrusive [um so aufdringlicher] does that which is ready-to-hand become—so much so, indeed, that it seems to lose its character of readiness-to-hand. It reveals itself as something just present-at-hand and no more, which cannot be budged without the thing that is missing" (103). Movement is blocked. Tools cannot be budged, leaving man encircled in a world of obtrusive objects. In paragraph 26 of *Being and Time*, dedicated to the spatiality of Being-in-the-world, Heidegger speaks of Dasein's "leeway": "Because Dasein is essentially spatial in the way of de-severance, its dealings always keep within an 'environment' which is deseveed from it within a certain leeway" (141). Equipment and Dasein in their interrelation create locations, open spaces, without being reduced to mere placeholders. The space of the ready-to-hand is—as a "region"—inconspicuous: "The readiness-to-hand which belongs to any such region beforehand has the *character of inconspicuous familiarity*, and it has it in an even more primordial sense than does the Being of the ready-to-hand. The region itself becomes visible in a conspicuous manner only when one discovers the ready-to-hand circumspectively and does so in the deficient modes of concern. Often the region of a place does not become accessible explicitly as such a region until one fails to find something in *its* place" (137–38). Heidegger emphasizes the ecstatic-horizontal temporality that allows for the entrance of Dasein into space. Because

Malicious Objects   151

of its temporal character, Dasein is "enspaced" (eingeräumt): it positions itself ecstatically in space, relating to the world, defined by Heidegger in this context as the whole of equipment: "Because Dasein as temporality is ecstatico-horizontal in its Being, it can take along with it a space for which it has made room, and it can do so factically and constantly. With regard to that space which it has ecstatically taken in, the 'here' of its current factical situation [Lage bzw. Situation] never signifies a position in space, but signifies rather the leeway of the range of that equipment totality with which it is most closely concerned—a leeway which has been opened up for it in directionality and de-severance" (420). Dasein requires leeway, legroom, and breathing space so as to ecstatically position itself. This position is not a neutral location in a three-dimensional Euclidean grid but is essentially tied to Dasein, positioning itself in a "region" (Gegend). Heidegger defines *region* as "the 'whither' for the possible belonging-somewhere of equipment which is ready-to-hand environmentally and which can be placed" (420). *Enspacing* happens in the act of Dasein relating itself to the region by means of ready-to-hand equipment. If the whole of equipment is interrupted by one element emerging as conspicuous, obtrusive, or obstinate, the "natural" relatedness of Dasein to its environment is affected.

For Heidegger, another mode that makes equipment perceivable is that of obstinacy:

> In our dealings with the world of our concern, the un-ready-to-hand can be encountered not only in the sense of that which is unusable or simply missing, but as something un-ready-to-hand which is *not* missing at all and *not* unusable, but which "stands in the way" of our concern. That to which our concern refuses to turn, that for which it has "no time," is something *un*-ready-to-hand in the manner of what does not belong here, of what has not yet been attended to. Anything which is un-ready-to-hand in this way is disturbing to us, and enables us to see the *obstinacy* of that with which we must concern ourselves in the first instance before we do anything else. With this obstinacy, the presence-at-hand of the ready-to-hand makes itself known in a new way as the Being of that which still lies before us and calls for our attending to it. (103–4)

Objects are not in their usual place, hindering progress, like the pedestrian in the street stepping into A.E.'s path. Instead of exerting a concerned circumspection, man has to cope with obstinate objects, rendering caring-for impossible: "In our concernful dealings, however, we not only come up against unusable things *within* what is ready-to-hand: we also find things which are missing—which not only are not 'handy' [handlich] but are not 'to hand' [zur Hand] at all. Again, to miss something in this way amounts to coming across something un-ready-to-hand" (103). As in the case of searching for a missing tool, one is never able to use the tool, since there is always something else to be done beforehand, like moving obstructing objects out of the way, which leaves the original task unfinished. In Vischer's world of obtrusive objects Heidegger's exceptional, phenomenologically revealing moment ceases to be an exception and becomes the rule and in fact a new form of concealment or habit.[87] According to Vischer, we live in a permanent state of exception, a permanent state of equipment breakdown.

In *Another One,* Vischer describes the loss of time over little annoyances and bagatelles, using the example of an hourlong search for misplaced glasses: "I had to waste my poor precious time in such doglike searching" (25). For Vischer, objects are most infuriating when they are needed most: "You might know that these miserable objects, these hedgehogs, these demons, like nothing better than hooking onto something, when you're in the biggest rush to finish up something that is necessary and reasonable!" (20). The more urgent and immediate the project or plan, the more resistant and defiant the object in its absence becomes, and the more pressing and wasteful the time spent looking for it appears: "I've got no time, absolutely no time for you!" (21). Objects do not go missing owing to the subject's lack of attention. The narrator emphasizes that the state of war between A.E. and the world of objects is not caused by his negligence: "Ineptitude, I realized, could not be the cause of this state of war in which he found himself with the bagatelle" (27). Things actively try to deceive and betray man. They lurk at every corner, waiting for man's attentiveness to weaken. The moment the "moral force of man's gaze" [moralische Gewalt des Menschenblickes] (30) declines, objects are empowered, threatening to damage or break down the established hierarchy between man and nature. By compelling man into a heightened state of attention to fend off its aggressiveness, the object prevents man from realizing the ideals of a higher sphere. "Who has the time?" A.E. asks, to be on a continuous lookout against the moment in which the object "pounces on" the subject like a wild tiger: "And like the tiger in the first moment when he, unobserved, sees and with a spring of rage pounces on his unfortunate prey, so is it with the accursed object" (30).

Malicious Objects

The lurking object escapes man's attention by hiding among other objects. The few times that A.E.'s searches are finally successful he realizes that what he was looking for was right in front of him, hidden in plain view by a crowd of similar-looking objects: "The object with its devilish humor especially loves to play hide and seek. Just as good, caring, protective nature paints some animals the same color as the ground on which they live and forms them in the likeness of that upon which they feed so that they are harder to find by their enemies . . . such is also the procedure of the demons: for example, a red-brown glasses case conceals itself on red-brown furniture" (31). Malicious objects are indistinguishable from their surroundings, concealing themselves from man's attention and access. Their cunning consists in a devious form of concealing their position within space. They camouflage themselves by becoming one with the environment, such that the distinction between the thing and its surrounding space can no longer be perceived. In these moments, the object's lurking does manifests itself, not in an aggressive pounce, but in a more passive form of concealment. In *Being and Time* Heidegger uses the example of spectacles to show how equipment in its ready-to-hand proximity conceals itself, escaping attention: "When, for instance, a man wears a pair of spectacles that are so close to him distantially that they are 'sitting on his nose,' they are environmentally more remote from him than the picture on the opposite wall. Such equipment has so little closeness that often it is impossible to find" (141). For Vischer, no systematic, rational approach, such as a goal-oriented search, can cope with malicious objects. They hide among others, camouflage themselves by becoming one with their surroundings, and move, apparently following their own devious will, out of sight. Pieces of paper slip into drawers where they don't belong, and slices of bread crawl to the edge of the table, waiting to jump, "but the spite of the object is above all to creep to the edge and then let itself fall" (31).

OBJECTS AND AGENCY: THE TWILIGHT OF SYMBOLIZATION

The demonic forces that seem to possess malicious objects have a history. For A.E., only knowledge of the metaphysical foundation of history allows for a historiography that properly renders the little, vexing disturbances of everyday life tolerable. The following section discusses Vischer's (failed) attempts to develop a theoretical discourse that would represent the history of malicious objects within a rational, logically consistent system. It furthermore analyzes the ascription of agency to objects, as performed in A.E.'s mythology of malicious objects, in relation to theories of language that emphasize the metaphorical foundations of all language (be it conceptual or literary).

Vischer's "primordial history" (Urgeschichte) of malicious objects begins with nature being created by a female "primordial being" [Urwesen] (69). All of nature and its creations can be traced back to this original being. Her character oscillates between good intentions and evil, demonic tendencies. She is simultaneously protective and destructive, "extremely ingenious, charming, extremely kind, and, at the same time, extremely frivolous and demonic, extremely cruel" (69). Intelligence and stupidity, reason and emotion, beauty and cruelty are inseparably intertwined, making nature's capricious actions random and unpredictable. Because of this duality, nature can appear beautiful, as in a "bird's plumage," or ugly, as in the "warthog, toad, tapeworm, lice, fleas, and bugs" (70). Analogously, nature is "actually positively cruel, as cruel as lovely, and in this respect it fully resembles the demonic woman, or rather it is the clearest proof that all this can derive only from a woman, specifically, from an ingeniously evil one" (70). Nature's wickedness is effortless, thoughtless, instinctive: "A wickedness so refined that a man might conceive of it only with extreme exertion in thought is brought about by a woman in an instant without any reflection: satanically guiltily, completely innocently" (70). Female nature is an incarnated paradox: innocent and guilty at the same time.

But human beings, under the guidance of a second deity, a male spirit of light, were able to create a superstructure of law, science, and culture. These institutions provide, according to A.E.'s private mythology of malicious objects, protection against vicious nature: "The same humanity discovered again and again, guided by a second, higher deity, a male spirit of light (of whom we will speak another time), things that were not in the grasp of the primordial woman and the spirits: law, the state, science, nonappetitive love, and art" (72). What A.E., in other contexts, describes as an antagonism of ideality and reality, culture and nature, here undergoes a mythological historicization. The split between human beings and things, subjects and objects, results from the struggle between a god and a goddess associated with evil spirits. The evil spirits are enraged by the enlightened inventions of mankind, but they are too weak to fight the god of light

Malicious Objects 155

directly, so they slip into objects, through which they carry out their vindictive struggle against the higher dispensation of reason and order: "But the spirits, the product of the ignominious slime, were furious and resolved to carry out a terrible revenge. They slunk into objects" (72). Evil, spirits rebelling against the higher order, occupy objects, which thus become malicious. These possessed objects deliberately and remorselessly cause pain and anguish for man, the representative of male enlightenment. Objects are merely the carriers or vessels of malicious demons, and the impulse to address them directly—instead of the possessing spirits—arises from a confusion: "It is yet to be taught that it is an inaccuracy in speech [ungenau gesprochen] to blame the possessed object instead of the demon that possesses it. This is simply in accordance with language and fantasy [sprach- und phantasiegemäß]; one cannot name both at the time [man kann nicht allemal zwei nennen]" (72). By accusing objects of malice and treating them as if they acted intentionally, one mixes up the possessing and the possessed, meaning and its carrier, message and medium, in a fantastic conflation of spirit and nature, the figural and the literal.

A.E., by highlighting the difficulty of simultaneously addressing object and spirit, echoes Paul de Man's analysis of the rhetorical status of anthropomorphism in Nietzsche's essay "On Truth and Lying in a Non-moral Sense." De Man points out that anthropomorphizing an entity by naming it goes beyond asserting a tropological proposition to wrongly establishing an identity.[88] Falsely accusing the object instead of the spirit in the moment of anger is an "inaccuracy in speech" (72) that confuses, in de Man's terms, what is "taken" and what is "given." It creates the mythology of the malicious object by giving a name to a tropological transference or projection. It "freezes the infinite chain of tropological transformations and propositions into one single assertion or essence which, as such, excludes all others."[89] Vischer maintains in the explanatory remarks on *Another One* in "Mein Lebensgang" that anthropomorphic projection and animation, equipping nature with a soul, are fundamental anthropological characteristics. The projection of agency onto random events accompanies human encounters with the world's recalcitrance. Again, Vischer uses the examples of an interrupted walk and of a catarrh:

> When I am making my way determinedly toward a destination and I stumble over a stone and fall, when in the midst of a heartfelt speech I am overcome by a fit of coughing so that I am stuck making curious fistula noises, it is, in itself, nothing other than a man in his willing

and doing and a piece of brute nature that is in no way concerned with the former but blindly gets in his way. But now if he has the least respect for himself, he would have to be completely without imagination not to curse the stone or the damned cough. He is thus obliged, by the impulse of the spirit to animate everything, to lend unconscious nature, or the piece of it that tripped him up, will and intention, malicious intention.[90]

This principal process of unconscious projection becomes visible in the moment of disruption. In these instances, Vischer advises, one should pay attention to oneself and one's mode of cognition, discerning the structural role that imagination plays in all of one's interactions with the world. The symbolic, indeed, fantastic, character of language becomes discernible. Not to animate nature in this way, which would mean not speaking metaphorically, is feasible only for someone "completely without imagination."

Already in the chapter on natural beauty in *Aesthetics*, Vischer had developed a corresponding concept of projection. Man's imagination, projecting consciousness onto things, is able to create beauty in nature: "The elements are represented as if they knew about the organic and human life already present outside them and rejoiced in nourishing and in giving pleasure to it or in jealously destroying it."[91] The aesthetic experience involves perceiving inanimate matter as if it were organic, even human life. *Unterschiebung*, the projection of an intention, transforms the ambiguous randomness of inorganic nature into necessary and beautiful entities.[92] By perceiving something as beautiful, man animates nature, thereby reducing its contingency. In his late writings on language and aesthetics, which can all be read as revisions and corrections of his early *Aesthetics*, Vischer situates modern aesthetic experience—as a form of symbolization—between the realm of the rational and the irrational, hovering between myth and reason, necessity and freedom: "The act of animating-projecting a soul [Akt der Seelenleihung] remains a necessary characteristic proper to humanity even when it has long since outgrown myth. Only now, with what we call reserve [Vorbehalt], the ego projected behind impersonal nature [das der unpersönlichen Natur untergeschobene Ich] is not made into a deity, indeed it is no further defined, no myths arise—but certainly something similar."[93] Symbolization, as an act of nonmythical "Seelenleihung," oscillating between the poles of freedom and necessity, claims a middle position.[94] It partakes in the realm of myth by its identification of image and meaning, signifier and signified, while at the same time it is free, having gained an ironic distance from the process of projection. While both myth and secular, merely aesthetic symbolization are founded in a confusion between image and meaning, they differ in how they relate to the symbol itself: "And so again: We call 'symbolic' something that was once believed as a myth, that which, without actual belief, but nevertheless passionately reinstating what was in the belief, is adopted and taken up as a free and aesthetic, yet not for that reason empty, instead meaningful, image of appearance" (435). Having recognized the mythological deities as projections of his or her imagination, the modern subject has lost his or her faith. What is left is a kind of "poetic faith" (427) that is simultaneously "not and yet nonetheless believing" (428). This belief without belief liberates the subject by loosening the bind of blind faith and the firm bond between signifier and signified. The free play with mythical symbols founds a "bright, liberated symbolization" (eine helle, freie Symbolik) that is simultaneously conscious and unconscious, enlightened and mythical: "The matter is now: the middle—one might also call it a peculiar twilight. It is the involuntary and nonetheless free, unconscious and yet in a certain sense indeed conscious animation of nature, the act of projection, by which we impute [unterlegen] our own souls and their moods to that which is soulless" (431–32). The symbol appears in the precarious twilight of exposed and disenchanted gods. In the middle ground—the realm of symbolization—things appear in twilight, where disenchantment and reenchantment are implicated and intertwined. The German word for twilight, *Zwielicht,* close to *Zweilicht,* must be read not only as "twilight" but also as a doubling or splitting of light. In this second interpretation, the process of symbolization into two mutually exclusive tendencies appears. It is simultaneously light and dark, unbound and limited. Symbolization is "dark-light" [dunkelhell] and "unfree-free" [unfreifrei] (433).

Poetic symbolization is a remainder of a mythological age when signifier and signified were believed to be identical, but it remains as an anthropological trait—"naturnotwendiger Zug der Menschheit" (435)—still active today. It is not only in poetry that the original identity between image and meaning persists, for "all of language is traversed by poeticizing expressions, which rest on this free-necessary deception [frei-notwendige Täuschung]" (433). Language rhetorically animates objects and is "thoroughly metaphorical [bildlich], even where it appears completely unmetaphorical [unbildlich]" (433). The twilight of symbolization is not restricted to a mythological past or poetic expressivity but affects any use of language, be it poetical or conceptual. Vischer's examples, in this context, are taken from colloquial language. Not surprisingly, some of them again contend with misbehaving objects that trigger the subject's projection of human traits: "All sorts of soulless things [Unbeseeltes jeder Art] are endowed with a will: the grape wants warmth, the nail does not want to come out (of the plank), the parcel does not want to go into the bag" (433).

Metaphor and anthropomorphism lie at the heart of the symbolic process, which cannot be limited to an earlier period of mankind's development or to the realm of aesthetic language uses. The imprecise discourse that A.E. claims to be responsible for mixing up objects and spirits is an anthropological and linguistic constant. All speaking takes place in the twilight of symbolization. It is always erroneous and improper. Inaccuracy "is a shortcoming only from the analytical standpoint, a shortcoming of knowledge. By the standards of the imagination, from the point of view of imagination-value, it is a great advantage, an energy for the image faculty [Energie des Bildvermögens]" (433). Symbolic language's imaginativeness, conceptualized by Vischer in energetic terms, compensates for its lack of precision. In this sense, A.E. is by no means a merely pathological case. His mythology of demonic spirits possessing objects pushes the universal anthropological activity of symbolization to a grotesque extreme. In "Mein Lebensgang," Vischer relates his theory of the symbol to its poetical incarnation in A.E.: "Now give this imputing, projecting, personifying play of the imagination [unterschiebenden, leihenden, personifizierenden Phantasiespiel], which every living person can sense in himself, the slightest push, such that one might consider it to be only slightly intensified, so that the game almost becomes serious [aus dem Spiel nahezu Ernst wird], as if the infuriated person half-believed in earnest [als glaubte der Geärgerte halb und halb wirklich] in some goblin behind the transgressive disruption—such a person is A.E., so is a good part of his character finished!"[95] The perception of objects as malicious originates in an experience of the *almost*. Playful imagination almost turns into earnest belief. Perception in the virtual mode of the "as if" is taken half-seriously:[96] "We all think and say a thousand times following very annoying accidents: it is indeed as though demons were plotting against me! One takes this 'as if' half-seriously, just as ancient mythology took similar incidents completely seriously—and thus one has A.E.!"[97] The primitive

Malicious Objects

mythology of deification and fetishization, which earnestly identifies thing and meaning, is lost. In modernity, its earnestness is replaced by an ironic half-serious "as if." Modern man, conscious of the tropological, anthropomorphic structure of all language, does not believe in the existence of demonic spirits possessing objects. For the modern, as for Wittgenstein, the idea of malicious objects is "a stupid anthropomorphism" (ein dummer Anthropomorphismus).[98]

A.E.—opposing this stance—takes the "as if" of poetic symbolization half-seriously, neither completely falling back into a mythological identification nor denouncing anthropomorphism as mere stupid confusion. For him, the seriousness of the mythological age is lost, so symbolization lacks the ability to console man's suffering, as it was envisioned by Friedrich Nietzsche in "On Truth and Lying in a Nonmoral Sense." For Nietzsche, man tries to cope with reality using reason and intuition. "They both [reasonable and intuitive man] desire to rule over life," claims Nietzsche, "the one by his knowledge of how to cope with the chief calamities of life by providing for the future, by prudence and regularity, the other by being an 'exuberant hero' who does not see those calamities and who only acknowledges life as real when it is disguised as beauty and appearance."[99] The "sublime happiness and Olympian cloudlessness" of the intuitive artist, according to Nietzsche, stems from "playing with earnest things."[100] The rule of art over life in the mode of poetic symbolization, a form of playful earnestness, appears in metaphorical visions, in the "immediacy of deception," protecting man from harm.[101] Anthropomorphic projections perform a decidedly ethical function. Nietzsche describes the symbolic production of art as a deceptive but necessary measure for man to survive. Affirmation of deception and lies leads to cheerfulness. Rational man, on the contrary, is "fearful of intuition" and no longer believes in the protective powers of the mythological, poetic symbolization. Enlightened man is honest, freed from deceptive illusions, and "governs himself by means of concepts!"[102] He shows patience and endurance in the face of adversity, denouncing the false promises of the "sublime happiness and Olympian cloudlessness" manifesting itself in the identity of word and meaning:

> This man, who otherwise seeks only honesty, truth, freedom from illusions, and protection from the onslaughts of things which might distract him, now performs, in the midst of misfortune, a masterpiece of pretence, just as the other did in the midst of happiness: he does not wear a twitching, mobile, human face, but rather a mask, as it

were, with its features in dignified equilibrium; he does not shout, nor does he even change his tone of voice. If a veritable storm-cloud empties itself on his head, he wraps himself in his cloak and slowly walks away from under it.[103]

The rational stoic, seeking only "honesty, truth, freedom from illusions," protects himself from the "onslaughts of things" by hiding behind a shielding mask, concealing his humanity. A.E. is neither the stoic man of science, guarded by pretense, nor an artist, living in blissful happiness in a world of "metaphorical visions."[104] Instead he shows both tendencies: he is an artist—the writer of a novella and an unfinished play—as well as a rational philosopher, constructing a classifying system of demonic forces. This opposition duplicates the distinction between the lower realm of female nature associated with spiteful demons and the higher, male realm of culture, as it was developed by A.E. in his conversations with the narrator of *Another One*. His life is made up of the constant struggle of a higher, Socratic realm of morality and freedom with a lower realm of matter and necessity. This struggle for dominance can never be resolved or transformed into a stable equilibrium,[105] so he can never, like Nietzsche's stoic figure, "wrap himself in a cloak and slowly walk away from under a veritable storm-cloud."

In *Another One*, the half-believed mythology of demons as an attempt to reduce contingency, to control and predict the randomness of natural events via their integration into an ordered system of symbolic representations, fails. A.E. is not a stoic, unaffected and emotionally detached from the random misfortunes of daily life, but someone who keeps losing his temper, bursting out in rage. Anger stems from his inability to resolve the tensions between art and science, intuition and rationality, metaphor and concept. In the instance of the malicious interruption, when man trips up and falls, the real calamities of life appear, which cannot be restrained by either poetic symbolization or rational conceptualization. The mask of pretense is torn away; neither stoicism nor aesthetic illusions nor any other program of self-governance can cope with the "onslaughts of things." Both art and science are exposed as inadequate, unable to redeem man's existence. For A.E., no one is safe from the pain and suffering of demonic corns or catarrh: "Didn't catarrh cause a devilish irritation in his throat, blur, cloud and stupefy his brain, no longer allowing him to think anything other than nonsense, falsity, and absurdity? Wasn't perhaps a burning corn giving him blistering dagger-stabs from the toes up into his heart and marrow?" (72–73). Brain, heart, and soul are painfully affected, leaving nothing but absurdity, injustice, and nonsense. Slight accidents rule even over heroes and demigods: "A hero can stumble on a straw! A demigod choke on a fish bone!" (73).

TAKING REVENGE AGAINST OBJECTS

For A.E., the only effective method to fight against the violent and antagonistic forces incarnated in malicious objects is to take revenge, to punish things in retaliation for the harm and injuries they set off. If one is attacked by malicious objects, one should, according to A.E., fight back. The vengeful onslaught of things, although it never fundamentally endangers the physical well-being of man, undermines his cheerfulness and in so doing gives rise to the need for retribution. The spirit of vengeance displayed by the objects is contagious, affecting also people under the pressure of things. The living human being and the inanimate thing approximate each other in the state of anger: "As I looked down at the lake, how it beat against the foot of the vertical rocks, it seemed to me that my fury was One thing with this stone and this raging tide and that I ought to be as defiant as those rocks and foam and as fierce as the face of the crashing waves" (44). In this passage, the narrator, who has gradually fallen more and more under the influence of A.E. with regard to objects, anthropomorphizes his anger: anger and object become *One* thing. In his rage, he resembles rocks, floods, and waves. Again, man, situated both in the world of nature and randomness and in the world of morality and freedom, appears in the form of a tropological identification. Living human being and inanimate rock resemble each other.

The primary method of taking revenge is based on what A.E. calls the execution of objects. When—after a long search—he finally discovers his glasses, his anger expresses itself in violence: "It was not easy to get the glasses out of the hole. The exertion in no way related to the worth of the object. Finally he succeeded. He held them up high and let them fall, shouting in a solemn tone: 'Death sentence! Supplicium!' He lifted his foot and stamped on them with his heel. Glass flew all over in little splinters and particles of dust" (21). A.E.'s anger is directed against an object with little or no value. Neither the fury generated during the long search, nor the violence meted out to the glasses once found, is in proportion to the inconvenience their absence posed. Instead of trying to claim his anger, A.E. escalates his poetico-mythic projection and takes revenge on the object as if it were a living being. The perception of the world as possessed by evil demons demands the destruction of all recalcitrant objects. The act of destruction resembles a judgment proclaimed by a court of law. A.E. is prosecutor, judge, and executor in one. As the object is sentenced to death like a human criminal, the act of projection—at the moment of the object's destruction—paradoxically reaches its anthropomorphic culmination. Who is really executed? Is it the object or the demon that possesses it? A.E. so earnestly believes in his projection that he is unable to clearly differentiate between image and meaning. The skepticism and ironic distance of the "as if" of poetic symbolization is lost, and he reverts to a mythic state in which signifier and signified object and evil spirit appear as one.

In contrast, the narrator of *Another One* is at least initially more skeptical. The mutual furious projection of vengeance as a tropological transfer of characteristics between subject and object leaves him in a state of suspension. His reaction to A.E.'s mythology of evil demons oscillates between laughter and anger: "I was only half-inclined to laugh at this sublime project. It dug and bored into me something like a fine thorn or, actually, two thorns piercing in opposing directions. . . . He may in the end be a major rogue [Kapitalschelm] who's making a fool of you" (42). Suspicion concerning the nature of A.E.'s sublime project makes it impossible for the narrator to laugh. He is not fully convinced that A.E.'s mythology is a purely idiosyncratic, mad product of imagination. Is mankind's struggle against malicious, vengeful objects the product of reason or imagination? Is A.E. a "major rogue," ridiculing the narrator, or does his private mythology reveal a deeper truth? Suspended between belief and skepticism, the narrator cannot decide whether A.E. believes in his poetic symbolization or not, whether his construct constitutes a metaphorical, anthropomorphic transfer or a substantial identity. Are A.E.'s historical narrative and eventually his angry outbursts rhetorical or literal? The half inclination of the narrator to believe in the myth of malicious demons echoes Vischer's remarks about the "as if" character of artistic symbolization. Hovering between seriousness and playfulness, art constructs and simultaneously voids symbols. The narrator experiences this oscillation physiologically as two stings piercing in opposite directions. He is suspended between laughter and anger in such a way that his ability to read A.E. is obstructed. Is the twitching in A.E.'s face while he develops his mythology of evil demons to be interpreted as an indication of irony, or is it a mere tic?

The narrator experiences this state of suspension between belief and skepticism, identity and transference, as a rupture of his very self. In A.E.'s diary notes, this model of a split subject is quite literally transformed into an image: "We are only images—really, literally only images" (391). We, as human beings, are a mere illusion, a fleeting representation, oscillating between creation and destruction: "We are in each moment woven, painted for the first time and also undone, wiped out again. But what comes into being each moment does not truly exist. We are not secure; we only oscillate much like a dream-image. We appear to be as solid as bone and iron although we are in fact so porous, merely fluctuating disintegration and recomposition" (391). Stability, permanence, and self-identity, the traditional conditions for the possibility of being a self, are lacking. The subject appears as a dream image,[106] never fully developed or gaining substance, transitory, hovering between illusion and dissolution. What seems solid is porous and fluid; it has no relation to a truthful and meaningful existence. Man: an anthropomorphism.

These insights into the transitional character of man, being created and destroyed within an instant, living from moment to moment without a definable essence, do not turn A.E. into a nihilist, denigrating or denying the existence of the self. Early in the novel he reports on his reading of Schopenhauer and agrees with Schopenhauer's ontological principles although he is critical of many other aspects of that philosopher's work, especially the idea of a permanent superstructure dominating the will. This realm of morality, although produced by man and under constant pressure from malicious nature, can provide provisional meaning and stability. Following Vischer, the subject is located between the realm of the irrational will and rational spirit, nature and culture. The self is positioned on the battlefield where these two antagonistic forces cross each other, struggling for dominance. In this struggle the human being is reduced to nothing more than a fluid image, painted and wiped out instantaneously.

THROWING THINGS

One prominent object that becomes the focus of A.E.'s revenge is a jug. The narrator reports, as A.E. again faces the resistance of unruly tableware, an instance of anger leading to the desire to destroy it: "The table was almost completely covered with dishes, side dishes, pots, bottles, glasses. An old sturdy earthenware jug held the water. I'd moved it around at least ten times, but it would not find its rightful place. A.E. had also, as I couldn't help but notice, long been irritated by it" (78–79). *Enspacing* the jug fails despite numerous attempts. The confined space of the table does not allow the jug to come to a stand. It has no leeway. The jug is the exemplary thing in Heidegger's discussion of the thing, which, attending to the etymology of the German *Ding*, he relates to a form of gathering and bringing into the open.[107] Its being, according to Heidegger, is that of an enspacement, the creation of an articulated space where it can appear: "If we think of the thing as thing, then we spare and protect the thing's presence in the region from which it presences."[108] What for Heidegger represents the thing par excellence causes vexation for Vischer: the jug does not gather, instead it bothers. It vexes A.E. because it continually moves from position to position: "This being crept from place to place [von Stelle zu Stelle], to whatever location was inconvenient for us" (79). Ruled and pressured by the jug, which always appears in inconvenient positions, the narrator reacts with rage and angrily addresses it as a living being: "The jug was no longer a jug for me but rather an animated, obnoxious being, a spirit-hooligan or hooligan-spirit [Geisterlümmel oder Lümmelgeist], his spout was a shameless snout, the raised tin cap an impudent face, the handle a defiant, mortised arm" (79). Here each feature of the jug is anthropomorphized and gains new meaning. It ceases to be a jug and, for the narrator, becomes a living being possessed by a malicious spirit. As a representative of a lower antagonistic force looking for revenge, the haunted jug needs to be destroyed. The narrator is "eager to treat the undoubtedly guilty being according to the rule of law and justice" (79). Rage against the object reacts to the painful disturbances of the daily routines. The human being fights back, initiating a permanent state of warfare. This struggle is fueled by the mutual need for a discharge of affect. In "Mein Lebensgang" Vischer says of A.E. that "fury at himself, disgust also at the guilty objects, fury at the guilty objects rushes over him, becoming half-mad: is it not human that a wild need for outward release [Entladung] emerges?"[109] The subject is split, angry not only with the object but with himself, with his inability to cope with the disruptive forces that permanently threaten his sense of self.

The impossibility of controlling this rage leads to an uncontrolled abreaction.[110]

Only violent destruction seems to be a satisfying means of dealing with the anger induced by misbehaving or missing tools and freeing the narrator from the pressures and restrictions that constrain his legroom. The endless endeavor of cleaning up and reordering resembles a metonymic chain of replacements. Signifiers, freed from an essential bond with the signified, enter a passionate, highly confusing economy of exchanges and substitutions. In this state of accelerated circulation, the subject is unable to allow the signifying object to appear in its proper place. Positioning the object in one location as a method to determine its meaning dissolves into a frantic, infinite process of replacement that never comes to rest. The inability to arrest the continuous tropological transformation leaves the subject only one option: to destroy the object and annihilate the material carrier of meaning. The unity of signifier and signified is not only torn apart but completely obliterated. The symbol shatters like A.E.'s glasses, leaving nothing but shards and splinters. Terminating symbolization in the form of the execution of objects stems from the act of projecting meaning. In the moment of anger, for the subject the "as if" character of poetic symbolization becomes unbearable. A.E. can no longer strike an ironic pose. What is supposed to be liberating and enlightening in the act of symbolization turns out to be confusing, overwhelming, and oppressive. The narrator describes the beginnings of his urge to punish the object: "But—prepared at an unconscious level [auf unbewußten Stufen vorbereitet]—something suddenly sprang up in me" (79). This is the moment when free, poetic symbolization is suddenly transformed into an earnest belief, when anger erupts and manifests itself as *something*. This "new sense" of the object confirms the unity of the subject and guarantees its ability to act: "And the worst was that I was not shocked for a moment by this godforsaken new sense that was magically attached to it, as I had been yesterday over the other ominous symptoms; rather, I was entirely at one with myself, completely sure and eager to treat the undoubtedly guilty being according to the rule of law and justice" (79). Rage against the object is the result of an earnest belief in anthropomorphism, which arises when one overlooks or forgets—to use Nietzsche's terminology—its figural foundation. It is an act of arresting and terminating the tropological constitution of anthropomorphism. In the angry outburst, the playful figural anthropomorphism is taken literally, creating the mythology of the malicious objects.

In Jacques Lacan's reading of Heidegger's essay "Das Ding," he (mis)translates jug—*der Krug*—as vase—*la vase*.[111] Both the jug and the vase function as symbols of symbolization, creating voids, empty spaces, that become locations for possible signification. For Heidegger, the jug's empty character consists in giving a form, in the act of holding: "How does the jug's void hold? It holds by taking what is poured in. It holds by keeping and retaining what it took in. The void holds in a twofold manner: taking and keeping. The word 'hold' is therefore ambiguous. Nevertheless, the taking of what is poured in and the keeping of what was poured belong together. But their unity is determined by the outpouring for which the jug is fitted as a jug. The twofold holding of the void rests on the outpouring."[112] The jug gives; its essence is that of a gift. Hollowness, around which the jug is built, allows for a dialectic of giving and receiving, of filling and emptying. It marks the site where a place, a *Stelle*, is opened up so that it can be filled and occupied with meaning.

Once the jug as a thing becomes recalcitrant and therefore is no longer at hand, once it cannot hold and pour water because, according to A.E.'s mythology, it sneaks toward the edge of the table and lets itself fall or constantly positions itself in inopportune places, the dialectic of giving and taking is interrupted. The ordered exchange of filling and emptying, that is, the economy of tropological transference, breaks down. The jug's function as a site allowing enspacing and signification is disrupted.

The philosophy and practice of executing malicious objects culminate in a scene depicting the narrator and A.E. jointly throwing tableware out the window of a restaurant: "Opposite the window, beyond the street, stood a massive granite block. . . . My aim wasn't bad, and the jug shattered upon it in countless shards and splinters. A.E. complimented me and grabbed a fruit vase; its fate was the same. We took turns with plates, platters, glasses and whatever came to hand" (86). Not just a single object but a whole collection of jugs, vases, and glasses shatters on the granite. Here anger is expressed if not replaced by a deliberate, calculated action. Things are not thrown in blind rage. The narrator aims, A.E. has time to compliment, and the two men follow an alternating, rhythmic order in the process of destroying objects. The execution's public character supports its ritualized, theatrical aspect. The restaurant window becomes a stage, with the narrator and A.E. as actors and some youths from the village as spectators: "Below, a circle of spectators had quickly formed, village youths who gathered and cheered before the unusual spectacle" (86–87). Rage is performed for an audience, it is planned—A.E. coolly purchases the tableware from the owner of the restaurant before the execution begins—and carefully staged. Nothing could be further from an unmediated, purely emotional outburst of anger. The narrator, who is initially overwhelmed by anger and on the point of spontaneously destroying the troublesome jug, is stopped by A.E.: "I jumped up: grabbed the sinner [the jug], rushed to the window and threw it open—but A.E. quickly held me back: 'Not yet, my dear man! I already know that you have made wonderful progress in your education, but it is not quite the time yet, there may still be some sort of adulation at play here. Wait! When it is time, I'll give the sign!'" (79). The execution is as much an act of deliberation and reflection as it is the result of wrath. Far from being an uncontrolled and spontaneous abreaction of angry energies, it takes place in a planned way. A.E. carefully calculates the moment of execution. It has to take place at the right time and at the right place to be successful.

What the throwing of tableware performs is a momentary return of the mythic belief in possessing spirits. Since one cannot speak about object and demon at the same time, as A.E. stated earlier, one must artificially stage a mythical relationship of objects and their meaning. A.E.'s and the narrator's execution of the tableware is an act of overcoming the blindness of believing in a mythical correspondence between signifier and signified, turning the mythical belief of the identity of thing and meaning into a performance that deliberately amplifies anger. The performance of destroying objects, as the physical carriers of meaning, exposes the forces of symbolization at work in all language. Since the destruction of the silverware is so obviously staged, it becomes questionable whether A.E. and the narrator perform the execution of objects in earnest or ironically. The impossibility of clearly distinguishing whether angry outbursts are earnest abreactions or rhetorically performed spectacles becomes evident in the reaction of the restaurant owner, who also observes the spectacle of the shattering of tableware in the street:

> The innkeeper looked on in shock, half angry, half laughing at this scene, which he nevertheless allowed to take place. One could read from his face that in his mind two forces were carrying out a proper battle: on the one hand, the feeling of the purposelessness

[Zweckwidrigkeit] of what was happening, the displeasure over such perverse activity [verkehrtes Handeln] and its brazenness; on the other, the respect for strangers who take the liberty of such extravagant waste, and the desire for amusement that such a scene as the last one gives rise to in every spectator. (89–90).

The innkeeper's reaction is ambivalent. He struggles between conflicting emotions: anger, respect, and joy. He is half-annoyed and half-amused, unable to ascribe a definite meaning to the spectacle that unfolds in front of him or to determine whether the actions of the narrator and A.E. are meant seriously. Is he witnessing a calculated, rhetorical amplification of anger or the energetic abreaction of a sudden rage without purpose?

The narrator further develops the relation between the execution of objects and A.E.'s theory of language during a short intermission in the "great drama of the pots" [große Töpfedrama] (90): "With much laughter calls were made for criminal justice: 'G'heibe! G'heibe!' A.E. had just picked up a nice carafe when this call was heard for the first time, he had even already extended for the throw, but he checked himself, grabbed with one hand the button of my coat, while the other, with the vessel, waited, held high in mid-swing, and gave me a short lecture concerning the word that the youths were shouting and that I, given the accent, would have, without his instruction, spelled *Keien*" (87). This scene proves again how the execution of objects goes beyond a mere destructive outburst of rage. A.E. stops mid-throw to give a lecture on the meaning of the word *G'heibe* that is being shouted by the village youth observing the devastation of the tableware. It turns out that it takes a certain amount of education to correctly understand its meaning. The effective implementation of the guilty verdict takes an element of reflection; otherwise it remains a form of private idiosyncrasy and vanity. Carrying out the death sentence against objects not only involves a public declaration of the judgment—"Supplicium! Death sentence!" (86)—but also a recognition of the audience's reactions. While the narrator is unable to understand the audience's shouts—he can only come up with the meaningless utterance "Keien"—A.E. is educated enough to be able to provide an interpretation of "G'heibe," which verifies the performance's achievement: "'*G'heien*,' as he taught in the pose described—spelled G, apostrophe, H, E, I, so actually *geheien*—from *heien* with the prefix *ge-*—means a) to throw; b) to bother (one says, 'Leave me *ung'heit*' in upper Swabia and Switzerland), also demonic haunting ('The devil

Malicious Objects 169

geheit mich', says Luther); c) an extremely delicate modification of the sense, which I learned in Swabia, *es g'heit mich*, means: I am uneasy, something pleasant has been missed or lost" (87). The word *G'heien* is characterized by a "very fine modification of its sense," split up into different meanings: to throw, to irritate (demonically), to feel uneasy, to have missed something. The shattered pieces of glass and porcelain generate shattered words. *G'heibe* needs to be spelled by A.E., broken into its most basic elements—letters—to bring out its meaning. This splitting of the word *G'heien*—if it is a word and not just the projection of A.E.—leaves several possible ways to read the act of execution. Do the boys outside the restaurant merely comment on the physical act of throwing, or are they able to comprehend the underlying intention of avenging the demonic assaults of the objects? Are they able to read the execution properly? The difficulty of understanding the boys' response is underlined by the laughter that accompanies their exclamations: "With much laughter calls were made for criminal justice: 'G'heibe! G'heibe!'" (87). What does the laughter stand for? Does it have to be read as a sign?

Fractured and fragmented language requires a specific skill of interpretation. To ascribe meaning to a shattered word like *G'heibe* requires an act of attribution. A.E. often projects meaning onto the meaningless sounds of his surroundings. Sounds mock him, interrupting his activities and causing him anger and pain. A door's creaking utters the Latin phrase "eo ipso," a judiciary-rhetorical term, meaning *by that very act*: "It has to be borne. There is some consolation. Now I no longer have to hear the door from my office into the chancellery creaking. Heavy oiling hardly helped at all. The whistling tone of the creaking always sounded quite clearly like 'eo ipso!'" (509). The squeaking door "clearly" speaks Latin. This shift from sound to meaning can also move in the opposing direction. There are several moments in the novel when A.E.'s discourse disintegrates into a series of unconnected words or even meaningless sounds. The scene in the horse carriage quoted in the beginning of this chapter exemplifies this disintegration from a mutual conversation into coughing, squeaking, and creaking, effectively terminating communication. A.E.'s voice creaks like the door of his office. At the climax of his angry speech he begins to cough, and his voice transforms itself into a high-pitched and inarticulate squealing. The squeaking door speaks, and man, the talking animal, squeaks. *Eo ipso*—by that very act—nonsense becomes sense, and sense nonsense. The establishment of a stable exchange between sound and meaning in an ordered system, as it was envisioned by A.E., fails. Combining concrete physical evils with abstract scientific, aesthetic, or rhetorical concepts leads to chaos. A systematic categorization of all evils in relation to their representations is unsuccessful: "There is no plan for the planless, no system for the systemless" (333). There is no authority that could order the entanglement of so many interjecting sounds and meanings. All attempts at a rational, calculating classification are in vain.

To these traversing interjections that resist determination there is only one exception. The narrator discovers one term in the chaotic "system for the systemless" that is able to relate word and physical interruption. It is the rhetorical concept of *amplificatio*: "At that moment my gaze fell on a place where a word stood that revived in me a memory-image that hovered in the dark distance. It was called *amplificatio*. I stared at it more intently. It is to be found in the rubric of rhetoric. . . . This *amplificatio* ought to stand on the chart as the centerpiece of combined actions. And this time he really succeeded in bringing the word together with the aforementioned combination: coughing, being stuck, tumbling" (333–34). Coughing, being stuck, and tumbling out of a driving carriage are brought together through *amplificatio*, a rhetorical device to intellectually and affectively implement the persuasive powers of discourse. Amplification constitutes a form of enlargement and exaggeration; it is "a graded enhancement of the basic given facts by artistic means, in the interest of the party."[113] What is naturally given is amplified in speech to create a certain affect in the listener. A prosecutor, for example, might paint the deeds of the accused in stark and harsh images in order to stir the emotions of the jury. After tumbling out of the carriage, A.E. regains his composure and voice, reacting to the mockery of his fellow travelers by cursing and evoking the rhetoric of amplification: "But the fallen man had quickly picked himself up. He stood, covered in dust, and shouted after us in a clear voice: 'Amplificatio, Ignoramuses, amplificatio!'" (11). It remains unclear what the word "ignoramuses," positioned between exclamations of *amplificatio*, refers to. What are the fellow travelers ignorant of? Do they lack knowledge of Switzerland's history (the topic of A.E.'s discourse), or do they misunderstand his sudden exit from the carriage as a laughable accident when it in fact was itself the enactment of the rhetorical device of *amplificatio* and was intended as the intensified expression of his argument? Was A.E.'s exit a jump, a planned event, integrated into a rhetorical system of ordered relations between words and actions so as to stir up the listener's emotions, or was it an accidental fall, a loss of control? Anger, in the first instance, would be less an immediate, uncontrollable emotional response than a form of rhetorical affection and self-affection.[114] The ambiguity of the rhetoric of anger shows itself in A.E.'s definition of *amplificatio*, which the narrator discovers in the unfinished classifying system of evils: "There were some names on it, names with which the ancient science of eloquence had designated certain parts of speech in Latin: *exordium, narratio, reprehension,* and the like. *Amplificatio* refers to an ostentatious turn of phrase at the close of a speech in which the speaker, by means of an abundance of images and proofs, smartly embellishes his wisdom one more time in order to go out with a bang [mit einem recht flotten Trumpf abzutreten]" (333–34). Amplification, in A.E.'s presentation of rhetorical doctrine, appears at the end of the speech as an overflowing abundance of images and conclusions before the speaker steps down. Stepping down, "in order to go out with a bang," can be read as an ironic allusion to A.E.'s fall from the carriage. In this case, stepping down is amplified into a tumble. Rage oscillates between a rhetorical act of self-affection, igniting and amplifying passions, and a cathartic abreaction. It takes place at the intersection of hermeneutics and energetics, where words as containers of meaning shatter like glass. The reaction of the reader, like that of the figure of the narrator in *Another One*, remains ambivalent. Should one laugh at A.E. or lose one's temper with him? *Amplificatio, Ignoramuses, amplificatio!*

CHAPTER FOUR

Igniting Anger

Heimito von Doderer and the Psychopathology of Everyday Rage

ANGRY RHYTHMS

Heimito von Doderer's 1962 novel *The Merowingians or The Total Family (Die Merowinger oder die totale Familie)* begins with a scene in the clinical practice of the psychiatrist Professor Dr. Horn. The patient, Dr. Bachmeyer, describes his ailment: "Rage, Professor. I suffer heavy attacks of rage that are terribly strenuous for me and extremely exhaust me."[1] Dr. Bachmeyer experiences rage as an exhausting disease that disrupts his psychological as well as physiological health and for this reason seeks treatment in Dr. Horn's "Neurological and Psychiatrical Clinic" (13). Rage constitutes a pathological deviance from the norm that requires clinical treatment, since its uncontrollable outbreaks are a threat to the patient's mental health. As with Vischer constant breakdowns of equipment characterize the human condition in modernity, for Doderer the accompanying emotion of rage becomes the most prominent example of the precarious interaction between human beings and things. Doderer, who had studied among other things psychology at the University of Vienna, was intimately familiar with the various psychological theories of the first half of the twentieth century.[2] This chapter traces the various cathartic treatments of anger presented by Doderer back to Julius Robert Mayer's theory of ignition and its application in such fields as poetics, philosophy, and psychoanalysis. Anger and rage, following Mayer, are conceptualized in terms of trigger mechanisms that seem to defy traditional ideas of causality.

The rage of Dr. Bachmeyer increases excessively when Dr. Horn asks about the cause of his angry eruptions. These outbursts manifest themselves in grotesque bodily reactions—kicking and stomping of the feet—and make it almost impossible for him to answer Dr. Horn's question: "Although Bachmeyer spoke the words that followed as urbanely and politely as the earlier ones, his fury seemed to swell precipitously, and he absolutely ground what he said between his teeth. At the same time, his voice became highpitched, almost falsetto. 'If I knew the reason, Professor, I probably wouldn't have come to you at all'" (14). In this incident, anger stems from the impossibility of knowing its causes. Anger for Bachmeyer is without ground. The inability to determine the reason for one's anger—its apparent groundlessness—becomes itself the reason or ground for an intensification, a "swelling" of rage. Again, as Uwe Japp remarks, "The groundlessness [Grundlosigkeit] of rage acts as its own intensification."[3] Groundlessness is the ground for anger. Doderer's insistence on the groundlessness of anger can be read as a variation of Martin Heidegger's phrase "Nothing is without ground" (Nichts ist ohne Grund)." When discussing the principle of causality in *The Principle of Reason (Der Satz vom Grund)*, Heidegger distinguishes between cause (Ursache) and reason (Grund): "Every cause is indeed some sort of reason, but not every reason has the character of being a cause that has an effect as a consequence."[4]

The fundamental ground of anger needs to be differentiated from mere inducements and occasions. Dr. Horn immediately recognizes his own mistake in confounding both notions: "Horn was not put off by this. He could just as well have said that he had not really intended to ask about the cause of the attacks of rage but only the occasion, and that the term 'cause' had been chosen inadvertently" (14). The subject can be aware only of the anger-inducing occasion; the deeper roots of rage are inaccessible or incomprehensible. To determine the grounds (i.e., reasons) for anger, a doctor's ability is required. This, at least, is the principle of traditional depth psychologies and psychoanalysis: to diagnose anger means to read its symptoms correctly. Reading in this context is defined by relating the symptoms as surface phenomena to deep, underlying psychic dynamics. Therapy has to go beyond the surface and analyze the depths of rage. Furthermore, it is successful only insofar as it establishes the ground on which the patient's affective outbursts rest. One entry in *Repertory: A Comprehension-Book of Greater and Lesser Life-Things (Repertorium:*

Ein Begreifbuch von höheren und niederen Lebens-Sachen)—a collection of aphorisms and short reflections on which Doderer worked from 1941 up to his death in 1966—speaks of fits of rage "without reason" (ohne Grund)."[5] Under the heading, "Fits of Rage, without Reason" (Wutanfälle, grundlose)," Doderer asserts: "Fits of rage that seem to be without reason are caused precisely by not knowing their reason, therefore they are of abysmal groundlessness" (Anscheinend grundlose Wutanfälle haben ihren Grund eben darin, daß man den Grund nicht kennt: daher sind sie von abgründiger Grundlosigkeit)."[6] In another passage from his diary *Tangents (Tangents)*, he speaks in a similar fashion of an "a priori rage" that is without reason or ground. As in the case of Dr. Bachmeyer, such groundless rage is caused by the very impossibility of determining its causes: "It is the rage of powerlessness not being able to determine its own causes" [es ist die Wut der Ohnmacht, ihren eigenen Grund zu finden] (273). If rage seems to have no cause, a successful treatment cannot be based upon the establishment of a causal relation between external, observable symptoms and the internal, mental states of the patient.

Dr. Horn's method of treating anger, in contradistinction to depth psychology and psychoanalysis, does not even attempt a hermeneutical reading of the psychic depths of the angry subject's unconscious. Instead it takes a purely psychophysical approach by controlling and directing the angry outbursts. Instead of a talking cure, with the cathartic expression of repressed traumas and desires relieving the patient of his or her pathologies, Dr. Horn's grotesque therapy increases the patient's anger in a controlled environment, transforming his stomping and kicking into a "march of anger" (16). This march of the angry patient to the music of the Coronation March from Giacomo Meyerbeer's opera *The Prophet*, is rhythmic and ordered. Led by a "nose-pincer" (15), the patient's movements are directed by a nurse while the treating doctor rhythmically hits the patient's head with a set of drumsticks. In addition, a number of little porcelain figurines are available to be smashed on the ground. Dr. Horn takes all these means to increase the intensity of the patient's rage for therapeutic ends: "Bachmeyer's stamping had considerably increased during this rage march, to the satisfaction of the Professor, who could, indeed, hope for some success in his therapeutic goal only through a powerful boiling-up and stirring-around of the fury" (17).[7] The notions of "boiling-up" and "stirring-around" hint at Horn's method of pushing anger to the limit at which it exhausts itself. The angry

Igniting Anger 175

patient has to "move through" his anger until—at the moment of its highest intensity—it starts to weaken and decrease. Against traditional ideas of expelling anger from the subject's affective economy or rationally attempting to control and pacify it in the mode of "working through," Dr. Horn encourages rage and goads its manifestations. His treatment consists in providing paths and directions for the angry energies. At a later stage in the novel, the simple march of anger is developed further into a "concept of the fury train, the spatial-locomotive therapy, the fury route" (323), which can treat several patients simultaneously by creating a "rhythmical, orderly fury" (16).

In Michel Foucault's terminology, this treatment could be called *dressage*. "At the centre" of dressage "reigns the notion of 'docility,' which joins the analyzable body to the manipulable body. A body is docile that may be subjected, used, transformed and improved."[8] The disciplinary power, represented by Dr. Horn, "trains the moving, confused, useless multitudes of bodies and forces into a multiplicity of individual elements—small, separate cells, organic autonomies, genetic identities and continuities, combinatory segments. Discipline 'makes' individuals; it is the specific technique of a power that regards individuals both as objects and as instruments of its exercise."[9] The comical crux of Doderer's parody of modern psychotherapy consists in the fact that Dr. Horn does not immediately soothe or alleviate rage but intensifies it, rejecting mainstream psychiatric treatments based on calming and pacifying the patient. Stefan Rieger, who characterizes modernity as ruled by "an all-embracing imperative of escalation" (einem allumfassenden Imperativ der Steigerung), analyzes these intensifications in the field of early twentieth-century psychology and psychotherapy.[10] He concludes: "The sciences pursue incremental fragmentation in their programmatic rejection of the concept of the whole person. Through fundamental procedures of simplification, formalization, and quantification, they manage to convert the human—that is, our corporeal, cognitive, and emotional faculties—into taxonomies."[11] Not surprisingly, Dr. Horn is described as "essentially a statistician" (152). The march of anger performs the rudimentization, formalization, and quantification that Rieger identifies as the main elements of modern psychological research. The method of treatment consists of a few discrete elements that are arranged according to general principles independent of the patient's mental state. The individual becomes a mere element, or "subelement,"[12] to use Doderer's terminology, in a serialized, rhythmic march of anger.

For Joseph Vogl, the violent eruption of running amok, in a similar fashion, is characterized by its affinity to statistical registration: "And in the end, what characterizes the Malaysian notion of running amok more than anything else is its absence of causality and history, as well as its normalcy. It becomes a figure and an event whose traceability is to be found less in stories and case studies than in mere lists and statistical diagrams."[13]

This focus on the scientific, objective treatment of anger and its representations in diagrams, statistics, and lists is premised on the bracketing of the question of individual responsibility. The origins of the angry outburst, if it is understood as a form of ignition, cannot be traced back to the conscious or unconscious intentions of a singular subject. Dr. Horn deals with averages, probabilities, and risks. His method exemplifies a tendency in the development of experimental psychology of which Doderer is highly critical. Psychological investigation no longer relies on models of introspection focusing on the inner state of individual subjects, as in the nineteenth century. The rise of the laboratory as the site of psychological research produces a new kind of knowledge. It is based on the experimenter's objective, quantifiable observations of the subject under controlled conditions. Kurt Danziger summarizes this change in the practice of psychological experimentation and the construction of the subject as follows: "Experimental subjects were not studied as individual persons but as examples that displayed certain common human characteristics. . . . They [the subjects] did not represent themselves but their common mental processes. These 'elementary' mental processes, as Wundt called them, were assumed to be natural objects that could be studied independently of the whole personality. All that was necessary were the restricted conditions of the laboratory and a certain preparation of the subject."[14] Horn transfers the restricted conditions of theoretical experimental research into the praxis of clinical treatment. Patients like Dr. Bachmeyer do not talk about their individual case histories, repressed memories, or childhood traumas but are stripped of their individuality and undergo a universally repeatable and applicable treatment that differs only in intensity depending on the concentration of anger in the subject. This is possible because Dr. Horn measures this anger and reduces it to an objective, quantifiable phenomenon.

In Dr. Horn's practice, therapy is based on the measurement of the angle between the patient's feet. The wider the angle, the stronger the rage. Dr. Bachmeyer's march of anger, for example, starts with

Igniting Anger

an angle of 140 degrees and ends with 90 degrees, "the foot angle of a normal human gait" (18). The psycho-pathological phenomenon of rage is reduced to a merely anatomical aberration that can be measured and tabulated. The success or failure of therapy is defined solely by the change in the foot angle. During his march Bachmeyer's foot angle began "rapidly to diminish and Bachmeyer's stamping now became steadily weaker" (17). For the feet to point straight ahead at an angle of 90 degrees, which defines the normal human gait, here comes to signify the normal human state of mind. The measure of what is normal and human is the right angle: 90 degrees.

This insensitive, mechanized form of treatment finds its absurd apex in the creation of a "little House of Fury" (312). This apparatus, which eventually replaces the "march of anger" and the "fury train," can automatically control the patient's angry outbursts: "The machine, once furnished with a well-defined grade of instrument, extracted from it every necessary intensification with an absolute constancy that was never to be achieved by hand" (249). The treatment of emotional conditions is completely automated: the necessary escalations are performed with mechanical consistency while the internal states of both the patient and the psychiatrist are entirely disregarded. Psychiatry turns into a "locksmithery of the soul."[15] The human body and the electrotechnical implementation of Horn's method in the form of the "little House of Fury" enter a symbiotic relationship. The psychiatrist turns into an engineer. Man and machine in this vision of automated healing form a system of negative feedback:

> The little house was conceived man-high, though adjustable in its height, padded inside with leather. The feet of the patient who stood in it were to repose on footrests that could swivel horizontally at the heel, rests that always conformed to the current foot angle of the patient. The movable rests, gliding along two quarter-circles and built-in rheostats (resistances), turned on and off the contacts for a stronger or lesser electric current which kept in operation a motor attached at the rear, as the propellant for the application—which then, becoming stronger or fainter, responded to each increase or decrease of the foot angle and reacted immediately to such changes, even to very fine deviations. The drumming-works of the application were mounted in a kind of hinged crash helmet and could be fed with whatever interchangeable instruments one chose—mallets, drumsticks, hammers. (248)

Emotional equilibrium is achieved in the controlled environment of a space that is strictly separated from all external influences. In the "little House of Fury," patient and machine reciprocally control each other's actions. The wider the foot angle, the stronger the electrically stimulated application. And in turn, the stronger the application, the lower the foot angle.

The "little House of Fury" is essentially a control mechanism. It is a parody of the classical definition of the modern individual as the product of self-referentiality. The self-reflexive mode of the modern subject is transformed into a form of psycho-cybernetics that does not have the capacity for self-reflection but is nevertheless capable of self-governing. The assembly of man and machine reciprocally observing and controlling each other is, quite literally, to draw on Foucault, a technology of the self. Stefan Rieger summarizes this constellation of technology and anthropology as follows: "What happens in the field of varying technologies of the self and self-behavioral theories appears to be nothing other than the seizing of a new control technology.... Whether based in magnetism or cybernetics, both serve the higher glory of a self that aims first and foremost to enable, through technico-pedogogical interventions, the condition of better self-proficiency, and may be called the enabling of the same."[16] Dr. Horn's invention sidesteps all models of reflection, introspection, or contemplation. Instead, technologies of the self are externalized, becoming mere technical artifacts, instruments that directly influence the body but not the psyche.

Dr. Horn's violent methods of anger control resemble—at a first glance—methods of treating mental patients in the early nineteenth century. One of the most prominent figures of early psychiatry was the German physician Ernst Horn.[17] Horn, the founder of the "authoritarian school of early psychiatry," initiated a treatment that involved often violent disciplinary actions to control and pacify the patient.[18] Its goal was the establishment of orderliness and regularity within the patient's psychic economy. According to the physician Johann Christoph Reil, a contemporary of Horn, "bring[ing] the actions of the sick person into an orderly system" was the first principle of such psychiatric treatment.[19] Beyond a strict regimen of daily routines, Horn used different devices that physically limited and restricted the patients' mobility, by attaching them to mechanisms that would, for example, force an insane person to sit or stand for extended periods of time. The most notorious of these devices were rotation beds and chairs that would spin the patient with up to 120 rotations per minute.[20] For Horn, physical means provided a necessary, if not sufficient, approach to curing mental disturbances: "The spiritual condition is so very much determined by the corporeal that, through the *improvement of bodily affliction*, we often simultaneously distance spiritual ones."[21] Dr. Horn's approach in *The Merowingians* is also determinately somatic; it is concerned only with observable, physical symptoms, not with the mental condition of the patient. Both the real and the fictitious Dr. Horn design specific apparatuses that mechanically influence the patient's body and eventually his mind. Mental health is created by the construction of serialized procedures that are measurable, continuous, and quantifiable.

CATHARTIC (SELF)-AFFECTIONS

In his 1876 essay "On Ignition" (Über Auslösung), the physicist and physician Julius Robert Mayer, who is best known as one of the discoverers of the first law of thermodynamics, discusses such phenomena as ignitions, explosions, and catalysis:[22] "Many natural processes occur when they are triggered by a stimulus. Such is the process that has been called 'ignition' by the new sciences. . . . Likewise, when we strike a match with a bit of frictional heat and initiate, by this burning match, any greater process of combustion, we have once again a simple example of 'ignition,' and such examples are suggested to us in unlimited abundance. With firearms, for instance, a little pull of the trigger yields a violent effect, and so on."[23] The processes Mayer mentions are characterized by a disproportion between cause and effect. It takes only a minimal amount of energy to effect maximum results. A spark is enough to ignite a fire, and a little pull of the trigger can make a deadly gun explode. These phenomena seem to contradict the principle of *causa aequat effectum*, according to which the cause equals the effect: "In an entirely different sense, however, we like to speak of cause and effect in the case of ignition not only when the cause is not equal or proportional to the effect but when there is absolutely no quantitative relation between cause and effect."[24] Even slight incidents or small amounts of energy can cause effects that are disproportionate in relation to the initial trigger. This disproportion can go so far as to create the illusion that an event happened "without cause."

Ignitions are not restricted to the realm of physics, but, according to Mayer, can also be found in the sciences of life: "Ignitions play a large and important role not only in inorganic nature . . . but also in the living world, that is, in physiology and psychology."[25] Physical as well as mental diseases are caused by a dysfunction, which hinders the proper ignition of the human being's energies. As Alwin Mittasch comments: "A comfortable feeling of health attests to an undisturbed apparatus of ignition [Auslösungsapparat], while alternatively, every disturbance in that apparatus will make itself known through very uncomfortable sensations."[26] Mayer rejects the idea that psychic phenomena based on processes of ignition can be suppressed artificially. He explicitly criticizes contemporary psychiatry for using force to control psychic ignitions: "It also clearly emerges from the aforesaid, which I wish to note here parenthetically, how preposterous it is to treat with such irresponsible casualness psychic afflictions and mental disorders (from which no mortal can be wholly spared), by stifling the so very necessary ignitions with straitjackets and restraining chairs and beds" (15). Ignitions are necessary for the psychic equilibrium of the self and should not be restrained. Dr. Horn's measures, while on the surface resembling the instruments of dressage criticized by Mayer, let rage ignite, albeit in an artificial, controlled environment. For him, rage cannot be suppressed, only directed and channeled.

If the phenomenon of rage cannot be traced back to a cause, Dr. Horn, echoing Mayer's doctrine of ignition, sees the only way of overcoming its violent outbursts as that of pushing it to its extremes and letting the surplus energy exhaust itself. Groundless fits of rage like ignition processes cannot be explained according to traditional models of cause and effect. Rage is an emotion that explodes suddenly, ignited by the smallest and most minute events. Bachmeyer explodes like a bullet: "Bachmeyer's eyes flashed like the ignition at the muzzle of a firearm" (14).[27]

One of the earliest readers of Mayer's theory of ignition was Friedrich Nietzsche. The book Nietzsche mentions explicitly is Mayer's *The Mechanics of Heat* (*Mechanik der Wärme*), which includes the two essays "Torricelle's Vacuum" (Die Torricellische Leere) and "On Ignition."[28] The essay on ignition, in particular, left a considerable impression on Nietzsche: "For me, 'On Ignition" is the most important and useful in Mayer's book."[29]

In *The Gay Science*, Nietzsche explicitly takes up Mayer's example of lighting a match in order to delineate his criticism of causality:

> *Two Kinds of Causes which are Confounded.*—It seems to me one of my most essential steps and advances that I have learned to distinguish the cause of an action generally from the cause of an action in

a particular manner, say, in this direction, with this aim. The first kind of cause is a quantum of stored-up force, which waits to be used in some manner, for some purpose; the second kind of cause, on the contrary, is something quite unimportant in comparison with the first, an insignificant hazard for the most part, in conformity with which the quantum of force in question "discharges" itself in some manner: the Lucifer-match in relation to the barrel of gunpowder. Among those insignificant hazards and Lucifer-matches I count all the so-called "aims," and similarly the still more so-called "occupations" of people: they are relatively optional, arbitrary, and almost indifferent in relation to the immense quantum of force which presses on, as we have said, to be used up in any way whatever. One generally looks at the matter in a different manner: one is accustomed to see the impelling force precisely in the aim (object, calling, &c.), according to a primeval error,—but it is only the directing force; the steersman and the steam have thereby been confounded.[30]

Mayer's theory of ignition provides the basis for Nietzsche's distinction between "impelling" and "directing" forces. Purposes, ends, and intentions are nothing more than the small fortuitous accidents that ignite the considerable latent forces of accumulated psychic energies. Morality, ideals, and virtue function as sparks lighting an "immense quantum" of drives. The adjective *ungeheuer,* oscillating between the meanings of "large," "immense," and "uncanny," points toward the Apollonian world of morality, which veils, according to Nietzsche, an uncanny, groundless realm of Dionysian drives. These urges lack direction. Anything, even the smallest detail, can ignite them, and the stable structure of the Apollonian world of forms is required to direct and channel them.

As the subtitle of *The Birth of Tragedy (Out of the Spirit of Music)* suggests, the art of music is the only medium in modern times that evokes the lost trance of the Dionysian cults. Nietzsche in *Twilight of the Gods* asserts: "Music, as we understand it nowadays, is likewise a total arousal and discharge of the emotions, and yet it is merely the remnant of a much fuller world of emotional expressions, a mere residuum of Dionysian histrionism."[31] In *The Gay Science*, Nietzsche explicitly relates the experience of energetic discharges in music to the ancient theory of catharsis. In antiquity, according to Nietzsche, music "was acknowledged to possess the power of unburdening the emotions, of purifying the soul, of soothing the *ferocia animi*" (59). Abreaction, purification, and alleviation, for Nietzsche, are elements of a "medical art" [Heilkunst)] (59). Musical trance makes life bearable, it offers a treatment for the miseries of life. For this "therapy of desire" (Nussbaum) to be successful, passionate discharges have to be activated, not suppressed. The first step in this treatment consists in intensifying and increasing the passions by "driving the frenzy and wantonness of their emotions to the highest pitch" (59). The result of this escalation after its final eruption, according to Nietzsche, soothes. Man's emotional economy is "freer and quieter afterwards" (59). Nietzsche writes: "Melos, according to its root, signifies a soothing agency, not because the song is gentle itself, but because its after-effect is gentle" (59). Especially useful for this task is music's rhythmic quality, which forces human and gods to become one: "Rhythm is a constraint; it produces an unconquerable desire to yield, to join in; not only the step of the foot, but also the soul itself follows the measure,—probably the soul of the Gods also, as people thought! They attempted, therefore, to *constrain* the Gods by rhythm, and to exercise a power over them; they threw poetry around the Gods like a magic noose" (59). Rhythmic music and poetry become means to cope with an environment that was thought to be animated by antagonistic demons: "And not only in the religious song, but also in the secular song of the most ancient times, the prerequisite is that the rhythm should exercise a magical influence; for example, in drawing water, or in rowing: the song is for the enchanting of the spirits supposed to be active thereby; it makes them obliging, involuntary, and the instruments of man" (59). The rhythmic qualities of song function as magical incantations, protecting humans from the demonic interruptions of everyday life. In the rhythmization of music and life, malicious objects come under a controlling magic spell. Human action, if performed rhythmically, is less prone to disruptions, an effect that created the superstition that poetry was "like a magic noose" with the power to quell the dangerous passions of the gods. "By means of it [poetry] even the maddened, revengeful Gods were treated for the purpose of a cure" (59). Curing humans and gods defines the *"superstitious utility"* (59) of poetry in its early stages.

In another context, Nietzsche again takes up Mayer's concept of ignition to suggest a therapy for psychic disorders: the affect of melancholy, for example, must be ignited, its forces activated, if it is to be overcome: "Many of our drives find their ignition in a forceful, mechanical activity, which *can* be purposefully chosen; without these activities corruptive and detrimental ignitions result. Hate, rage, sexual desires etc. can be put to use and they can be transformed into useful activities. Examples of such activities are wood cutting, delivering letters, or plowing. One has to rework [umarbeiten] one's drives. . . . All displeasure [Missmut] has to be ignited."[32] Nietzsche differentiates between useful and useless, even detrimental, ignitions. Since urges cannot be suppressed, their energy needs to be directed toward useful activities. Drives need to be transformed into work. Happiness and cheerfulness are results of this treatment: "By igniting a force, which was painfully accumulated and compressed, happiness is produced."[33] Again, Nietzsche is interested in the utility of psychic energies. The discharge of energies is not only the source of artistic creativity but also a method for humans to create a moral, that is, energetic, equilibrium within themselves. Only after the ignition of suppressed energies is it possible to live freely and happily. Nietzsche indirectly quotes Mayer's treatise on ignition, which claims: "It is not necessarily given that the activities committed *in ira* must be impractical and destructive. If the impatient person vents his anger, for instance, on a log of firewood that he's cutting up and splitting, he is still committing an externally purposive act [zweckmäßige Handlung] while he blows off steam."[34] Angry energies can be transfigured and sublimated in an act of discharge. Ignitions not only maintain mental and physical health but can also be utilized for practical ends.

Living the good life, in this sense, would mean, not following abstract doctrines of morality that preach the extirpation of passions and drives, but igniting oneself. Self-ignition consists in the useful discharge of the uncanny driving energies by an appropriate directing force. This release is experienced as pleasurable; it relieves the pain of blocked energies and ultimately leads to happiness. There is not only a "gay science" but also a cheerful, energetic morality. Any ethics that is based on notions of self-restraint and self-control leads, according to Nietzsche, to a permanent, that is, pathological, state of irritability: "Those moral teachers who first and foremost order man to get himself into his own power, induce thereby a curious infirmity in him,—namely, a constant sensitiveness with reference to all natural strivings and inclinations, and as it were, a sort of itching" (115). The attempt to control urges and desires produces, not ataraxia, health, and happiness, but a form of intensified sensitivity. As in the case of Jean Paul's overattentive figure of Siebenkäs, the imperative to constantly observe and control one's affects—one of the central principles of Stoic philosophy—creates disequilibrium. The more one tries to monitor one's passions and keep them in check, the more one starts to itch, exposing a dissonance between moral and energetic imperatives.

Nietzsche's philosophy of affects does not attempt to extirpate them but rather to use and direct them for cathartic ends. Contra the Stoics, it does not follow the ideal of moderation and restraint.[35] Nietzsche's "therapy of desire" turns the philosopher into a psychologist or physio-psychologist. Affects are an inextricable part of the whole human being. Hence they have to be taken "as factors which, fundamentally and essentially, must be present in the general economy of life (and must, therefore, be further enhanced if life is to be further enhanced)."[36] Philosophers as psychologists and physicians detect and affirm those passions that enhance and intensify life. "Where are the new physicians of the soul?" Nietzsche asks in *The Dawn of Day*, by which he means those who understand that "the worst disease of mankind has arisen from the struggle against diseases, and apparent remedies have in the long run brought about worse conditions than those which it was intended to remove by their use."[37] Their diagnosis would prescribe the intensification of life, as opposed to the struggle to calm and control the passions, which would heighten the subject's sensitivity, allowing all irritations and innervations to ignite.

One of the main influences on Nietzsche's theory of tragedy was Jacob Bernays's 1857 study *On Catharsis: From Fundamentals of Aristotle's Lost Essay on the "Effect of Tragedy" (Grundzüge der verlorenen Abhandlung des Aristoteles über die Wirkung der Tragödie)*, which for the first time related Aristotle's poetics to his politics (especially book 8 of the *Politics*) and rhetoric. It opposes the prevailing understanding of the tragic affects of *eleos* and *phobos* in moral terms as it had been proposed by Lessing and his followers. For Lessing, fear and compassion were meant to bring about a purification of the audience's affects. In section 78 of the *Hamburg Dramaturgy (Hamburgische Dramatugie)*, Lessing defines *catharsis* as follows: "Purification rests in nothing else than in the transformation of passions into virtuous habits."[38] Tragic affects are in the service of virtue and morality. For Jacob Bernays, this moralistic definition of tragedy reduces tragedy to a "moral house of correction that must keep in readiness the remedial method conducive for every irregular turning of pity and fear."[39] Bernays opposes Lessing's classicist interpretation of Greek tragedy and replaces it with a medical model. Against the idea of theater as a moral institution, he identifies the main impact of tragedy as its ability to "solicit" affects. To illustrate the mode of tragic solicitation, Bernays refers not only to medical models but also to natural science: "In the same way that a fire is ignited when a

Igniting Anger 185

combustible agent comes close to it, a tragic action—assembled from sad and terrifying events—ignites an outbreak of the same affects in every spectator of natural disposition."[40] Tragedy triggers—to use Mayer's terminology—an outbreak of passions within the audience. Like a chemical reaction, the viewer's reactions are ignited. Tragedy functions like a match setting fire to the audience. It solicits an explosion of affect. Not unlike Nietzsche a few years later in *The Birth of Tragedy*, Bernays places the origin of tragedy in the "realm of ecstatic occurrences, which often took place in Greek and Oriental antiquity."[41] In religious, cultic events such as Dionysian rites, the natural affectability of human beings, according to Bernays and Nietzsche, is channeled and transformed into "stable forms of appeasement."[42] Nietzsche at one point in *The Birth of Tragedy* describes the transfiguration of the Dionysian forces into Apollonian images in the tragedy explicitly as a "discharge" (Entladung): "This insight leads us to understand Greek tragedy as a Dionysian chorus which discharges itself over and over again in an Apolline world of images."[43]

Far from being a purely aesthetic phenomenon, the ecstatic eruptions in "Oriental" and Greek antiquity for Bernays constitute forms of "ecstatic catharsis."[44] They solicit affects to (re)-create a psychic equilibrium, resembling medical (i.e., "somatic") methods of purification: "In the same way cathartic means function as a form of therapy, ecstatic Olympian songs affect the ecstatic element in a soliciting manner which, in turn, charges against the fetters of consciousness."[45] After this ecstatic solicitation, the human being returns to the "Ruhe und Fassung des geregelten Gemüthszustandes."[46] In this context, those passages in Nietzsche that seem to affirm the Stoic doctrine of self-government can be read differently. Self-ignition must be understood not as a sheer *laisser aller* but as the controlled discharge of energies. In paragraph 188 of *Beyond Good and Evil*, Nietzsche makes clear that any morality, even one beyond good and evil, "is, as opposed to *laisser aller*, a bit of tyranny."[47] With the notion of tyranny, Nietzsche takes up his criticism of Stoic doctrine as "self-tyranny" but reverses his judgment.[48] Against the decadent morality of weakness, he installs a new ethos that is "stoic, tough, tyrannical," for which, as Barbara Neymeyr has described, it is necessary to produce forms of "productive catharsis."[49] It is the sovereignty of the "free spirit" to actively and voluntarily ignite his or her passions, thereby releasing pent-up affects and desires in a controlled fashion that become artistically as well as therapeutically effective.

Cathartic discharges follow their own rules; they must not be misunderstood as the subject uninhibitedly letting go. "Every artist," according to Nietzsche, "knows how far from any feeling of letting himself go his 'most natural' state is—the free ordering, placing, disposing, giving form in the moment of 'inspiration'—and how strictly and subtly he obeys thousandfold laws precisely then, laws that precisely on account of their hardness and determination defy all formulation through concepts (even the firmest concept is, compared with them, not free of fluctuation, multiplicity, and ambiguity)."[50] Nietzsche takes seriously the famous Stoic motto of *secundum naturam vivere*. For him, nature consists in affectual energies ruling human behavior. As the "last Stoic," he affirms these natural forces; hence he lives according to nature. This morality beyond good and evil involves, not extirpating or calming passions, but transfiguring them. There is no rational (i.e., intellectual) method, according to Nietzsche, that would be able to eliminate affects from the psychic economy of human beings.

In some of Nietzsche's late fragments he differentiates between two different types of ignition, depending on whether the stimulus for a discharge comes from the outside or from the inside: "Even the smallest organism constantly generates a force, which has to be ignited: either from the fullness of the organism itself, ... or from a stimulus from the outside."[51] In another aphorism Nietzsche takes up the distinction between auto- and hetero-affection and transforms it into the opposition between active and reactive forces: "One aspect of *my* values: whether derived from fullness or from desire? ... whether from accumulated force, 'spontaneous,' or merely reactive, stimulated ... ?"[52]

The ability to ignite oneself spontaneously, not in reaction to an outer stimulus, constitutes a form of sovereignty over the self. In a letter to Heinrich Köselitz (Peter Gast) from July 23, 1885, Nietzsche discusses the phenomenon of wanting to answer one's own letters: "From my own life of writing letters I know that phenomenon all too well, which I call 'self-answering' [Selbstbeantwortung] ... , this natural 'release' [Auslösung] (creation of personal sovereignty)."[53] The "natural release" of "personal sovereignty" is based on a self-referential form of auto-affection. Nietzsche describes to Köselitz how he was driven, upon rereading a letter that he had already sent, to answer himself with a new letter. It is not Köselitz, to whom the letter was originally addressed, who ignites Nietzsche's personal sovereignty, but Nietzsche himself. With this image of the self responding

Igniting Anger

to itself, Nietzsche presents the model of the self as self-igniting. It is this moment of ignition that differentiates Nietzsche's model from classical theories of self-reflection. The self is nothing more than a series of self-ignitions, expressions of affective energies that are transfigured, (re)presented, and anthropomorphized. "The discharge," following Armin Schäfer and Joseph Vogl, "*is* the act of signification."[54] Nietzsche reduces communication, understood as a form of "signaling," to a processes of ignition:[55] "greatest error in judging human beings: we evaluate them according to their impact, applying the measure of effectus aequat causam. But the human being only stimulates other human beings. It is dependent on what is available within other human beings in order for the gunpowder to explode or that stimulus is almost negligible. Who would hold a quick match responsible for its after-effect of destroying a city?"[56] This model of communication as the transmittal of stimuli and signals can be compared to Nietzsche's model of "self-response," which also needs to be understood as auto-affection resembling a match that ignites latent explosive energies. Again, there is no proportionate relationship between cause and effect. The model of *effectus aequat causam*, which Mayer rejected as insufficient to explain ignition processes, fails to account for the highly explosive acts of self-ignition and self-signification. In *Ecce Homo*, Nietzsche condenses this doctrine of self-ignition to the famous line: "I am no man, I am dynamite."[57] The idea of an "I" as a formed, substantial entity is the result of self-ignition, the transfiguration of psychic energies into images and words. Nietzsche characterizes the unstable existence of such a Dionysian human being as follows: "The essential feature remains the facility in transforming, the inability to refrain from reaction (—a similar state to that of certain hysterical patients, who at the slightest hint assume any role). It is impossible for the Dionysian artist not to understand any suggestion; no outward sign of emotion escapes him, he possesses the instinct of comprehension and of divination in the highest degree, just as he is capable of the most perfect art of communication. He enters into every skin, into every passion: he is continually changing himself."[58] The Dionysian human is no subject in the strict sense; he or she lacks a stable *Gestalt*. Being is becoming, which is to say, in a state of continuous metamorphosis. Any affective suggestion is enacted and performed. The whole "system of passions" is being represented, imitated, transfigured, and transformed. It is the act of self-ignition as self-affection, according to Nietzsche, that constitutes the *essence* of a true ethical human being. It does not follow abstract norms or rules but in the process of self-affection instantiates subjectivity. The self exists only as these moments of self-ignition when psychic powers erupt and manifest themselves in anthropomorphism, metamorphosis, and metaphor. The discharge of psychic energies appears as a transfiguration; the "I" is nothing more than a metaphor. A Stoic subject, on the other hand, exercises a form of self-tyranny; it arrests the "mobile army of metaphors, metonymies, anthropomorphisms" into a rigid, inflexible form.[59] Self-government turns into a form of tyranny. The Stoics perceive the self and the world "persistently" and "rigidly-hypnotically."[60] Their fluidity and vitality are reduced and eventually annihilated by the "tyrannical drive" of philosophy.[61]

The function of cathartic discharges is at the heart of another discourse of abreaction: psychoanalysis. Josef Breuer's treatment of his patient Bertha Pappenheim, better known in psychoanalytic literature as Anna O., is widely considered to be the origin of psychoanalysis.[62] In treating Anna O., who was considered to suffer from hysteria, Breuer discovered that for traumatic memories to lose their negative influence, the patient needed to "abreact" its surplus energies. Anna O. herself called this method of removing psychic affections the "talking cure" or "chimney sweeping."[63] In cooperation with Sigmund Freud, Breuer published his findings in the short treatise "The Mechanism of Hysterical Phenomena" (1893). It was republished in 1895 as part of *Studies on Hysteria*. Breuer and Freud write: "The fading of a memory or the losing of its affect depends on various factors. The most important of these is *whether there has been an energetic reaction to the event that provokes an affect*. By 'reaction' we here understand the whole class of voluntary and involuntary reflexes—from tears to acts of revenge—in which, as experience shows us, the affects are discharged. . . . The injured person's reaction to the trauma only exercises a completely 'cathartic' effect if it is an *adequate* reaction—as, for instance, revenge."[64] Language becomes the medium through which affective energies are being discharged. It is the surrogate of a physical outburst. Therapy consists in releasing unconscious traumas by an act of transfiguration and translation. What is crucial about these abreactions in the mode of linguistic expression is that they happen energetically. For the talking cure to be successful, that is, for symptoms to disappear, the patient's narration needs to reenact the original psychological intensity of the trauma: "It soon emerged, as though by chance, that this process of sweeping the mind clean could accomplish more than the merely temporary relief of her ever-recurring mental confusion. It was actually possible to bring about the disappearance of the painful symptoms of her illness, if she could be brought to remember under hypnosis, with an accompanying expression of affect, on what occasion and in what connection the symptoms had first appeared."[65] Freud mentions one of his female patient's abreaction of anger as an example of this amplified and intensified cathartic discourse. After the patient gave "further energetic expression to the anger she had held back," she was relieved of her hydrophobia.[66] Energetic expressions of anger function as means to treat hysterical disorders. In the therapeutical session, the analyst provides a framework within which the patient is able to affect him- or herself.

The poetical and theatrical elements in cathartic psychotherapy, as they are documented in Anna O.'s notion of "private theatre" and Breuer's identification of abreacting with tragic performance, show the proximity of aesthetic and medical discourses in catharsis, as Jacob Bernays's interpretation of Aristotle's poetics had shown.[67] In *Studies on Hysteria*, Breuer describes Anna O.'s state as follows: "She had gone entirely without food the whole time, was full of anxiety and her hallucinatory *absences* were filled with terrifying figures, death's heads and skeletons. Since she acted these things through as though she were experiencing them and in part put them into words, the people around her became aware to a great extent of the content of her hallucinations."[68] Anna O. enacts and performs her hallucinations like a play filled with stage props. Using the expression "acting through," Breuer hints at the similarities between hysterical attacks and ancient tragedy. Both represent, perform, and abreact passions.

Cathartic psychotherapy, in this sense, is "in no way a modern method of treatment" as Freud in a lecture from 1904 claims: "On the contrary, it is the most ancient form of therapy in medicine."[69] Günter Gödde sees these old therapies of desire as being not in the Stoic tradition but in a tradition of what Paul Rabbow calls "enthusiastic mysticism."[70] Gödde summarizes these methods of *Seelenführung* as follows: "The affections should not be enclosed and suppressed in the inner soul, but rather opened and discharged externally."[71]

In antiquity, the exemplary place for the creation and representation of affects is the stage. Following Horace's dictum, "If you would have me weep, you must first of all feel grief yourself," it is necessary for the actor, in order to be convincing, to create within himself the emotions he wishes to convey.[72] The affection of the audience originates in the self-affection of the actor. In the same sense, the cure from anger is based on the controlled, rhythmic auto-affection of the patient. According to Henry F. Ellenberger, hysteria—the mental disorder for which cathartic abreaction was first invented—shows "dramatizing tendencies."[73] The hysteric person resembles an actor insofar as both produce an affect in order to influence themselves and an audience. Stavros Mentzos summarizes this self-affective performance as follows: "Hysterical symptoms are very much oriented toward the audience. They are frequently performances that aim to impress, influence, and convince the spectator in a particular way. Indeed, they have an appellative character about them" and "Not only the spectator, but more importantly the patient himself must be convinced of this falsified exhibition of self-representation."[74] Hysteria follows the ancient model not only of drama but also of rhetoric. It performs in order to persuade and influence, by instigating passions within the recipient. But according to Horace's doctrine of drama and Quintilian's doctrine of self-affection for public speech, the audience can be affected only if the performer is affected as well. Any type of affection presupposes an act of self-affection. The following section will discuss one of Doderer's many grotesque representations of self-affective procedures in *The Merowingians*. The "pouch stab," discussed in the next section, ridicules psychotherapies based on models of cathartic discharges, exposing them as primitive, quasi-animistic doctrines.

INTENSIFICATIONS: THE POUCH STAB

Surprisingly, Doderer does not mention the term *catharsis* in the context of Dr. Horn's psychiatric practice but instead uses it to characterize a different model of anger management. This method, called the "pouch stab," is the invention not of a physician or psychologist but of a bureaucrat, the civil servant Dr. Schajo. It functions as follows:

> On a solid support there are displayed two shelves, one above the other—something like those one has in a laboratory for test tubes or *eprouvettes*—on each of which sits a row of grey leather pouches held on by strips of wood and stuffed full of red glass beads of the smallest caliber. The belly of each pouch is painted with a red ring in the middle that surrounds and points out the so-called "sensitive spot." From the pouches there stick out little rods with tiny plaques on which can be written, as required, "Attorney, Dr. N.N.," "Passport Office," "Foreign Exchange Control Bureau," "Revenue Office," and so forth,

Igniting Anger 191

> corresponding to the need at hand. . . . The pouch stabber takes his place opposite the apparatus and puts the point of the instrument, somewhat leaning on it, precisely against the "sensitive point" of the pouch in question at the moment. In such a position, now remaining motionless, the stabber is obliged to have all the fury toward the object collect until it swells up to an almost unbearable and nearly suffocating dimension; only then can the puncture occur, which experience shows brings immediate deep relief, but only perfect when the instrument is drawn back, while simultaneously from the pierced opening pours out a thin tinkling stream of red glass beads into the tin channel, which roll down into the collection container until the pouch is deflated. (198–99)

As in the case of Dr. Horn's "march of anger," the pouch stab starts with an artificial intensification of the patient's anger. When all his or her rage is focused in the point of the needle, the stab into the pouch allows for its controlled discharge. At the moment of its highest intensity, anger is set free. Angry energies depart the body like the red pearls pouring out of the pouch. Here anger is, to use a phrase from Doderer's *Repertory*, carried to its extreme: "Fits of rage must be carried to their extreme to lose their sting" [Wutanfälle müssen auf die Spitze getrieben werden, damit diese ab breche] (272). The German phrase "auf die Spitze treiben," which is usually translated as "carrying to the extreme," literally means "driven to the point." The metaphor of "Spitze" refers not only to a peak or pinnacle but also to a barb, sting, or point. For anger to be released, it needs to be pushed to the extreme, gathered in the "very end of a finely filed knitting needle."[75] The concentration of anger in the tip of a needle for Dr. Schajo, in contradistinction to Dr. Horn's purely somatic approach, serves as a psychic technique: "The pouch stab necessitated spiritual concentration if at the same time that the red beads were to flow, with a light tinkle, in a cathartic stream into the collection container, the paroxysm of anger should be dispersed" (262). Concentration functions as a form of gathering and collection; the patient must collect his or her attention and focus it on the tip of the needle.

Dr. Schajo's method of igniting and calming anger focuses on one's ability to self-affect. It is not the outside intervention of a psychiatrist that produces the soothing discharge but an act of the pouch stabber him- or herself. In the entry "Artificial Fits of Rage" (Wutanfälle, künstliche) from *Repertory*, Doderer elaborates further on the creation of artificial fits of rage as forms of self-affection: "One can determine the cause of anger only if one produces it artificially. One could write a whole tract entitled 'On the Means to Produce Rage and Fury within Oneself Artificially and to Increase It to Its Highest Intensity'" (272). Anger is an affect that the subject can artificially induce; it is the result of an auto-affection that is used to create a cathartic abreaction.

While these lines discuss artificial rage attacks in epistemological terms as ways of determining the essence of rage, the closing sentences of the same entry, after having described an example of auto-affected anger, allude to possible ethical implications: "From now on [after the artificially induced fit of rage], it will never again be possible to accept rage as an irresistible destiny, if it should appear again" (274). As with Dr. Schajo's method, artificially induced fits of rage function as technologies of the self. By artificially inducing anger, the subject is able to cope with future annoyances in a more controlled fashion. If anger can be created intentionally, it is not "irresistible" (unwiderstehlich) but can be directed and abreacted in a controlled manner. In contrast to Dr. Schajo and his followers, the Bartenbruch family, a.k.a. the Merowingians, in Doderer's novel, who are characterized by their choleric outbursts and uncontrolled rage, are represented by a specific type of sword that lacks a sharp tip: "The pommel bore no parrying-shaft, or rather, pommel and parrying-shaft were the same; that is, there was on it no such cross-hilt as could be seen in the swords of the succeeding Carolingian epoch, and then on those of the entire Middle Ages, somewhat like that hilt on Charlemagne's sword in the Paris Louvre; this last mentioned also had a sharp point, or *Ort* (the old Germanic word for the tip of a weapon). The Bartenbruch sword, as an exclusively slashing weapon, had a round *Ort*" (46). What the Bartenbruchs and especially Childerich III constitutionally lack is the ability to focus their anger. The proper place to release anger is not the rounded "Ort" of the medieval, anachronistic sword of the Merowingians but the sharp tip of a needle.[76] Martin Heidegger's essay "Language in the Poem," in *On the Way to Language*, provides the following etymology of the German word *Ort:* "Originally the word 'site' suggests a place in which everything comes together, is concentrated, supremely and in the extreme. Its gathering power penetrates and pervades everything."[77] The English translation misses Heidegger's reference to a weapon. The original German reads: "Urspünglich bedeutet der Name 'Ort' die Spitze des Speers. In ihr läuft alles zusammen. Der Ort versammelt zu sich ins Höchste und Äußerste."[78] The "Ort," or tip of the spear, is a place

Igniting Anger 193

of gathering. On the tip of the needle of the pouch stabbers all their affects and passions are gathered and intensified to the most extreme point. Anger ignites and so is discharged. Childerich III, on the other hand, who is said to resemble a round pouch, lacks this pointed solution; [79] he suppresses his rage only to have it explode in an uncontrollable fashion: "The unequaled attacks of rage—that some day would violently rock his mature years—remained there for him, in the face of the extreme external pressure, pushed deep inside himself; and how violent this pressure must have been, to frighten such fury into secret caverns!" (36–37). There is no controlled cathartic release for Childerich's wrath. His sword is rounded and therefore cannot penetrate like a sharp needle the hidden caves and pouches of the self, where the accumulated anger is stored.

In German, the French word *pointe*, denoting the tip of the needle, refers to a specific literary device: "The striking ending of jokes, epigrams, short stories, and anecdotes is usually called the *Pointe*."[80] Ernst Robert Curtius identifies *pointe* with the rhetorical terms *acutus* and *acumen*: "The word *pointe* ('point') is the French equivalent for the 'pointed' diction or thought which the Romans designated by *acutus* and *acumen*."[81] Emil Kraepelin, one of the main representatives of German nineteenth-century psychiatry, defines the *pointe* as a sudden release of psychic energies in the act of laughing: "The intensification of successive contrast that is achieved by the tension of expectation may be designated by *pointe*. The term describes the unexpected bursting of incompatible associations upon each other [aufeinanderplatzen], the sudden paradoxical solution of a psychic state of stress. It is the intensification [Zuspitzung] of the *pointe* upon which the effective laughter that arises from successive comic contrast especially depends."[82] The comic effect is the product of a "Zuspitzung" (intensification), of the recipient's anticipation. This heightened expectation intensifies the contrast between what Lessing in his theory of the epigram calls "expectation" (Erwartung) and "resolution" (Aufschluß). For Lessing, who used the French word *pointe* for the first time in a German poetological context, the *pointe* is a "special feature of a good resolution."[83]

The exemplary genre for writing as a form of sharpening culmination is what Doderer idiosyncratically calls "shortest story" (Kürzestgeschichte), an intensification of the "short story" (Kurzgeschichte).[84] Wendelin Schmidt-Dengler characterizes these "shortest stories" as instances of a "radical depsychologization."[85] Their laconic and reductive qualities that refuse an immediate understanding function as irritants for the reader. "Shortest stories" often lack a punchline, as Torsten Buchholz points out, but still needle the reader. His or her expectations are disappointed; reading leaves any recipient angry or amused without ever being able to come to a conclusive, *good* resolution.[86] In the context of Doderer's narratives of violent rage, the English translation of *pointe* as "punchline" has to be taken seriously. Several stories end with people being punched or slapped in the face. Doderer's poetics is one of provocation that tries to achieve the reader's irritation but not a plausible conclusion of a narrative. His literary technique, by radically dissolving the connection between expectation and resolution, produces the sort of psychosomatic irritation characteristic of the mechanical practices and devices Dr. Horn employs.

Sigmund Freud, in an added footnote to *Jokes and Their Relation to the Unconscious (Der Witz und seine Beziehung zum Unbewußten)*, discusses a specific type of tendentious joke that he calls the "shaggy-dog story" (Aufsitzer):

> These extreme examples have an effect because they rouse the expectation of a joke, so that one tries to find a meaning concealed behind the nonsense. But one finds none, they really are nonsense. Under the influence of that play of mirrors it has become possible, one moment long, to liberate the pleasure in nonsense. These jokes are not entirely without a purpose; they are a "take-in," and give the person who tells them a certain amount of pleasure in annoying and misleading his hearer. The latter than damps his annoyance by determining to tell them himself later on.[87]

While the narrator of a shaggy-dog story experiences pleasure, the listener, who cannot make sense of the story, can overcome his anger only by imagining becoming a narrator him- or herself.[88] Doderer's concept of sharpening culmination and intensification echoes the process of the listener turning into a narrator, the recipient becoming a producer. Shaggy-dog stories, like sharp epigrams or pointed "shortest stories," function as irritants that trigger an affective reaction within the recipient and spur on his or her own productivity.

In the unpublished draft of an introduction to the *Repertory*, Doderer takes up the idea of ignition and applies it to the structural composition of the book:

> This is an encyclopedia, but not a dictionary of philosophical concepts. . . . I would like to say that it is only a collection of irritants, initiating a tension that cannot be relinquished if one wants

Igniting Anger 195

> to establish the proper distance to any matter. Paradoxically, this distance can be created by either approaching or retreating, which equals the golden mean, the *section aurea* between proximity and distance. It is like the most beneficial adjustment of the telescope or microscope (one has to turn them until one sees clearly), the proper distance between burning glass and cigarette (if one has no matches or wants to light the cigarette with a magnifying glass for fun). It focuses the combustion point onto that which is combustible, thereby suddenly and sharply lighting the spark. (12)

The book as a dictionary functions as a collection of irritants. Its aim is not the gathering and imparting of information, but the creation of a tension and irritation within the reader. It creates sparks aimed at igniting the reader. In its "Small Preliminary Remark on a Literary Conversation" (Kleine Vorbemerkung zu einer literarischen Unterhaltung), Doderer defines the *Repertory* as a dictionary and an irritant, comparing it to a pharmaceutical: "Here, the only aim is to present a basic foundation, made up of irritants and stimulants, i.e., medicines, irritants in the sense of 'to anger,' to annoy" (17). The *Repertory*'s aim is to provoke, irritate, and annoy the reader. It is the highest goal of a writer, according to Doderer, to ignite a reaction within the listener or reader: "The most beautiful compensation for a writer is to be a *déclic* for the reader or listener" (17). In a diary entry from 1944, Doderer discusses the *déclic* of anger in terms of recalcitrant objects: "Anger caused by a small trifle (which objectively would not be more than a trigger, in French a *déclic*), like a breakfast ruined by an indolent waitress or other caricatures of domestic misfortune, functions as the inserted sparkplug for everything we have on our mind."[89] Doderer reformulates the difference between "cause" (Grund) and "occasion" (Anlass), which Dr. Horn in the opening scene of *The Merowingians* is unable to determine, in terms of a *déclic* caused by a malicious object. Objects function as irritants and triggers, releasing the subject's inner tensions.

In the novel *The Strudlhof Steps or Melzer and the Depth of the Years (Die Strudlhofstiege oder Melzer und die Tiefe der Jahre)*, Doderer describes an anthology of epigrams by the Arab poet Omar Chajjâm as an ensemble of explosives: "The epigrams stood alone, only one on each page of the book, which seemed like the most appropriate way to arrange the quatrains, with their compression of content, since it gave them enough room, so to speak, in which to explode, whereupon they did not just fill the thoughts of the reader but also went on to overrun the blank part of the page, as it were. These little poems, indeed, acted like the overflowing contents of a strongbox crammed full and now having its lid pried off."[90] The poems of Omar Chajjâm are explosives waiting for ignition. Their content is so condensed that they require the space of a whole page to contain their eruptive force. Analogously, the printed edition of the *Repertory* is marked by blank pages so as to allow the reader to note his or her own thoughts and reflections triggered by reading the text. The *Repertory* becomes, in its own description, a "book for the reader to continue" (18).[91] It functions as a stimulant, influencing the reader to become productive. The novel *The Strudlhof Steps*, despite its considerable length, could be characterized—as Rudolf Helmstetter has remarked—as epigrammatic in the sense that "small forms" like "aphorisms, maxims, apercus, bon mots, and psychological reasonings of the narrator and the novel's figures" are integrated within the overarching narrative.[92] The novel, following Helmstetter, displays a dialectics between "narrative concretization and aphoristic concretization" as an "ornamental counterpoint."[93]

André Jolles's description of rhetorical emblems as a "duality of artwork and object of utility" also fits Doderer's model of epigrammatic writing.[94] Literature, in this sense, should be not so much read as applied to everyday life. Julius Zihal, the protagonist of Doderer's novel *The Lighted Windows, or the Humanization of the Bureaucrat Julius Zihal (Die erleuchteten Fenster oder die Menschwerdung des Amtsrates Julius Zihal)*, is exemplary as a reader for whom books function as instruments that—like a perspective or a microscope—affect one's relation to one's environment. Reading for Zihal goes beyond mere aesthetic pleasure or hermeneutic understanding. Instead, his reading allows for the institution of an immediate and self-evident connection "between his life and his book."[95] Zihal is able to become human by apperceiving reality: that is, by establishing a proper relationship between subject and object.[96] The book becomes an article of daily use, an object of utility: "We've learned earlier that he [Zihal], as a serious person, rejected the reading of novels, for instance. . . . He read just that one book—but knew how to use it; and that alone we consider decisive. For him that book was a useful tool and not some cultural plus to be added to others, a sorry and at the same time silly role that the best works of literature are often forced to play by their readers" (92). The one and only book Zihal uses is neither literary nor philosophical but a so-called *Dienstpragmatik*, a manual that regulates the application of Austrian civil service law. In

Igniting Anger

this sense, it resembles the encyclopedic approach of the *Repertory*. Neither text narrates stories, instead instructing the reader on how to apply abstract concepts to concrete situations. Both store knowledge and advise how to use this knowledge in everyday life.

Zihal's method of reading dissolves concepts, thereby rendering them useful for his personal life: "Zihal, on the other hand, had the ability to dissolve those almost totally hardened concepts that were in the book, to make the buds from which they had once come swell and burst [schwellen und platzen zu lassen] into flower a second time, to repeat their development to a certain extent, but with regard to a different subject matter. And in that way he developed form, arrived at an inner configuration [innrer Gestalt]" (92). Zihal reenacts the creation of concepts by igniting them. The invention and reinvention (in the act of reading) of concepts is based on the dynamic dialectics of swelling and bursting. Like anger, a concept has to be blown up to enter the life of the human being in a different, living form. Reading the *Repertory* as a manual for personal *Bildung* requires the ability to use the content of the book against the grain as irritants, transforming the reader's psychic economy. The "humanization" of Julius Zihal rests to a certain degree on his ability "not only to know something, but to dissolve that knowing in the warmth of his life"(93). Reading, for Zihal, constitutes a technology of the self, which is primarily concerned not with (self-)knowledge but with self-cultivation. While "his anger knew no bounds" [Sein Grimm ohne Boden] (107), he now—after having read the *Dienstpragmatik*—regained his footing: "Ground beneath the feet! Home ground!" [Boden unter den Füßen! Der Boden der Heimat!] (97). Becoming human, following Zihal's model, overcomes "groundless fits of rage." It involves the ignition of abstract concepts in order to acquire an individual, living language able to express a new and different morality. Becoming human means (re)gaining language. The (re)birth of the human Zihal is identical to the (re)birth of a new language. In this sense, Zihal's reading of the civil service manual and his eventual transformation resemble poetic acts.

In the essay "The Language of the Poet" (Die Sprache des Dichters) from 1931, Doderer discusses the creation of a new, poetic language in modernity in terms of a return to a primitive, prehistoric stage: "Whoever wants to arrive at language needs to return to where it once arose. That means, he must, at least for a period of his life, have been a primitive. In today's civilization this becomes increasingly easier, because it is on the decline and resembles a dangerous wilderness, even including its loneliness. In a certain sense, our big cities soon will be more malicious [tückisch] than the jungle."[97] The original poetic language, which is characterized by the "magic of the word," functioned to protect the human being from a dangerous environment that was beyond his control.[98] Man's existence, threatened by malicious forces—Doderer uses the verb *tückisch*[99]—is not specific to the primeval wilderness of prehistoric time but repeats itself in the experience of the modern metropolis. It is the poet's task to create a language that copes with the shocks and alienation of a disenchanted world. Poetical language as "designation" (Bezeichnung) and "expression" (Ausdruck) originates in an act of magical invocation.[100] The first word, according to Doderer, was an "incantation" (Beschwörungsformel).[101]

The belief in the magic origins of language in general and of poetry in particular is not Doderer's invention but has a long history. Friedrich Nietzsche, in the context of arguing for the cathartic qualities of music in *The Gay Science*, points to the enthralling and enchanting powers of song: "And not only in the religious song, but also in the secular song of the most ancient times, the prerequisite is that rhythm should exercise a magical influence; for example, in drawing water, or in rowing: the song is for the enchanting of the spirits supposed to be active thereby; it makes them obliging, involuntary, and the instruments of man" (118). It is the rhythmization of everyday activities like drawing water or rowing that protects them from being disturbed.[102] In song, tools and instruments lose their recalcitrant character; they function properly. The practices of everyday life resemble art forms, they function as *arts de faire* in the strict sense.[103] For the primitive mind, following Nietzsche and other ethnologists of the time, all objects are possessed by spirits. Therefore, the human being must overcome their malicious intentions before being able to use objects as tools and instruments. For Nietzsche in *The Gay Science,* this conjuring of demonic objects marks the origin of poetry: "*Every* action is dependent on the assistance of spirits: magic song and incantation appear to be the original form of poetry" (118–19). The origin of poetry in song stems from a "superstitious utility" (117).

In *The Merowingians*, the usefulness of superstition, or the belief in a quasi-animistic influence of the human mind over a recalcitrant environment, is exemplified by Dr. Schajo's pouch stab. In addition to the cathartic qualities of the pouch stab, Doderer offers another explanation for its therapeutic successes. According to this account, the pouch stab originates in a magical worldview characterized by what Freud calls "omnipotence of thoughts":[104] "Pouch stabbing is thousands of years old. Science knows of it: as the 'Magic of the Effect of Analogies' [Analogiehandlungszauber]; that is, in its mimicry form. One gets oneself a likeness of the person against whom the harmful magic is to be directed, and pierces through it where the one concerned is to be sickened; along with curses and sayings, naturally" (200). The efficacy of Dr. Schajo's method, according to this interpretation, is not based on a medico-theatrical catharsis or a psychological process of concentration; instead it relies on the primitive belief in magic. In a footnote referring to Hanns Bächtold-Stäubli's *Concise Dictionary of German Superstition (Handwörterbuch des deutschen Aberglaubens)*, Doderer discusses the source of the peculiar magic power of the pouch stab. Bächtold-Stäubli defines "the magic of the effect of analogies" as follows: "The concept 'magic of analogy' should be understood here as that magic which is intended to achieve the represented in actuality through a *representation* carried out by the subject, in this case the magician. In this way, both the representation and the expected reality in its appearance are in parallel with each other and should be thought of as being magically connected."[105] One subsection of the article on *Analogiezauber* is dedicated to mimic forms of magic called *Analogiehandlungszauber*. It examines a medium that creates a "connection between mimic representation and reality."[106] This medium "can be an *image* [Bild] that represents a person. With this image, one creates actions through which, analogously, the person himself is influenced.... But also a piece of clothing of the person in question, an item of his, or something taken from his body (hair, nails, or sweat on a piece of cloth) can serve as an object with which the magical act can be conducted."[107] The mimetic relationship between magic practice and its effects, performed by Dr. Schajo's pouch stabbers, includes an act of naming. Each pouch is labeled with the name of the subject or institution it is supposed to represent. The emphasis on the importance of naming points out that in magic there is no need for an equivalent relation between cause and effect, image and reality: "The likeness need not in any way be lifelike or even similar. It must only be named expressly and christened in some way cursedly with the name of he who is to be harmed or slain" (148). In an excursus, Doderer remembers an "anger pouch" (Grimmbeutel) from his childhood that functioned as an occasion of discharge only after it was given the name of the person it stood for: "In addition, this author remembers from his childhood that he and his favorite sister, with whom he grew up, used a so-called 'anger pouch.' It was a sack stuffed with something or other. In certain situations one threw oneself upon it and beat it, not without—and this seems here the important part—first giving it the name of the person who had caused the attack of anger" (201). Neither the pouches of Dr. Schajo nor those from the narrator's youth show any likeness with the real agents who caused wrath, exemplifying how in Dr. Schajo's hands superstition and animism become powerful tools to alleviate and calm the patient's angry outbursts.

Dr. Schajo's method of the pouch stab makes the underlying projective structure of anger explicit. What children, primitives, and paranoids do unintentionally becomes a quasi-scientific, psychological method of self-control. On the one hand, anthropomorphic projections function to protect the subject from a world that is experienced as alien and dangerous, while on the other hand they enhance, in an almost Stoic fashion, the ability to control one's affects. The anthropomorphic, animistic core of the pouch-stabbing treatment is underlined by the narrator when he identifies the concept of the "revenge doll" (Rachepuppe) as the core of Dr. Schajo's treatment: "Still, the core of the matter, that is, the pouch stab, originated in the revenge doll that one pierced through. It was usually made of wax and the piercing was usually done with a red-hot needle and with concentrated cursing" (201). It turns out that the pouch stab is not a modern psychological form of self-cultivation but an ancient, primitive belief in magic. Dr. Schajo's patients react to the shocking experiences of a disenchanted world by projecting acts of reenchantment. Their belief in magic could be described, to use a phrase from Hermann Bausinger, as "regressions initiated by technology."[108] This form of regression must be understood, not as sheer antimodern resentment, but as an inherent moment of modernity itself. For Bausinger, animistic beliefs in magic or demons are not mere archaic "relics which have survived the strange world of technology and mechanics in an unbroken tradition, but regressions caused by technology itself."[109] This *dialectic of enlightenment*, the emergence of mythical thought at the heart of technological progress, manifests itself in Doderer's writing in two instances. The first is animating affective projection in the face of an obstinate environment. The second consists in the psychological treatment of such affective conditions. Anger management reveals itself to be essentially related to this primitive-magical practice of reenchantment. The treatment of anger by the pouch stab, which on the surface appears to be a variation of standard cathartic abreactions, is at its core as animistic as the ascription of agency to inanimate objects.

CAUSES: THE SPECTER OF OLD VISCHER

In *The Psychopathology of Everyday Life*, Sigmund Freud introduces the term *parapraxis* (Fehlleistung). The subtitle of the book lists some of these faulty actions and misperformances: *Forgetting, Slips of the Tongue, Bungled Actions, Superstitions and Errors*. In the eighth chapter, dedicated to a discussion of "Bungled Actions" (Vergreifen), Freud describes the cramped space of his office, filled with numerous antique figurines. One day despite his usual care he clumsily throws down the lid of his inkstand. At first the destruction of the inkstand seems inadvertent. But upon closer examination, Freud realizes that the breaking of the little piece of equipment is more than a random coincidence. Instead it reveals a deeper, unconscious motivation: "The explanation was not hard to find. Some hours before, my sister had been in the room to inspect some new acquisitions. She admired them very much, and then remarked: 'Your writing table looks really attractive now; only the inkstand doesn't match. You must get a nicer one.' I went out with my sister and did not return for some hours. But when I did I carried out, so it seems, the execution of the condemned inkstand."[110] Freud interprets the sister's judgment of the writing utensil as a call for its execution. For him, the sister condemned and sentenced the object. Hence his action "was only apparently clumsy; in reality it was exceedingly adroit and well-directed."[111] The term *execution,* as Freud points out himself, is a reference to Friedrich Theodor Vischer's novel *Another One*: "A third breakage was connected with less serious matters; it was only the disguised 'execution'—to borrow an expression from Vischer's *Another One*—of an object which no longer enjoyed my favour."[112] The object is not simply destroyed but sentenced and executed as if it were a human subject responsible for a crime. Faulty actions like the apparently accidental destruction of the inkwell reveal a deeper motivation that manifests itself in an anthropomorphic projection.

Parapraxis expresses unconscious wishes that can be made manifest by analysis but are also often, Freud suggests, attested to in humor and in the superstition of traditional proverbs: "Dropping, knocking over and breaking objects are acts which seem to be used very often to express unconscious trains of thought, as analysis can occasionally demonstrate, but as may more frequently be guessed from the superstitious of facetious interpretations popularly connected with them."[113] In this context, Freud calls his own "attack of destructive fury" a "sacrifice."[114] The psychopathology of everyday life can be analyzed properly only when seemingly primitive animistic or anthropomorphic explanations are not ruled out as simply irrational. Jacques Derrida writes: "The superstitious person is sensitive to the precariousness of the contextual circumscriptions of the epistemological frames, the *constructs* and *artifacts* that enable us, for life's convenience and for the mastery of limited networks of knowledge and technics, to separate the psychic from the physical or the inside from the outside."[115] To cope with the radical contingency of the real, humans create psychic "constructs" and material "artifacts." For the rational mind these spheres are supposedly distinct and do not intersect, while from a superstitious perspective—and that of psychoanalysis—the border between subject and object, the mental and the physical, is porous. Psychoanalysis and superstition share "the compulsion not to allow chance as chance but to interpret it."[116] They both look for hidden motivations and do not allow for randomness. They share a compulsion to interpret. But while in superstition and paranoia the subject looks for causes outside him- or herself, the psychoanalyst, namely Freud, knows that these external determinations actually originate within the psyche: "In this way our parapraxes make it possible for us to practise all those pious and superstitious customs that must shun the light of consciousness owing to opposition from our reason, which has now grown skeptical."[117] The act of throwing the inkwell to the ground for Freud is neither merely clumsy nor bad luck but the fulfillment of an unconscious wish. Parapraxis is always a meaningful event. There is no erroneous action performed by the subject that does not signify. When it comes to human actions, there are no accidents, only symptoms.

For Freud, superstition "is nothing but psychology projected into the external world."[118] The superstitious person projects his or her unconscious thoughts and intentions onto the outside world. He or she is primarily concerned, not with epistemological questions of the relation between contingency and necessity, but, as Derrida puts it, with "the *believing attitude* before the effects of change."[119] Freud's discussion of superstition in everyday life is analogous to his analysis of primitive animistic thought and its resemblance to paranoia. In "Totem and Taboo," he explains the belief in spirits and demons as a form of projection: "Spirits and demons . . . are only projections of man's own emotional impulses. He turns his emotional cathexes into persons, he peoples the world with them and meets his internal mental processes again outside himself."[120] The primitive, as well as the superstitious or the paranoid mind, confuses "an ideal connection for a real one," thereby projecting his or her affects into the outside world.[121] Such "magical technique[s]" typically take the form of personification and anthropomorphism.[122]

Nietzsche, like Freud, takes up the contemporary ethnological discourse on the primitive mind and applies it to modern, which is to say rationalized, Western culture. He argues that the belief in free will and the complementary belief in causality are types of magic. This kind of projection turns the human being into a powerful magician who can control his or her surroundings. If this control fails and the will cannot immediately be transformed into an action, the human being, according to Nietzsche, invents different malicious agents interfering with his or her actions: "If for once our endeavors fail, it must have been caused by an antagonistic being [feindlichem Wesen], which, using magic, placed an obstacle between will and deed. To will the good and to do the wrong: One ascribes this to the devil, another to sinfulness, while a third perceives it as punishment for the guilt of earlier lifetimes. They all interpret it in a moral and demonic fashion."[123] The confusion of "ideal" and "real" connections in animistic thinking offers Doderer a model against which he can develop his concept of apperception, the key notion of his epistemology, psychology, and aesthetics. In an entry from *Tangents* dated December 17, 1944, Doderer discusses the concepts of objects and objectivity. The objective perception of things, apperception, consists, in the first section of the entry, in a "separation of objects" (Ablösung der Objekte) from the subject (263): "It is our separation from the objects by which they become what they are, as when one carefully retreats from out of a thorn-shrubbery" (262). To perceive the world objectively, one has to remove oneself from it, disentangling oneself from the world of objects and avoiding their thorny nature. Here, Doderer understands perception as a form of distancing oneself from the physical obstinacy of things. The final section of the entry offers a different doctrine of perception, which is related to the idea of the demonic as suggested by Nietzsche: "At contra: this demonic, i.e., this way of experiencing each and every thing as if it were a part of our body, is simultaneously a necessary cohabitant of the more gifted life. It actually appears to me to be a type of intestinal flora of the spirit without which it could not finish its chemical processes" (263). In the following entry of the *Tangents* from December 19, in contradistinction to the earlier entry, it is precisely the "chemical" quality, indicating a merging of subject and object, that defines true, "existential apperception" [existenzielle Apperzeption] (265). Perceiving objects from a distance, as described in the earlier entry, is now nothing more than a "purely formal cognition," which differs from an "existentially altering perception" or an "apperception" proper (264). Apperception, according to Doderer, is the experience of objects as integral to the subject, as if indeed they were somehow chemically combined. Apperception, "which derives from *aperte percipere*—to perceive openly" (264), involves an approach to reality similar to that of animism. The separation between subject and object, body and spirit, animate and inanimate, becomes porous, in a manner reminiscent of what Freud, in *Totem and Taboo*, referred to as the "general overvaluation ... of all mental processes."[124]

In one of the aforementioned entries of the *Repertory*, Doderer describes a form of punishment for recalcitrant objects: "Also, one should enrich fits of rage by placing small objects—for example, pens, lighters, or saucers that have, because of their behavior, caused anger—into a specifically assigned wire cage, carrying the sign: 'Dishonorable Discharge because of Malice' [Entehrende Außer-Dienst-Stellung wegen Tücke]. From outside the cage one can threaten the delinquents inside with objects suitable to destroy them: for example, a hammer" (273). The notion of the "dishonorable discharge" (Entehrende Außer-Dienst-Stellung) of the offending object has its roots in Austrian civil service law. In one of several passages in *The Lighted Windows*, Doderer mentions the "Guidelines for Effecting Handbook of Administrative Practices Regulations concerning Suspension of Duties" [Durchführungsvorschrift zu den Bestimmungen der Dienstpragmatik über die Außerdienststellung] (94). Like a human civil servant, an object that fails in its service can be dismissed and retired. It is capable of experiencing honor and fear; it reacts to threats and punishments. This demonic interpretation of things culminates in the idea of spiteful, malicious objects.

The persecution, indictment, and punishment of inanimate objects, as grotesque as it may sound, has a long legal tradition. In ancient Greek law, if there was no human to whom a criminal act could be assigned, animals as well as inanimate objects were tried and sentenced. Plato, imagining an ideal legal system, allows for the possibility of an ax to be the willful perpetrator of a crime: "if an animate thing cause loss of a human life—an exception being made for lightning or other such visitations of god—any object which causes death by its falling upon a man or his falling against it shall be sat upon in judgment by the nearest neighbor, at the invitation of the next of kin, who shall hereby acquit himself and the whole family of their obligation; on conviction the guilty object is to be cast beyond the frontier."[125] Banishment as punishment is not limited to human criminals but can also be used against inanimate objects. Since in Greek legal thought the polis needs to be purged from the pollution of a crime, the ax as an instrument of a crime was, for example, tried in court: "It was when Erechtheus was king of Athens that the ox-slayer first killed an ox at the altar of Zeus Polieus. Leaving the axe where it lay he went out of the land into exile, and the axe was forthwith tried and acquitted."[126] It was necessary to determine the perpetrator of a crime, whether it was man, animal, or object, because the identification of a responsible agent was crucial for successfully cleansing the city of its moral pollution. Only if the Furies could direct their avenging wrath against an individual would they not turn against the community. The focus of the trial in the Prytaneum was on reinstating the "moral equilibrium," as Walter H. Hyde remarks, and not so much on the individual motives of the defendant or the circumstances of the crime.[127] The practice of putting objects on trial negotiates between the individual and society as well as between the divine violence of the Furies and the realm of human laws. Cornelia Vismann, in her essay "Schuld ist das Ding," analyzes several moments in the history of law when objects have become the subjects of legal proceedings. For Vismann, the court presents one of those places where the distribution of agency between subjects and objects is discussed in a paradigmatic fashion: "The ceremonialized trial of the knife enacts the power of things. It presents the thing's stage, which demands its secretly working power. . . . If the court on the thing goes too far, it becomes clear that the thing has power over human actions. This power is negotiated before the court."[128] In an article entitled "A Problem for Pericles," Ferdinand Fairfax Stone discusses the need to determine a responsible perpetrator in ancient law, recapitulating the accidental death of a young man hit by a javelin. After discussing the possible guilt of the javelin thrower, Plutarch, who narrates the episode, also ponders the possibility of the javelin's being responsible. Stone concludes his argument by pointing toward issues raised by the case, which have not lost any of their relevance today: "We do not know what resolution Pericles and Protagoras made of the problem of the javelin-killed lad, but we do know that their analysis raised questions that we still debate: What is an 'accident'? What do we mean by 'fault'? . . . What can we say of *causalité* in a world of complicated relationships?"[129]

In an oblique reference to the court of the Prytaneum, Aristotle, in *The Athenian Constitution*, speaks of the need to prosecute "the doer" even if one does not know who did it: "When the killer is unknown, a suit is entered against 'the doer of the deed.'"[130] This unknown guilty "doer" can be an individual human, an inanimate object, or an animal. Law requires that cause and effect be determinable. If the direct cause cannot be determined, the orator needs to create a passionate, lively "legal fiction." Hence trials against inanimate objects are not the sign of "the animism of primitive man" or an irrational mind-set, as some legal scholars attempt to argue.[131] The legal resolution of a homicide, even if it happened inadvertently or without an easily distinguishable human perpetrator, requires an agent who can be held responsible and consequently punished. As Michael Gagarin states in his comment on Antiphon's *Tetralogies*: "One cannot argue . . . that the killer cannot be known; someone must be available to satisfy the avenging spirit."[132]

Legal scholars trace these "symbolic functions of legal actions against objects" in antiquity through the Middle Ages to modern forfeiture laws: "Evidence suggests that, throughout the medieval period, legal actions against both inanimate objects and animals were widespread. Indeed, it appears that the origin of such trials extends as far back as ancient Greece. . . . We may see that these legal actions performed social functions for the community that are not necessarily so different from the function of modern forfeiture law."[133] What underlies the "legal fiction" that objects can become responsible as legal subjects and therefore can be forfeited is the belief in the possibility of inanimate objects being held responsible for certain deeds. Legal historians like Paul Schiff Berman argue against the dismissal of this tradition of forfeiture and deodand laws as unenlightened and irrational by stressing its symbolic function: the restoration and preservation of an established community. Comparing ancient trials against things with modern forfeiture procedures, Berman concludes: "I argue that such legal proceedings permitted the community to heal itself after the breach of a social norm by creating a narrative whereby a symbolic transgressor of the established order was deemed to be 'guilty' of a 'crime' and cast beyond the boundaries of the society."[134]

The healing of the community between objects and subjects in Doderer's universe of recalcitrant objects is achieved not only by a quasi-legal procedure but also by the threat of immediate violence. While in the aforementioned *Repertory* entry the threat of a violent destruction is never actualized, Doderer's narrator in the story "The Intimidation" (Die Einschüchterung), part of "Eight Fits of Rage" (Acht Wutanfälle), makes short work of the offending object. After having burned himself with a hot teapot, the narrator reacts by "executing" it:

> I carefully put down the teapot and again put water in the kettle, which was above the gas flame in the kitchen. I also prepared the tea caddy and another porcelain teapot. I emptied the one that had bitten me by pouring out the fresh tea that was inside, and I let the biter cool off. Finally lining it up opposite a framed picture under glass—its blinking glance on my misfortune made me suspicious that it was in collusion with the biting teapot—I now grabbed the teapot, went about four meters away from the picture, and threw the teapot like a discus with a powerful turn from my hips. I let the corpses lay there *in situ* for four hours.[135]

The breaking of dishes resembles the scene from Vischer's *Another One* in which the narrator and the protagonist of the novel throw dishes out of the window of a restaurant.[136] The subject, experiencing the malice of the object, acts as persecutor, judge, and executioner and in the process creates a private, phantasmagoric court. Here, justice—the moral and emotional equilibrium of the subject as well as that of the household (oikos) and the state (polis)—is reestablished. In the final passage of "The Intimidation," the angry outburst functions as a threat and fulmination, reestablishing the subject's control over the situation. Not only is the guilty teapot destroyed, but the other household objects are intimidated, their malice held in check by their fear of destruction: "After the throw I had growled only one time briefly and threateningly. But there was no doubt that the executive scene [exekutive Vorgang] in the room had been taken in *ad notam* by countless penduculated eyes. For I was spared for nearly a whole year thereafter from all of the tricks and jeers, bites, insubordination, and malice [Tücken] of the present objects."[137] Objects are not merely destroyed but executed. The term *execution,* from the Latin *executio,* literally translating as "action of carrying something into effect," must be read not only as a juridical category but also as a psychological one. It designates the subject's attempt to regain autonomy and self-possession, the ability to carry out his or her intentions without the interruption of malicious objects, reestablishing the law of *causa aequat effectum.*

In a *Tangents* diary entry from May 6, 1945—two days before the end of World War II—Doderer, serving as an officer in the German air force, attempts to delineate an etiology of his recurring fits of rage: "I suspect that, in the end, my rage is nothing other than a mirror of my current weakness and unproductivity, and therefore the worst kind: what has been called a 'powerless rage' [ohnmächtige Wut]" (313). In moments of weakness and unproductivity, the subject temporarily loses the ability to act, feeling powerless and impotent, which in turn ignites outbursts of anger. The term *powerless rage* reappears in the *Repertory,* where it designates the worst type of rage: "The artificially generated rage now becomes a powerless one and therefore one of the worst kinds" (174). This lack of self-mastery features prominently in the subject's relation to household objects, which seem to him malicious, actively interfering with his intentions, as in this excerpt from *Tangents:* "When I get angry with small objects because of their malice [Tücken], then I ascribe to them, in animistic or demonological fashion, evil and common intentions. Alone in my room, I triumph, shouting sardonically, if the cord of the curtain does not succeed in secretly wrapping itself up with the flower vase. Therefore, once the curtain is pulled up, the vase does not fall and tumble to the ground. Whether in these moments old Vischer was haunting me or I was haunting myself can today no longer be determined" (313). Malice is not the inherent quality of the pernicious things themselves, which interrupt the subject's intentions, but rather the projection of the impotent, weak subject. Projecting agency in the form of malicious intentions is an "executive process" [exekutive Vorgang] to reduce or efface the even greater threat of contingency, that is, radical groundlessness.[138] From this perspective, the seemingly random movements of household items like curtains or vases appear to be more than merely resistant or recalcitrant. They act against the subject, as if animated by malicious spirits. In other contexts Doderer

Igniting Anger

further develops this theory of animistic and demonic imputation in the state of rage.

In *The Merowingians*, copies of Vischer's novel *Another One* are distributed as a kind of shibboleth identifying the members of the mysterious organization Hulesch & Quenzel, the sole purpose of which consists in the production and distribution of dysfunctional objects, creating outbursts of anger and rage.[139] The agents of Hulesch & Quenzel strategically place anger-inducing objects in the everyday life of several of the main characters, among them the protagonist Childerich von Bartenbruch, who is afflicted by uncontrollable fits of rage. These objects are recalcitrant by design; they are produced to fail. Malfunction here reveals, not a flaw or defect of an object, but its purpose. The articles of Hulesch & Quenzel function by not functioning, they succeed by failing. Doderer inserts into the novel a catalog of several of Hulesch & Quenzel's anger-inducing objects:

> No. 10729. HORROR CHAIR. Especially effective with tea guests. Cause not immediately to discern. Sudden shortening of a leg that restores itself when one investigates. Spilling tea as good as guaranteed.
>
> No. 10730. SAUCERS, PNEUMATIC. Stick a few seconds to the tea cup.
>
> No. 10731. CAPS OF BOTTLES, TOOTHPASTE TUBES, ETC., ETC. Made of highly elastic materials, bounce when dropped. Devil's dance on the stone floor of a bathroom, roll to the furthest corner. (169)

What appears to humans as malicious objects, obstinate instruments that seem to act against the subject's intentions are artificial creations that are industrially produced and distributed.[140] In this context, Doderer's notion of malicious objects differs from that of Vischer. Vischer, according to Doderer, "believed he had discovered a general quality of life altogether" (164). In contrast, for Doderer, the object's malice is no universal phenomenon: "Further, we know now that all this has to do with something that has been manipulated, that is, brought to life artificially" (164). The artificial character of malicious objects, which for Vischer is a transhistorical occurrence, Doderer identifies as a specifically modern experience: "But as we know today, Hulesch & Quenzel is a modern institution of artificial vexations, entirely "l'art pour l'art," and its results are in no way to be considered merely a fundamental quality of life" (166–67). Doderer reveals

Vischer's metaphysical theory of objects possessed by demons interfering with the human being's *Lebenswelt* as the product of a secret organization, its members consisting of "designers, technologists, lab assistants, industrial representatives and agents" (169). These representatives of modernity's technological progress create the illusion of malicious objects populating the world. Their inventions, at first glance, are not meant to facilitate and improve everyday life. On the contrary, each newly developed device developed by Hulesch & Quenzel disrupts the ability of humans to use technology undisturbed. The disclosure of the world as a "break in that referential totality in which circumspection 'operates'" is engineered and distributed.[141] The angry ego in Vischer and Doderer results from being cornered by the obstinacy of a world filled with industrially produced artifacts, machines, and devices that, despite the claim of their usefulness and facilitation of everyday life, create an adversarial space where they tend to dictate to people their gestures and movements. "Horror chairs," for example, are characterized by a malicious design that makes it impossible for the perturbed and angry user to identify the reason for their obstinacy: "Sudden shortening of a leg that restores itself when one investigates" (169). Hulesch & Quenzel's equipment not only fails but hides its flaws, what *Tangents* describes as the object's "holding itself in."

The theoretical principle informing Hulesch & Quenzel's method of "particularized torture" [Detailpeinigungen] (163–64) consists in the reduction of the human existence into an ensemble of small, abstract parts. Hulesch & Quenzel represent the idea of analysis, understood in its etymological sense as the resolution of anything into discrete elements. In his diary, Doderer calls this a "dismantling-like thought" (zerlegungsweises Denken).[142] As a scientific principle, it also informs Dr. Horn's march of anger, which Doderer describes as an assembly of "anger elements" (Wutelemente). Human life in its wholeness is broken up, dissected, and thereby becomes disposable for therapeutic or malicious interventions. The organization of Hulesch & Quenzel uses the analytic framework of modern science, not to improve the everyday life of man, but to disrupt it. It represents

> a principle of life's entirety being divided into ever smaller parts and particles of parts, so that the multitude of curves in our existence (which, indeed, as we know, exhibit not one actual and literal straight stretch) disappear, and with them also the verve that otherwise carries us through such curves. Even more, it demonstrates that perhaps even the circular line is formed only of countless tiniest straight ones.

> Every situation, then, immediately breaks down into these straight ones when the firm Hulesch & Quenzel goes into action. That such has to amount in the end to particularized torture goes without saying. (163–64)

By subsuming the curvature of one's life to discrete plottable elements on a graph, one loses a sense of the continuity and integrity of one's life. The focus on detail and the minute, ever-increasing process of splitting life into small parts leads not to an improvement of one's situation but to an inability to deal with the irregularities of the everyday. Life's movement is perceived, not as a continuous motion, but in the mathematical sense as a set of small jumps and gaps. Every situation falls apart, split into distinct parts that lack coherence.

Hulesch & Quenzel, despite their seemingly malicious intentions to torture and torment random subjects, follow a hidden, "metaphysical" plan and are engaged in a pedagogical project. Malicious objects are a means to an end: to cure man of his anger. The crest of the organization contains a heraldic motto summarizing its educational intentions: "The coat of arms displays the head of smiling Big Quenzel in the decorative style, over which spreads Hulesch's pinions. On the lower rim one reads the heraldic motto, in English: TAKE IT EASY! This expresses the actual educational intention of the institute. But in the entrance hall one finds still a second text, somewhat below the huge, colorful coat of arms, in raised letters of marble: POST RABIEM RISUS (After fury, grin). One sees here the great dignity of the whole business clear" (168). Horror chairs, pneumatic saucers, and other recalcitrant objects are used to create artificial vexations. The subjects that are exposed to these infernal artifacts undergo an intensification followed by a transformation of their anger, which eventually, as in the case of Dr. Horn's march of anger, results in an alleviation and relief of rage: "POST RABIEM RISUS." The ignition of anger follows a therapeutic doctrine: after the cathartic discharge of anger, the human being laughs and grins. The subject, one might say, reaches a state of relaxation and, to use Martin Heidegger's terminology, *Gelassenheit* in relationship to the objects of his environment.[143] For the late Heidegger, the mode of "releasement toward things" [Gelassenheit] represents the possibility of existing securely in a world of technologically produced, recalcitrant objects: "Releasement toward things and openness to the mystery belong together. They grant us the possibility of dwelling in the world in a totally different way. They promise us a new ground and foundation upon which we can stand and endure in the world of technology without being imperiled."¹⁴⁴ While for Heidegger *Gelassenheit* offers human beings in modernity a foundation, in Doderer's world of industrially produced recalcitrant objects a new ethics of dealing with objects relies on the repeated ignition of groundless fits of rage. Heidegger's definition of the thing as "gathering" appears in the epilogue of the novel when the narrator attempts to explicate the principle of the "total family": "What does the philosopher say? 'Aus dem Dingen des Dinges ereignet sich und bestimmt sich auch erst das Anwesen des Anwesenden,' and: 'Wie aber west das Ding? Das Ding dingt. Das Dingen versammelt.' These sentences give in utmost brevity and pregnancy a complete theory of the total family" (412–13). The Heidegger quote functions like a *pointe* needling the reader.¹⁴⁵ Not only does Childerich's project of a total family—very much like Heidegger's total philosophy of gathering—fail, but the place where humans and things gather is not the "Ort" of a rounded, archaic sword, or the Germanic "Ding" or "thing" as a place of gathering, but the tip of piercing needles, pricks, and barbs. Heidegger's late philosophy, understood as an attempt to overcome traditional concepts of the object, resembles Childerich's grotesque and eventually disastrous project of creating a total family. The following section of this chapter takes up Doderer's notion of the "total family" as he transfers it into the realm of politics. Here his idea of "totality" reappears in the essay "Sexuality and the Total State" (Sexualität und totaler Staat), in which Doderer explicitly links individual pathologies like uncontrollable rage to larger historical, sociological, and political tendencies.

THE NECESSARY AND THE SUPERFLUOUS

Around 1948, Doderer began to work on an essay that he would ultimately, in 1951, entitle "Sexuality and the Total State." Despite several attempts to publish the piece in the *Merkur* and other journals, it was not until after his death in 1966 that it appeared in a collection of essays, tracts, and speeches, *The Return of the Dragons (Die Rückkehr der Drachen)*. In this essay, Doderer discusses more analytically the relation of the "refusal to apperceive" and other pathologies in relation to modernity. In the pseudologicial realm of modernity the difference between the necessary and the superfluous loses its validity: "In the pseudologic space, the difference between the necessary and the superfluous, in the spirit of Johann Nestroy, is lost."¹⁴⁶ This failure to make distinctions defines the modern, total state: "One criticizes this [the failure to differentiate] as one of the failures of the total state: its overorganization."[147] In the state of overorganization, everything is equally necessary and superfluous. There is no criterion that would guarantee a differentiation between what is essential and what is accidental.

Nestroy's 1836 play *The Two Sleepwalkers or the Necessary and the Superfluous (Die beiden Nachtwandler oder Das Notwendige und das Überflüssige)* tells the story of a poor rope maker who is granted every wish as long as he wishes only for the necessary but not for the superfluous. The rope maker proceeds to formulate more and more wishes and inevitably crosses the line between the necessary and the superfluous. Nestroy's play, a version of the fairy tale "The Fisherman and His Wife," is a reflection on the possibility of happiness. What leads to the rope maker's downfall is his inability to distinguish between the necessary and the superfluous. While in Nestroy's comedy this inability is due to individual greed and hubris, in the total state individual blindness is generalized, a characteristic of the whole social structure. Here the individual's subjective incapacity to apperceive reality is prohibited by the creation of a second, abstract reality. In the essay "Literalness as the Cornerstone of Reality" (Wörtlichkeit als Kernfestung der Wirklichkeit), Doderer asserts: "Here we are dealing with the creation of a second reality. We recognize it as objectively projected, that is, as externalized forcefully in the ideological total state."[148] Psychology and politics can be analyzed in terms of the same opposition: apperception versus the refusal to apperceive.

In *The Merowingians*, Doderer's description of Dr. Horn's treatment ridicules modern psychology's belief in the possibility of an objective, scientific method in the humanities. The recurring characterization of psychology as the "locksmithery of the soul" in Doderer's diaries points in a similar direction.[149] The danger of splitting hairs, the "overorganization" of statistical methodologies, threatens psychologists' ability to apperceive the reality of their patients' afflictions concretely. Modern psychology functions according to the same pseudologic as the total state, subsuming concrete reality under abstract concepts. In the chapter "Professor Horn's Terrible Suspicion; Horn Succumbs to Avarice," the narrator ironically explicates Dr. Horn's grotesque treatment, interpreting especially the method of measuring foot angles, as a mad form of statistics: "Following his spiritual bent, Horn was essentially a statistician. Because of the inherent and ever-existent danger of hair-splitting, the use of statistics as a method can very easily lead to mental illness; indeed, some maintain that it is generally a symptom of such. This illness manifests itself especially when a person is no longer able to differentiate the indispensable from the superfluous (on the whole, one can notice this within any totalitarian state [Totalstaat]" (152). The belief that statistics provide a viable model for analyzing human behavior reflects a condition indistinguishable from madness. The statistician is unable to separate the necessary from the superfluous; hence he cannot determine the reason for pathological emotional states.

In a short series of brief reflections, "The Bare Room" (Das kahle Zimmer), written in 1942/43, Doderer takes up Nestroy's distinction between the necessary and the superfluous, relating it to the question of whether humans can perceive reality clearly and concretely. Such a perception would bring humans into the proximity of things, to use a Heideggerian formula, in which subject and object, inside and outside, are in close proximity, if only for brief intervals. According to *Tangents*: "The human being may have, in these seconds of proximity, i.e., the seconds of created clarity and beginning reality [hergestellten Anschaulichkeit und beginnenden Wirklichkeit], already thrown a newly measured glance [neu bemessenden Blick] upon the necessary and the superfluous" (218). The subject's apperceptive gaze distinguishes between the necessary and the superfluous. For Doderer, it is in dreams and memories that the necessary and the superfluous are most clearly differentiated:[150] "And indeed, every gripping tale as well as every bar of symphonic music tastes and sounds 'like rising memory' that was not intended [ungerufen], naturally. Only this kind remembers and renews: it paradoxically appears as something new out of something already experienced. Only the dreams of deep sleep are not called [nicht . . . gerufen] by this day. An eye, which opened suddenly many years ago, looks straight at us from these dreams. Here the selection between the necessary and the superfluous has already been made."[151] Doderer takes up the notion of "rising memories" (aufsteigende Erinnerungen) from his friend and teacher Hermann Swoboda. For Swoboda, freely rising memories "are those that do not appear as causally induced, but rather have established themselves by means of inadequately realized perceptions in our unconscious, in order to arise in consciousness as laws that are at first unknown. Freely rising memories distinguish themselves above all as unintentional [ungerufen]."[152] As a form of *mémoire involontaire*, the thoughts and images that appear in the subject's consciousness cannot be (re)produced intentionally.[153] They rise freely, seemingly without connection to the subject's present state. They are not solicited by a determinable occurrence. Hence they appear to be without ground. For Doderer, Swoboda's concept of memory is closely connected to a specific relationship of man to things; he writes in *Tangents* that "in the basic network, there are also things interlaced, I mean objects of the material type. It reminds me of a gigantic ball of wool my little sister once owned, which from time to time as a reward for the knitting child would reveal a new, most charming toy, like a doll made of porcelain, a few dice or something like that" (203). In "On the Walls of Kursk" (Auf den Wällen von Kursk)—written around the same time as "The Bare Room"—Doderer reminisces about his childhood as a time when he had an intense, almost pathological relationship to things: "Today I look beyond the small, magical stage, alluring as life itself, of my Christmas table from those days, which is spiritually decidedly less valuable. I see my technical world in many things, also in books, blank and delicate. I *had* these things—I simply *had* them, I did not ask from where they came nor what they meant—and I related to them at once in an intensive way, perhaps even touching upon the pathological" (167). The child relates to objects differently than the grownup does. To be in possession of a thing implies in this context a proximity between subject and object that not only borders on the pathological but also has the magic power of theater. For the child, things are inscribed with a force that goes beyond function and meaning. They appear on the magical stage of the Christmas table, enticing the child as if they were animated and speaking in a language that cannot be reduced to a mere medium of communication. The child entertains a quasi-animistic relationship to the objects in his environment. Its intensity cannot be rendered in terms of semantic meaning or reduced to a rational explanation of its origins. Albert Paris Gütersloh's writing provides another example of such a language of things: "Here, [in Gütersloh's novel *Eine sagenhafte Figur*], we see removed from language all remnants of its communicative function."[154]

Language, devoid of its function as a means to communicate, as in Gütersloh, becomes the medium in which the subject can establish an intense, childlike relationship to the world of objects as "concrete reality" (anschauliche Wirklichkeit).[155] Setting language's instrumentality aside creates a deeper understanding transcending traditional concepts of means and ends: "The communicative function of language, central for its social relevance, is only a side branch. The hand must dig deeper if it wants to reach the taproot of language."[156] Discovering the roots of concrete reality involves moving beneath the prevailing forms of instrumental reason and communication. This move coincides with the newly measured perception of the necessary and the superfluous—a perception that, according to *Tangents,* "lacks Nestroy's consolidated cheerfulness but not his depth" (218). Against traditional interpretations of Nestroy as a writer of popular and superficial comedies, Doderer stresses the epistemological and ethical depth of Nestroy's plays. They express a "consolidated cheerfulness" (konsolodierte Heiterkeit) that allows humor to serve as a key element for a certain mode of apperception. Cheerfulness is not opposed to depth. On the contrary, it allows apperceiving the present and the past openly, providing the foundation for a true *Menschwerdung* (humanization).

Apperception, writes Doderer in *Tangents,* implies an explicit ethical imperative. The concrete clearness of apperception facilitates the subject's ability to live the good life without following abstract rules or regulations. Once one makes the decision to apperceive, "then we are redeemed with life before it can even begin, and we will remain redeemed and entangled with it, no matter how it progresses, because a common aura encloses us and the external world" (216). In the act of apperception, subject and object are deeply entangled, and the inner life of the mind and the outer world of reality are reconciled. The result is the acceptance of one's life with all its vagaries. In apperception, life gains a coherence and necessity that cannot be guaranteed by traditional morality. Humans and things do not stand in opposition to each other but form a continuum, almost like a chemical compound, thereby affording the possibility for a coherent biography. Coming to terms with the world is identical to coming to terms with oneself. The subject is not trapped or constrained by reality's recalcitrant objects but accepts and approves of them as an integral part of him- or herself. Therefore, the apperceptive character does not attempt to change reality; he is not a revolutionary but by definition conservative. The conservative takes life as it is, while the revolutionary conceives of it as a "product that one could attain."[157]

In "Sexuality and the Total State," Doderer expands the idea of apperception from individual psychology and ethics into the realm of history and politics. Here he denounces the political revolutionary who lacks the ability "to endure the situation (both inner and outer) just as it is, without resisting perception, but simply absorbing the full reality of the situation precisely as it is."[158] The revolutionary is characterized, according to Doderer, by a certain type of stupidity: he or she is unable to differentiate between the necessary and the superfluous. Political programs and ideologies turn away from the concrete reality of life toward abstract and artificial constructs. This involves the fantasy of being in possession of the "solely rational and binding system of concepts, from which one could directly reach its concretion."[159]

The totalizing, overorganizing tendencies of modernity become paradigmatic in the character of the Prussian bureaucrat who, in his blind obedience to written rules, lacks the ability to differentiate between the necessary and the superfluous. Alfred Weber, in the article "The Civil Servant" (Der Beamte) from 1910, describes bureaucracy as a system "that spreads itself over all work and all creation with a dead face-to-face and dead successiveness, with a coming-together bit by bit, but with a soullessness for each other."[160] Bureaucracy poisons and destroys all forms of individuality. Natural, organic coherence and interconnectedness are replaced by abstract schematization.[161] Doderer dramatizes the asymmetrical relationship of the powerless individual to the "overorganization" of the bureaucratic system of the total state. For Doderer, bureaucracy is inherently malicious, causing highly theatrical fits of rage. One entry in *Tangents*, entitled "Fits of Rage (Medium Strength)" (Wutanfälle [mittlere Stärke]), written on May 4, 1945, states: "I am, by the way, aware of the fact that my anger, as soon as I simply come near an administrative office, could be described as an a priori one" (312). In the pseudological space of the total state, the individual's apperception of reality is structurally obstructed and impeded. Hence the mere proximity of an office exposes an *a priori rage*. This is a type of anger that is independent of any actual, empirical experience—it is not about individual malicious civil servants—and that formally structures the subject's apperception of the world. While in Kant the a priori transcendental conditions of apperception open up the possibility of experience, a priori rage for Doderer is a "refusal to apperceive."

It is the antagonism between a rigid, abstract concept and the fluctuating realities of given facts that ignites Doderer's angry eruptions and renders manifest the bottomless latency of a priori rage. Doderer does not just lament the loss of an immediate access to an organic, concrete reality in the age of instrumental reason and totalitarian ideologies; he celebrates the often violent reemergence of the particular, of that which refuses to be integrated into the systematic technologies of bureaucratic control. His work investigates those moments when the "overorganization" reveals itself in failures, interruptions, and disturbances. The *Tangents* entry from May 4 continues: "In rage, I thoroughly refuse to apperceive. During these five years 'with the Prussians' I have accumulated a readiness for anger that shocks me. I probably always had these tendencies within me: while I was performing a certain task, following a rigid plan, that would not always correspond with the given situation, I would be disturbed. This disturbance and the following modification of my plans would easily make me lose control as a result of anger" (312–13). Anger is the refusal to apperceive. During Doderer's service in the German army it comes to an accumulation of angry energies that can be ignited by the slightest incident. For Doderer, the seemingly inconsequential task of obtaining new underpants from the German army brings out his a priori rage:

> Today an extraordinarily bad day. In the morning and in the afternoon, I ran several errands to complete my outfit. In order to do so, I had to visit several administrative offices to retain so-called coupons. In this area, fits of rage are for me, so it seems, inevitable. . . . Six times I had to climb the stairs so as to reach third-floor offices in two opposing enormous administrative buildings (room number 323 here and room number 401 over there). After I was finally able to purchase underpants with those coupons and tried them on at home, I realized that they would have fit a man with the belly of a tub but were twice too wide for me. (311–12)

The German army is unable to provide the individual soldier with the necessary equipment; it cannot separate the necessary from the superfluous. In March 1946, Doderer reminisces about the infamous German annexation of Austria in March 1938: "Eight years ago today, Austria lost its independence and found itself under Prussian-German rule. Swarms of military overflowed 'Greece's tender border,' installing administrative offices. They assessed, ruled, and administered, transforming everything more and more, as we were forced to realize. And how quickly did they replace our yellow mailboxes with their red ones, while right after them the torturers in plainclothes arrived, the agents of the people of the judges and executioners (413)." Doderer, quoting Karl Kraus's transformation of a "people of poets and thinkers" (Volk der Dichter und Denker) into a "people of judges and executioners" (Volk der Richter und Henker), remembers the German torturers.[162] But for Doderer, not only the judges and executioners are torturers; civilians,—that is, civil servants and administrators—fill these roles as well. The interconnectedness of "assessing" (taxieren), "ruling" (schalten), and "administrating" (verwalten) characterizes the total state, which is defined, not by a specific ideology or political form of organization, but by the conflation of rule and administration, of *walten* and *verwalten*. Here, Doderer is in line with Theodor W. Adorno, who in *Minima Moralia* claims: "By tracing the absolutely particular interests of each individual, the nature of the collective in a false society can be most accurately studied."[163] Doderer's violent outbursts of rage constitute more than just a mere idiosyncrasy or pathology; they can be read as a symptom of the aggression inherent in the false society of the total state. Adorno continues: "One need only observe outbursts in which the individual asserts himself energetically against his environment, for instance rage. The enraged man always appears as the gang-leader of his own self, giving his unconscious the order to pull no punches, his eyes shining with the satisfaction of speaking for the many that he himself is. The more someone has espoused the cause of his own aggression, the more perfectly he represents the repressive principle of society. In this sense more than in any other, perhaps, the proposition is true that the most individual is the most general."[164] Adorno's critique of the rationalization of reason revolves around the diagnosis of late capitalism as the blind reduction of the individual to the general: that is, the suppression of the nonidentical and incommensurable by instrumental reason. In moments of anger and rage, structural violence personifies itself in the furious individual. But while in Doderer rage equals the refusal to perceive openly, Adorno sees a potential of liberation in rage if it is sublimated into creative energy: "Talent is perhaps nothing other than successfully sublimated rage, the capacity to convert energies once intensified beyond measure to destroy recalcitrant objects, into the concentration of patient observation.... Does not the artist himself feel himself, amid the transports of creation, brutalized, 'working furiously'? Indeed, is not such fury necessary to free oneself from confinement and the fury of confinement?"[165] Transforming intense anger caused by recalcitrant objects into a *furor poeticus*, converting anger's destruction into production—poiesis—allows the subject to free him- or herself from the constraints and confinement imposed on it by a world of resistant, if not malicious objects. For Adorno, fury and artistic inspiration are closely related and contain the promise of freedom and liberation, while in the case of Doderer, the angry subject dissociates him- or herself more and more from reality by getting lost in the "second reality" of "pseudological space."[166]

Adorno's focus on the unconscious aggressive libidinal forces that manifest themselves in rage and consequently in art, and that carry the possibility of a liberation, echoes Doderer's explanation for the hatred of Germans. Under the title "Hatred of Germans, Its Origins" (Deutschenhass, seine Ursachen), written in December 1944 in *Tangents*, Doderer typifies Germans as being able to act only directly and consciously, a limitation that leads to inhumanity: "The German constantly acts in extension of his conscious thought (because this on its own can, in the end, lead to nothing but action) and thereby always ends up in the same trajectory, namely that of inhumanity" (260). Germany's enemies perceive this schematic and inhuman approach, exemplified in the impersonal bureaucratic system that erases all individuality, with horror and disgust: "Germany's enemies, who in their practice are not always human themselves, have at least kept the remainder of an indirect and unconscious, that is, highly personal, relationship to life, which, as long as it is alive, jumps like a rabbit in stride. To align and stretch out such zigzagging into a straight line produces horror and disgust" (260). The lack of apperception, which for Doderer happens unconsciously, leads directly into the inhumanity of the total state. Here everything is conscious and abstract, devoid of an immediate relationship to life. Its incalculable fluctuations are brought under the rule of measure and order. Life's irregularities are "fixed, vexed," and "tormented" ["fixiert, vexiert," and "tormentiert"] (295). The zigzagging of everyday life, which relates to concrete reality, is painfully straightened out into an abstract line that excludes anything that is not consciously assessed and valued. The Germans replace a qualitative relationship to life, which Doderer often describes in terms of an analogy of inside and outside (referring to Thomas Aquinas's concept of *analogia entis*), with a quantitative relationship that allows immediate action.

After World War II, for Doderer the Austrian civil servant serves as an example of a successful analogical combination of inside and outside, form and content. In the 1947 essay "Rosa Chymica

Austriaco-Hispanica," Doderer delineates an idea of Austria as a chemical compound of different political and historical tendencies, personified by the figure of the Viennese civil servant: "When today an Austrian civil servant carefully adds one sheet of paper to the other, lightning quick, unconscious and discreet, thereby implicating the nuclear core of a 'Chief and State Plays' in this minor act, he gains form and decor."[167] The juxtaposition of Austria to Germany is exemplified by the difference between German government agency and Austrian civil service. The Austrian civil servant of Doderer's imagination creates order, not by following abstract rules, but by a gesture encapsulating knowledge that transcends the blind application of laws. In the careful method of arranging pieces of paper, a different form of administration appears. "Quick," "unconscious," and "discreet," the Austrian civil servant is embedded within a time-space continuum, connecting past, present, and future as well as central Europe and the rest of the world. He is the anachronistic remnant of the Habsburg Empire's idea of convention and politeness. Adorno in *Minima Moralia*, written around the same time as Doderer's reflections, defines this form of tact as "the discrimination of differences."[168] German bureaucracy, by contrast, is marked by a "false elaboratedness" (falsche Ausführlichkeit,) trying to account for even the minutest details but thereby losing a sense of form and confounding the superfluous with the necessary.[169] The German principles of impoliteness and directness support, to quote Adorno again, "what is most universal, naked external power, to triumph even in the most intimate constellation."[170] For Doderer in his postwar essays, the idea of Austria, as personified in the civil servant, constitutes a place of intersecting geographical, ethnographical, and political tendencies, a "golden section" between heterogeneous forces and influences. The Viennese administration is the site of overlap and interference, creating "chemical moments" (chymische Augenblicke), where inside and outside, past and present, coincide and where the subject, as well as the institution, apperceives concrete reality.[171] The Austrian bureaucratic system is not *overorganized* like the Prussian one but appears in "ideal balance" (idealischer Balance).[172] Form and content are one; the civil servant's discretion can unconsciously differentiate between what is superfluous and what is necessary. In the context of this imaginary ideal of Austrian bureaucracy, it is not surprising that it is Dr. Schajo, a civil servant, who invents and performs the most humane and gentle form of anger treatment.

In *The Merowingians*, the torments of German bureaucracy in Austria do not end in 1945 but show a lasting impact that only fades away slowly:

> In the Thousand Year Reich at that time, and much more so after its expiration, the offices displayed an uncanny virulence that has somewhat abated since then, at least, so that many of these institutions have returned to that calm, self-serving existence that in better times they once led; without wanting, continuously, to prove to themselves and the public their necessity and indispensability, that no one believed in anyway. But around 1950, it had not yet come so far. The fine "zilking" of the civil servants penetrated the sleep of the people, who lived in unceasing defensive foreboding of having to sacrifice many hours to waiting through visits in public offices in order to prevent official intervention and damage. (111–20)[173]

The archaic verb *zilken*, which Grimm's dictionary defines as "peeping, bleeping, cries of young birds," must be understood as a form of needling and prodding that manifests itself in unnecessary delays and other bureaucratic harassments.[174] Most of Dr. Horn's rage-sick patients "were delivered to him by way of the public offices and agencies with which they . . . were continuously involved" (25). Or, to put it more bluntly: "Trembling with rage, people came from the public offices" (26). It is not only the *zilken* itself that causes rage, but even more the people's constant attempts to fend off bureaucratic intrusions, resembling Siebenkäs's desperate efforts to block out the noise of his wife sweeping the floor. In the context of cathartic therapies of rage, Doderer, in *Repertorium,* imagines a visit to a post office as a possible trigger for the ignition and abreaction of anger. He describes this "means of creating, with skill and diligence, fury and wrath from within themselves and then increasing both to their highest power of affect" (273) as follows: "We can, for example, imagine a postal worker, who from his counter window suddenly utters a poisonous insolence against us. We have not said a word, we remain silent, we diplomatically control ourselves. The counter window is suddenly being thrown down. Already, the imaginative rage swells. We move on to the supervisor, still calm and collected, reporting the incident politely. But the supervisor immediately interrupts, taking the side of the postal worker. We keep still, stating only the facts because we intend to pursue the issue to the next person in command and, if necessary, even further" (273–74). Just imagining an encounter with a hostile civil servant is enough to artificially induce rage, making the

Igniting Anger

subject go postal. Artificially induced outbreaks of anger make it possible to determine the "essence of rage" (273) and provide a model of dealing with real instances of vexation. After one has intensified an artificial rage to its highest degree, it turns into "a powerless one and therefore one of the worst kind. . . . But never again will it be possible from now on to accept fully and completely, like an irresistible fate, the condition that we were ourselves in a position to artificially bring about" (274). The imagination—as a means to ignite and abreact anger—is in the service, like the institute of Hulesch & Quenzel, of an "educational intention" (168). Exercising anger provides a pedagogical means by which human beings can exist in a hostile environment. Once the subject has experienced the power of creating powerlessness, he or she can use this insight against future fits of rage. In these moments, what is described in *Repertorium* as the "ridiculousness of matter" (272) becomes visible and the "great dignity of the whole business" in the *Merowingians* (168) becomes readable: POST RABIEM RISUS.

Epilogue

> Much will be gained if [psychoanalysis] can succeed in transforming hysterical misery into common unhappiness.
> —Josef Breuer and Sigmund Freud, *Studies on Hysteria*

THE ENERGETIC IMPERATIVE

Around 1900, following Julius Robert Mayer's research on the laws of thermodynamics and his later discovery of processes of ignition, the German chemist Wilhelm Ostwald developed a general theory of *energetics*. It broadened and expanded the first two laws of thermodynamics, which state the conservation of energy and the general tendency toward entropy, beyond the realm of physics, mechanics, and chemistry to the life sciences and even the social sciences and the humanities, as the title "The Energetic Foundations of Cultural Studies" (Die energetischen Grundlagen der Kulturwissenschaft) from 1909 suggests.[1] Ostwald introduces a "classification of pure sciences"[2] that differentiates between sciences of order (logic, mathematics, geometry), sciences of energy (mechanics, physics, chemistry), and sciences of life (physiology, psychology, cultural studies). The latter two types of science (energy and life), according to Ostwald's schema, are ruled by a specific concept of energy.

In the programmatic article "The Energetic Imperative," Ostwald describes his approach as the "application of the second principle of energetics to all events and especially to all human actions."[3] This universal application of energetics refers to a doctrine that classifies all life forms (plants, animals, humans), as well as inanimate machines, as energy-transforming entities: "All events in the world can be described in terms of a transformation of energy out of its present state into other forms."[4] Energy is transformed, utilized for "specific purposes of life."[5] The more efficiently this transformation is realized, the better the purposes achieved. Ostwald transfers this rule of efficiency in the process of energy transformation to human life:

> For the person who sets himself this task—to treat the whole of nature and even his fellow man as efficiently and purposefully as possible—there follows a general rule for such comportment. This rule instructs him to convert free energy as efficiently, that is to say, as thoroughly, as possible into the form desired for the purpose and to check constantly on the configuration and settings and, where necessary, amend them so that the magnitude of purposive energy that is gained from a given magnitude of free energy in raw form is as large as possible. One can summarize this general tendency, or rather this general task of all human doing and acting, in a short phrase, which I, with reference to the Kantian categorical imperative, have suggested calling the *energetic imperative* and which reads: Don't squander any energy, exploit it.[6]

Ostwald's slight shift from "universal tendency" (allgemeine Tendenz) to "universal task" (allgemeine Aufgabe) demonstrates his move from a strictly descriptive model to a prescriptive one. Efficiency in utilizing energy provides a measure not only for hierarchically distinguishing higher from lower forms of life, and advanced technology from primitive tools, but moreover functions as the "most universal rule of all human action."[7] By explicitly referring to Immanuel Kant's categorical imperative, Ostwald translates the descriptive laws of thermodynamics into prescriptive rules of morality. Ethics consists of relating to others (as well as to nature) in the most purposeful way. Therefore it is one's ethical task to convert energy as efficiently as possible. To relate to others ethically, that is, efficiently, one has to constantly control and correct one's own energetic economy. Living the good life requires modes of self-examination and self-correction, guaranteeing the most purposeful utilization of the limited resource of free energy. Rage and other emotional eruptions in this context must be understood as inefficient, useless conversions. The angry individual does not follow the energetic imperative: energy is squandered instead of being exploited. In the essay "Practical Philosophy" (Praktische Philosophie), Ostwald cites an episode from the life of one of his readers (a businessman) who was able to control his anger using the energetic imperative: "Since I have become acquainted with the energetic imperative, I've done much better business than before. For I am, unfortunately, a somewhat nervous man and used to react furiously in the conflicts that inevitably arise with my business associates, and I lost in this way many valuable relationships. When I now want to get worked up, I say to myself: don't squander any energy! And can then settle the matter, which on many occasions has already afforded me considerable advantage."[8] It is no coincidence that Ostwald narrates the story of a businessman to exemplify his energetic ethics. The development and application of the energetic imperative must be placed within a larger context of attempts to rationalize and improve the productivity of capitalist industrial society. The emblem of this ideology of efficiency is Frederick Winslow Taylor's *Principles of Scientific Management*.[9] Managing the self according to an energetic imperative, rather than being an abstract moral law, is part of a rationalizing program directed at making the life of the individual subject to economic imperatives. Self-government and self-regulation do not create a free, autonomous self but are in the service of practices that shape subjects to become more productive elements of capitalist society. Not surprisingly, in stating his generalizing claims, Ostwald highlights the relationship of science, aesthetics, and ethics to economy: "We should not have to switch over our spirit [Geist] when we move from science to art, and we should be able to apply the same principles for our ethical action as for our economic activity."[10] From this perspective, the self is not an end in itself but always the means toward an end. Kant's definition of the categorical imperative states: "Act in such a way that you treat humanity, whether in your own person or in the person of any other, never merely as a means to an end, but always at the same time as an end."[11] In contrast, Ostwald's expansion of energetics into the realm of ethics calls for a treatment of humanity in oneself and in others as a means to increase the efficiency of energy conversion; human beings are therefore never ends in themselves. To act ethically means to preserve and utilize the scarce resource of energy as efficiently as possible.

PSYCHOTECHNICS AND ITS DISCONTENTS

The applicability of energetic principles in the realm of ethics and all other "Kulturwissenschaften," as defined by Ostwald, stems from a fundamental analogy of human beings and other animals to machines. They all function as "transformers of energy" (Energietransformatoren).[12] In the essay "Machines and Organisms" (Maschinen und Lebewesen) Ostwald identifies the conversion of raw energy for specific purposes as the principle that governs organisms as well as machines: "Both machines and organisms are transformers of energy, and their purpose is to convert energies as efficient as possible."[13] The less energy is wasted, that is, not used for a purpose, the higher the efficiency of a machine: "The more the use energy [Nutzenergie] gained from the same amount of raw energy [Rohenenergie], the better the machine."[14] Humans and machines adhere to the same principle of making use of energy in the most efficient way. Just as there are more and less intelligent people, whom Ostwald differentiates according to their (in)ability to transform nutrition into mental work, there are more and less efficient machines, characterized by different energy efficiencies. Hence the development of technology and the evolution of organisms can be compared, "since we know that the same task is at stake in both cases, namely the most efficient transformation of energy, a task that is not accomplished all at once but over the slow course of a progressive approximation."[15] "Social Energeticism" (Rabinbach), in this sense, must be understood as a form of Social Darwinism. The ethical imperative to use energy as efficiently as possible is a call for a process of adaptation. The full and complete transformation of energy is the unattainable telos that all machines and humans strive for: "One grasps that the thing *can* be better made and also, therefore, that it *must* be better made."[16] Humans, animals, and machines exist under the constant pressure to improve, to increase their efficiency by minimizing the loss of energy. For Stefan Rieger, quoting Niklas Luhmann, this "capacity for enhancement of the human" (Steigerbarkeit des Menschen) marks a specifically modern moment in the history of subjectivity: "*Psychical capabilities, competences, cognitive complexity, achievements in developmental logic and so on* have come to be the focus of human's capacity for enhancement, which has its center in the concretion of discursive events and therefore beyond mere metaphorics."[17] Psychic abilities and competences are not natural to human beings; one must cultivate, train, and organize them according to specific rules and procedures. The self becomes an object of continuous reflection, intervention, and adjustment. These strategies of self-improvement can be described in terms of Michel Foucault's *The History of Sexuality* as a form of *care of the self.*

Around 1900, these *technologies of the self* manifest themselves most explicitly in the field of psychotechnics. Hugo Münsterberg, a German American psychologist, coined this term in *Basics of Psychotechnology (Grundzüge der Psychotechnik)* from 1914 to describe the field of applied psychology, which aimed to determine and improve the mental and physical aptitude of workers to perform in their workplace. The goal of psychotechnics, according to Münsterberg, is a "transformation of the psycho-physical capacity for performance" of the worker.[18] "The task of psychotechnics," summarizes Andreas Killen, "was to bring about the closest possible meshing of the human with the mechanical agents of productivity, thus to better integrate workers into the social-technical circuitry of modern industrial civilization."[19]

The improvement of the worker's mental and physical capacities must not be misunderstood as a mere disciplinary force relation: it was also aimed at individualizing the self. The goal of psychotechnicians like Hugo Münsterberg and Fritz Giese was a transformation of the worker's psyche that would not be experienced as limiting or encroaching. This aspect differentiated their theories from those of Taylor, for example, who represented for most European and especially German proponents of psychotechnology an approach that did not sufficiently take the individual human being's abilities and needs into account. In fact, psychotechnics can appear as the exact opposite of merely disciplinary measures of regulation, namely as the realization of the individual's potential, in that it aims at promoting self-fulfillment and the attainment and enjoyment of autonomy. To reach this state of happiness, living as a free individual, the self has to acquire certain "ways of inspecting oneself, accounting for oneself, and working upon oneself."[20] Regulation and standardization are not applied from an outside authority but emanate from the self. The relationship between power and individual is not exclusively repressive but productive. Psychotechnics attempts to install a government of individualization by the self for the self. The subject becomes its own object on which it can perform different operations of control, regulation, and management. These individualizing technologies "enable one to construe a form of family life, education, or production that simultaneously maximizes the capacities of individuals, their personal contentment, and the efficiency of the institution."[21] As an ensemble of procedures of objectification and subjectification, psychotechnics expands the reach of applied psychology from the field of scientific management in the industrialized workplace to the "everyday individuality of everybody."[22] The whole human being in all its relations (to itself and others) falls under the imperative of self-government. Andreas Killen writes: "The German science of work would replace the 'human motor' model with a concern for the 'whole person,' body and mind."[23] The production and codification of individuality do not take place only in specific disciplinary institutions like the jail, the asylum, or the clinic as analyzed by Foucault. Instead, as a psychotechnics of the self, "psychopower" extends to all aspects of the social as well as the psychic life of every human being.[24] To reach the goal of maximum efficiency, human beings must design their encounters with tools and machines of their work environment as well as of their everyday life in such a way as to produce as little friction and discontent as possible. Self-rationalization becomes a mode of training body and mind to prepare the self to interact with machines with the least possible disruption. For this to happen, man and machine have to resemble each other. Psychotechnology, according to Friedrich Kittler, "relays psychology and media technology under the pretext that each psychic apparatus is also a technological one."[25]

In "Civilization and Its Discontents," published in 1930, Sigmund Freud discusses the possibility of technology to protect the life of the individual, among other things, "from the external world, which may rage against us with overwhelming and merciless forces of destruction."[26] Freud in this context defines technology broadly as an "art of living" (79) that includes techniques "recommended by the various schools of worldly wisdom" (77). Technology in this broad sense, therefore, refers not only to tools, instruments, and machines but also to various *technologies of the self*. In this sense, it is reminiscent of psychotechnics, another expansive concept of technology. Fritz Giese in *Psychotechnik* maintains that its method has "in no way only to do with technics, with industry."[27] Freud as well as Münsterberg, Giese, and others attempts to provide practical solutions and treatments for the deficiencies, anxieties, and discontents of modern industrialized society. Is happiness for the individual human being possible, and how can it be achieved?

In the second section of "Civilization and Its Discontents," Freud asks what human beings generally understand as the meaning of life: "We will therefore turn to the less ambitious question of what men themselves show by their behavior to be the purpose and intention of their lives. What do they demand of life and wish to achieve in it? The answer to this can hardly be in doubt. They strive after happiness, they want to become happy and to remain so" (76). As James Strachey reports, Freud had originally intended to give his essay the title "Das Unglück in der Natur."[28] Maybe one reason why Freud became reluctant to give his essay this name can be found in the ambiguity of the German word *Unglück*. While Freud's text mostly deals with *Unglück* in the sense of misfortune and being unhappy, the word can also denote accidents, mishaps, or disasters. It is this catastrophic element of modern culture, understood as the uncontrollable intrusion of contingency, about which Freud, at least in this essay, is conspicuously silent.[29] The phenomenon Freud is interested in appears not only as *Unglück* in the sense of "accident" or "disaster" but as an experience of anxiety in the most *behaglich* (comfortable, homely) environment, as part of the everyday life of the *normal* human being. Much like the words *heimlich* und *unheimlich* as Freud analyzes them, *behaglich* und *unbehaglich* cannot be separated.[30]

Freud's interest in the (im)possibility of happiness in modernity, switching from the realm of nature to that of culture, becomes even more apparent in a handwritten list of possible titles for the different sections of "Civilization and Its Discontents:" "'Das Streben nach dem Glück" (The Striving for Happiness), "Die Quellen des Leidens" (The Sources of Suffering), "Glücksverlust bei Triebbeherrschung" (Loss of Happiness from the Control of Instinct), "Das Glück in der Liebe" (Happiness in Love), and "Die Kultur als Leidensquelle" (Civilization as a Source of Suffering).[31] As Ilse Grubrich-Simitis notes, the one notion missing from this list is "Unbehagen."[32] Despite all technological advances, the life of the individual human being is still characterized by feelings of discomfort, anxiety, and unhappiness:

> During the last few generations mankind has made an extraordinary advance in the natural sciences and in their technical application and has established his control over nature in a way never before imagined. The single steps of this advance are common knowledge and it is unnecessary to enumerate them. Men are proud of those achievements, and have a right to be. But they seem to have observed that this newly-won power over space and time, this subjugation of the forces of nature, which is the fulfillment of a longing that goes back thousands of years, has not increased the amount of pleasurable satisfaction which they may expect from life and has not made them feel happier. (87–88)

Freud does not argue against technology's advances. On the contrary, "By his science and technology, man has brought about on the earth, on which he first appeared as feeble animal organism and on which each individual of his species must once more make its entry ('oh inch of nature!') as a helpless suckling—these things do not only sound like a fairy tale, they are an actual fulfillment of every—or of almost every—fairy-tale wish" (91).

The omnipotence and omniscience that primitives project into their gods, modern man "almost" embodies himself:

> Long ago he [man] formed an ideal conception of omnipotence and omniscience, which he embodied in his gods. To these gods he attributed everything that seemed unattainable to his wishes, or that was forbidden to him. One may say, therefore, that these gods were cultural ideas. Today he has come very close to the attainment of this ideal, he has almost become a god himself. Only, it is true, in the fashion in which ideals are usually attained according to the general judgment of humanity. Not completely; in some respects not at all, in others only half way. Man has, as it were, become kind of prosthetic God. When he puts on all his auxiliary organs he is truly magnificent; but those organs have not grown on to him and they still give him much trouble at times. (91–92)

It is exactly those auxiliary organs that make the human "truly magnificent" but that also "give him much trouble." Avital Ronell observes: "The 'almost' in this sentence provides a space for a somewhat striking difference, marking the incompletion of any subject's ration of infinity. Freud's rhetoric does not depict man attaining a "poore inch" of self-inflating divinity; rather, the detachable tool itself is inspired with divinity. Only the 'almost' belongs to man, whereas the 'become a god himself' attaches properly to his 'auxiliary organs.'"[33]

The human being as an ensemble of animate and inanimate matter, humanity and divinity, man and machine, itself becomes an uncanny being. As in E. T. A. Hoffmann's tale "The Sandman"—Freud's paradigmatic figuration of the uncanny—the various technological "extensions of man" do not lead to a harmonious amalgamation of man and machine. Despite the divine inspiration of the tool, writes Ronell, human beings remain in the realm of the "almost." Anxiety, defined in a Freudian sense as an affective response to danger, caused by an uncontrollable environment, returns. The inability to project a complete image of the self that would harmoniously amalgamate the human being and technology can be traced back to Freud's own prosthetic existence. Because of his oral cancer, which destroyed part of his soft palate, he had to wear a prosthesis. Ernest Jones reports on the pain and irritation caused by it: "The huge prosthesis, a sort of magnified denture or obturator, designed to shut off the mouth from the nasal cavity, was a horror; it was labeled 'the monster.' . . . Then for the instrument to fulfill its purpose of shutting off the yawning cavity above, and so make speaking and eating possible, it had to fit fairly tightly. This, however, produced constant irritation and sore places until its presence was unbearable. But if left out for more than a few hours the tissues would shrink, and the denture could no longer be replaced without being altered."[34] Where human being and inanimate object, subject and prosthesis, come into contact, "sore places" occur. The technical artifact, inserted to improve the everyday life of the cancer patient Freud, becomes "unbearable": a "monster" has invaded his body. The prosthesis, in the sense of the Latin word *monstrum*, becomes a sign designating an aberrant occurrence outside the natural order. Furthermore, it is anthropomorphized and animated, taking the shape of a hideous creature on the border of life and death, causing—in addition to physical harm—emotions of anxiety, fear, and terror. The fairy tale of a complete fulfillment of all wishes turns into a nightmare populated by monsters, uncanny figurations, and fantastic incarnations of the repressed.

In this sense, the prosthesis inserted into Freud's jaw paradigmatically shows how technology cannot be reduced to the "outer" environment of human beings. As an "extension of man," it becomes part of the imaginary constitution of the human being's identity.[35] The self, in the Lacanian sense, is not a given but the product of a projection creating a specific imaginary body image. Analogously, the self as the product of self-regulatory and self-governing procedures, as analyzed by Foucault, constantly needs to produce images of itself, anticipating the future goals of self-sufficiency and autonomy. It becomes, in the literal sense of the words a project and a projection. *Technologies of the self* rely on specific imaginings of wholeness and identity and therefore create simulations of the self, virtual realities of a harmonious interaction between man and his extensions.[36] As Freud's use of "the monster" to describe his prosthesis indicates, these virtual realities can appear in the form of malicious objects, fantasies invested with affect. As much as one attempts to utilize one's imaginings so as to produce a stable relation between subject and object, psychic system and environment, it becomes clear that these anthropomorphized images can take on a life on their own. Like Michel Serres's parasite, phantoms, monsters, and other uncanny figurations infiltrate the imaginary mapping of the self.[37] They interrupt the psychic system, functioning as a "mischievous operator and, in the final analysis, provocative participator."[38]

VIRTUAL ENGINEERING

Ostwald's theory of energetics and Freud's psychoanalytic conceptualization of psychic energies are symptomatic of a more general turn from a mechanical to an energetic worldview at the turn of the century. In *Ströme und Strahlen: Das langsame Verschwinden der Materie um 1900*, Christoph Asendorf has shown how in various fields such as art, philosophy, physics, medicine, and architecture "nervous geometries" of energetic flows and currents, vibrations and waves replace concepts of solid matter.[39]

Nevertheless, it is the real, the resistance of matter (Benjamin), its obtrusiveness and obstinacy, that provokes the subject to produce virtual realities of the world and of him- or herself. Virtuality as a "conjectural practice" in this sense must not be misunderstood as a "Farewell to the Corporeal" (Abschied vom Körperlichen) or the absence of material reality; on the contrary, it follows from the interaction between subject and object, system and environment, body and world.[40] Things do not simply disappear, transformed into electric currents or abstract economies of exchange. As Asendorf notes of Georg Simmel's *Philosophy of Money*, things transformed into circulating commodities leave "a light feeling of uncanniness in the face of the sheer 'quantity' of things—he [Simmel] speaks of the 'independence' of the things crowded around, of their service as fetishes, of a feeling that the things interfere with one's freedom."[41] The seemingly fantastic ascription of malicious agency to inanimate objects can be interpreted as a reaction to this experience of the uncanny. It is a manifestation of a human tendency to produce virtual realities in the face of an antagonistic, inhospitable lifeworld. The turn from a mechanical to an energetic worldview, or, in Ernst Cassirer's terms, from substance to function, coincides with the recurrence of seemingly irrational, fantastic images.[42] Fantasy in this context must not be misunderstood as a mere *terminus technicus* from the tradition of idealist aesthetics. Instead, one could, following Stefan Rieger, speak of the universalization of imagination, which he calls *virtuality*.

From Laurence Sterne to Jean Paul, Friedrich Theodor Vischer, and Heimito von Doderer, the interruption of daily routines by unexpected, random occurrences and the accompanying affects of anger and rage are compensated for by the production of fictions. These virtual realities can take such different shapes as Uncle Toby's hobbyhorse, Siebenkäs's humor, A.E.'s mythology of malicious objects, and

Epilogue

Dr. Horn's cathartic anger treatment. Imagination, which, in this tradition exceeds the realm of aesthetics, functions as therapy. Freud in "Analysis of a Phobia in a Five-Year-Old Boy" stresses the importance of "anticipatory ideas" in the therapeutic process of psychoanalysis: "In a psycho-analysis the physician always gives his patient (sometimes to a greater and sometimes to a lesser extent) the conscious anticipatory ideas by the help of which he is put in a position to recognize and to grasp the unconscious material."[43] According to Rieger's study of the history of virtuality in the early twentieth century, the various modes of anger management, projective humor, or aesthetic imagination discussed here expose a fundamental anthropological modality: "The way in which people interact with the world and with each other, the way in which they perceive things, in which things present themselves or make themselves visible, even to the way in which they shape their lives, . . .—all this is only comprehensively describable in terms of what is at once conceived of and called *virtuality*."[44] Central to these virtual modes of dealing with the world and dealing with oneself are the notions of imagination, fantasy, and projection.[45] The self is not a substantial entity but produces itself in a process of pro-jecting.

The ascription of malice to objects as a form of "metaphorical regulation" (bildhafter Steuerung), as a mode of coping with reality, is based on the ability to produce fantasies and simulacra.[46] The private mythology developed by the protagonist in Vischer's *Another One*, for example, not only provides an explanation for the series of accidents afflicting him but also depotentializes their threatening insistence. Accidents, although still painful, at least have a reason: they are based on the hostile intentions of evil spirits possessing the objects of everyday life. What is real and manifest, the resistance of matter, appears in the form of that which is merely possible, virtual.

The engineer Henry Petroski points out that what governs the invention and design of new objects is not the commonsensical principle "Form follows function" but the principle "Form follows failure": "What form does follow is the real and perceived failure of things as they are used to do what they are supposed to do. Clever people in the past, whom we today might call inventors, designers, or engineers, observed the failure of existing things to function as well as might be imagined. By focusing on the shortcomings of things, innovators altered those items to remove the imperfections, thus producing new, improved objects."[47] By focusing on the "shortcomings of things," the engineer can envision a new and improved object. The failure of a tool makes the engineer imagine a better model. Failure, accidents, and catastrophes trigger the invention of new, improved objects whose former flaws and imperfections have been eliminated. The idea of an "evolution of things" contests the Platonic model of *techne,* which perceives of every object only as the manifestation of a stable, unchanging idea. For Ernst Cassirer in the 1930 essay "Form and Technology" (Form und Technik), technology exposes the principal difference between idea and its manifestation, the ideal and the real. The act of invention requires the inventor to compare what is with what is possible. The evolution of things "does not simply take place under the constant supervision, the regulation and tutelage of the real; rather, it demands that we constantly go back from the 'real' to the realm of the 'possible' and regard the real itself under the image of the possible."[48]

To develop a new tool, for example, the inventor must compare and measure the actual artifact with his or her idea of it. The "adequatio rei et intellectus" is not immediately given but needs to be produced in a process of continuing adaptation between idea and reality. Hence engineering could be characterized as a technique of the virtual, a project directed toward an open future, imagining what could be. Cassirer writes: "Technical production never binds itself to this pure facticity, to the given face of object; rather, it operates according to the law of a pure anticipation, a foresight, that reaches into the future and brings about a new future."[49] What the engineer imagines and eventually produces are not mere subjective fantasies, detached from reality, but instead things that appear as objective, that are virtual but by no means indeterminate or vague: "Technology does not ask in the first instance about what is, but about what *can* be. But this 'can' does not indicate any mere supposition or conjecture; rather, it expresses itself as an assertive claim and an assertion of certainty."[50]

The history of things is always also a history of virtual things, imaginary artifacts without which there would be no technological progress. In an essay entitled "The Concept of Reality and the Possibility of the Novel" (Wirklichkeitsbegriff und Möglichkeit des Romans), Hans Blumenberg mentions one type of "Wirklichkeitsbegriff," based on the resistance of matter: "Reality," is understood as "that which is not compliant to the subject and offers him resistance. . . . Reality is here the completely and utterly unavailable, that which does not allow itself to be treated as mere material for manipulation and so subordinated to the constant regulation of appearances. Instead, it is only apparently and temporarily taken into the service of technologization, in order then to reveal itself, according to its own overwhelming laws [überwältigende Eigengesetzlichkeit] and its tyrannizing power over its producers, as a *factum brutum*."[51] Although Blumenberg develops this characterization of a specifically modern relationship between reality and virtuality in the context of a discussion of the genre of the novel, he nevertheless points out a more general anthropological insight. His *pointe* consists in showing that resistance is not reducible to sheer matter and that one's own projections, imaginations, and constructions gain independence. The human being as a "phantom-producing animal" (Rieger) falls under the tyranny of his or her own fantasies. Instead of alleviating the pains of everyday life, constructs like malicious objects gain a life of their own. Virtuality produces its own resistance. Virtual reality is anything but the phantasmatic space in which everything is possible. To quote Anselm Haverkamp's reconstruction of the relationship between latency and representation: "Not everything is possible; rather, everything shows in this kind of possibility the unreality of every possible realization. In reality, this flood of the possible is the flood of unrealized afterimages, a postmodern gallery of the phantasms of modernity, upon the backside of which reality becomes real in another way."[52]

In *Traces (Spuren)*, a collection of short stories, reflections, and observations, Ernst Bloch identifies the "backside of things" as the specific site that allows for the perception of the unrealized potential of things in modernity. Bloch examines an "ungeheuerliches Gefühl" (uncanny feeling) that accompanies the human being's encounter with everyday objects. This experience of the uncanny expresses itself in questions like: "What do things do without us? How does the room look once we have left?"[53] Where one is most at home is where the uncanny often lurks. Tools and instruments that are hiding in their smooth functionality reappear in uncanny, anxiety-inducing forms as malicious objects. They not only have an unfulfilled potential to improve and increase their functionality but are also characterized by an ability, lurking on their backside, to turn into demonic, uncanny figures.

In the vignette "The First Locomotive," Bloch narrates an incident during the invention of the first locomotive by George Stephenson that brings out the uncanny character of technology that is hidden beneath its smooth surface: "Only the accident recalls it [the uncanny character of technology] to memory: the crack of the crash, the bang of the explosion, the screams of crushed people, in short an ensemble that lacks a civilized railway schedule."[54] In accidents, the idyllic harmony between human beings and inanimate artifacts, between idea and reality, is violently disrupted. The "backside of things" appears suddenly and violently, turning against human beings.[55] While the gothic tradition of ghost stories is irrevocably over, for Bloch, in modernity uncanniness appears within the technological artifacts themselves.[56] In the everyday, normal functioning of modern urban society is concealed a *"magical sphere"* of demonic, uncanny apparitions: "Nonetheless, the more advanced and unfrivolous technology is, the more mysteriously it mingles with the realm of taboo, with mists and vapors, unearthly velocity, golem-robots, and bolts of lightning. And so it comes into contact with things that were formerly conceived of as belonging to the *magical sphere*."[57] After witnessing the physical destruction his invention caused as well as the psychological devastation (several people, among them a priest, went mad), Stephenson improved the locomotive by putting it on tracks, thereby channeling and directing its otherwise uncontrollable force: "But Stephenson had understood everything and built a new machine on tracks and with a driver's cab. In this way its demonic power was set on the right track; indeed it is, in the final instance, almost organic. The locomotive now runs as if on blood, hisses as if out of breath, a tamed cross-country animal in the grand style [ein großes Überlandtier großen Stils], which makes one forget the golem."[58] Putting the locomotive on tracks not only controls the movement of the machine but also has a psychological effect. It appears as an animal. Technology becomes "almost organic," its demonical underside tamed. It does not appear as a golem, as the product of a human inventor, but as a *natural*, living being. Coping with the violent, often traumatic intrusion of technology into the lifeworld of human beings (as in Bloch's presentation of Stephenson) does not consists only in the improvement of technology itself but also always implies psychological as well as rhetorical modes similar to those of anthropomorphization and personification. Technological progress, far from overcoming seemingly primitive beliefs and mythical explanations, instead reenchants the world. The demons of technology cannot be extirpated or dissolved by rational discourse but produce new "fantastic" ascriptions and projections. Hence not only the engineer whose machines fail but even more the successful engineer feels a certain uneasiness with regard to his inventions: "And although no inventor acts like a magician in terms of either character or method, still the inventor's *successes* are not only wonder-inspiring but *uncanny.*"[59] Successful technological invention and magic, although not identical, show a certain affinity. The engineer's technique resembles that of magic, causing wonder and fear. Technological projects, much like visions and literary fantasies, gain a life of their own. The "demon" of technology is given a face, its violence tamed. Nevertheless, the success of technological projections and prosopopeias carries with it an irreducible experience of the uncanny. Every invention implies, according to Paul Virilio, the invention of an accident.[60] Every object threatens to become malicious. Virtuality, understood as a mode to cope with the resistance of matter, cannot escape a different form of obstinacy—that of its fantastic imaginations.

UNCANNY CYBERNETICS

During the middle of the twentieth century, cybernetic programs of self-regulation introduced a model of feedback control to cope with disruptions, accidents, and mishaps. This cybernetic turn installed a program of general reciprocity that is applicable to physical and social systems, to organisms and human beings. Self-governing systems are all "constructed by a common move—the translation of the world into a problem of coding, a search for a common language in which all resistance to instrumental control disappears and all heterogeneity can be submitted to disassembly, reassembly, investment and exchange."[61] What appears as disruption, disturbance, or blockage, because of the system's self-reflexive flexibility, can be translated (i.e., integrated) into a process of equalization. Its stability rests, not on inelastic rigidity, but on flexible adaptation and correction. These methods of self-observation and self-improvement, characterized by Foucault as modes of caring for oneself, reappear—minus their subjective overtones—as technological implementations of self-governance. Technologies of the self, understood as the "task of testing oneself, examining oneself, monitoring oneself in a series of clearly defined exercises," are, according to Foucault, "central to the formation of the ethical subject."[62] It is exactly these modes of testing, examining, and monitoring that not only define methods of caring for the self but reach their apex in the processes of cybernetic self-regulation.

Norbert Wiener, in *The Human Use of Human Beings* (1950), emphasizes the importance of effective communication to achieve a satisfactory degree of control for psychic as well as social systems:

> The process of receiving and of using information is the process of our adjusting to the contingencies of the outer environment, and of our living effectively within that environment. The needs and the complexity of modern life make greater demands on this process of information than ever before, and our press, our museums, our scientific laboratories, our universities, our libraries and textbooks, are obliged to meet the needs of this process or fail in their purpose. To live effectively is to live with the adequate information. Thus, communication and control belong to the essence of man's inner life, even as they belong to his life in society.[63]

Living, for Wiener, means adjusting to the "contingencies of the outer environment," so as to function "effectively." This cybernetic vision of governmentality relies on systems functioning according to the principles of feedback control. Rosenblueth, Wiener, and Bigelow, in their groundbreaking paper "Behavior, Purpose, and Teleology" (1943), define feedback as follows:

> In a broad sense [feedback] may denote that some of the output energy of an apparatus or machine is returned as input; an example is an electrical amplifier with feed-back. The feed-back is in these cases positive—the fraction of the output which reenters the object has the same sign as the original input signal. Positive feed-back adds to the input signals, it does not correct them. [...] The term feed-back is also employed in a more restricted sense to signify that the behavior of an object is controlled by the margin of error at which the object stands at a given time with reference to a relatively specific goal. The feed-back is then negative, that is, the signals from the goal are used to restrict outputs which would otherwise go beyond the goal.[64]

The models of positive and negative feedback loops allow the subject to conceptualize exceptional emotional states like anger, as well as strategies to cope with them. If a small disturbance enters a positive feedback loop, it leads to a rapid increase of the emotional intensity, causing an escalation of rage. If, on the other hand, the psychic system functions according to the principles of a negative feedback model, small disruptions do lead, not to an intensification or escalation of the disturbance, but to a corrective adjustment. Emotional equilibrium is restored. Cybernetics as a form of ethics proposes modes of living the good life and therefore primarily focuses on negative feedback control as a means of stabilization.[65] While negative feedback loops progressively adjust to the uncontrollable contingencies of the environment, positive feedback amplifies those disturbances, creating instability and eventually loss of control.

The proximity of self-regulation—as conceptualized in cybernetics—to more wide-ranging theories of governmentality in general, and to ethics in particular, can already be found in theories of biological regulation from the nineteenth and early twentieth centuries.[66] Like Ostwald's energetic imperative, the concept of homeostasis allows for the description of self-regulatory systems in organisms, the psyche, and social systems. Homeostasis, as defined by the American physiologist and biologist Walter Cannon, represents a "general principle of stabilization," constituted by "devices for maintaining constancy." In organisms, "the corrective agencies act, in the main, through a special portion of the nervous system which functions as a regulatory mechanism. For this regulation it employs, first, storage of materials as a means of adjustment between supply and demand, and, second, altered rates of continuous processes in the body."[67] Georges Canguilhem summarizes the influence of these biological models of regulation in cybernetics as follows: "The line of descent is well known: Claude Bernard *qui genuit* Cannon *qui genuit* Rosenblueth *apud* Wiener."[68] Already in its title, Cannon's most influential text, *The Wisdom of the Body*, first published in 1932, attempts to bridge the gap between the physiological and the psychological, between biology and ethics.[69] For Cannon, the body represents a specific type of wisdom; it not only has knowledge of itself but also is able to apply and make use of this knowledge. Much as a sage might use principles and philosophical doctrines to order and rule over his life, the body possesses an ability to regulate, govern, and stabilize itself.

In the last chapter of *The Wisdom of the Body*, Cannon explicitly calls for an application of the concept of biological homeostasis to society at large. For him, the "body physiologic" and the "body politic" cannot be separated. In the very last sentence, Cannon declares: "Just as social stabilization would foster the stability, both physical and mental, of the members of the social organism, so likewise it would foster their higher freedom, giving them serenity and leisure, which are the primary conditions for wholesome recreation, for the discovery of a satisfactory and invigorating social *milieu*, and for the discipline and enjoyment of individual aptitudes."[70] Jacques Lacan criticizes Freud precisely for his uncritical use of a homeostatic concept of the psyche. In *The Ego in Freud's Theory and in the Technique of Psychoanalysis, 1954–1955,* Lacan states that Freud conceptualizes psychic reality as follows: "There is a close precinct, within which a certain equilibrium is maintained, through the action of a mechanism which we now call homeostasis, which absorbs, moderates the irruption of quantities of energy coming from the external world."[71] According to Lacan, Freud believes that the psychical and physical systems of the human being function according to the same laws, namely those of "inertia" (Freud's term for homeostasis, a concept he does not invoke explicitly): that is, a dynamic model of charges, accumulations, and discharges of energy. But this regulatory model of the psycho-physical organization of the subject, which Lacan compares to the "equilibration of a machine," poses problems for Freud, which he addresses in *Beyond the Pleasure Principle*.[72] Here the symmetrical, complementary relationship between physical and psychical processes becomes questionable. What interrupts, according to Lacan, "has something disturbing about it. It is dissymmetrical. It doesn't quite fit. Something in it eludes the system of equations and the evidence borrowed from the forms of thought of the register of energetics as they were introduced in the middle of the nineteenth century."[73] It is precisely the unconscious that insistently returns in the form of a compulsion to repeat. This "insistence"—Lacan's enigmatic translation of Freud's notion of *Wiederholungszwang* (compulsion to repeat)—disrupts the belief in the establishment of a stable identity of the self. All attempts at (self)-regulation are affected by the insistence of the unconscious. In other words, the "law of regulation" as "discharge and return to the position of equilibrium" cannot account for the (re)emergence of uncanny, anxiety-inducing phenomena like *Unbehagen* (uneasiness) or *Unglück* (balefulness). Freud in "The Uncanny" explicitly ties the insistent experience of the compulsion to repeat to that of the uncanny:

> How exactly we can trace back to infantile psychology the uncanny effect of such similar recurrences is a question I can only lightly touch on in these pages; and I must refer the reader instead to another work [i.e., *Beyond the Pleasure Principle*, which he was writing at the same time]. For it is possible to recognize the dominance in the unconscious mind of a "compulsion to repeat" proceeding from the instinctual impulses and probably inherent in the very nature of the instincts—a compulsion powerful enough to overrule the pleasure principle, lending to certain aspects of the mind their demonic character. . . . All these considerations prepare us for the discovery that

Epilogue

whatever reminds us of this inner "compulsion to repeat" is perceived as uncanny.[74]

As the Sandman, an uncanny specter and *revenant*, returns to terrorize and finally destroy the life of Nathanael, the protagonist of Hoffmann's tale *The Sandman*, the malice and mischief of everyday objects continues to haunt a figure like A.E. from Vischer's novel *Another One*. Here it is the "insistence of the familiar which gives rise to what is uncanny."[75] Although in Vischer's demonology Hoffmann's terror is domesticated and ironized, the repetitive, returning quality of the uncanny remains. The compulsion to repeat beyond the pleasure principle disturbs the logic of an equilibrium produced by an organized series of charges and discharges. The uncanniness of malicious objects is beyond the pleasure principle insofar as it represents "the principle of regulation which enables us to inscribe the concrete functioning of man considered as a machine in a coherent system of symbolic formulations."[76] An object that "doesn't quite fit" intrudes into the regulatory system of the pleasure principle, repeatedly cropping up. As "when the little pegs refuse to go into the little holes," these instances of interruption, resisting their smooth integration into a symbolic order, cause anxiety.[77] This anxiety can manifest itself in feelings of horror (in the case of the uncanny), laughter (in jokes), or anger (in the experience of malicious objects). Rather than overcoming demonic chance, the circular logic of self-regulation creates phantoms, monsters, and demons, uncanny figurations of the repressed. They are the representations of that which refuses to be regulated and governed by "mechanisms of equilibration, of harmonization and of agreement."[78] It is in literary phantasms, slapstick routines, or pathological emotional outbursts like computer rage, that malicious objects crop up, disobeying the laws of presence and absence, the human and the machine, the animate and inanimate.

NOTES

INTRODUCTION: HOW (NOT) TO DO THINGS WITH DOORS

1. See Heidegger, *Being and Time*, 96–97: "The Greeks had an appropriate term for 'Things': pragmata—that is to say, that which one has to do with in one's concernful dealings (praxis). . . . We shall call those entities which we encounter in concern 'equipment.' In our dealings we come across equipment for writing, sewing, working, transportation, measurement."
2. See Hörisch, *Wissen der Literatur*.
3. For a discussion of the term *poetics of knowledge*, see Vogl, *Poetologien des Wissens*.
4. Doderer, "Kleine Vorbemerkung," 17.
5. Adorno, *Minima Moralia*, 40.
6. Adorno, "On Subject and Object," 140.
7. Ibid., 147.
8. The notion of "object agency" has lately been developed in such diverse fields as the sociology of scientific knowledge, anthropological aesthetics, and literary theory. See Latour, "Where Are the Missing Masses?"; Gell, *Art and Agency*; Brown, "Thing Theory."
9. Adorno, "On Subject and Object," 140.
10. Ibid.
11. Latour, "Where Are the Missing Masses?," 227. For a discussion of the similarities and differences between Adorno and Latour, see Highmore, *Ordinary Lives*, 67–72.
12. Latour, "Where Are the Missing Masses?," 235.
13. Ibid., 236.
14. Heidegger, "Thing," 172; Heidegger, *Being and Time*, 96.
15. Ibid., 97.
16. Ibid., 107, 105.
17. Ibid., 104.
18. Ibid.
19. Ibid., 102.
20. Grimm, *Deutsches Wörterbuch*, 1528.
21. Wittgenstein, *Vermischte Bemerkungen*, 136: "Die 'Tücke' des Objekts ist ein dummer Anthropomorphismus."

22. In this sense, the belief in the magical powers of malicious objects resembles—in reverse—forms of fetishization. Recently, theories of the fetish have been read as a paradigm for a new and different history of modernity. See Apter and Pietz, *Fetishism as Cultural Discourse*; Böhme, *Fetischismus und Kultur*.

23. Latour, *We Have Never Been Modern*, 129.

24. Galen, "Diagnosis and Cure," 38.

25. Ibid.

26. Recently Latour has expanded his epistemology into the realm of politics. See Latour, *Politics of Nature*.

27. Lacan, *Ethics of Psychoanalysis*, 103.

28. Ibid.

29. Foucault, "Technologies of the Self," 18.

30. See Brewer and Porter, *Consumption*.

31. Porter, *Flesh*, 291.

32. Nussbaum, *Therapy of Desire*.

33. On moral management as psychotherapy, see Porter, "Shaping Psychiatric Knowledge"; Foucault, *Madness and Civilization*. An important figure in the tradition of mechanical models is John Brown, for whom diseases originate in an imbalance of human excitability. See J. Brown, *Elements of Medicine*, 126.

34. For a discussion of the relationship between philosophy, anthropology, and medicine, see Riedel, *Anthropologie des jungen Schiller;* Koschorke, *Körperströme und Schriftverkehr*. On treatments of the whole human being, see Schings, *Ganze Mensch*.

35. Foucault, *Madness and Civilization*, 187–88.

36. Duncan Large gives an account of Germany's fascination with Sterne. He writes: "The German-speaking world took Sterne to its bosom in the late 1760s in the waning of the late Enlightenment period, and the two have never ever really fallen out since. Sterne has proved somewhat of a man for all seasons, constantly reperceived, reinvented, reappropriated by successive generations of German intellectuals and the broader reading public." See Large, "'Sterne-Bilder,'" 70.

37. See Michelsen, *Laurence Sterne*.

38. Uwe C. Steiner, although not mentioning Doderer, proposes a similar genealogy of the "literary knowledge of the thing," from the eighteenth to the twentieth century. See Steiner, "Widerstand im Gegenstand," 245: "Es gibt also ein Wissen vom Ding, das (noch) kein wissenschaftliches bzw. literaturwissenschaftliches ist. Das erhärtet ein Blick auf die epische Tradition. Ich beziehe mich hauptsächlich auf jenen Traditionsstrang, der sich mindestens zu Laurence Sterne und Jean Paul zurückverfolgen lässt und der 1878 kulminiert, als der gewesene Hegelianer Friedrich Theodor Vischer seinen bis in die 1920er Jahre eminent erfolgreichen Roman *Auch Einer* veröffentlicht."

39. Sterne, *Life and Opinions*, 646.

40. See Fleming, *Pleasures of Abandonment*.

41. Sterne, *Life and Opinions*, 184.

42. Ibid., 2.

Notes

43. Ibid., 182–83.
44. Jean Paul, "Über die natürliche Magie."
45. Müller, *Jean Pauls Ästhetik,* 81–86.
46. Cf. Tismar, *Gestörte Idyllen.*
47. For a discussion of the ambiguous status of the term *pharmakon,* see Derrida, "Plato's Pharmacy."
48. Vischer, *Auch Einer,* 509.
49. Jacques Derrida, "My Chances," 26.
50. Brown, *Sense of Things,* 5.
51. The quote here is from ibid., 4.
52. Vischer, "Mein Lebensgang," 511.
53. For a discussion of Jean Paul's influence on nineteenth-century aesthetics in general and Vischer in particular, see Müller, "Zur Bedeutung Jean Pauls." On the nineteenth-century discussion of projection, see Müller-Tamm, *Abstraktion als Einfühlung.*
54. Derrida, "My Chances," 25.
55. Sigmund Freud, *Psychopathology of Everyday Life,* 163.
56. Ibid.
57. Derrida, "My Chances," 20.
58. Freud, *Psychopathology of Everyday Life,* 257.
59. Ibid., 20.
60. Blumenberg, "Lebenswelt und Technisierung," 35. For a discussion of the technical artifact of the door as a cultural signifier, see Siegert, "Türen."
61. Blumenberg, "Lebenswelt und Technisierung," 36.
62. Ibid.
63. Ibid., 37.
64. Mayer, "Über Auslösung," 12.
65. Ibid., 16.
66. Bernays, "Grundzüge der verlorenen Abhandlung," 74.
67. Bernays, "Aristotle," 160.
68. One subcategory of the tendentious joke is the so-called *Aufsitzer* (shaggy-dog story), which etymologically is connected to *Aufsässigkeit* (obstinacy), the notion Heidegger uses to illustrate recalcitrant equipment.
69. Freud, *Jokes,* 136.
70. Ibid., 137.
71. Weber, *Legend of Freud,* 126.
72. Nietzsche's breakdown in Turin, compassionately embracing a horse, uncannily resembles the scene in Vischer's *Auch Einer* in which Albert Einhardt gets fatally injured while trying to protect a horse from being beaten. See Grimm, "Embracing Two Horses."
73. Nietzsche, *Ecce Homo,* 326.
74. Nietzsche, *Gay Science,* 139.
75. Ibid.
76. Cf. Mittasch, *Friedrich Nietzsche als Naturphilosoph;* Brusotti, *Leidenschaft der Erkenntnis.*
77. Nietzsche's theory of self-ignition not only is rooted in his reception of Mayer's "On Ignition" but also can be traced back to rhetorical models

of self-affection. For a reconstruction of these methods of self-affection in rhetoric, see Campe, "Affizieren und Selbstaffizieren," 135–52.

78. See Ostwald, *Energetische Imperativ*. See also Rieger, *Individualität der Medien*.

79. Rieger, *Individualität der Medien*, 13.

80. Doderer, *Merowingians*, 5.

81. Doderer, *Repertorium*, 273.

82. In this context, *The Merowingians* can be read as a variation of Heidegger's interpretation of the doctrine of "nihil est sine ratione" in *Der Satz vom Grund [The Principle of Reason]*. See Heidegger, *Principle of Reason*.

83. Doderer, "Sexualität und totaler Staat."

84. Luft, *Eros and Inwardness*, 158.

85. Heidegger, *Being and Time*, 97; Heidegger, "Origin of the Work," 26.

86. Doderer, *Merowingians*, 412. For an English translation of Heidegger, see the translator's notes: "'From the thinging of the thing it comes to pass and just then determines also the presence of the present.' 'But how does the thing present? The thing things. The thinging assembles.'"

87. Ibid., 413.

88. Heidegger, "Thing," 179.

89. Heidegger, *What Is a Thing?*, 38.

90. Heidegger, *Discourse on Thinking*, 54.

91. Ibid.

92. Ibid., 25.

93. Ibid., 54.

94. "New autochthony" in ibid., 53.

95. See Hörl, "Offene Maschine," 54.

96. Doderer, *Merowingians*, 168. Doderer, using Latin and English to represent ancient Rome and Anglo-American modernity, gestures toward an uncanny correspondence between Stoic anger control and the industrialized production of objects.

1. "WHEN THINGS MOVE UPON BAD HINGES": STERNE AND STOICISM

1. Sterne, *Life and Opinions*, 10–11; this and subsequent citations in the chapter are to Melvin and Joan New's edition and are given parenthetically in the text.

2. Cf. Brewer and Porter, *Consumption*. Michael Rosenblum points out Sterne's importance for the history of literary representations of the everyday. See Rosenblum, "Why What Happens," 171: "Unlike Fielding and Reynolds, Sterne sees that the quotidian is compatible with having a story worth the telling. Although the representation is not fully 'promiscuous' in the sense that Johnson fears and contemporary critics admire . . . , it nevertheless makes a contribution to the history of the everyday, a beginning at least in giving representation to what Lefebvre describes as 'the immense wealth that the humblest facts of everyday life contain.'"

3. See Hamilton, *Accident*, 69–128. Ernst Bloch in *Spuren* imagines a household diametrically opposed to that of Shandy Hall. Here, in the piece "Das Haus des Tags," human beings and things live in harmony. See Bloch, *Spuren*, 162–63: "Oder wenn das Land am menschlichen Haus teilnimmt, wie einmal sehr deutlich bei einem Freunde wurde, mit einem Einklang von innen und außen, der auch draußen ein Haus vortäuschte oder gab, eben unsres. Das ist eine Erinnerung, die zunächst hierher gehört, als scheinbares oder wirkliches Korrektiv der Ding-Einwohnung ohne Unfall, ohne Endlosigkeit ohne Verwirrung. . . . Ein höchst heiteres Kreisen ging fühlbar zwischen Drinnen und Draußen, Schein und Tiefe, Kraft und Oberfläche. 'Hören Sie', sagte da mein Freund, 'wie gut das Haus in Gang ist.' Und man hörte die Ruhe, das richtig Eingehängte, wie es läuft, die wohlbekannte Kameradschaft mit den Dingen."

4. For a discussion of Stoic ethics in *Tristram Shandy*, see Norton, "Moral in Phutatorius's Breeches." See also Lanham, *Tristram Shandy*, 1–18.

5. Bhushan, *Introduction to Tribology*, xvii. Bhushan further notes the importance of tribology for modern, industrialized society: "Sliding and rolling surfaces represent the key to much of our technological society. Understanding of tribological principles is essential for the successful design of machine elements" (xvii).

6. Ibid.

7. Lamb, *Sterne's Fiction*, 57.

8. See Lamb, "Sterne's System of Imitation."

9. Lacan, *Ego in Freud's Theory*, 302.

10. Ibid., 301.

11. Wellbery, "Zufall der Geburt," 304. For a discussion of the effects of contingency in narratology in general, see Wellbery, "Contingency."

12. McMaster, "'Uncrystallized Flesh and Blood,'" 202.

13. Norton, "Moral in Phutatorius's Breeches," 408.

14. See Bergson, "On Laughter," 85: "In the first place, this view of the mechanical and the living dovetailed into each other makes us incline towards the vaguer image of *some rigidity or other* applied to the mobility of life, in an awkward attempt to follow its lines and counterfeit its suppleness. Here we perceive how easy it is for a garment to become ridiculous. It might almost be said that every fashion is laughable in some respect. Only, when we are dealing with the fashion of the day, we are accustomed to it that the garment seems, in our mind, to form one with the individual wearing it. We do not separate them in imagination. The idea no longer occurs to us to contrast the inert rigidity of the covering with the living suppleness of the object covered; consequently, the comic here remains in a latent condition. It will only succeed in emerging when the natural incompatibility is so deep-seated between the covering and the covered that even an immemorial association fails to cement this union."

15. Brown and Kushner, "Eruptive Voices," 549.

16. Hamilton, *Accident*, 134.

17. Joan and Melvyn New, the editors of the Florida Edition of the works of Laurence Sterne, remark on the term *twelve-penny oath:* "According to

the Profane Oaths Act of 1746, the penalties for swearing were determined by the class of speaker rather that the oath uttered. Twelve pence was the fine for the lower orders; gentlemen paid more. Sterne would have been familiar with the act, since it was required to be read in church on four Sundays each year" (Sterne, *Life and Opinions*, 667 n.).

18. Benveniste, "Blasphémie et l'euphémie."
19. Ibid., 256.
20. Brown and Kushner, "Eruptive Voices."
21. Agamben, *Sacrament of Language*, 42–43.
22. Ibid., 47.
23. Ibid.
24. McMaster quotes the preface to *John Andrews*, where Henry Fielding espouses a similar theory of comic catharsis. See McMaster, "'Uncrystallized Flesh and Blood,'" 97: "The Ridiculous, he [Fielding] tells us, arises from the exposure of affectation, which strikes the reader with the comic emotions of 'surprise and pleasure' (to balance Aristotle's pity and terror), and thereby purges away 'spleen, melancholy, and ill affections.'"
25. Porter, "Against the Spleen," 91: "Within the fields of medicine and the life-sciences, for example, mechanistic dualism—far more subtle in any case than knock-about denunciations of it would allow—did not carry the day. Rather, the classical framework, heavily indebted to Hippocrates, Aristotle and Galen, retained great vitality, and traditional medical categories, such as ideas of the humours, non-naturals, and the vital and animal spirits, complexions and temperaments, remained integral."
26. Lamb, *Sterne's Fiction*, 7.
27. Cf. Nussbaum, "Aristotle on Emotions." Studies in emotions and affects in Hellenistic philosophy include Sorabji, *Emotion*; Gill, *Structured Self*; Graver, *Stoicism and Emotion*.
28. Nussbaum, "Aristotle on Emotions," 309.
29. Ibid., 306.
30. Martha Nussbaum has shown how Aristotle makes no technical distinction between *phantasia* and *doxa*. See Nussbaum, "Aristotle on Emotions," 307: "Further pursuit of the question shows clearly, however, that no technical distinction between phantasia and believing is at issue in any of these analyses of emotion: *phantasia* is used, in the rare cases where it is used, simply as the verbal noun of *phainesthai*, 'appear.' The passage contains no suggestion that *phantasia* is being distinguished from *doxa*, belief. And indeed Aristotle feels free to use belief words such as *dokein* and *oiesthai* in connection with his analyses of emotions."
31. Ibid., 307.
32. Lamb, *Sterne's Fiction*, 57.
33. Aristotle, *Art of Rhetoric*, 173.
34. Ibid., 267.
35. Lamb, *Sterne's Fiction*, 57.
36. See Wellbery, "Zufall der Geburt," 309 n. 26.
37. For an account of the human body's differentiation into different spheres, see Myer, "Tristram," who gives an overview of the various

Notes

physiological models circulating in the eighteenth century. She quotes E. M. W. Tillyard on the role of the upper regions (i.e., the brain) in controlling the body: "The brain rules the top of man's body, and is the seat of the rational and immortal part. The animal spirits are the executive agents of the brain through the nerves and partake both of the body and of the soul" (Tillyard, *Elizabethan World Picture*, 64, quoted in Myer, "Tristram," 102).

38. Sterne quotes verbatim these mental faculties from Rabelais's *Gargantua and Pantagruel*, where they are mentioned as being endowed to the soul by animal spirits. See Myer, "Tristram," 106: "For Rabelais, the animal spirits endow us with 'imagination, discourse, judgement, resolution, deliberation, ratiocination and memory.'"

39. Brown and Kushner, "Eruptive Voices," 544.

40. Ibid., 522. For a further discussion of 'narrative speech acts' in *Tristram Shandy*, see Mahler, "'Doing' Things with Words."

41. See Lanham, *Tristram Shandy*, 65: "The terrible maledictions become a consort of viols, a peaceful home entertainment in the great age of amateurism."

42. Brown and Kushner, "Eruptive Voices," 550.

43. Ibid., 539.

44. See Lamb, "Sterne's System of Imitation," 141: "No matter how exempt from the stream of vulgar ideas or the common road of thinking Walter thinks he is, and no matter how oddly he assembles his theories and applies them, it is evident from Chambers's *Cyclopaedia*, Burton's *Anatomy of Melancholy*, and Obadiah Walker's *Of Education* that his ideas once dwelt in other heads. He makes this point himself when he praises Ernulphus's anathema as a digest and institute of all possible modes of swearing and defies anyone 'to swear *out* of it.' Not that Ernulphus is original on this account: he merely provides the meeting point between all prior and all subsequent knowledge of oath-making (as Slawkenbergius does in the field of noses) to show that there is nothing new under the sun and that all is imitation."

45. Coleridge, *Fire, Famine, and Slaughter*, quoted in Montagu, *Anatomy of Swearing*, 67. For a discussion of the steam engine as a metaphor for human characteristics in the nineteenth and early twentieth centuries, see Rabinbach, *Human Motor*.

46. Patrick, "Psychology of Profanity," 126, quoted in Montagu, *Anatomy of Swearing*, 73.

47. Ricoeur, *Freud and Philosophy*, 66.

48. See Lanham, *Tristram Shandy*, 64: "Further, the recitation's mechanistic inflexibility, its final *inapplicability* to the private life, is emphasized by the mechanical insertion of (*Obadiah*) where needed, and by the supplying of the proper pronominal equivalents throughout in the same kind of parantheses."

49. Brown and Kushner, "Eruptive Voices," 550.

50. Thomas, *Religion and the Decline*, 75–76.

51. Ibid., 504.

52. Lanham, *Tristram Shandy*, 65.

53. For a reconstruction of rhetorical methods of self-influence, see Campe, "Affizieren und Selbstaffizieren."

54. See Campe, *Affekt und Ausdruck.*

55. Lausberg, *Handbook of Literary Rhetoric,* 359. Quintilian, whom Lausberg paraphrases, names this figure *evidentia.*

56. Lanham, *Tristram Shandy,* 25.

57. Melvyn and Joan New explain that trunk-hose were "loose-fitting breeches of the previous century, sometimes stuffed with wool, as opposed to the tighter breeches of the eighteenth century, which could not be stuffed" (Sterne, *Life and Opinions,* 642 n.).

58. The list of possible objects to be displayed includes "a scar, an axe, a sword, a pink'd-doublet, a rusty helmet, a pound and a half of pot-ashes in an urn, or a three-halfpenny pickle pot,—but above all, a tender infant royally accoutred" (Sterne, *Life and Opinions,* 167). An eloquent orator has the ability to pull out an infant from underneath his mantle, repeating and mimicking the moment of birth. Again Sterne chooses the discourse of origin, paternity, and genealogy to explicate his model of rhetorical veiling/unveiling as performance. Striking eloquence and giving birth resemble each other.

59. Cervantes Saavedra, *History of the Renowned Don Quixote,* 125.

60. Ibid., 76.

61. Sterne's rootedness in the doctrines and rhetorical practices of the Church of England is discussed by Bowden, *Yorick's Congregration.*

62. Locke, *Essay concerning Human Understanding,* 92.

63. Traugott, "Shandean Comic Vision," 147.

64. Arthur H. Cash identifies Sterne's contemporary physician Dr. Francis Topham as Didius. See Cash, *Laurence Sterne,* 289.

65. For a questioning of Locke's influence on Sterne, a commonplace in Sterne scholarship, see Day, "*Tristram Shandy.*"

66. In this sense he could be called an "amiable humorist." See Tave, *Amiable Humorist,* 166–67: "To make a general distinction, amiable humor measured reality not, as the satirist tends, by an ideal against which reality is terribly wanting, nor did it, in the manner of the sentimentalist, deny or falsify the gap between the real and the ideal. It accepted the difference with a liberal tolerance, or unlike both satirist and sentimentalist, it found the ideal in the varied fullness of the real with all its imperfections."

67. For a discussion of Sterne's theory of animal spirits, see Myer, "Tristram."

68. On Walter's unsuccessful research, see New, "Sterne and the Narrative."

69. Wellbery, "Zufall der Geburt," 316.

70. Ibid., 312.

71. Ibid.

72. Ibid., 313.

73. Lacan, *Language of the Self,* 39. For a Lacanian interpretation of Tristram Shandy, discussing the status of the absent father, see Macksey, "'Alas, Poor Yorick.'" See also Wilson, "'And Let Me Go On.'"

Notes

74. For a feminist reading of the relation between language and gender in *Tristram Shandy*, see Ruth Perry, "Words for Sex." See also Harries, "Words, Sex, and Gender." For a discussion of gender and its relation to eighteenth-century theories of procreation, see Harvey, "Substance of Sexual Difference."

75. For a discussion of Tristram's perceived circumcision and the medical discourse on the topic of circumcision in eighteenth-century Great Britain, see Darby, "Oblique and Slovenly Initiation."

76. For a discussion of the status of rumor in *Tristram Shandy*, see Stovel, "*Tristram Shandy*."

77. For a cultural and literary history of sash windows in the seventeenth and eighteenth centuries, see Ramsey, "Literary History."

78. Seneca, "On Anger," 219. Similar passages not only can be found throughout *De Ira* but also are commonplaces in Cicero and Plutarch. In *De Ira* 3.40, anger and rage with a slave reach a gruesome climax when Vedius Pollo tries to punish a slave by feeding him to large lampreys. See Seneca, "On Anger," 349: "When one of his slaves [of Vedius Pollo] had broken a crystal cup, Vedius ordered him to be seized and doomed him to die, but in an extraordinary way—he ordered him to be thrown to the huge lampreys, which he kept in a fish-pond.... It was really out of cruelty." Only the intrusion of the *deified Augustus*—a divine intervention—saves the slave's life. For a discussion of the relationship between anger and the institution of slavery in antiquity, see Harris, *Restraining Rage*, 317–36.

79. Harris, *Restraining Rage*, 327.

80. For the status of polite discourse adhering to the laws of decorum in the eighteenth century, see Potkay, *Fate of Eloquence*.

81. Melvyn and Joan New point toward the practical problems that arose in eighteenth-century England from this sense of decorum for male midwives and their patients. A contemporary pamphlet *Man-Midwifery Analysed* from 1764 states: "I desire every woman ... to consider whether she be strictly entitled to the appellation of ... a modest woman, after she has admitted a male operator thus to insult her person" (Sterne, *Life and Opinions*, 624 n.).

82. Quintilian, *Institutio Oratoria*, 3:209.

83. Ibid., 197.

84. Ibid.

85. Ibid.

86. Ibid.

87. See New, "Sterne, Warburton."

88. See "Meaning of 'Point Blank,'" posted on *The Phrase Finder* by Bill Shope, May 17, 2003, www.phrases.org.uk/bulletin_board/20/messages/1416.html.

89. Burckhardt, "Tristram Shandy's Law," 73.

90. The world of Tristram could be described as one of falling objects. See Molesworth, *Chance*, 190: "Just about everything in Tristram Shandy, it seems, is either sinking, winding down, running to exhaustion, interrupted, cut short, or dropping off."

91. Burckhardt, "Tristram Shandy's Law," 81.

92. Sterne, *Sentimental Journey*, 36.

93. Locke, *Essay concerning Human Understanding*, 95.
94. Stedmond, *Comic Art*, 82.
95. Lanham, *Tristram Shandy*, 55.
96. Burckhardt, "Tristram Shandy's Law," 80. For a classic interpretation of Sterne's digressive and interruptive style, see Shlovsky, "Parodying Novel," 66–89.
97. Burckhardt, "Tristram Shandy's Law," 80.
98. Traugott, *Tristram Shandy's World*, 28.

2. ANNOYING BAGATELLES: JEAN PAUL AND THE COMEDY OF THE QUOTIDIAN

1. Goethe, *Truth and Fiction*, 1:237–38.
2. Campe, "Schreibszene."
3. For a discussion of the term *materiality* that differs from Roland Barthes's in his discussion of the "materiality of the signifier," see Mücke, "Imaginary Materiality of Writing."
4. Jean Paul, "Komet," 1004. Subsequent page citations to this work are given parenthetically in the text.
5. See Koschorke, *Körperströme und Schriftverkehr*.
6. Ibid., 217: "Strömen induziert Seele."
7. Ibid., 315.
8. Shaftesbury, "Letter concerning Enthusiasm," 2. For a discussion of the idea of auto-affection in rhetoric, see Campe, "Affizieren und Selbstaffizieren."
9. Jean Paul, *Horn of Oberon*, 38 (German, *Vorschule der Ästhetik*, 59). Subsequent citations to this work are given parenthetically in the text, with the page of the English translation followed by the page of the German original in brackets.
10. Dengel-Pelloquin, *Eigensinnige Geschöpfe*, 240.
11. Tismar, *Gestörte Idyllen*, 37.
12. Jean Paul, *Wedded Life*, 280 (German, *Siebenkäs*, 287). Subsequent citations to this work are given parenthetically in the text, with the page of the English translation followed by the page of the German translation in brackets.
13. Jean Paul, *Konjektural-Biographie*, 1057.
14. Campe, "Schreibstunden," 133. See also Kreienbrock, "Lauern des Objekts."
15. Koschorke, *Körperströme und Schriftverkehr*, 247–48.
16. Paul Fleming concisely summarizes the function of fantasy in anticipating the future: "Fantasy hovers between the present and a desired future, and this anticipated time—this time of fantasy—reflects back upon the present, transfiguring it. This bending back of the anticipated future onto the present could be called Jean Paul's theory of affective reflection. The anticipation of still further pleasure casts an aura around the present joy, producing 'the amalgam of the present with fantasy,' in which one savors at once the present moment and its future possibilities." See Fleming, *Pleasures of Abandonment*, 32.

Notes 255

17. See Bergengruen, *Schöne Seelen, groteske Körper*, 65: "Geld und Körper stehen nicht nur in einem metaphorischen, sondern auch in einem kausalen Zusammenhang. Der Geldmangel und der daraus resultierende Streit mit Lenette machen den an sich geldverachtenden Siebenkäs krank am (physischen) Körper und melancholisch."

18. See Frey, "Wissen um Trieb."

19. Tissot, *Von der Gesundheit der Gelehrten*, 73.

20. Platner, *Anthropologie für Aerzte*, xv-xvii. Immanuel Kant differentiates his own late *Anthropology from a Pragmatic Point of View [Anthropologie in pragmatischer Absicht]* from this type of physiological anthropology by stressing the moral aspects and rejecting all epistemological aspirations. For a discussion of Platner's influence on Jean Paul, see Kosenina, *Ernst Platners Anthropologie*.

21. See Pross, *Jean Pauls geschichtliche Stellung*, 156: "wird die animistische Physiologie in Jean Pauls Werk zur Grundlage der Poesie umgestaltet."

22. See Koschorke, *Körperströme und Schriftverkehr*, 404; Müller, *Jean Pauls Ästhetik*, 224.

23. Mauser, "Anakreon als Therapie?," 109. Götz Müller points out that there is barely any other literary ouevre, "in dem so viele Kuren stattfinden, in dem so viele Therapien diskutiert und praktiziert werden. . . . Das Werk Jean Pauls kennt Heilungen des gestörten Leibes und der gestörten Seele durch die Täuschung, die Einfühlung, den Choc und den Schrecken oder auch durch die magnetische Kur." See Müller, *Jean Pauls Ästhetik*, 15.

24. Fleming, *Pleasures of Abandonment*, 83.

25. Jean Paul, *Life of Quintus Fixlein*, 299–300 (German, *Leben des Quintus Fixlein*, 185). Subsequent citations of this work in this chapter are given parenthetically in the text, with the English page citation followed by the German in brackets.

26. Fleming, *Pleasures of Abandonment*, 83.

27. Bergson, "Laughter," 68.

28. Ibid., 67.

29. Forschner, *Stoische Ethik*, 119. See also the discussion of Epictetus in Sterne's *Tristram Shandy* in chapter 1.

30. See Simon, "Universum des Schreibens," 155: "Hier wird das Aufhören in der Tat zum Auf-Hören. Das Ende der Pragmatik ist der Beginn des poetischen Hörens. Wo im Drinnen der Schreibszene nur gedacht werden kann, wird das Draußen zum Unglück. Die poetische Phatik ist hier an dem Punkt, wo das Hören aufhört, um poetisch beginnen zu können."

31. Reil, *Rhapsodieen*, 120.

32. Blanchot, "Literature," 317.

33. See Fleming, *Pleasures of Abandonment*, 81: "In Jean Paul, all pleasure occurs a bit out of time, in either the anticipated joy or the memory of the past expectation. 'Today' is savored by anticipating the next day; when tomorrow arrives and becomes 'today,' it is enjoyed by recalling yesterday's anticipation of 'today.' Stripped of any sense of possibility, the present moment represents the time of melancholy, the dead time, in which Saturn tightens its rings around one's breast. Only by infusing the present with a

sense of the future or with a past anticipation, can one transform the temporal ring of melancholy into a magical circle of pleasure."

34. Marcus Aurelius, *Meditations,* 3, quoted in Hadot, *Philosophy,* 228.
35. Epictetus, "Enchiridion," 221.
36. See section "The Idyll as Stoic Remedy."
37. Jean Paul, "Über die natürliche Magie, " 200. Subsequent citations to this work are given parenthetically in the text.
38. Ibid.
39. Hadot, *Philosophy.*
40. See Harris, *Restraining Rage,* 375: "The most important of the new techniques [of anger control] was *daily self-examination.*"
41. Seneca, "On Anger," 110. For the relation of the Delphic precept "Know thyself" to this form of Stoic reflection, see Foucault, *Hermeneutics of the Subject.*
42. Epictetus, "Enchiridion," 221.
43. Hadot, *Philosophy,* 227.
44. Lunch is then the reverse of breakfast. Siebenkäs has to wait for his wife while the hot food is already on the table: "rauchte ein solcher Schmaus über das Tischtuch: so konnte Siebenkäs gewiß hoffen, daß seine Frau einige hundert Dinge mehr vor dem Essen wegzuarbeiten habe als sonst—Der Mann sitzt dort und ist willens anzuspießen—blickt umher, gedämpft anfangs, dann grimmig—wird doch seiner Meister auf einige Minuten lang—denket inzwischen neben dem Braten bei so guter Muße seinem Elende nach—tut endlich den ersten Donnerschlag aus seinem Gewitter und schreiet: 'Das Donner und Wetter! ich sitze schon ein Säkulum da, und es friert alles ein—Frau, Frau!'" (2:283).
45. Jean Paul, "Freudenbüchlein," 33.
46. Page numbers here are to the German original, and English translations are my own (since this addendum to *Life of Quintus Fixlein* has not been translated).47. Fleming, *Pleasures of Abandonment,* 82.
48. Beresford, *Miseries of Human Life,* 232.
49. Ibid., 1–2.
50. The *Freudenbüchlein* was never published during Jean Paul's life and was only made available for the first time in Ernst Behrendt's *Historical-Critical Edition* in 1934.
51. G. Müller, *Jean Pauls Ästhetik,* 205.
52. On the influence of Sterne on Jean Paul, see Michelsen, *Laurence Sterne.*
53. Jean Paul, "Museum," 967.
54. Jean Paul, "Freudenbüchlein," 12.
55. Ibid., 15.
56. Fleming, *Pleasures of Abandonment,* 61.
57. Cf. Tismar, *Gestörte Idyllen;* Wuthenow, "Gefährdete Idylle." Cf. Meyer-Siekendieck, *Affektpoetik,* 352–56.
58. Jean Paul, "Life of the Merry Masterkin," 113 (German, *Leben des vergnügten Schulmeisterleins,* 461). Subsequent citations to this work are given parenthetically in the text, with the page of the English translation

followed by the page of the German original in brackets. For a reading of this passage, see Kommerell, *Jean Paul*, 287.

59. Panofsky, "Et in Arcadia Ego," 237.
60. Kittler, *Discourse Networks*, 110.
61. Ibid.
62. Ibid.
63. Foucault, *Madness and Civilization*, 187–88.
64. Ibid., 187.
65. See Müller, *Jean Pauls Ästhetik*, 213.
66. This scene echoes Wutz's last moments before his death, when he surrounds himself with his collection of toys, "Rudera und Spätlinge seiner verspielten Kindheit" (1,455). In the moment of dying, be it imagined or real, Fixlein and Wutz are transported back to their childhood.
67. See Barry, "Natural Palingenesis."
68. Kommerell, *Jean Paul*, 283. See also Meyer, *Typus des Sonderlings*.
69. Kommerell, *Jean Paul*, 284.
70. Epictetus, "Enchiridion," 227.
71. Reil, "Zerfallen der Einheit unseres Körpers," 583.
72. Jean Paul, "Über die Tugend," 353. Jean Paul, in this text from 1788/89, refers to Kant's *Groundwork of the Metaphysics of Morals [Grundlegung der Metaphysik der Sitten]*. See Köpke, *Erfolglosigkeit*, 216–25.
73. Kant, *Anthropology*, 155–56. Kant's speculations regarding the etymological derivation of *hallucinari* from the Latin word for "big toe," *allex*, have been refuted.
74. Koschorke, *Körperströme und Schriftverkehr*, 215.
75. Reil, *Rhapsodieen*, 49–50.
76. Kant, *Anthropology*, 152: "The principle of *apathy*—namely that the wise man must never be in a state of affect, not even in that of compassion with the misfortune of his best friend, is an entirely correct and sublime moral principle of the Stoic school."
77. Reil, *Rhapsodieen*, 383–84.
78. Roller, *Irrenanstalt*, 258. Horn, Heinroth, and Neumann held opposing positions that supported the often violent restriction and suppression of affective outbursts in therapy. For a discussion of Ernst Horn, the second director and first practicing psychiatrist of the Charité in Berlin, see chapter 4.
79. This form of health must be understood not only in terms of the psyche but also in a very physical sense. Unrepressed anger improves digestion. See Kant, *Anthropology*, 161: "Health is promoted mechanically by nature through several affects. *Laughing* and *crying* in particular belong here. Anger is also a fairly reliable aid to digestion, if one can scold freely (without fear of resistance), and many a housewife has no other emotional exercise than the scolding of her children and servants."
80. Kant, *Anthropology*, 159.
81. Ibid., 153.
82. Ibid.
83. Ibid., 154.

84. Stahl, *Theorie der Heilkunde*, 1:199.
85. Ibid., 1:198–99.
86. Ibid., 1:89.
87. Jean Paul, "Frage," 952–53.
88. For a discussion of the relationship between philosophy, anthropology, and medicine in the late eighteenth century, see Riedel, *Anthropologie des jungen Schiller*. On treatment of the whole person, see Schings, *Ganze Mensch*. *Der philosophische Arzt* was also the name of a prominent medical journal of the time.
89. See Schings, "Philosophische Arzt."
90. Zückert was not only one of Germany's most prominent physicians but also the first translator of Laurence Sterne's *Tristam Shandy* in 1765.
91. Zückert, *Von den Leidenschaften*, 64.
92. Ibid., 50.
93. Ibid., 64.
94. The term *Schweif* as a noun can mean "tail," but as a verb also implies a digressive, aimless movement. For a discussion of Jean Paul's digressive, *schweifend* style of writing, see Schestag, "Bibliographie."
95. The editor of "Der Komet," Norbert Miller, remarks: "ungewohnten: Die zweite Reimersche Ausgabe setzt die nicht notwendige, zum folgenden nicht stimmige Konjektur: 'angewohnten'" (Jean Paul, "Komet," 1311). My reading of the passage would support Reimer's choice of "accustomed." It is precisely because Süptitz is too accustomed and used to reflecting that he fails to put on his shirt, not because he is unaccustomed to reflection.
96. Schweikert, *Jean Pauls "Komet,"* 84. See also Michelsen, *Laurence Sterne*, 354.
97. Herder's notion of *Besonnenheit* resists an immediate translation into English. It can be rendered as "reflection," "attentiveness," "deliberateness," "prudence."
98. Herder, "Essay on the Origin," 115–16.
99. Richards, "Rhapsodies on a Cat-Piano," 713.
100. Reil, *Rhapsodieen*, 100.
101. Ibid., 102.
102. Ibid., 109–10.
103. See the section "Recalcitrant Writing" in this chapter.
104. La Bruyère, *Characters*, 273.
105. Bergk, *Kunst*, 7–8, quoted in Koschorke, *Körperströme und Schriftverkehr*, 198.
106. Bergk, *Kunst*, 7.
107. Reil, *Ueber die Erkenntniss*, 558, quoted in Müller, *Jean Pauls Ästhetik*, 238.
108. See "Besonnenheit," in Ritter, Gründer, and Gabriel, *Historisches Wörterbuch der Philosophie*, 850. On the relationship between instinct and reflection, see Müller, *Jean Pauls Ästhetik*, 59–60.
109. Kommerell, *Jean Paul*, 302–3.
110. Ibid., 302.

111. Jean Paul, *Titan*, 2:441 (German, *Titan*, 767). For Karlheinz Stierle, stumbling while walking functions as an example for his taxonomy of the comical. See Stierle, "Komik der Handlung," 240: "Ein triviales Beispiel—aber eine Systematik des Komischen kann auf triviale Beispiele nicht verzichten—ist die Komik des Stolperns, die daraus hervorgeht, daß die Füße plötzlich einem eigenen Willen zu gehorchen scheinen und daß im Fallen das Ganze gleichsam zum Objekt seines Teils wird."

112. For a discussion of this context in Jean Paul's early satirical writings, see Schmidt-Biggemann, *Maschine und Teufel*.

113. Jean Paul, *Titan*, 354. Ironically—or consequently—Schoppe's life ends in madness and insanity. See Wiethölter, *Witzige Illuminationen*.

114. Tieleman, *Chrysippus' On Affections*, 108–9.

115. See Forschner, *Stoische Ethik*, 123: "eine Person, deren Impulse nicht exzessiv sind, ist wie ein Mensch, der spazierengeht; seine Beine gehorchen seiner Absicht, sind Schritt für Schritt unter Kontrolle; eine Person, deren Impulse exzessiv sind, ist wie ein Läufer; dieser, einmal in Bewegung, vermag nicht mehr anzuhalten, wann er will; er schießt übers Ziel hinaus."

116. Grimm, *Deutsches Wörterbuch*, 18: 2791: "[Stiefelknecht] als schimpfwort: der kandidat war informator und . . . taufen und hölle predigen wird der stiefelknecht, kriecher und schmeichler."

117. Jean Paul, *Invisible Lodge*, 338 (German, *Unsichtbare Loge*, 361). See Bergengruen, *Schöne Seelen, grosteske Körper*, 90.

118. Fleming, *Pleasures of Abandonment*, 21.

119. Kommerell, *Jean Paul*, 318.

120. Ibid., 309.

121. Ibid., 309–10.

122. For a discussion of Kommerell's reception of Jean Paul, see Fleming, "Crisis of Art."

123. The editor, Norbert Miller, notes: "Die erwähnte Szene kommt in der Form gar nicht im 'Don Quixote' vor, worauf zuerst Joseph Müller in 'Das Wesen des Humors' . . . hingewiesen hat" (1210).

124. Fleming, *Pleasures of Abandonment*, 45.

125. In the *Vorschule*, Jean Paul states: "Übrigens haben wir später außer unserer Definition des Lächerlichen noch etwas zu suchen, das noch schwerer gefunden wird, nämlich die Ursache, warum uns dasselbe, obgleich als die Empfindung einer Unvollkommenheit, doch Vergnügen gewährt, und zwar nicht nur in der Dichtkunst—welche auch auf den Schimmel Blüten und an dem Sarge Blumenstücke gibt—, sondern im trockenen Leben selber" (5,:104). For the relationship of life and literature, see Stierle, "Komik der Handlung," 237: "Erst im Bereich der komischen Funktion wird die Vielfalt der komischen Möglichkeiten und Kombinationen offenbar, wird das Komische in seiner Vielgestaltigkeit und in seinen extremsten Möglichkeiten durch die dichterische Imagination erfahrbar gemacht. So ist es kein Zufall, daß am Anfang der modernen Beschäftigung mit dem Komischen die tiefsinnigen Einsichten eines Schriftstellers, Jean Pauls nämlich, stehen, denen die späteren Theorien oft mehr verdanken als sie zu erkennen geben und daß, auch wo das

Komische Gegenstand anthropologischen, philosophischen, psychologischen Interesses wurde, die einsichtigsten komischen Paradigmen literarischen Gestaltungen des Komischen entnommen sind."

126. Bergengruen, *Schöne Seelen, groteske Körper*, 214.
127. Blair, *Lectures on Rhetoric*, 417, quoted in Wasserman, "Inherent Values," 441.
128. Ibid., 440.
129. de Man, "Anthropomorphism," 247.
130. Herder, "Essay on the Origin," 133.
131. Ibid.
132. Stierle, "Komik der Handlung," 242.
133. Ibid.
134. Ibid.
135. Vischer, "Über das Erhabene," 179.
136. It is interesting to note that in the context of this diatribe Süptitz downplays the affective effects of his afflictions, while in the letter to his wife in the "Enklave" emotions of anger and rage are much more prominent.
137. Friedrich Theodor Vischer in the novel *Auch Einer* develops a similar system of little annoyances and vexations caused by malicious demons. See chapter 3 below.
138. Mesmer, *Mesmerismus*, 111. See Tatar, *Spellbound*; Mackay, "Religious Significance"; Müller, *Jean Pauls Ästhetik*, 38ff.; Müller, "Literarisierung des Mesmerismus."
139. Gmelin, *Ueber den Thierischen Magnetismus*, 27–28, quoted in Müller, *Jean Pauls Ästhetik*, 47.
140. The Swiss psychiatrist Ludwig Binswanger describes the notion of "extravagance" (Verstiegenheit) as a mode of failed human existence. See Binswanger, "Extravagance," 343: "Extravagance is, in fact, rooted in a certain disharmony in the relation between rising upward and striding forth. If we call such a relation 'anthropologically proportionate' when it is 'successful,' then we must speak of Extravagance as a form of anthropological disproportion, as a 'failure' of the relationship between height and breadth in the anthropological sense. . . . 'Extravagance' is conditioned by the fact that the Dasein has 'gotten stuck' at a certain experiential locus [Er-Fahrung] from which it can no longer, to use a phrase from Hofmannsthal, 'strike its tent,' from which it can no longer break out. Robbed of *communio* and *communicatio*, the Dasein can no longer widen, revise, or examine its 'experiential horizon' and remains rooted to a 'narrow minded,' i.e., sharply limited, standpoint." Freudel is trapped under his wig. His Dasein, to use Binswanger's Heideggerian terminology, has reached a place from which there is no way back. The loss of orientation within the text of his sermon leads to a precarious, inflexible situation from which there is no possibility of progress; he is cornered. While Binswanger analyzes extravagance strictly within his existential approach to psychoanalysis, in Jean Paul the extravagant hero is more than a mere pathological case. He represents a paradigmatic instance of a failed embodiment (Kommerell) that lies at the heart of comical projection. What he does in a comic fashion is, to quote a footnote

from Binswanger, "to see the psychic and the spiritual as already inherent in the corporeal appearances, and vice versa." Despite all attempts to think of a successful community of body and soul, extravagant figures like Siebenkäs, Süptitz, and Freudel show how human existence, exposed to the vexations of everyday life, cannot come to terms with its *Lebenswelt*. They are stuck in a narrow and cramped place where malicious objects subvert any ability to live the good life and remain excluded from the redemptive qualities of idyllic anticipation or humorous projection.

3. MALICIOUS OBJECTS: FRIEDRICH THEODOR VISCHER AND THE (NON)FUNCTIONALITY OF THINGS

1. "Mind Where You Put Your Feet," *Punch, or The London Charivari*, November 29, 1879, reprinted in Schlaffer and Mende, "Friedrich Thedor Vischer," 91. Two months later, in January 1880, Vischer responded to *Punch* with an article entitled "Podoböotismus, 'Punch' und Reichskanzler," criticizing the British publication for purposefully missing the point by relating the lament over the lack of manners to Chancellor Bismarck's foreign policies and the lack of freedom of press in Germany. In the following extract Vischer quotes from and answers the *Punch* article (Vischer, "Podoböotismus," 366–72): "'When one thinks of all that Prince Bismarck, for instance, has set foot on! And such big boots as he wears too—and so far from clean as they are sometimes! Suppose Herr Vischer looked a little beyond the railway carriage! But *Punch*, in his insolent and insular freedom, forgets there is the Correctional Police-Rod in pickle for the backs of all who dare impiously to poke fun at the awful Chancellor of the Empire, whose will is law,—justice to the contrary notwithstanding,—and whose warning to his critics in the press, short, sharp, and decisive, is 'Shut up, or be shut up.' . . . It's very funny. Herr 'Punch' indulges himself in what otherwise occurs to a reader or a writer out of distraction: . . . diversion to a different subject. For the symbolic jackboots of the chancellor of the Reich have absolutely nothing to do with the very real ones worn by train passengers, such as the studded hiking boots of the parson of whom we spoke. And they have just as little to do with the German train code—or with the media laws."
2. Vischer, "Podoböotismus," 366.
3. Bergson, "Laughter," 84.
4. Vischer, "Podoböotismus," 367.
5. Ibid.
6. Ibid.
7. Ibid.
8. Certeau, *Practice of Everyday Life*, 111. For a cultural history of train travel, see Schivelbusch, *Railway Journey*. See also Harrington, "Railway Journey," 230: "The railway journey was not merely an event or a process; it was a shared cultural location through which the ill-defined but potent anxieties associated with the advent of mass transportation were focused, collected and transmitted. It constituted the paradigmatic experience of the railway age, serving as a link between the public, externalized, shared fears and anxieties provoked by the railway and the private, internal trauma of the

individual railway traveler, confronted with the dangers and discomforts, and industrialized stresses of train travel."

9. Vischer, *Auch Einer,* 48. Subsequent citations to this work are given parenthetically in the text.

10. In another passage, A.E. laments the superficiality of all Hamlet interpretations, which, he says, miss the real, physiological cause for Hamlet's melancholia: "He [A.E.] was just getting into *Hamlet* and fervently occupied with demonstrating how it was in fact proof of the shallowness of all previous accounts of his vacillation and hesitation, to have acknowledged his spiritual rather than physiological obstruction. All significant passages in this immortal drama are, however, announced with blistering script: every inch, a haemorrhage" (78).

11. Rapp, *Briefwechsel zwischen Strauss und Vischer,* 52.

12. Hermann Lang, quoted in Schlaffer and Mende, "Friedrich Theodor Vischer," 63–64.

13. For a general criticism of contemporary fashion, see Vischer, "Mode und Cynismus."

14. Moritz Lazarus, quoted in Schlaffer and Mende, "Friedrich Theodor Vischer," 39.

15. For a history of the misfit in German literature, see Meyer, *Typus des Sonderlings.*

16. Heidegger, "Origin of the Work," 32.

17. Ibid.

18. Ibid., 63.

19. Derrida, "Restitutions," 265.

20. Schapiro, "Still Life."

21. Derrida, "Restitutions," 275.

22. Vischer, "Podoböotismus," 370.

23. In antiquity, the people of Boeotia were considered to be stupid and dull compared to their intelligent and witty neighbors from Attica.

24. Vischer, "Podoböotismus," 368.

25. Ibid.

26. Ibid., 374.

27. Heidegger, "Origin of the Work," 33.

28. Ibid., 32–33.

29. Ibid., 33.

30. Derrida, "Restitutions," 320.

31. Ibid., 313.

32. Heidegger, "Origin of the Work," 35.

33. Ibid.

34. Heidegger, *Introduction to Metaphysics,* 41.

35. Heidegger, "Origin of the Work," 23.

36. Ibid., 32–33.

37. Ibid., 33.

38. Ibid., 39. For a discussion of the relation of Heidegger's theory of art to the idea of the museum, see Babich, "From van Gogh's Museum," 169.

39. Heidegger, "Origin of the Work," 33.

Notes

40. Here Heidegger plays with the difference between "stehen" and "stellen," pointing toward his notion of "Gestell."

41. In the 1950 lecture "Das Ding," Heidegger discusses the thing in terms of a certain hollowness. See Heidegger, "Thing," 167: "The emptiness, the void, is what does the vessel's holding. The empty space, this nothing of the jug, is what the jug is as the holding vessel."

42. Heidegger, *Introduction to Metaphysics*, 34.

43. It is difficult to render the German word *eigentlich* in English. Possible translations include "actually," "intrinsic," "literal," "proper," "real," and "underlying."

44. Heidegger, "Origin of the Work," 63.

45. Ibid., 54.

46. Ibid., 44.

47. Heidegger, *Introduction to Metaphysics*, 26.

48. See Husserl, *Ding und Raum*.

49. Freud, "Civilization and Its Discontents," 70–71.

50. Heidegger, *What Is a Thing*, 78.

51. Ibid., 85, trans. Ben Robinson.

52. Ibid., 88, trans. Ben Robinson.

53. Weber, "Upsetting the Setup," 72.

54. For a discussion of these terms as translations of *Gestell*, see ibid., 71: "This tension [between verb and noun in the term *Gestell*] resounds in the word proposed by Lacoue-Labarthe to render Gestell: installation. I would like to suggest another possibility, one that has the virtue of pointing towards the lexical 'root' of Gestell, stell: emplacement. If I prefer this word to 'installation', it is because it signifies not so much the setting-up of an apparatus as the set-up tout court, 'the assignment or appointing of a definite place.'"

55. While the melancholic flaneur in the tradition of Poe and Baudelaire loses his way and eventually himself in the crowd of the modern metropolis, Vischer's hero rages at the impossibility of taking an uninterrupted walk through the city without being exposed to the shocks of human beings as well as things stepping into his path.

56. David Hume uses the example of billiard balls to attack traditional models of causality. See Hume, *Hume's Enquiries*, 29–30: "When I see, for instance, a Billiard-ball moving in a straight line towards another; even suppose motion in the second ball should by accident be suggested to me, as the result of their contact or impulse; may I not conceive, that a hundred different events might as well follow from that cause? May not both these balls remain at absolute rest? May not the first ball return in a straight line, or leap off from the second in any line or direction? All these suppositions are consistent and conceivable. Why then should we give the preference to one, which is no more consistent or conceivable than the rest? All our reasonings *a priori* will never be able to show us any foundation for this preference."

57. On the relation of the notions of *Riß*, *Umriß*, and *reißen* to drawing, see Heidegger, "Origin of the Work," 58.

58. Certeau, *Practice of Everyday Life*, 93.

59. Oesterle, "Verübelte Geschichte," 73.

60. Vischer, "Mein Lebensgang," 519.
61. Vischer, *Aesthetik*, 1:120.
62. Vischer, "Mein Lebensgang," 519.
63. Ibid.
64. A blurred and characterless "Gewirre und Gekleckse" was—not by chance—the typical contemporary critical assessment of Vischer's novel. According to Berthold Auerbach, the organization of the novel is characterized by "decomposition, destruction of form" and the "dissolution of the fable." See Auerbach, "Wissen und Schaffen," 272. For an overview of the history of the controversial reception of Vischer's novel, see Grimm, "Zur Wirkungsgeschichte."
65. Oesterle, "Verübelte Geschichte," 71.
66. Vischer, "Mein Lebensgang," 519.
67. Vischer, "Über das Erhabene," 109.
68. Ibid.
69. Ibid., 107.
70. Oesterle, "Verübelte Geschichte," 76.
71. Ibid.
72. Ibid., 75.
73. Vischer, *Aesthetik*, 403. Here Vischer obviously takes up Jean Paul's discussion of the sublime and the ridiculous in *Vorschule der Ästhetik*.
74. Ibid.
75. Ibid., 407.
76. Ibid.
77. Ibid., 410.
78. Ibid., 412.
79. Ibid., 413.
80. Cf. Tismar, *Gestörte Idyllen*. See also chapter 2 above, the section "The Idyll as Stoic Remedy."
81. Ingrid Oesterle argues for the proximity of Hegel's *List der Vernunft* und Vischer's *Tücke des Objekts*. See Oesterle, "Verübelte Geschichte," 79: "Solange die Vernunft im Prozeß der Geschichte unangefochten ihre Zwecke zu verwirklichen schien, solange konnte sie auch das Widerstrebende—und sei es mit List—sich gefügig machen. Seit 1848 aber, so ist im *Auch Einer* erkennbar, scheitert auch die noch so listige Vernunft an Widerständen, die der Schwabe Vischer dem Schwaben Hegel kontrapunktisch und kongenial zur 'List der Vernunft' im Begriff der 'Tücke des Objekts' entgegenhält."
82. Earlier in the novel, the existence of physiological annoyances like sneezing, coughing, and spitting challenges the existence of a divine creator: "'Living-searching-spitting! . . . Oh, we are born to search, to unravel knots, to see the world with foot corns and agh! to sneeze, to cough, to spit. . . . Indeed, man changes into a slimy mollusk, debased to a stubborn oyster, a repository, a shameful vessel for fermenting glandular fluids, a muzzle-machine, in the throat a serrated scraper, a nest for demons, which, with their fine nails, tickle the larynx all night long, the eyes bleary, the brain hollow, dull, distraught, the nerves agitated by poison, . . . and there is supposed to be a God" (26).

83. In the addendum to "Mein Lebensgang," Vischer explains the focus on the physiological ill of the catarrh in *Auch Einer*. See Vischer, "Mein Lebensgang," 512: "Among the evils a man deals with, one must be brought center stage as is stipulated by a well-known poetic law. Catarrh is without question one of the most burdensome, not only because it distresses, as is obvious, the breathing organs, but because it also afflicts the brain (it clouds the site of thought), and because one is sick but cannot rightly claim to be ill, and finally because its symptoms are unseemly."

84. For Vischer's reception and analysis of Shakespeare in general and *Hamlet* in particular, see Vischer, "Shakespeares Hamlet."

85. For a discussion of the term *broken teleology,* see Sorg, *Gebrochene Teleologie,* and Ajouri, *Erzählen nach Darwin.*

86. Heidegger, *Being and Time,* 107. Subsequent citations to this work are given parenthetically in the text.

87. In a similar vein, Hans Blumenberg points to the inability of Husserl's late phenomenology of *Lebenswelt* to account for the intrusions of technology. See Blumenberg, "Lebenswelt und Technisierung," 37: "Der Zusammenhang von Lebenswelt und Technisierung ist komplizierter, als Husserl ihn gesehen hat. Der von Husserl analysierte Prozeß der Verdeckung des Entdeckten erreicht erst darin sein Telos, daß das im theoretischen Fragen unselbstverständlich Gewordene zurückkehrt in die Fraglosigkeit. Ungleich vollkommener als durch die Mimikry der Gehäuse wird das Technische als solches unsichtbar, wenn es der Lebenswelt implantiert ist."

88. De Man, "Anthropomorphism," 242.

89. Ibid., 241.

90. Vischer, "Mein Lebensgang," 510–11.

91. Vischer, *Aesthetik,* 2:31.

92. The word *Unterschiebung* is difficult to translate into English. Its meaning oscillates between "projection," "supposition," and (false) "attribution."

93. Vischer, "Das Symbol," 4:435. Subsequent citations to this work are given parenthetically in the text. For a discussion of Vischer's motivation for revising his *Aesthetics,* see Ajouri, *Erzählen nach Darwin,* 176: "Die Gründe für die Selbstkritik sind vielfältig. Bedenken gegenüber der eigenen Ästhetik begleiteten die Ausarbeitung des Werks schon von Beginn an. In den 1850er Jahren schließlich entwickelte sich eine formalistische Schule der Ästhetik mit dem Protagonisten Robert Zimmermann. Es kam zu einer lang anhaltenden Kontroverse zwischen Zimmermann und Vischer über Form und Gehalt in der Kunst; Vischer hielt zwar an der Einheit von Form und Inhalt fest, blieb gleichwohl von der Kritik der Formalisten an der idealistischen Ästhetik nicht unbeeinflußt. Auch gehört Vischers Selbstkritik in die Neukantianische Bewegung hinein, da er in seinen späten Schriften die Schönheit, einst objektiv in der Natur gesucht, nun nicht mehr als Objekt, sondern als Art der Anschauung konzipiert."

94. *Seelenleihung* literally translates as "lending of the soul."

95. Vischer, "Mein Lebensgang," 511.

96. Hans Vaihinger in 1911 will use the notion of the "as if" to develop his principle of fictionalism. For Vaihinger, fictions have an important practical value and should therefore be utilized. Vaihinger claims: "An idea whose theoretical untruth or incorrectness, and therewith its falsity, is admitted, is not for that reason practically useless; for such an idea, in spite of its theoretical nullity may have great practical importance." See Vaihinger, *Philosophy of "As If,"* viii.

97. Vischer, "Mein Lebensgang," 511.
98. Wittgenstein, *Vermischte Bemerkungen*, 136.
99. Nietzsche, "On Truth and Lying," 152.
100. Ibid., 153.
101. Ibid.
102. Ibid.
103. Ibid.
104. Ibid.
105. For a discussion of this antagonistic struggle in relation to Nietzsche's concepts of the Apollonian and the Dionysian as developed in *The Birth of Tragedy,* see Oelmüller, *Friedrich Theodor Vischer.*
106. For a discussion of the relation of metaphorization and the dream in Vischer, see his last essay "The Dream" (Der Traum), written roughly ten years before Freud's *Interpretation of Dreams.*
107. Heidegger, "Thing," 172: "To be sure, the Old High German word thing means a gathering, and specifically a gathering to deliberate on a matter under discussion, a contested matter."
108. Ibid., 179.
109. Vischer, "Mein Lebensgang," 522.
110. For a discussion of the relationship between executions and cathartic abreactions, see chapter 4.
111. For a reading of this mistranslation, see Schwenger, *Tears of Things.*
112. Heidegger, "Thing," 169.
113. Lausberg, *Handbook of Literary Rhetoric,* 118.
114. Campe, "Affizieren und Selbstaffizieren."

4. IGNITING ANGER: HEIMITO DODERER AND THE PSYCHOPATHOLOGY OF EVERYDAY RAGE

1. Doderer, *Merowingians,* 14. Subsequent citations to this work are given parenthetically in the text.
2. See Luehrs-Kaiser, "'Schnürlzieherei der Assoziationen.'"
3. Japp, "Mikrologie der Wut," 39.
4. Heidegger, *Principle of Reason,* 21.
5. The meaning of the German word *Grund* oscillates between "ground," "reason," and "cause."
6. Doderer, *Repertorium,* 273. Subsequent citations to this work are given parenthetically in the text.
7. The grotesque therapy of the "march of anger" can be read as a parody of Hugo Schwerdtner's theory of "Ausdrucksbewegungen." See Schwerdtner,

"Ausdrucksbewegungen," 293–94: "Therapie: Durch eine ganz bestimmte Bewegungstherapie werden im Kranken Ausdrucksbewegungen ausgelöst. Der Patient bekommt z.B. die Aufgabe, ein musikalisches Thema durch ein, diesem adäquaten Bewegungsthema darzustellen. Diese Methode hat den Vorteil, ein unwissentliches Verfahren zu sein; der Patient wird, ohne daß er die therapeutische Absicht merkt, das, was ihn seelisch bewegt, zum Ausdruck bringen. Dadurch wird funktionell für die gehemmte psychische Energie ein Ablauf geschaffen; inhaltlich kommt es zu einer Projektion der überwertigen Komplexe. Diese werden viel wirksamer abreagiert durch die Umsetzung in die Tat, als durch Unmsetzung durch Worte." Quoted in Rieger, Ästhetik des Menschen, 238.

8. Foucault, *Discipline and Punish*, 136.
9. Ibid., 170.
10. Rieger, "Steigerungen," 417.
11. Ibid., 420.
12. See the chapter "Elements and Sub-Elements" in Doderer, *Merowingians*, 233–34.
13. Vogl, "Gesetze des Amok," 83.
14. Danziger, *Constructing the Subject*, 52.
15. Doderer adopts this expression from his friend and teacher Hermann Swoboda, a professor of psychology at the University of Vienna and a vocal critic of positivistic experimental psychology. See Doderer, *Tagebücher*, 2:881: "About Swoboda one has to say that he would not recognize a science without a back of the head [Hinterkopf]. For the psychology of the Kraepelin school he found the fitting expression 'locksmithery of the soul.'" For Swoboda's influence on Doderer, see Walter, "Verlieben, nicht erleuchten."
16. Rieger, *Kybernetische Anthropologie*, 20. See also the section "Uncanny Cybernetics" in the Epilogue below.
17. Gerald Sommer convincingly presents the similarities between the real and the fictitious Dr. Horn. See Sommer, "Prof. Dr. Anonymus Horn."
18. See Shorter, *History of Psychiatry*, 14–15: "An authoritarian stream [of psychology], however, arose at the same time in the figure of Ernst Horn, a 32-year-old army doctor who had gone into teaching and who became in 1806 the associate director of Berlin's Charité Hospital.... The order he imposed ... was not just tidy and appealing to the bureaucratic mind, it was therapeutic as well. He dictated a regimen of military drilling to the patients, inserted tight daily schedules to replace endless idleness, and installed a general sense of limits that helped give patients the feeling of being able to control their lives."
19. Reil, *Rhapsodieen*, 232.
20. For a precise description of these treatments, see Sommer, "Prof. Dr. Anonymus Horn," 293ff.
21. Horn, *Öffentliche Rechenschaft*, 217, quoted in Sommer, "Prof. Dr. Anonymus Horn," 292.
22. The classic study on the discovery of the First Law is still Kuhn, "Energy Conservation." G. A. Zimmermann, in the translator's introduction

to Rudolf Schmidt's *Theories of Darwin*, discusses Mayer's term *ignition*, for which it is difficult to find a suitable English translation. See Schmidt, *Theories of Darwin*, 333: "Auslösung is a word originated by modern mechanical science, and means (1.) Slight mechanical operations of detaching and the like, by which another and more important action, whose forces were heretofore restrained, can be set into activity: e.g., the pressure which sets in motion a machine, previously at rest, is Auslösung, the pressure on the trigger of a gun is Auslösung; the friction of a match which is the beginning of a great fire is Auslösung. (2.) This idea may now be applied to chemical processes: e.g., a glass of sugar-water will remain sweet unless some foreign element is introduced into it, but the moment it receives a fermenting substance either by chance, from the air, or with intention, then the sugar water is brought into a process of chemical decomposition, and from this there results Auslösung; but from the introduction of the fermenting agent into the sugar-water is Auslösung. (3.) Von Mayer applies this idea to psycho-physical relations of life, and says: when the will acting through the agency of the motor nerves sets in motion the muscles, this is Auslösung."

23. Mayer, "Über Auslösung," 12.
24. Ibid.
25. Ibid.
26. Mittasch, *Friedrich Nietzsche als Naturphilosoph*, 115.
27. Stefan Rieger discusses the prominence of energetic models of the psyche in the first half of the twentieth century and concludes: "Im energetischen Korrelat findet die Moderne ihr allgemeinstes Rechenprinzip und ihren kleinsten gemeinsamen Nenner. *Denkökonomie und Energieprinzip*, die Entdeckung von *persönlicher Energie* und ein *psychoenergetischer Vitalismus* sind die Folge." See Rieger, "Steigerungen," 420.
28. For a discussion of Mayer's influence on Nietzsche, see Mittasch, *Friedrich Nietzsche als Naturphilosoph*, 102–49.
29. Nietzsche, *Briefwechsel*, 85, quoted in ibid., 114.
30. Nietzsche, *Gay Science*, 147. Subsequent citations to this work are given parenthetically in the text.
31. Nietzsche, *Twilight of the Gods*, 11.
32. Nietzsche, *Nachgelassene Fragmente, 1880–1882*, 453.
33. Nietzsche, *Nachgelassene Fragmente, 1887–1889*, 20.
34. Mayer, "Über Auslösung," 15–16.
35. See Neymeyr, "'Selbst-Tyrannei'"; see also Kofman, *Nietzsche et la scène philosophique*, 165–88.
36. Nietzsche, "Beyond Good and Evil," 221.
37. Nietzsche, *Dawn of the Day*, 56.
38. Lessing, *Hamburg Dramaturgy*, 193. For Lessing's doctrine of compassion, see Schings, *Mitleidigste Mensch*. See also Türk, "Interruptions."
39. Bernays, "On Catharsis," 321.
40. Bernays, "Grundzüge," 62.
41. Ibid., 64. Jean Bollack stresses this archaic, preaesthetic origin of Bernays's therapeutic concept of catharsis: "La *katharsis* thérapeutique ne pouvait donc être le fait de la construction esthétique. La cure ne se faisait pas au

moment d'une lecture ou d'un spectacle. C'était uns autre chose encore, plus archaïque, qui agissait par ce biais." See Bollack, *Jacob Bernays*, 50. See also Wilm, "Grenzen tragischer Katharsis," 40–42.

42. Bernays, "Grundzüge," 64.
43. Nietzsche, *Birth of Tragedy*, 44.
44. Bernays, "Grundzüge," 65.
45. Ibid., 64.
46. Ibid., 64–65.
47. Nietzsche, "Beyond Good and Evil," 290.
48. Ibid., 206.
49. Neymeyr, "Selbst-Tyrannei," 92.
50. Nietzsche, *Beyond Good and Evil*, 290–91.
51. Nietzsche, *Nachgelassene Fragmente, 1880–1882*, 493.
52. Nietzsche, *Nachgelassene Fragmente, 1885–1887*, 537. For a discussion of the dialectics of active and reactive in Nietzsche, see Deleuze, *Nietzsche and Philosophy*, 36–67.
53. Nietzsche, *Briefe von Nietzsche, 1885–1886*, 68.
54. Schäfer and Vogl, "Feuer und Flamme," 203.
55. See Siegert, *Passagen des Digitalen*, 369–83.
56. Nietzsche, *Nachgelassene Fragmente, 1880–1882*, 541–42.
57. Nietzsche, *Ecce Homo*, 782.
58. Ibid., 68.
59. Nietzsche, "On Truth and Lying," 146.
60. Nietzsche, "Beyond Good and Evil," 206.
61. Ibid.
62. See Ellenberger, *Discovery of the Unconscious*, and Ellenberger, "Story of 'Anna O.'"
63. Breuer, "Krankengeschichte Bertha Pappenheim," 360.
64. Freud and Breuer, "On the Psychical Mechanism," 8.
65. Freud, "Five Lectures," 13.
66. Ibid.
67. Breuer, "Fräulein Anna O.," 22.
68. Ibid., 27.
69. Freud, "On Psychotherapy," 258.
70. Rabbow, *Seelenführung*, 280–300, quoted in Gödde, "Therapeutik und Ästhetik," 78.
71. Gödde, "Therapeutik und Ästhetik," 78.
72. Horace, "Art of Poetry," 400.
73. Ellenberger, *Discovery of the Unconscious*, 353.
74. Stavros Mentzos, "Hysterie," 775, 778.
75. In a *Commentarii* entry from August 31, 1960, Doderer identifies a certain type of individual like Pépin and the nurse Helga—both figures in *The Merowingians*—with sharp nails biting into the flesh of life: "Es gibt Leute, die wie krumme Nägel im Fleische des Lebens stecken: sie gehören mit der Beißzange ausgerissen. Aber, da niemand sie auszureißen vermag, obwohl der Riß hier noch viel berechtigter wäre als beim Beutelstich, bleiben sie in unserem armen gequälten Leben, wie steckengebliebene Bienenstachel, statt

zertreten zu werden." See Doderer, *Commentarii,* 2:250. Doderer's mention of a bee sting points to a possible source for the figure of Dr. Schajo in *The Merowingians.* It was the Hungarian entomologist Karl Sajo—in German pronounced "Schajo"—who in his 1909 study *Unsere Honigbiene* gives an entomological account of the bee sting. In the chapter "Stechapparate, bzw. Giftstachel," he analyzes the structure of the sting, resembling a barb, which remains stuck within the body: "Die Widerhaken sind so angebracht, daß der Stachel, wenn er einmal in einen Körper hineingestoßen wurde, steckenbleibt und gar nicht oder nur schwer zurückgezogen werden kann." See Sajo, *Unsere Honigbiene.*

76. For a discussion of the status of needles and pricks in the history of psychophysics, see Rieger, "Stiche des Wissens."

77. Heidegger, "Language in the Poem," 159.

78. Heidegger, "Spache im Gedicht," 37.

79. Doderer, *Merowingians:* "At fifteen he looked like a sad little bag" (36).

80. Müller, "*Pointe* in German Research," 225. See also Müller, *Theorie der Pointe*. Etymologically, the word *pointe* is related to the Latin *punctum*, a translation of the Greek *stigme*. See Schäffner, "Point," 57: "The point is a *semeion*, as in Euclid's Elements, the most inconspicuous of all signs: a *stigme*, as previously found in Aristotle's *Physics*, whose Latin translation *punctum* has been preserved in in the words *Punkt/point/punto*: the point is a puncture, a hole actually, from which the world of magnitude and extensions seems to fall out, an operation of discontinuity and interruption, and at the same time the beginning and the end of all continuous magnitudes."

81. Curtius, *European Literature,* 294.

82. Kraepelin, "Zur Psychologie des Komischen," 360.

83. Müller, "Pointe," 226. For a discussion of Doderer's use of the *pointe* in relation to the short prose of Johann Peter Hebel, see Buchholz, "Hebel-Wirkung."

84. See Schmidt-Dengler, "Tangenten an die Moderne."

85. Ibid., 58.

86. For a discussion of Doderer's method of irritating the reader, see Sommer, *Heimito von Doderer,* 41–106. See also Uwe Japp's interpretation of the short story "Erzählung" in "Mikrologie der Wut," 40–41: "Alles läuft, wie es bei Wutanfällen, besonders solchen ohne Grund, zu sein pflegt, auf eine Manifestation des Nicht-Wissens hinaus, einen Eklat der Ohnmacht. Während die Wut mit allen Insignien einer aggressiven Irrationalität ('Hohn, Haß und Bitternis') auf dem Schauplatz erscheint, bleibt der Grund—wie so oft—verborgen. Freilich besteht die Pointe der Geschichte gerade darin, dass der Wutanfall gar nicht (jedenfalls nicht narrativ) zum Austrag kommt, vielmehr in die ergebnislose Reflexion auf das Ereignis umkippt."

87. Freud, *Jokes,* 170.

88. For an enlightening interpretation of Freud's footnote, see Weber, *Legend of Freud,* 138–58.

89. Doderer, *Tangenten,* 259. Subsequent citations to this work are given parenthetically in the text.

90. Doderer, *Strudlhof Steps*, 76–77.

91. The editor, Dietrich Weber, comments: "Um das Weiterschreiben zu begünstigen und dem Leser ausreichend Raum für Marginalien und eigene Beiträge zu bieten, sah er sogar vor, das Buch nach Art mittelalterlicher Bücher mit weißem Papier durchschossen erscheinen zu lassen. In der vorliegenden Ausgabe wird wenigstens an den Übergängen von Buchstabe zu Buchstabe Platz gelassen für alle diejenigen, die den Autor beim Wort nehmen wollen." See Weber, "Einleitung des Herausgebers," 17.

92. Helmstetter, *Ornament der Grammatik*, 377.

93. Ibid., 385.

94. Jolles, *Einfache Formen*, 169, quoted in Helmstetter, *Ornament der Grammatik*, 385.

95. Doderer, *Lighted Windows*, 102. Subsequent citations to this work are given parenthetically in the text.

96. For a discussion of the term *apperception,* see the sections "Causes: The Specter of Old Vischer" and "The Necessary and the Superfluous" in this chapter.

97. Doderer, "Sprache des Dichters," 195–96.

98. Ibid., 196.

99. Ibid.

100. Ibid.

101. Ibid.

102. See Bücher, *Arbeit und Rhythmus*.

103. See Certeau, *Practice of Everyday Life*.

104. Freud, "Totem and Taboo," 75.

105. Bächtold-Stäubli, *Handwörterbuch*, 1:385.

106. Ibid., 1:391.

107. Ibid., 1:394.

108. See the chapter "Technology as a Release Mechanism for Regressions," in Bausinger, *Folk Culture*, 25–32.

109. Ibid., 25.

110. Freud, *Psychopathology of Everyday Life*, 167.

111. Ibid.

112. Ibid., 170.

113. Ibid., 173.

114. Ibid., 169.

115. Derrida, "My Chances," 25–26.

116. Freud, *Psychopathology of Everyday Life*, 258.

117. Ibid., 175.

118. Freud, *Psychopathology of Everyday Life*, 258. For a discussion of the term *projection,* see Müller-Tamm, *Abstraktion als Einfühlung*, 146–213.

119. Derrida, "My Chances," 24. What Derrida calls a "believing attitude" could be described in Daniel Dennett's terms as an "intentional stance." See Dennett, *Intentional Stance*.

120. Freud, "Totem and Taboo," 92.

121. Ibid., 79.

122. Ibid.

123. Nietzsche, *Nachgelassene Fragmente, 1880–1882*, 120. See Brusotti, *Leidenschaften der Erkenntnis*, 56–64.

124. Freud, "Totem and Taboo," 85.

125. Plato, *Laws of Plato*, 263–64.

126. Ibid., 153.

127. Hyde, "Prosecution of Animals," 698. See Berman, "Rats, Pigs," 296: "For the Greeks, guilt and punishment had to be ascribed to some person or thing lest the Furies, avenging spirits of the dead person, create misfortunes throughout the land. Indeed, whether the killing was intentional or premeditated seems to have been irrelevant, for the primary purpose was to remove the moral pollution in the air created by the murder."

128. Vismann, "Schuld ist das Ding," 18.

129. Stone, "Problem for Pericles."

130. Aristotle, *Athenian Constitution*, 103.

131. The quote is from Berman, "Anthropological Approach," 34. MacDowell, arguing against these interpretations, stresses the positive results of the Prytaneum. MacDowell, *Athenian Homicide Law*, 89: "The existence and procedure of this court are an outstanding example of the operation of ritual in Athenian homicide law. Yet it is not on that account to be regarded as entirely absurd and pointless. If someone was killed by an object, an animal, or an unknown person, it was desirable that the state should take note of the manner of his death, and take any steps that were practicable to see that no one else died in the same way in the future. The court served some of the purposes of a modern coroner's court."

132. Gagarin, *Antiphon the Athenian*, 111.

133. Berman, "Anthropological Approach," 4.

134. Ibid., 46.

135. Doderer, "Acht Wutanfälle," 311–12.

136. See chapter 3 above.

137. Doderer, "Acht Wutanfälle," 312.

138. Doderer, "Acht Wutanfälle," 312.

139. For a discussion of the relationship between Vischer and Doderer, see Schmid-Bortenschlager, "Doderers 'Merowinger.'" See also Löffler, "Zur Metaphysik."

140. See Hermann-Trentepohl, "Hulesch & Quenzel," 78.

141. Heidegger, *Being and Time*, 107.

142. Doderer, *Commentarii*, 91.

143. The German word *Gelassenheit* is difficult to translate. Possible translations include "calmness," "imperturbability," and "serenity."

144. Heidegger, *Discourse on Thinking*, 55.

145. The following sentences in *The Merowingians* must be read not only as a commentary on the whole novel but especially as a comment on Heidegger's philosophy of the thing: "At last, the Captain took the pipe out of his mouth and said agreeably: "Excuse me, Doctor, but that whole thing is a mighty piece of nonsense." "Yes, of course, of course nonsense!" cried Doctor Döblinger, delighted that at last he had been understood by this valued reader. "What else?! And what besides nonsense?! All madness" (413).

146. Doderer, "Sexualität und totaler Staat," 294.
147. Ibid.
148. Doderer, "Wörtlichkeit," 200.
149. See Doderer, *Tagebücher, 1920–1939*, 881: "About Swoboda one has to say that he would not recognize a science without a back of the head [Hinterkopf]. For the psychology of the Kraepelin school he found the fitting expression 'locksmithery of the soul.'"
150. This can be read as an ironic allusion to Freud's *Interpretation of Dreams*, where often the seemingly inessential and accidental reveals essential truths.
151. Doderer, "Grundlagen und Funktion," 158.
152. Luehrs-Kaiser, "'Schnürlzieherei der Assoziationen,'" 290.
153. In the essay "Foundations and Function of the Novel" [Grundlagen und Funktion des Romans], Doderer highlights Proust's concept of memory as crucial for his theory of the novel. See Doderer, "Grundlagen und Funktion," 157: "Die fundamentale Bedeutung des Gedächtnisses für die Haltung des Epikers hat uns Marcel Proust durch sein gewaltiges Werk praktisch demonstriert" (Marcel Proust's enormous work has practically demonstrated the fundamental importance of the memory for the the mental constitution of the epic writer). For a discussion of Proust's influence on Doderer, see Schröder, *Apperzeption und Vorurteil*, 162–68.
154. Doderer, "Wörtlichkeit," 198.
155. Ibid.
156. Ibid.
157. Doderer, "Sexualität und totaler Staat," 284.
158. Ibid., 164.
159. Ibid., 286.
160. Weber, "Beamte," 1321.
161. According to Niels Werber's reading, Weber describes "die Bürokratie als komplexe Organisationsform, statt als quasi dramatisches Interaktionssystem von—je nach Rolle bösartigen oder gutmütigen—Bürokraten." See Werber, "Bürokratische Kommunikation," 313.
162. In *The Merowingians* Doderer further modifies the phrase into "Denker und Drescher" (130).
163. Adorno, *Minima Moralia*, 45.
164. Ibid.
165. Ibid., 109.
166. Doderer defines the notions of "second reality" and "pseudological space" so broadly that all forms of the modern state, whether fascism, socialism, or parliamentary democracy, can be subsumed under them, so that these notions lose any critical power.
167. Doderer, "Rosa Chymica Austriaco-Hispanica," 235.
168. Adorno, *Minima Moralia*, 37.
169. Doderer, "Sexualität und totaler Staat," 294.
170. Adorno, *Minima Moralia*, 37.
171. Doderer, "Rosa Chymica Austriaco-Hispanica," 232.
172. Ibid., 234.

173. For Doderer, the underlying psychological structure of a generalized refusal to apperceive did not disappear with the end of the Nazi regime but remained to exercise an "uncanny insistence." The project of "humanization" (Menschwerdung), therefore, must be understood as a way of overcoming this insistence. All of Doderer's comments on the Third Reich have to be read against the background of his own involvement with Nazism and his anti-Semitism in the thirties and forties. He joined the Austrian branch of the German Nazi Party as early as April 1, 1933, and remained a member until 1945. In the context of this study, all of the manifold political as well as biographical implications of Doderer's own "refusal to perceive" and his attempts in the fifties and sixties to come to terms with them (and whether they were successful or merely superficial) cannot be analyzed sufficiently. For a discussion of Doderer's political involvements, see Sommer, "In die 'Sackgasse,'" and Sommer, "Entbehrliche Dr. Hartog."

174. Grimm, *Deutsches Wörterbuch*, 1273. See Koller, "Von Abergeil bis Zilken"; McInnes, "Literary Onomastics"; Winterstein, "Torpedierung und Apologie," 319.

EPILOGUE

1. For the prehistory of Ostwald's concept of *energetics*, see Rabinbach, *Human Motor*.
2. Ostwald, "Wissenschaftsgeschichtliche Stellung der Energetik," 100.
3. Ostwald, "Energetische Imperativ," 83. See Rabinbach, *Human Motor*, 182: "No area of human endeavour was untouched by the laws of energy. The entire effort of civilization, Ostwald maintained, was devoted to converting raw energy into available energy. . . . All progress can thus be measured by the efficiency of energy conversion, by the elimination of waste, and by the coordination of energies to maximize efficiency."
4. Ostwald, "Energetische Imperativ," 83.
5. Ibid., 84.
6. Ibid., 85.
7. Ibid.
8. Ostwald, "Praktische Philosophie," 126.
9. See Rabinbach, *Human Motor*, 254: "Significantly, the German reception of Taylor's ideas was smoothed by their presentation in the language of energetics. The German translation (1912) of his study, *Principles of Scientific Management*, was introduced as a 'system of budgeting human labor power,' and its translator, the Berlin engineer Rudolf Roesler, remarked on many parallels between Taylor's ideas and those of Wilhelm Ostwald, whose *Der energetische Imperativ* appeared the previous year."
10. Ostwald, "Wie der energetische Imperativ entstand," 14.
11. Kant, *Grounding for the Metaphysics*, 30–31.
12. Ostwald, "Maschinen und Lebewesen," 135.
13. Ibid., 130. Against traditional histories of technology that attempted to explain organisms in terms of technology—most famously represented by

Notes

Ernst Kapp's *Organprojektion*—Ostwald reverses the perspective and conceptualizes machines in terms of organisms.

14. Ibid., 131.
15. Ibid., 132.
16. Ibid., 133.
17. Rieger, *Individualität der Medien*, 12.
18. Münsterberg, *Grundzüge der Psychotechnik*, 389, quoted and translated in Rabinbach, *Human Motor*, 192.
19. Killen, "Weimar Psychotechnics," 60.
20. Rose, *Inventing Our Selves*, 17.
21. Ibid., 114.
22. Foucault, *Discipline and Punish*, 191.
23. Killen, "Weimar Psychotechnics," 60–61.
24. The term *psychopower*, analogous to Foucault's notion of *biopower*, was coined by Jackie Orr. See Orr, *Panic Diaries*.
25. Kittler, *Gramophone, Film, Typewriter*, 160.
26. Freud, "Civilization and Its Discontents," 77. Subsequent citations to this work are given parenthetically in the text.
27. Giese, *Psychotechnik*, 7.
28. See Strachey, "Editor's Introduction," 59–60: "The original title chosen for it [*Das Unbehagen in der Natur*,] by Freud was '*Das Unglück in der Natur*' ('Unhappiness in Civilization'); but '*Unglück*' was later altered to '*Unbehagen*'—a word for which it was difficult to choose an English equivalent, though the French '*malaise*' might have served. Freud suggested '*Man's Discomfort in Civilization*' in a letter to his translator, Mrs. Riviere; but it was she herself who found the ideal solution of the difficulty in the title that was finally adopted."
29. See Brunner, "Naked Mother."
30. See Freud, "Uncanny." "What interests us most in this long excerpt is to find that among its different shades of meaning the word '*heimlich*' exhibits one which is identical with its opposite, '*unheimlich*.' What is *heimlich* thus comes to be *unheimlich*."
31. Grubrich-Simitis, *Back to Freud's Texts*, 168.
32. Ibid.
33. Ronell, *Telephone Book*, 88.
34. Jones, *Life and Work of Freud*, 3:95. For a discussion of Freud's prosthetic existence, see Wills, *Prosthesis*, 92–129, and Ronell, *Telephone Book*, 88.
35. McLuhan, *Understanding Media*. In the chapter "The Gadget Lover: Narcissus as Narcosis," McLuhan discusses technology in terms of amputation and prosthesis.
36. See Johnson, *Persons and Things*, 89: "Organic form might always have been a fantasy."
37. Cf. Serres, *Parasite*.
38. Assad, *Reading with Michel Serres*, 18.
39. Asendorf, *Ströme und Strahlen*, 119.
40. Jacques Lacan suggests replacing the notion of human sciences with that of "conjectural sciences." See Lacan, *Ego in Freud's Theory*, 296. On

the "farewell to the corporeal," see Kamper, "Corpus absconditum," 445, quoted in Rieger, *Kybernetische Anthropologie*, 108.

41. Asendorf, *Batteries of Life*, 133.
42. Cassirer, *Substanzbegriff und Funktionsbegriff*.
43. Freud, "Analysis of a Phobia," 104.
44. Rieger, *Kybernetische Anthropologie*, 108–9.
45. On the history of the term *projection* in nineteenth-century philosophy, physiology, ethnology, and psychology, see Müller-Tamm, *Abstraktion als Einfühlung*.
46. Rieger, *Kybernetische Anthropologie*, 109.
47. Petroski, *Evolution of Useful Things*, 20.
48. Cassirer, "Form und Technik," 176.
49. Ibid., 177.
50. Ibid., 176. In a similar vein, Blumenberg perceives rhetoric as a technique dealing with what is possible, not with what is. See Blumenberg, "Anthropological Approach."
51. Blumenberg, "Wirklichkeitsbegriff und Möglichkeit," 53–54.
52. Haverkamp, *Figura Cryptica*, 17.
53. Bloch, *Spuren*, 172.
54. Ibid., 161.
55. For a discussion of the traumatic experience of the railway accident in the nineteenth century, see Fischer-Homberger, "Eisenbahnunfall." See also Harrington, "Railway Accident." For the cultural significance of the railway and especially the railway journey in the nineteenth century, see Schivelbusch, *Railway Journey*.
56. See Bloch, "Technology and Ghostly Apparitions," 315: "Whereas the failure of an electric bulb does not betray the existence of any spirit world acting to suppress the light, but only the existence of a short-circuit or a power-station shutdown."
57. Bloch, "Anxiety of the Engineer," 310.
58. Bloch, *Spuren*, 161.
59. Bloch, "Anxiety of the Engineer," 312.
60. Virilio, *Original Accident*, 10: "To invent the sailing ship or steamer is to *invent the shipwreck*. To invent the train is *to invent the rail accident* of derailment. To invent the family automobile is to produce the *pile-up* on the highway."
61. Haraway, "Cyborg Manifesto," 164.
62. Foucault, *Care of the Self*, 68.
63. Wiener, *Human Use of Human Beings*, 17–18.
64. Rosenblueth, Wiener, and Bigelow, "Behavior, Purpose, and Teleology," 18.
65. See Foerster, "Ethics and Second-Order Cybernetics."
66. See Foucault, "Governmentality."
67. Cannon, *Wisdom of the Body*, 303. On Cannon's concept of homeostasis, see Tanner, "'Weisheit des Körpers.'"
68. Canguilhem, "Development of the Concept," 82.

Notes

69. See Cannon, *Wisdom of the Body*, xiv–xv: "In 1923, the late Professor E. H. Starling, of University College, London, gave the Harveian Oration before the Royal College of Physicians. . . . His oration he entitled 'The Wisdom of the Body.' Only by understanding the wisdom of the body, he declared, shall we attain that 'mastery of disease and pain which will enable us to relieve the burden of mankind.' Because of my own convictions coincide with those of Professor Starling, and because the facts and interpretations which I shall offer illustrate his point of view, I have chosen to give the title of his oration to the present volume."

70. Ibid., 324. Tanner, in "'Weisheit des Körpers,'" 144–45, summarizes this interaction of physis and thesis, nature and culture, in Cannon as follows: "Menschen sind biologisch auf Kultur angewiesen. Sie sind nicht nur ein Körper—sie 'haben' auch einen, sie verwenden ihn als ursprüngliches Artefakt und machen ihn zum Gegenstand von Reflexion und Intervention."

71. Lacan, *Ego in Freud's Theory*, 60. See also Laplanche and Pontalis, *Language of Psycho-Analysis*, 342: "When Freud—as well as Breuer—postulates a law of constancy as part of the groundwork of psychology, he is only confronting in his turn a requirement which was very widely acknowledged in the scientific circles of the latter part of the nineteenth century—namely, the call to extend the most general principles of physics, in so far as these stand at the very basis of all science, to psychology and psychophysiology."

72. Lacan, *Ego in Freud's Theory*, 60.
73. Ibid., 61.
74. Freud, "Uncanny," 237.
75. Cixous, "Fiction and Its Phantoms," 542.
76. Lacan, *Ego in Freud's Theory*, 62.
77. Lacan, *Ethics of Psychoanalysis*, 103.
78. Lacan, *Ego in Freud's Theory*, 90.

BIBLIOGRAPHY

Adorno, Theodor W. *Minima Moralia.* Trans. E. F. N. Jephcott. London: Verso, 1978.

———. "On Subject and Object." Trans. Andrew Arato and Eike Gebhardt. In *The Adorno Reader,* ed. Brian O'Connor, 137–54. Oxford: Wiley-Blackwell, 2000.

Agamben, Giorgio. *The Sacrament of Language: An Archaeology of the Oath.* Ed. Adam Kotsko. Stanford: Stanford University Press, 2011.

Ajouri, Philipp. *Erzählen nach Darwin: Die Krise der Teleologie im literarischen Realismus: Friedrich Theodor Vischer und Gottfried Keller.* New York: De Gruyter, 2007.

Apter, Emily, and William Pietz, eds. *Fetishism as Cultural Discourse.* Ithaca: Cornell University Press, 1993.

Aristotle. *Art of Rhetoric.* Trans. John H. Freese. Cambridge, MA: Harvard University Press, 1924.

———. *The Athenian Constitution.* Trans. P. J. Rhodes. New York: Penguin Books, 1984.

Asendorf, Christoph. *Batteries of Life: On the History of Things and Their Perception in Modernity.* Trans. Don Reneau. Berkeley: University of California Press, 1993.

———. *Ströme und Strahlen: Das langsame Verschwinden der Materie um 1900.* Giessen: Anabas, 1989.

Assad, Maria L. *Reading with Michel Serres: An Encounter with Time.* Albany: State University of New York Press, 1999.

Auerbach, Berthold. "Wissen und Schaffen: Aphorismen zu Friedrich Vischer's 'Auch Einer.'" *Deutsche Rundschau* 19 (1879): 269–95.

Babich, Babette. "From van Gogh's Museum to the Temple at Bassae: Heidegger's Truth of Art and Schapiro's Art History." *Culture, Theory and Critique* 44, no. 2 (2003): 151–69.

Bächtold-Stäubli, Hanns, ed. *Handwörterbuch des deutschen Aberglaubens.* Vol. 1. Berlin: De Gruyter, 1927.

Barry, Kelly. "Natural Palingenesis: Childhood, Memory and Self-Experience in Herder and Jean Paul." *Goethe Yearbook* 6 (2007): 1–25.

Bausinger, Hermann. *Folk Culture in a World of Technology.* Trans. Elke Dettmer. Bloomington: Indiana University Press, 1990.

Benveniste, Émile. "La blasphémie et l'euphémie." In *Problèmes de linguistique générale,* 2:255–56. Paris: Gallimard, 1974.

Beresford, James. *The Miseries of Human Life, or The Last Groans of Timothy Testy and Samuel Sensitive.* London: William Miller, 1807.

Bergengruen, Maximilian. *Schöne Seelen, groteske Körper: Jean Pauls Dynamisierung der Anthropologie.* Hamburg: Meiner, 2003.

Bergk, J. A. *Die Kunst, Bücher zu lesen: Nebst Bemerkungen über Schriften und Schriftsteller.* Jena: Hempelsche Buchhandlung, 1799.

Bergson, Henri. "On Laughter." In *Comedy,* ed. Wylie Syper, 61–190. Garden City, NY: Doubleday Anchor Books, 1956.

Berman, Paul Schiff. "An Anthropological Approach to Modern Forfeiture Law: The Symbolic Function of Legal Actions against Objects." *Yale Journal of Law and the Humanities* 11 (1999): 1–46.

———. "Rats, Pigs, and Statues on Trial: The Creation of Cultural Narratives in the Prosecution of Animals and Inanimate Objects." *NYU Law Review* 69 (1994): 288–326.

Bernays, Jacob. "Aristotle on the Effect of Tragedy." Trans. Jennifer Barnes and Jonathan Barnes. In *Articles on Aristotle,* ed. Jonathan Barnes, Malcolm Schofield, and Richard Sorabji, 4:154–65. London: Duckworth, 1979.

———. "Grundzüge der verlorenen Abhandlung des Aristoteles über Wirkung der Tragödie." In *Zwei Abhandlungen über die Aristotelische Theorie des Drama,* 1–118. Berlin: Hertz, 1880.

———. "On Catharsis: From Fundamentals of Aristotle's Lost Essay on the 'Effect of Tragedy.'" *American Imago* 61, no. 3 (2004): 319–41.

Bhushan, Bharat. *Introduction to Tribology.* New York: John Wiley, 2002.

Binswanger, Ludwig. "Extravagance." In *Being-in-the-World: Selected Papers of Ludwig Binswanger,* trans. Jacob Needleman, 342–49. London: Basic Books, 1963.

Blair, Hugh. *Lectures on Rhetoric and Belles Lettres.* 2nd ed. London: Strahan, Cadell, Creech, 1787.

Blanchot, Maurice. "Literature and the Right to Death." Trans. Lydia Davis. In *The Work of Fire,* 300–344. Stanford: Stanford University Press, 1995.

Bloch, Ernst. "The Anxiety of the Engineer." In *Literary Essays,* trans. Andrew Joron, 304–13. Stanford: Stanford University Press, 1998.

Bibliography

———. *Spuren.* Frankfurt: Suhrkamp, 1985.

———. "Technology and Ghostly Apparitions." In *Literary Essays,* trans. Andrew Joron, 314–20. Stanford: Stanford University Press, 1998.

Blumenberg, Hans. "An Anthropological Approach to the Contemporary Significance of Rhetoric." Trans. Robert M. Wallace. In *After Philosophy? End or Transformation,* ed. Kenneth Baynes, James Bohman, and Thomas McCarthy, 423–58. Cambridge, MA: MIT Press, 1987.

———. "Lebenswelt und Technisierung unter Aspekten der Phänomenologie." In *Wirklichkeiten in denen wir leben,* 7–54. Stuttgart: Reclam, 1981.

———. "Wirklichkeitsbegriff und Möglichkeit des Romans." In Ästhetische und Metaphorologische Schriften, ed. Anselm Haverkamp, 47–74. Frankfurt: Suhrkamp, 2001.

Böhme, Hartmut. *Fetischismus und Kultur: Eine andere Theorie der Moderne.* Hamburg: Rowohlt, 2006.

Bollack, Jean. *Jacob Bernays: Un homme entre deux mondes.* Villeneuve d'Ascq: Nord, 1998.

Bowden, Martha F. *Yorick's Congregation: The Church of England in the Time of Laurence Sterne.* Newark: University of Delaware Press, 2007.

Breuer, Josef. "Fräulein Anna O." In *Studies on Hysteria,* vol. 2 of *The Standard Edition of the Complete Works of Sigmund Freud,* ed. and trans. James Strachey, 21–48. London: Hogarth, 1955.

———. "Krankengeschichte Bertha Pappenheim." In *Physiologie und Psychoanalyse in Leben und Werk Josef Breuers,* ed. Albrecht Hirschmüller, 348–64. Bern: Huber, 1978.

Breuer, Josef, and Sigmund Freud. *Studies on Hysteria.* Vol. 2 of *The Standard Edition of the Complete Works of Sigmund Freud.* Ed. and trans. James Strachey. London: Hogarth, 1955.

Brewer, John, and Roy Porter, eds. *Consumption and the World of Goods.* London: Routledge, 1993.

Brown, Bill. *A Sense of Things: The Object Matter of American Literature.* Chicago: University of Chicago Press, 2003.

———. "Thing Theory." *Critical Inquiry* 28, no. 1 (2001): 1–22.

Brown, John. *The Elements of Medicine, or A Translation of the Elementa Medicinae Brunonis.* 2 vols. London: Johnson, 1786.

Brown, Kate E., and Howard I. Kushner. "Eruptive Voices: Coprolalia, Malediction, and the Poetics of Cursing." *New Literary History* 32 (2001): 537–62.

Brunner, José. "The Naked Mother or, Why Freud Did Not Write about Railway Accidents." *Psychoanalysis and History* 9, no. 1 (2007): 71–82.

Brusotti, Marco. *Die Leidenschaft der Erkenntnis: Philosophie und ästhetische*

Lebensgestaltung bei Nietzsche von "Morgenröthe" bis "Also sprach Zarathustra." Berlin: De Gruyter, 1997.

Bücher, Karl. *Arbeit und Rhythmus.* Leipzig: Hirzel, 1896.

Buchholz, Torsten. "Die Hebel-Wirkung auf die Kurzprosa oder Doderers vergrabene Pfunde im Schatzkästlein." In *"Schüsse ins Finstere" Zu Heimito von Doderers Kurzprosa,* ed. Gerald Sommer and Kai Luehrs-Kaiser, 87–96. Würzburg: Königshausen und Neumann, 2001.

Burckhardt, Sigurd. "Tristram Shandy's Law of Gravity." *ELH* 28, no. 1 (1961): 70–88.

Campe, Rüdiger. *Affekt und Ausdruck: Umwandlungen der rhetorischen Rede im 17. und 18. Jahrhundert.* Tübingen: Niemeyer, 1990.

———. "Affizieren und Selbstaffizieren: Rhetorisch-anthropologische Näherungen ausgehend von Quintilian *Institutio oratoria* VI 1–2." In *Rhetorische Anthropologie: Studien zum Homo Rhetoricus,* ed. Josef Kopperschmidt, 135–52. Munich: Fink, 2000.

———. "Schreibstunden in Jean Pauls Idyllen." In *Fugen: Deutsch-Französisches Jahrbuch für Text-Analytik,* ed. Manfred Frank, Friedrich A. Kittler, and Samuel Weber, 1:132–70. Olten: Walter, 1980.

———. "Schreibszene: Schreiben." In *Paradoxien, Dissonanzen, Zusammenbrüche: Baustellen offener Epistemologie,* ed. Hans Ulrich Gumbrecht and Karl Ludwig Pfeiffer, 759–72. Frankfurt: Suhrkamp, 1991.

Canguilhem, Georges. "The Development of the Concept of Biological Regulation in the Eighteenth and Nineteenth Centuries." In *Ideology and Rationality in the History of the Life Sciences,* trans. Arthur Goldhammer, 81–102. Cambridge, MA: MIT Press, 1988.

Cannon, Walter. *The Wisdom of the Body.* New York: Norton, 1963.

Cash, Arthur H. *Laurence Sterne: The Early and Middle Years.* London: Methuen, 1975.

Cassirer, Ernst. "Form und Technik." In *Gesammelte Werke,* ed. Tobias Berben, 17:139–84. Hamburg: Meiner, 2004.

———. *Substanzbegriff und Funktionsbegriff: Untersuchungen über die Fragen der Erkenntniskritik.* 1910. Reprinted as vol. 6 of *Gesammelte Werke,* ed. Birgit Recki. Hamburg: Meiner, 2000.

Certeau, Michel de. *The Practice of Everyday Life.* Trans. Steven Rendall. Berkeley: University of California Press, 1984.

Cervantes Saavedra, Miguel de. *The History of the Renowned Don Quixote de la Mancha.* Vol. 1. Trans. Peter Motteux. Rev. John Ozell. London: Kowper, 1771.

Cixous, Hélène. "Fiction and Its Phantoms: A Reading of Freud's 'Das Unheimliche.'" *New Literary History* 7, no. 3 (1976): 525–48.

Coleridge, Samuel Taylor. *Fire, Famine, and Slaughter.* London, 1798.

Curtius, Ernst Robert. *European Literature and the Latin Middle Ages.* Trans. Willard R. Trask. Princeton: Princeton University Press, 1973.

Danziger, Kurt. *Constructing the Subject: Historical Origins of Psychological Research.* Cambridge: Cambridge University Press, 1990.

Darby, Robert. "An Oblique and Slovenly Initiation: The Circumcision Episode in Tristram Shandy." *Eighteenth-Century Life* 27, no. 1 (2003): 72–84.

Day, W. G. "*Tristram Shandy*: Locke May Not Be the Key." In *Laurence Sterne: Riddles and Mysteries,* ed. Valerie Grosvenor Myer, 75–83. London: Vision Press, 1984.

Deleuze, Gilles. *Nietzsche and Philosophy.* London: Continuum, 1986.

de Man, Paul. "Anthropomorphism and Trope in the Lyric." In *The Rhetoric of Romanticism,* 239–62. New York: Columbia University Press, 1984.

Dengel-Pelloquin, Elsbeth. *Eigensinnige Geschöpfe: Jean Pauls poetische Geschlechter-Werkstatt.* Freiburg: Rombach, 1999.

Dennett, Daniel. *The Intentional Stance.* Cambridge, MA: MIT Press, 1989.

Derrida, Jacques. "My Chances / *Mes Chances*: A Rendezvous with Some Epicurean Stereophonies." In *Taking Chances: Derrida, Psychoanalysis and Literature,* ed. Joseph H. Smith and William Kerrigan, trans. Irene Harvey and Avital Ronell, 1–32. Baltimore: Johns Hopkins University Press, 1984.

———. "Plato's Pharmacy." In *Dissemination,* trans. Barbara Johnson, 67–186. London: Continuum Press, 2004.

———. "Restitutions." In *The Truth in Painting,* ed. Geoff Bennington and Ian McLeod, 255–382. Chicago: University of Chicago Press, 1987.

Doderer, Heimito von. "Acht Wutanfälle." In *Die Erzählungen,* ed. Wendelin Schmidt-Dengler, 310–15. Munich: Biederstein, 1972.

———. *Commentarii 1957 bis 1966: Tagebücher aus dem Nachlass.* Vol. 2. Ed. Wendelin Schmidt-Dengler. Munich: Biederstein, 1986.

———. "Grundlagen und Funktion des Romans." In *Die Wiederkehr der Drachen,* ed. Wendelin Schmidt-Dengler, 149–75. Munich: Biederstein, 1970.

———. "Kleine Vorbemerkung zu einer literarischen Unterhaltung." In *Repertorium: Ein Begreifbuch von höheren und niederen Lebens-Sachen,* ed. Dietrich Weber, 5–18. Munich: Biederstein, 1969.

———. *The Lighted Windows or The Humanization of the Bureeaucrat Julius Zihal.* Trans. John S. Barrett. Riverside, CA: Ariadne Press, 2000.

———. *The Merowingians, or The Total Family.* Trans. Vinal Overing Binner. Los Angeles: Sun and Moon Press, 1996.

———. *Repertorium: Ein Begreifbuch von höheren und niederen Lebens-Sachen*. Ed. Dietrich Weber. Munich: Biederstein, 1969.

———. "Rosa Chymica Austriaco-Hispanica: Voraussetzungen österreichischer Lyrik." In *Die Wiederkehr der Drachen*, ed. Wendelin Schmidt-Dengler, 231–36. Munich: Biederstein, 1970.

———. "Sexualität und totaler Staat." In *Die Wiederkehr der Drachen*, ed. Wendelin Schmidt-Dengler, 275–98. Munich: Biederstein, 1970.

———. "Die Sprache des Dichters." in *Die Wiederkehr der Drachen*, ed. Wendelin Schmidt-Dengler, 194–97. Munich: Biederstein, 1970.

———. *The Strudlhof Steps or Melzer and the Depths of the Years*. Trans. Vincent Kling. Munich: C. H. Beck, 1999. www.doderer-gesellschaft.org/english/pdf/The_Strudlhof_Steps.pdf.

———. *Tagebücher, 1920–1939*. Vol. 2. Ed. Wendelin Schmidt-Dengler, Martin Loew-Cadonna, and Gerald Sommer. Munich: Beck, 1996.

———. *Tangenten: Tagebuch eines Schriftstellers*. Munich: Biederstein, 1964.

———. "Wörtlichkeit als Kernfestung der Wirklichkeit." In *Die Wiederkehr der Drachen*, ed. Wendelin Schmidt-Dengler, 198–204. Munich: Biederstein, 1970.

Ellenberger, Henry F. *The Discovery of the Unconscious: The History and Evolution of Dynamic Psychiatry*. New York: Basic Books, 1970.

———. "The Story of 'Anna O.': A Critical Review with New Data." In *Beyond the Unconscious: Essays of Henry E. Ellenberger in the History of Psychiatry*, ed. Mark S. Micale, 254–72. Princeton: Princeton University Press, 1993.

Epictetus. "Enchiridion." In *Discourses and Selected Writings*, ed. and trans. Robert Dobbin. London: Penguin Books, 2008.

Fischer-Homberger, Esther. "Der Eisenbahnunfall von 1842 auf der Paris-Versailles-Linie: Traumatische Dissoziation und Fortschrittsgeschichte." In *Die Unordnung der Dinge: Eine Wissens- und Mediengeschichte des Unfalls*, ed. Christian Kassung, 45–84. Bielefeld: Transcript, 2009.

Fleming, Paul. "The Crisis of Art: Max Kommerell and Jean Paul's Gestures." *MLN* 115, no. 3 (2000): 519–43.

———. *The Pleasures of Abandonment: Jean Paul and the Life of Humor*. Tübingen: Königshausen und Neumann, 2006.

Forschner, Maximilian. *Die stoische Ethik: Über den Zusammenhang von Natur-, Sprach-, und Moralphilosophie im altstoischen System*. Stuttgart: Klett-Cotta, 1981.

Foucault, Michel. *The Care of the Self*. Trans. Robert Hurley. New York: Vintage Books, 1988.

Bibliography

———. *Discipline and Punish: The Birth of the Prison.* Trans. Alan Sheridan. London: Allen Lane, 1977.

———. "Governmentality." Trans. Rosi Breidotti. Rev. Colin Gordon. In *The Foucault Effect: Studies in Governmentality*, ed. Graham Burchell and Colin Gordon, 87–104. Chicago: University of Chicago Press, 1991.

———. *The Hermeneutics of the Subject: Lectures at the Collège de France, 1981–1982.* Ed. Frédéric Gros. Trans. Graham Burchell. New York: Picador, 2005.

———. *Madness and Civilization: A History of Insanity in the Age of Reason.* Trans. Richard Howard. New York: Vintage Books, 1973.

———. "Technologies of the Self." In *Technologies of the Self*, ed. Luther H. Martin, Huck Gutman, and Patrick H. Hutton, 16–49. Amherst: University of Massachusetts Press, 1988.

Freud, Sigmund. "Analysis of a Phobia in a Five-Year-Old Boy." In *Two Case Histories*, vol. 10 of *The Standard Edition of the Complete Psychological Works of Sigmund Freud*, ed. and trans. James Strachey, 1–150. London: Hogarth, 1978.

———. "Civilization and Its Discontents." In *The Future of an Illusion, Civilization and Its Discontents and Other Works*, vol. 21 of *The Standard Edition of the Complete Psychological Works of Sigmund Freud*, ed. and trans. James Strachey, 64–145. London: Hogarth, 1961.

———. "Five Lectures on Psycho-Analysis." In *Five Lectures on Psycho-Analysis, Leonardo da Vinci and Other Works*, vol. 11 of *The Standard Edition of the Complete Psychological Works of Sigmund Freud*, ed. and trans. James Strachey, 3–55. London: Hogarth, 1957.

———. *Jokes and Their Relation to the Unconscious.* Vol. 8 of *The Standard Edition of the Complete Psychological Works of Sigmund Freud.* Ed. and trans. James Strachey. London: Hogarth, 1905.

———. "On Psychotherapy." In *A Case of Hysteria, Three Essays on Sexuality and Other Works*, vol. 7 of *The Standard Edition of the Complete Psychological Works of Sigmund Freud*, ed. and trans. James Strachey, 257–68. London: Hogarth, 1953.

———. *The Psychopathology of Everyday Life.* Vol. 6 of *The Standard Edition of the Complete Psychological Works of Sigmund Freud.* Ed. and trans. James Strachey. London: Hogarth, 1901.

———. "Totem and Taboo." In *Totem and Taboo and Other Works*, vol. 13 of *The Standard Edition of the Complete Psychological Works of Sigmund Freud*, ed. and trans. James Strachey, 1–161. London: Hogarth, 1955.

———. "The Uncanny." In *An Infantile Neurosis and Other Works*, vol. 17 of *The Standard Edition of the Complete Psychological Works of*

Sigmund Freud, ed. and trans. James Strachey, 217–56. London: Hogarth, 1955.

Freud, Sigmund, and Josef Breuer. "On the Psychical Mechanism of Hysterical Phenomena: Preliminary Communication." In *Studies on Hysteria,* vol. 2 of *The Standard Edition of the Complete Psychological Works of Sigmund Freud,* ed. and trans. James Strachey, 1–18. London: Hogarth, 1955.

Frey, Christiane. "Wissen um Trieb und Laune: Zu einem Widerspruch in Anthropologie und Ästhetik des 18. Jahrhunderts." In *Kulturen des Wissens im 18. Jahrhundert,* ed. Ulrich Johannes Schneider, 391–98. Berlin: De Gruyter, 2008.

Gagarin, Michael. *Antiphon the Athenian: Oratory, Law, and Justice in the Age of the Sophists.* Austin: University of Texas Press, 2002.

Galen. "The Diagnosis and Cure of the Soul's Passions." In *On the Passions and Errors of the Soul,* trans. Paul W. Harkins. Columbus: Ohio State University Press, 1963.

Gell, Alfred. *Art and Agency: An Anthropological Theory.* Oxford: Clarendon Press, 1998.

Giese, Fritz. *Psychotechnik.* Breslau: Hirt, 1928.

Gill, Christopher. *The Structured Self in Hellenistic and Roman Thought.* Oxford: Oxford University Press, 2006.

Gmelin, Eberhard. *Ueber den Thierischen Magnetismus: In einem Brief an Herrn Geheimen Rath Hoffmann in Mainz.* Tübingen: Heerbrandt, 1787.

Gödde, Günter. "Therapeutik und Ästhetik: Verbindungen zwischen Breuers und Freuds kathartischer Therapie und der Katharsis-Konzeption von Jacob Bernays." In *Grenzen der Katharsis in den modernen Künsten: Transformationen des aristotelischen Modells seit Bernays, Nietzsche und Freud,* ed. Martin Vöhler and Dirck Linck, 63–93. Berlin: De Gruyter, 2009.

Goethe, Johann Wolfgang. *Truth and Fiction: Relating to My Life.* Vol. 1. Trans. John Oxenford. New York: Lovel, Coryell, 1882.

Graver, Margaret. *Stoicism and Emotion.* Chicago: Chicago of University Press, 2007.

Grimm, Jacob, and Wilhelm Grimm. *Deutsches Wörterbuch.* 1854–72. Reprint, Munich: Deutscher Taschenbuchverlag, 1999.

Grimm, Reinhold. "Embracing Two Horses: Tragedy, Humor, and Inwardness; or, Nietzsche, Vischer, und Julius Bahnsen." *Nietzsche-Studien* 18 (1989): 203–20.

———. "Zur Wirkungsgeschichte von Vischers 'Auch Einer.'" *Gestaltungsgeschichte und Gesellschaftsgeschichte,* ed. Helmut Kreuzer, 352–81. Stuttgart: Metzler, 1969.

Grubrich-Simitis, Ilse. *Back to Freud's Texts: Making Silent Documents Speak*. Trans. Philip Slotkin. New Haven: Yale University Press, 1996.

Hadot, Pierre. *Philosophy as a Way of Life: Spiritual Exercises from Socrates to Foucault*. Oxford: Blackwell, 1995.

Hamilton, Ross. *Accident: A Philosophical and Literary History*. Chicago: University of Chicago Press, 2007.

Haraway, Donna. "A Cyborg Manifesto: Science, Technology, and Socialist-Feminism in the Late Twentieth Century." In *Simians, Cyborgs and Women: The Reinvention of Nature*, 149–81. New York: Routledge, 1991.

Harries, Elizabeth W. "Words, Sex, and Gender in Sterne's Novels." *The Cambridge Companion to Laurence Sterne*, ed. Thomas Keymer, 111–24. Cambridge: Cambridge University Press, 2009.

Harrington, Ralph. "The Railway Accident: Trains, Trauma and Technological Crises in Nineteenth-Century Britain." In *Traumatic Pasts: History, Psychiatry, and Trauma in the Modern Age, 1870–1930*, ed. Mark S. Micale and Paul Lerner, 31–56. Cambridge: Cambridge University Press, 2001.

———. "The Railway Journey and the Neuroses of Modernity." In *Pathologies of Travel*, ed. Richard Wrigley and George Revill, 229–60. Amsterdam: Rodopi, 2000.

Harris, William V. *Restraining Rage: The Ideology of Anger Control in Classical Antiquity*. Cambridge, MA: Harvard University Press, 2001.

Harvey, Karen. "The Substance of Sexual Difference: Change and Persistence in Representations of the Body in Eighteenth Century England." *Gender and History* 14, no. 2 (2002): 202–23.

Haverkamp, Anselm. *Figura Cryptica: Theorie der literarischen Latenz*. Frankfurt: Suhrkamp, 2002.

Heidegger, Martin. *Being and Time*. Trans. John Macquarrie and Edward Robinson. New York: Harper and Row, 1962.

———. *Discourse on Thinking*. Trans. John M. Andersen and E. Hans Freund. New York: Harper and Row, 1966.

———. "Language in the Poem." In *On the Way to Language*, trans. Peter D. Hertz, 159–98. New York: Harper and Row, 1971.

———. "The Origin of the Work of Art." In *Poetry, Language, Thought*, trans. Albert Hofstadter, 15–86. New York: Harper and Row, 1971.

———. *The Principle of Reason*. Trans. Reginald Lilly. Bloomington: Indiana University Press, 1991.

———. "Die Spache im Gedicht." In *Unterwegs zur Sprache*, 35–82. Stuttgart: Neske, 1959.

———. "The Thing." In *Poetry, Language, Thought*, trans. Albert Hofstadter, 161–84. New York: Harper and Row, 1971.

———. *What Is a Thing?* Trans. W. B. Barton and V. Deutsch. South Bend, IN: Regnery/Gateway, 1967.

Heine, Heinrich. "The Romantic School." Trans. Helen Mustard. In *The Romantic School and Other Essays*, ed. Jost Hermand and Robert C. Holub, 1–127. New York: Continuum, 1985.

Helmstetter, Rudolf. *Das Ornament der Grammatik in der Eskalation der Zitate: "Die Strudlhofstiege," Doderers moderne Poetik des Romans und die Rezeptionsgeschichte*. Munich: Fink, 1995.

Herder, Johann Gottfried. "Essay on the Origin of Language." Trans. Alexander Gode. In *Jean-Jacques Rousseau, Johann Gottfried Herder: Origin of Language: Two Essays*, ed. and trans. John H. Moran and Alexander Gode, 85–166. Chicago: University of Chicago Press, 1986.

Hermann-Trentepohl, Henning. "'Hulesch & Quenzel und das 'Waarentheater': Die Verschwörung der Dinge als Krisensymptom der Moderne am Beispiel von Heimito von Doderers Roman *Die Merowinger*." In *"Die Wut des Zeitalters ist tief": Die Merowinger und die Kunst des Grotesken bei Heimito von Doderer*, ed. Christoph Deupmann and Kai Luehrs-Kaiser, 69–78. Würzburg: Königshausen und Neumann, 2010.

Highmore, Ben. *Ordinary Lives: Studies in the Everyday*. London: Routledge, 2010.

Horace. "The Art of Poetry." Trans. Eduard Henry Blakeney. In *The Complete Works of Horace*, ed. Caspar J. Kraemer Jr., 397–412. New York: Book League of America, 1938.

Hörisch, Jochen. *Das Wissen der Literatur*. Munich: Fink, 2007.

Hörl, Erich. "Die offene Maschine: Heidegger, Günther und Simondon über die technologische Bedingung." *MLN* 123, no. 3 (2008): 632–55.

Horn, Ernst. *Öffentliche Rechenschaft über meine zwölfjährige Dienstführung als zweiter Arzt des Königl. Charité-Krankenhauses zu Berlin, nebst Erfahrungen über Krankenhäuser und Irrenanstalten*. Berlin: Realschulbuchhandlun, 1818.

Hume, David. *Hume's Enquiries*. Ed. L. A. Selby-Bigge and P. H. Nidditch. Oxford: Clarendon, 1975.

Husserl, Edmund. *Ding und Raum: Vorlesungen 1907*. Ed. Karl-Heinz Hahnengreß and Smail Rapic. Hamburg: Meiner, 1991.

Hyde, Walter W. "The Prosecution of Animals and Lifeless Things in the Middle Ages and Modern Times." *University of Pennsylvania Law Review* 64 (1916): 696–700.

Japp, Uwe. "Mikrologie der Wut: Affektive Aufgipfelungen in Heimito von Doderers Kurzprosa." *Text und Kritik* 150 (2001): 37–47.

Jean Paul. "Frage über das Entstehen der ersten Pflanzen, Tiere und Menschen."

In *Sämtliche Werke,* ed. Norbert Miller and Wilhelm Schmidt-Biggemann, 2/1:928-54. Munich: Hanser, 1976.

———. "Freudenbüchlein oder Ars Semper Gaudendi." In *Historisch-kritische Ausgabe,* ed. Preußische Akademie der Wissenschaften, 2/4. Weimar: Hermann Böhlaus Nachfolger, 1934.

———. *Horn of Oberon: Jean Paul Richter's School for Aesthetics.* Trans. Margaret R. Hale. Detroit: Wayne State University Press, 1973.

———. *The Invisible Lodge.* Trans. Charles T. Brooks. New York: Henry Holt, 1883.

———. *Der Komet.* In *Werke,* ed. Norbert Miller, vol. 6: 563-1036. Munich: Hanser, 1963.

———. *Selberlebensbeschreibung.* In *Werke,* ed. Norbert Miller, 4:1025-80. Munich: Hanser, 1962.

———. *Leben des Quintus Fixlein.* In *Werke,* ed. Norbert Miller, 4:7-259. Munich: Hanser, 1962.

———. *Leben des vergnügten Schulmeisterleins Maria Wutz in Auenthal.* In *Werke,* ed. Norbert Miller, 1:422-62. Munich: Hanser, 1960.

———. *Life of Quintus Fixlein.* In *Army-Chaplain Schmelzle's Journey to Flaetz and Life of Quintus Fixlein,* trans. Thomas Carlyle, 113-319. 1827. Reprint, Columbia, SC: Camden House, 1991.

———. "Life of the Merry Masterkin Maria Wutz in Auenthal: A Kind of Idyll." Trans. Erika Casey. In *Jean Paul: A Reader,* ed. Timothy Casey, 83-114. Baltimore: Johns Hopkins University Press, 1992.

———. "Museum." In *Jean Paul: Sämtliche Werke. Abt. II: Jugendwerke und vermischte Schriften,* ed. Norbert Miller and Wolfgang Schmidt-Biggemann, 877-1048. Munich: Hanser, 1976.

———. *Siebenkäs.* In *Werke,* ed. Norbert Miller, 2:7-565. Munich: Hanser, 1959.

———. *Titan: A Romance.* 2 vols. Trans. Charles T. Brooks. London: Trübner, 1863.

———. "Über die natürliche Magie der Einbildungskraft." In *Werke,* ed. Norbert Miller, 4:195-205. Munich: Hanser, 1962.

———. "Über die Tugend." In *Sämtliche Werke,* ed. Norbert Miller und Wilhelm Schmidt-Biggemann, 2/1:346-53. Munich: Hanser, 1976.

———. *Die Unsichtbare Loge.* In *Werke,* ed. Norbert Miller, 1:422-62. Munich: Hanser, 1960.

———. *Vorschule der Ästhetik.* In *Werke,* ed. Norbert Miller, 5: . Munich: Hanser, .

———. *Wedded Life, Death, and Marriage of Firmian Stanislaus Siebenkäs,*

Parish Advocate in Burgh of Kuhschnappel (A Genuine Thorn Piece). Trans. Alexander Ewing. London: Bell and Sons, 1897.

Johnson, Barbara. *Persons and Things.* Cambridge, MA: Harvard University Press, 2010.

Jolles, André. *Einfache Formen.* 4th ed. Tübingen: Niemeyer, 1968.

Jones, Ernest. *Life and Work of Freud.* Vol. 3. New York: Basic Books, 1957.

Kamper, Dietmar. "Corpus absconditum: Das Virtuelle als Spielart der Absenz." In *Kommunikation Medien Macht,* ed. Rudolf Maresch and Niels Werber, 445–46. Frankfurt: Suhrkamp, 1999.

Kant, Immanuel. *Anthropology from a Pragmatic Point of View.* Ed. and trans. Robert E. Louden. Cambridge: Cambridge University Press, 2006.

———. *Grounding for the Metaphysics of Morals.* Trans. James W. Ellington. Indianapolis: Hackett, 1981.

Kapp, Ernst. *Grundlinien einer Philosophie der Technik.* Braunschweig: Westermann, 1877.

Killen, Andreas. "Weimar Psychotechnics between Americanism and Fascism." In *The Self as Project: Politics and the Human Sciences,* ed. Greg Eghigan, Andreas Killen, and Christine Leuenberger, 48–71. Chicago: Chicago University Press, 2007.

Kittler, Friedrich. *Discourse Networks: 1800/1900.* Trans. Michael Mettler and Chris Cullen. Stanford: Stanford University Press, 1990.

———. *Gramophone, Film, Typewriter.* Trans. Geoffrey Winthrop-Young and Michael Wutz. Stanford: Stanford University Press, 1999.

Kofman, Sarah. *Nietzsche et la scène philosophique.* Paris: Inédit, 1979.

Koller, Erwin. "Von Abergeil bis Zilken: Zu Wortwahl und Wortbildung in Doderers Roman 'Die Merowinger.'" In *Studien zur Literatur des 19. Und 20. Jahrhunderts in Österreich: Festschrift für Alfred Doppler zum 60. Geburtstag,* ed. Johann Holzner, Michael Klein, and Wolfgang Wiesmüller, 219–29. Innsbruck: Kowatsch, 1981.

Kommerell, Max. *Jean Paul.* Frankfurt: Klostermann, 1933.

Köpke, Wulf. *Erfolglosigkeit: Zum Frühwerk Jean Pauls.* Munich: Fink, 1977.

Koschorke, Albrecht. *Körperströme und Schriftverkehr: Mediologie des 18. Jahrhunderts.* Munich: Fink, 1999.

Kosenina, Alexander. *Ernst Platners Anthropologie und Philosophie: Der philosophische Arzt und seine Wirkung auf Johann Karl Wezel und Jean Paul.* Würzburg: Königshausen und Neumann, 1989.

Kraepelin, Emil. "Zur Psychologie des Komischen." In *Philosophische Studien,* ed. Wilhelm Wundt, 2:327–69. Leipzig: Engelmann, 1885.

Kreienbrock, Jörg. "Das Lauern des Objekts: Schreibszenen bei Jean Paul und Friedrich Theodor Vischer." *Zeitschrift für Deutsche Philologie* 129, no. 4 (2010): 515–31.

Kuhn, Thomas. "Energy Conservation as an Example of Simultaneous Discovery." In *Critical Problems in the History of Science,* ed. Marshall Clagett, 321–56. Madison: University of Wisconsin Press, 1959.

La Bruyère, Jean de. *The Characters of Jean de la Bruyère.* Trans. Henri van Laun. Oxford: Oxford University Press, 1963.

Lacan, Jacques. *The Ego in Freud's Theory and in the Technique of Psychoanalysis, 1954–1955.* Trans. Sylvana Tomaselli. Vol. 2 of *The Seminar of Jacques Lacan,* ed. Jacques-Alain Miller. New York: Norton, 1988.

———. *The Ethics of Psychoanalysis, 1959–1969.* Trans. Dennis Porter. Vol. 7 of *The Seminar of Jacques Lacan,* ed. Jacques-Alain Miller. New York: Norton, 1992.

———. *The Language of the Self: The Function of Language in Psychoanalysis.* Trans. Anthony Wilden. New York: Dell, 1975.

Lamb, Jonathan. *Sterne's Fiction and the Double Principle.* New York: Cambridge University Press, 1989.

———. "Sterne's System of Imitation." In *Laurence Sterne,* ed. Marcus Walsh, 138–60. London: Pearson, 2002.

Lanham, Richard A. *Tristram Shandy: The Games of Pleasure.* Berkeley: University of California Press, 1973.

Laplanche, Jean, and Jean-Bertrand Pontalis. *The Vocabulary of Psychoanalysis.* Trans. Donald Nicholson-Smith. London: Hogarth Press, 1973.

Large, Duncan. "'Sterne-Bilder': Sterne in the German-Speaking World." In *The Reception of Laurence Sterne in Europe,* ed. Peter Jan de Voogd and John Neubauer, 68–84. London: Continuum, 2004.

Latour, Bruno. *Politics of Nature: How to Bring the Sciences into Democracy.* Trans. Catherine Porter. Cambridge, MA: Harvard University Press, 2004.

———. *We Have Never Been Modern.* Trans. Catherine Porter. Cambridge, MA: Harvard University Press, 1993.

———. "Where Are the Missing Masses? The Sociology of a Few Mundane Artifacts." In *The Object Reader,* ed. Fiona Candlin and Raiford Guins, 229–54. London: Routledge, 2009.

Lausberg, Heinrich. *Handbook of Literary Rhetoric: A Foundation for Literary Study.* Ed. David E. Orton and R. Dean Anderson. Trans. Matthew T. Bliss. Leiden: Brill, 1998.

Lessing, Gotthold Ephraim. *Hamburg Dramaturgy.* Trans. Helen Zimmern. New York: Dover, 1962.

Locke, John. An *Essay concerning Human Understanding*. Ed. Pauline Phemister. Oxford: Oxford University Press, 2008.

Löffler, Henner. "Zur Metaphysik der Tücke des Objekts." In *"Die Wut des Zeitalters ist tief": Die Merowinger und die Kunst des Grotesken bei Heimito von Doderer*, ed. Christoph Deupmann and Kai Luehrs-Kaiser, 79-92. Würzburg: Königshausen und Neumann, 2010.

Luehrs-Kaiser, Kai. "'Schnürlzieherei der Assoziationen': Doderer als Schüler Freuds, Bühlers und Swobodas." In *Gassen und Landschaften: Heimito von Doderers 'Dämonen' vom Zentrum und vom Rande aus betrachtet*, ed. Gerald Sommer, 279-92. Würzburg: Königshausen und Neumann, 2004.

Luft, David S. *Eros and Inwardness in Vienna: Weininger, Musil, Doderer*. Chicago: University of Chicago Press, 2003.

MacDowell, Douglas M. *Athenian Homicide Law in the Age of the Orators*. Manchester: Manchester University Press, 1963.

Mackay, A. T. "The Religious Significance of Animal Magnetism in the Later Works of Jean Paul." *German Life and Letters* 23 (1969–70): 216–25.

Macksey, Richard. "'Alas, Poor Yorick': Sterne Thoughts." *MLN* 98, no. 5 (1983): 1006–20.

Mahler, Andreas. "'*Doing' Things with Words*: Laurence Sternes Tristram Shandy und die Praxis des narrativen Sprechakts." *Anglia: Zeitschrift für Englische Philologie* 127, no. 1 (1997): 41–64.

Marcus Aurelius. *The Meditations of the Emperor Marcus Aurelius*. Ed. and trans. A. S. L. Farquharson. Oxford: Blackwell, 1944.

Mauser, Wolfram. "Anakreon als Therapie? Zur medizinisch-diätetischen Begründung der Rokokodichtung." *Lessing Yearbook* 20 (1988): 87–120.

Mayer, Julius Robert. "Über Auslösung." In *Julius Robert Mayer über Auslösung*, by Wilhelm Ostwald, 9–18. Weinheim: Verlag der Chemie, 1953.

McInnes, Malcolm. "Literary Onomastics and Heimito von Doderer, or: 'Wie kann man Scheichsbeutel heißen?'" *Seminar: A Journal of Germanic Studies* 23, no. 2 (1987): 156–57.

McLuhan, Marshall. *Understanding Media: The Extensions of Man*. Cambridge, MA: MIT Press, 1994.

McMaster, Juliet. "'Uncrystallized Flesh and Blood': The Body in *Tristram Shandy*." *Eighteenth-Century Fiction* 2 (1990): 197–214.

Mentzos, Stavros. "Hysterie." In *Die Psychologie des 20. Jahrhunderts*, ed. Uwe H. Peters, 10: 770–90. Munich: Kindler, 1980.

Mesmer, Friedrich Anton. *Mesmerismus oder System der Wechselwirkungen. Theorie und Anwendung des thierischen Magnetismus als allgemeine Heilkunde zur Erhaltung des Menschen*. Ed. Karl Christian Wolfart. 1814. Reprint, Amsterdam: Bonset, 1966.

Meyer, Herman. *Der Typus des Sonderlings in der deutschen Literatur.* Frankfurt: Fischer, 1993.

Meyer-Siekendieck, Burkhard. *Affektpoetik: Eine Kulturgeschichte literarischer Emotionen.* Würzburg: Königshausen und Neumann, 2005.

Michelsen, Peter. *Laurence Sterne und der deutsche Roman des 18. Jahrhunderts.* Göttingen: Vandenhoeck und Ruprecht, 1962.

"Mind Where You Put Your Feet." *Punch, or The London Charivari,* November 29, 1879. Reprinted in "Friedrich Theodor Vischer," ed. Heinz Schlaffer and Dirk Mende, special issue, *Marbacher Magazin* 44 (1987): 91.

Mittasch, Alwin. *Friedrich Nietzsche als Naturphilosoph.* Stuttgart: Kröner, 1952.

Molesworth, Jesse. *Chance and the Eighteenth-Century Novel: Realism, Probability, Magic.* Cambridge: Cambridge University Press 2010.

Montagu, Ashley. *The Anatomy of Swearing.* New York: Macmillan, 1967.

Mücke, Dorothea von. "The Imaginary Materiality of Writing in Poe's 'Ligeia.'" *Differences: A Journal of Feminist Cultural Studies* 11, no. 2 (1999): 53–75.

Müller, Götz. *Jean Pauls Ästhetik und Naturphilosophie.* Tübingen: Max Niemeyer, 1983.

———. "Die Literarisierung des Mesmerismus in Jean Pauls Roman 'Der Komet.'" In *Jean Paul im Kontext: Gesammelte Aufsätze,* ed. Wolfgang Riedel, 45–58. Würzburg: Königshausen und Neumann, 1996.

———. "Zur Bedeutung Jean Pauls für die Ästhetik zwischen 1830 und 1848 (Weisse, Ruge, Vischer)." In *Jean Paul im Kontext: Gesammelte Aufsätze,* ed. Wolfgang Riedel, 7–28. Würzburg: Königshausen und Neumann, 1996.

Müller, Ralph. "The *Pointe* in German Research." *Humor* 16, no. 2 (2003): 225–42.

———. *Theorie der Pointe.* Paderborn: Mentis, 2003.

Müller-Tamm, Jutta. *Abstraktion als Einfühlung: Zur Denkfigur der Projektion in Psychophysiologie, Kulturtheorie, Ästhetik und Literatur der frühen Moderne.* Freiburg: Rombach, 2005.

Münsterberg, Hugo. *Grundzüge der Psychotechnik.* Leipzig: Barth, 1914.

Myer, Valerie Grosvenor. "Tristram and the Animal Spirits." In *Laurence Sterne: Riddles and Mysteries,* ed. Valerie Grosvenor Myer, 99–114. London: Vision Press, 1984.

New, Melvyn. "Sterne and the Narrative of Determinateness." *Eighteenth-Century Fiction* 4, no. 4 (1992): 315–29.

———. "Sterne, Warburton, and the Burden of Exuberant Wit." *Eighteenth-Century Studies* 15 (1982): 245–74.

Neymeyr, Barbara. "'Selbst-Tyrannei' und 'Bildsäulenkälte': Nietzsches kritische Auseinandersetzung mit der stoischen Moral." *Nietzsche-Studien* 38 (2009): 65–92.

Nietzsche, Friedrich. "Beyond Good and Evil." In *Basic Writings of Nietzsche*, ed. and trans. Walter Kaufman, 181–435. New York: Modern Library, 1968.

———. *The Birth of Tragedy*. Ed. Raymond Geuss and Ronald Speirs. Trans. Ronald Speirs. Cambridge: Cambridge University Press, 1999.

———. *Briefe Januar 1880–Dezember 1884*. Vol. 3, pt. 1, of *Briefwechsel: Kritische Gesamtausgabe*. Ed. Giorgio Colli and Mazzino Montinari. Berlin: De Gruyter, 1981.

———. *Briefe Januar 1885–Dezember 1886*. Vol. 3, pt. 3, of *Briefwechsel: Kritische Gesamtausgabe*. Ed. Giorgio Colli and Mazzino Montinari. Berlin: De Gruyter, 1982.

———. *The Dawn of the Day*. Trans. J. M. Kennedy. New York: Russell and Russell, 1964.

———. *Ecce Homo*. Trans. R. J. Hollingdale and Walter Kaufmann. New York: Random House, 1967.

———. *The Gay Science*. Trans. Walter Kaufmann. New York: Random House, 1974.

———. *Nachgelassene Fragmente, 1880–1882*. Vol. 9 of *Sämtliche Werke: Kritische Studienausgabe*, ed. Giorgio Colli and Mazzino Montinari. Berlin: De Gruyter, 1980.

———. *Nachgelassene Fragmente, 1885–1887*. Vol. 12 of *Sämtliche Werke: Kritische Studienausgabe*, ed. Giorgio Colli and Mazzino Montinari. Berlin: De Gruyter, 1980.

———. *Nachgelassene Fragmente, 1887–1889*. Vol. 13 of *Sämtliche Werke: Kritische Studienausgabe*, ed. Giorgio Colli and Mazzino Montinari. Berlin: De Gruyter, 1980.

———. "On Truth and Lying in a Non-moral Sense." In *The Birth of Tragedy*, ed. Raymond Geuss and Ronald Speirs, trans. Ronald Speirs, 139–53. Cambridge: Cambridge University Press, 1999.

———. *Sämtliche Werke: Kritische Studienausgabe*. 15 vols. Ed. Giorgio Colli and Mazzino Montinari. Berlin: De Gruyter, 1980.

———. *Twilight of the Gods: How to Philosophize with a Hammer*. Trans. Duncan Large. Oxford: Oxford University Press, 1998.

Norton, Brian Michael. "The Moral in Phutatorius's Breeches: Tristram Shandy and the Limits of Stoic Ethics." *Eighteenth-Century Fiction* 18, no. 4 (2006): 405–23.

Nussbaum, Martha. "Aristotle on Emotions and Rational Persuasion." In

Essays on Aristotle's Rhetoric, ed. Amelie Oksenberg Rorty, 303–23. Berkeley: University of California Press, 1996.

———. *The Therapy of Desire: Theory and Practice in Hellenistic Ethics.* Princeton: Princeton University Press, 1994.

Oelmüller, Willi. *Friedrich Theodor Vischer und das Problem der Nachhegelschen Ästhetik.* Stuttgart: Kohlhammer, 1959.

Oesterle, Ingrid. "Verübelte Geschichte: Autobiographische Selbstentblössung, komische Selbstentlastung und bedingte Selbstbehauptung in Friedrich Theodor Vischers Roman *Auch Einer*." In *Vom Anderen und vom Selbst: Beiträge zu Fragen der Biographie und Autobiographie,* ed. Jost Hermand and Reinhold Grimm, 71–93. Königstein: Athenäum, 1982.

Orr, Jackie. *Panic Diaries: A Genealogy of Panic Disorder.* Durham: Duke University Press, 2006.

Ostwald, Wilhelm. *Der energetische Imperativ.* Leipzig: Akademische Verlagsanstalt, 1912.

———. "Die wissenschaftsgeschichtliche Stellung der Energetik," In Wilhelm Ostwald, *Der energetische Imperativ*, 98–102. Leipzig: Akademische Verlagsgesellschaft, 1912.

———. "Maschinen und Lebewesen." In Wilhelm Ostwald, *Der energetische Imperativ*, 130–35. Leipzig: Akademische Verlagsanstalt, 1912.

———. "Wie der energetische Imperativ entstand." In Wilhelm Ostwald, *Der energetische Imperativ*, 1–24. Leipzig: Akademische Verlagsanstalt, 1912.

Panofsky, Erwin. "Et in Arcadia Ego." In *Philosophy and History: The Ernst Cassirer Festschrift,* ed. Raymond Klibansky and H. J. Paton, 223–54. New York: Harper, 1963.

Patrick, G. T. W. "The Psychology of Profanity." *Psychological Review* 8, no. 2 (1901): 113–27.

Perry, Ruth. "Words for Sex: The Verbal-Sexual Continuum in *Tristram Shandy*." *Studies in the Novel* 20 (1988): 27–42.

Petroski, Henry. *The Evolution of Useful Things.* New York: Vintage Books, 1994.

Platner, Ernst. *Anthropologie für Aerzte und Weltweise.* Leipzig: Dykische Buchhandlung, 1772.

Plato, *The Laws of Plato.* Trans. A. E. Taylor. London: J. M. Dent and Sons, 1934.

Porter, Roy. "Against the Spleen." In *Laurence Sterne: Riddles and Mysteries,* ed. Valerie Grosvenor Myer, 85–96. London: Vision Press, 1984.

———. *Flesh in the Age of Reason.* London: Allen Lane, 2003.

———. "Shaping Psychiatric Knowledge: The Role of the Asylum." In

Medicine in the Enlightenment, ed. Roy Porter, 256-73. Amsterdam: Rodopi, 1995.

Potkay, Adam. *The Fate of Eloquence in the Age of Hume.* Ithaca: Cornell University Press, 1994.

Pross, Wolfgang. *Jean Pauls geschichtliche Stellung.* Tübingen: Niemeyer, 1975.

Quintilian. *Institutio Oratoria.* Vol. 3. Trans. H. E. Butler. Cambridge, MA: Harvard University Press, 1920.

Rabbow, Paul. *Seelenführung: Methodik der Exerzitien in der Antike.* Munich: Kösel, 1954.

Rabinbach, Anson. *The Human Motor: Energy, Fatigue, and the Origins of Modernity.* New York: Basic Books, 1990.

Ramsey, Rachel. "The Literary History of the Sash-Window." *Eighteenth-Century Fiction* 22, no. 2 (2009–10): 171–94.

Rapp, Adolf, ed. *Briefwechsel zwischen Strauß und Vischer.* Vol. 1. Stuttgart: Klett, 1952.

Reil, Johann Christoph. *Rhapsodieen über die Anwendung der psychischen Curmethode auf Geisteszerrüttungen.* Halle: Curtsche Buchhandlung, 1803.

———. *Ueber die Erkenntniss und Cur der Fieber: Besondere Fieberlehre.* Vol. 4. *Nervenkrankheiten.* 2nd ed. Halle: Curtsche Buchhandlung, 1805.

———. "Das Zerfallen der Einheit unseres Körpers im Selbstbewußtseyn." In *Beyträge zu einer Curmethode auf psychischem Wege,* ed. Johann Christoph Reil and Johann Christoph Hoffbauer, 4:550-85. Halle: Curtsche Buchhandlung, 1808.

Richards, Richard J. "Rhapsodies on a Cat-Piano, or Johann Christian Reil and the Foundations of Romantic Psychiatry." *Critical Inquiry* 24, no. 3 (1998): 700–736.

Ricoeur, Paul. *Freud and Philosophy: An Essay on Interpretation.* Trans. Denis Savage. New Haven: Yale University Press, 1970.

Riedel, Wolfgang. *Die Anthropologie des jungen Schiller: Zur Ideengeschichte der medizinischen Schriften und der "Philosophischen Briefe."* Würzburg: Königshausen und Neumann, 1985.

Rieger, Stefan. *Die Ästhetik des Menschen: Über das Technische in Leben und Kunst.* Frankfurt: Suhrkamp, 2002.

———. *Die Individualität der Medien: Eine Geschichte der Wissenschaft vom Menschen.* Frankfurt: Suhrkamp, 2001.

———. *Kybernetische Anthropologie: Eine Geschichte der Virtualität.* Frankfurt: Suhrkamp, 2003.

———. "Steigerungen: Zum Verhältnis von Mensch, Medium, Moderne." In

Konzepte der Moderne, ed. Gerhard von Graevenitz, 417-39. Stuttgart: Metzler, 1999.

———. "Stiche des Wissens: Zur Genealogie der Psychophysik." In *Stigmata: Poetiken der Körperinschrift,* ed. Bettine Menke and Barbara Vinken, 355-71. Munich: Fink, 2004.

Ritter, Joachim, Karlfried Gründer, and Gottfried Gabriel, eds. *Historisches Wörterbuch der Philosophie.* Vol. 1. Basel: Schwabe, 1971.

Roller, Christian Friedrich Wilhelm. *Die Irrenanstalt nach all ihren Beziehungen dargestellt.* Karlsruhe: Müller'sche Hofbuchhandlung, 1831.

Ronell, Avital. *The Telephone Book: Technology, Schizophrenia, Electric Speech.* Lincoln: University of Nebraska Press, 1989.

Rose, Nikolas. *Inventing Our Selves: Psychology, Power, and Personhood.* Cambridge: Cambridge University Press, 1996.

Rosenblueth, Arturo, Norbert Wiener, and Julian Bigelow. "Behavior, Purpose, and Teleology." *Philosophy of Science* 10 (1943): 18-24.

Rosenblum, Michael. "Why What Happens in Shandy Hall Is Not 'A Matter for the Police.'" In *Critical Essays on Laurence Sterne,* ed. Melvyn New, 159-74. New York: G. K. Hall, 1998.

Sajo, Karl. *Unsere Honigbiene.* 15th ed. Stuttgart: Franckh'sche Verlagshandlung, 1909.

Schäfer, Armin, and Joseph Vogl. "Feuer und Flamme: Über ein Ereignis des 19. Jahrhunderts." In *Kultur im Experiment,* ed. Sven Dierig, Peter Geimer, and Henning Schmidgen, 191-211. Berlin: Kadmos, 2004.

Schäffner, Wolfgang. "The Point: The Smallest Venue of Knowledge in the 17th Century (1585–1665)." In *Collection, Laboratory, Theater: Scenes of Knowledge in the 17th Century,* ed. Helmar Schramm, Ludgar Schwarte, and Jan Lazardzig, 57-74. Berlin: De Gruyter, 2005.

Schapiro, Meyer. "The Still Life as a Personal Object: A Note on Heidegger." In *Theory and Philosophy of Art: Style, Artist, and Society: Selected Papers,* 4:135–42. New York: George Braziller, 1994.

Schestag, Thomas. "Bibliographie: Für Jean Paul." *MLN* 113, no. 3 (1998): 465-523.

Schiller, Friedrich. "Was kann eine gute stehende Schaubühne eigentlich wirken? (Die Schaubühne als eine moralische Anstalt betrachtet)." In *Sämtliche Werke,* ed. Gerhard Fricke and Herbert G. Göpfert, 5:818-30. Munich: Hanser, 1959.

Schings, Hans-Jürgen, ed. *Der ganze Mensch: Literatur und Anthropologie im 18. Jahrhundert.* Stuttgart: Metzler, 1994.

———. *Der mitleidigste Mensch ist der beste Mensch: Poetik des Mitleids von Lessing bis Büchner.* Munich: Beck, 1980.

———. "Der philosophische Arzt." In *Melancholie und Aufklärung:*

Melancholiker und ihre Kritiker in Erfahrungsseelenkunde und Literatur des 18. Jahrhunderts, ed. Hans-Jürgen Schings, 11–40. Stuttgart: Metzler, 1977.

Schivelbusch, Wolfgang. *The Railway Journey: The Industrialization of Time and Space in the 19th Century.* Berkeley: University of California Press, 1986.

Schlaffer, Heinz, and Dirk Mende, eds. "Friedrich Thedor Vischer." Special issue. *Marbacher Magazin* 44 (1987).

Schmid-Bortenschlager, Sigrid. "Doderers 'Merowinger' und Vischers 'Auch Einer': Ein Vergleich." In *Dialog der Epochen: Studien zur Literatur des 19. und 20. Jahrhunderts,* ed. Eduard Beutner et al., 124–33. Vienna: Bundesverlag, 1987.

Schmidt, Rudolf. *The Theories of Darwin and Their Relation to Philosophy, Religion, and Morality.* Trans. G. A. Zimmermann. Chicago: Janson and McClurg, 1885.

Schmidt-Biggemann, Wilhelm. *Maschine und Teufel: Jean Pauls Jugendsatiren nach ihrer Modellgeschichte.* Freiburg: Alber, 1975.

Schmidt-Dengler, Wendelin. "Tangenten an die Moderne: Zur Poetik der kleinen Form: Heimito von Doderer und die 'Wiener Gruppe.'" In *"Schüsse ins Finstere" Zu Heimito von Doderers Kurzprosa,* ed. Gerald Sommer and Kai Luehrs-Kaiser, 53–62. Würzburg: Königshausen und Neumann, 2001.

Schröder, Hans-Joachim. *Apperzeption und Vorurteil: Untersuchungen zur Reflexion Heimito von Doderers.* Heidelberg: Winter, 1976.

Schweikert, Uwe. *Jean Pauls "Komet": Selbstparodie der Kunst.* Stuttgart: Metzler, 1971.

Schwenger, Peter. *The Tears of Things: Melancholy and Physical Objects.* Minneapolis: University of Minneapolis Press, 2006.

Schwerdtner, Hugo. "Die Ausdrucksbewegungen im Dienste der Psychotherapie: Vorläufige Mitteilungen über eine neue Behandlungsart der Psychoneurosen." *Medizinische Klinik: Wochenschrift für praktische Ärzte* 23 (1926): 293–94.

Seneca. "On Anger." In *Moral and Political Essays,* ed. and trans. John M. Cooper and J. F. Procopé. Cambridge: Cambridge University Press, 1995.

Serres, Michel. *The Parasite.* Trans. Lawrence R. Schehr. Minneapolis: University of Minnesota Press, 2007.

Shaftesbury, Anthony, Earl of. "Letter concerning Enthusiasm." In *Characteristics of Men, Manners, Opinions, Times, with a Collection of Letters,* vol. 1. Basel: Tourneisen and Legrand, 1790.

Shlovsky, Viktor. "A Parodying Novel: Sterne's Tristram Shandy." Trans.

John W. Isaak. In *Laurence Sterne: A Collection of Critical Essays*, ed. John Traugott, 61–79. Englewood Cliffs, NJ: Prentice-Hall, 1968.

Shorter, Edward. *A History of Psychiatry: From the Era of the Asylum to the Age of Prozac*. New York: John Wiley and Sons, 1997.

Siegert, Bernhard. *Passagen des Digitalen: Zeichenpraktiken in den neuzeitlichen Wissenschaften, 1500–1900*. Berlin: Brinkmann und Bose, 2003.

———. "Türen: Zur Materialität des Symbolischen." *Zeitschrift für Medien- und Kulturforschung* 2, no. 1 (2010): 151–70.

Simon, Ralf. "Das Universum des Schreibens in Kuhschnappel (Jean Paul, *Siebenkäs*—Roman Jakobson)." In *"Mir ekelt vor diesem tintenklecksenden Säkulum": Schreibszenen im Zeitalter der Manuskripte*, ed. Martin Stingelin, 140–55. Munich: Fink, 2004.

Sommer, Gerald. "Der entbehrliche Dr. Hartog oder die 'große Flut' überflüssigen Geredes: Anmerkungen zu 'Die Dämonen der Ostmark.'" In *Gassen und Landschaften: Heimito von Doderers 'Dämonen' vom Zentrum und vom Rande aus betrachtet*, ed. Gerald Sommer, 223–35. Würzburg: Königshausen und Neumann, 2004.

———. *Heimito von Doderer: "Technische Mittel": Fragmente einer Poetik des Schreibhandwerks*. Vienna: Braumüller, 2006.

———. "In die 'Sackgasse' und wieder heraus: Über den zur Romantendenz erhobenen Antisemitismus in Heimito von Doderers 'Aide mémoire.'" In *Gassen und Landschaften: Heimito von Doderers 'Dämonen' vom Zentrum und vom Rande aus betrachtet*, ed. Gerald Sommer, 39–72. Würzburg: Königshausen und Neumann, 2004.

———. "Prof. Dr. Anonymus Horn—Fiktion und Geschichte der Psychotherapie in Heimito von Doderers Roman *Die Merowinger*." In *"Die Wut des Zeitalters ist tief": Die Merowinger und die Kunst des Grotesken bei Heimito von Doderer*, ed. Christoph Deupmann and Kai Luehrs-Kaiser, 283–98. Würzburg: Königshausen und Neumann, 2009.

Sorabji, Richard. *Emotion and Peace of Mind: From Stoic Agitation to Christian Temptation*. Oxford: Oxford University Press, 2002.

Sorg, Klaus-Dieter. *Gebrochene Teleologie: Studien zum Bildungsroman von Goethe bis Thomas Mann*. Heidelberg: Winter, 1983.

Stahl, Georg Ernst Stahl. *Theorie der Heilkunde*. 2 vols. Ed. K. W. Ideler. Berlin: Enslin, 1831.

Stedmond, John. *The Comic Art of Laurence Sterne*. Toronto: University of Toronto Press, 1967.

Steiner, Uwe C. "Widerstand im Gegenstand: Das literarische Wissen vom Ding am Beispiel Franz Kafkas." In *Literatur, Wissenschaft und Wissen seit der Epochenschwelle um 1800: Theorie—Epistemologie—komparatistische*

Fallstudien, ed. Monika Neuhofer and Thomas Klinkert, 237–52. Berlin: De Gruyter, 2008.

Sterne, Laurence. *The Life and Opinions of Tristram Shandy, Gentleman.* 2 vols. Ed. Melvyn New and Joan New. *The Works of Laurence Sterne.* Gainesville: University of Florida Press, 1978.

———. *A Sentimental Journey and Continuation of the Bramine's Journal.* Ed. Melvyn New and W. G. Day. *The Works of Laurence Sterne.* Gainesville: University of Florida Press, 2002.

Stierle, Karlheinz. "Komik der Handlung, Komik der Sprachhandlung, Komik der Komödie." In *Das Komische, Poetik und Hermeneutik,* ed. Wolfgang Preisendanz and Rainer Warning, vol. 7. Munich: Fink, 1976.

Stone, Ferdinand Fairfax. "A Problem for Pericles." *California Law Review* 59, no. 3 (1971): 782–83.

Stovel, Bruce. "*Tristram Shandy* and the Art of Gossip." In *Laurence Sterne: Riddles and Mysteries,* ed. Valerie Grosvenor Myer, 115–25. London: Vision Press, 1984.

Strachey, James. "Editor's Introduction." In Sigmund Freud, *The Future of an Illusion, Civilization and Its Discontents and Other Works,* vol. 21 of *The Standard Edition of the Complete Psychological Works of Sigmund Freud,* ed. and trans. James Strachey, 59–63. London: Hogarth, 1961.

Tanner, Jakob. "'Weisheit des Körpers' und soziale Homöostase: Physiologie und das Konzept der Selbstregulation." In *Physiologie und industrielle Gesellschaft: Studien zur Verwissenschaftlichung des Körpers im 19. und 20. Jahrhundert,* ed. Philipp Sarrasin and Jakob Tanner, 129–69. Frankfurt: Suhrkamp, 1998.

Tatar, Maria. *Spellbound: Studies on Mesmerism and Literature.* Princeton: Princeton University Press, 1978.

Tave, Stuart M. *The Amiable Humorist: A Study in the Comic Theory and Criticism of the Eighteenth and Early Nineteenth Centuries.* Chicago: University of Chicago Press, 1960.

Thomas, Keith. *Religion and the Decline of Magic: Studies in Popular Beliefs in Sixteenth and Seventeenth Century England.* London: Weidenfeld and Nicolson, 1971.

Tieleman, Teun. *Chrysippus' On Affections: Reconstruction and Interpretation.* Leiden: Brill, 2003.

Tillyard, E. M. W. *The Elizabethan World Picture.* London: Chatto and Windus, 1943.

Tismar, Jens. *Gestörte Idyllen: Eine Studie zur Problematik der idyllischen Wunschvorstellungen am Beispiel von Jean Paul, Adalbert Stifter, Robert Walser und Thomas Bernhard.* Munich: Hanser, 1973.

Tissot, Samuel August David. *Von der Gesundheit der Gelehrten.* Zurich: Füeßlin, 1768.

Traugott, John. "The Shandean Comic Vision of Locke." In *Laurence Sterne: A Collection of Critical Essays,* ed. John Traugott, 126-47. Englewood Cliffs, NJ: Prentice-Hall, 1968.

———. *Tristram Shandy's World: Sterne's Philosophic Rhetoric.* Berkeley: California University Press, 1954.

Türk, Johannes. "Interruptions: Scenes of Empathy from Aristotle to Proust." In *Deutsche Vierteljahrsschrift für Literaturwissenschaft und Geistesgeschichte* 82, no. 3 (2008): 448-78.

Vaihinger, Hans. *The Philosophy of "As If."* Trans. C. K. Ogden. London: Routledge and Kegan, 1935.

Virilio, Paul. *The Original Accident.* Trans. Julie Rose. Cambridge: Polity Press, 2007.

Vischer, Friedrich Theodor. *Aesthetik, oder Wissenschaft des Schönen.* Vol. 1. Reutlingen: Carl Mäcken, 1846.

———. *Auch Einer: Eine Reisebekanntschaft.* Frankfurt: Insel, 1987.

———. "Mein Lebensgang." In *Kritische Gänge,* ed. Robert Vischer, 6:439-536. Munich: Meyer und Jessen, 1922.

———. "Mode und Cynismus: Beiträge zur Kenntnis unserer Kulturformen." *Kritische Gänge,* ed. Robert Vischer, 5:367-417. Munich: Meyer und Jessen, 1920.

———. "Podoböotismus oder die Fußflegelei auf der Eisenbahn." In *Kritische Gänge,* ed. Robert Vischer, 3:366-72. Berlin: Meyer und Jessen, 1920.

———. "Shakespeares Hamlet." In *Kritische Gänge,* ed. Robert Vischer, 6:57-120. Munich: Meyer und Jessen, 1922.

———. "Das Symbol." In *Kritische Gänge,* ed. Robert Vischer, 4:420-456. Munich: Meyer und Jessen, 1922.

———. "Der Traum." In *Kritische Gänge,* ed. Robert Vischer, 6:459-88. Munich: Meyer und Jessen, 1922.

———. "Über das Erhabene und Komische: Ein Beitrag zu der Philosophie des Schönen." In *Kritische Gänge,* ed. Robert Vischer, 4:3-158. Munich: Meyer und Jessen, 1922.

Vismann, Cornelia. "Schuld ist das Ding." *Gesetz. Ironie: Festschrift für Manfred Schneider,* ed. Rüdiger Campe and Michael Niehaus, 11-22. Heidelberg: Synchron, 2004.

Vogl, Joseph. "Gesetze des Amok: Über monströse Gewöhnlichkeiten." *Neue Rundschau* 111, no. 4 (2000): 77-90.

———, ed. *Poetologien des Wissens um 1800.* Munich: Fink, 1999.

von Foerster, Heinz. "Ethics and Second-Order Cybernetics." *Cybernetics and Human Knowing* 1, no. 1 (1992): 9–20.

Walter, Robert. "Verlieben, nicht erleuchten: Die erleuchteten Fenster und die Anthropologie Hermann Swobodas." In *"Er las nur dieses eine Buch": Studien zu Heimito von Doderers "Die erleuchteten Fenster,"* ed. Stefan Winterstein, 343–58. Würzburg: Königshausen und Neumann, 2009.

Wasserman, Earl R. "The Inherent Values of Eighteenth-Century Personification." *PMLA* 65, no. 4 (1950): 435–63.

Weber, Alfred. "Der Beamte." In *Die Neue Rundschau: XXIter Jahrgang der freien Bühne*, ed. Oscar Bie, 1321–39. Berlin: S. Fischer, 1910.

Weber, Dietrich. "Einleitung des Herausgebers." In Heimito von Doderer, *Repertorium: Ein Begreifbuch von höheren und niederen Lebens-Sachen*. Ed. Dietrich Weber, 5–18. Munich: Biederstein, 1969.

Weber, Samuel. *The Legend of Freud*. Expanded ed. Stanford: Stanford University Press, 2000.

———. "Upsetting the Setup: Remarks on Heidegger's 'Questing after Technics.'" In *Mass Mediauras: Form, Technics, Media*, 55–75. Stanford: Stanford University Press, 1996.

Wellbery, David. "Contingency." In *Neverending Stories: Toward a Critical Narratology*, ed. Ann Fehn, Ingeborg Hoesterey, and Maria Tartar, 237–57. Princeton: Princeton University Press, 1992.

———. "Der Zufall der Geburt: Laurence Sternes Poetik der Kontingenz." In *Kontingenz*, ed. Gerhard von Graevenitz, Poetik und Hermeneutik 17, 291–317. Munich: Fink, 1998.

Werber, Niels. "Bürokratische Kommunikation: Franz Kafkas Roman *Der Proceß*." *Germanic Review* 73, no. 4 (1998): 309–26.

Wiener, Norbert. *The Human Use of Human Beings: Cybernetics and Society*. Boston: Houghton Mifflin, 1954.

Wiethölter, Waltraud. *Witzige Illuminationen: Studien zur Ästhetik Jean Pauls*. Tübingen: Niemeyer, 1979.

Wills, David. *Prosthesis*. Stanford: Stanford University Press, 1995.

Wilm, Marie-Christin. "Die Grenzen tragischer Katharsis: Jacob Bernays' *Grundzüge der verlorenen Abhandlung des Aristoteles* (1857) im Kontext zeitgenössischer Tragödientheorie." In *Grenzen der Katharsis in den modernen Künsten: Transformationen des aristotelischen Modells seit Bernays, Nietzsche und Freud*, ed. Martin Vöhler and Dirck Linck, 21–50. Berlin: De Gruyter, 2009.

Wilson, Mitchell. "'And Let Me Go On': Tristram Shandy, Lacanian Theory, and the Dialectic of Desire." *Psychoanalysis and Contemporary Thought* 9 (1986): 335–72.

Winterstein, Stefan. "Torpedierung und Apologie der Amtsehre." In *"Er las nur dieses eine Buch": Studien zu Heimito von Doderers "Die Erleucheten Fenster,"* ed. Stefan Winterstein, 237–341. Würzburg: Königshausen und Neumann, 2009.

Wittgenstein, Ludwig. *Vermischte Bemerkungen.* Ed. Georg Henrik von Wright. Frankfurt: Suhrkamp, 1987.

Wuthenow, Rolf Rainer. "Gefährdete Idylle." *Des Luftschiffers Gianozzo Seebuch: Mit Illustrationen von Emil Pretorius und Jean-Paul-Aufsätzen von R. R. Wuthenow.* Frankfurt: Insel, 1979.

Zückert, Johann Friedrich. *Von den Leidenschaften.* 2nd ed. Berlin: Mylius, 1768.

INDEX

abreaction, 188–89
absentmindedness, 75–76
accidents: *versus* judgments, 39–40; secularization, 23
aesthetic pleasure, vexations and, 85
Aesthetics (Vischer), sublime, 143–47
affects, 81–2; auto-affection, 186; cathartic self-affections, 179–90; composure guided by reason, 87–88; hetero-affection, 186; necessity, 184; stage and, 189–90
Agamben, Giorgio, *The Sacrament of Language: An Archaeology of the Oath*, 35–36
amplificatio, 170–71
anger. *See also* rage: Aristotle on, 38; *déclic*, 195; devil and, 100; energetic imperative and, 226–27; groundlessness and, 173; medical theory, 99; responsible agent, 38–39; Seneca on, 253; as a shock, 98–99; statistics, 175–78; suppression, 97–98; violent destruction and, 165–66
anger management: Aristotle, 38; depictions of failure, 10; Doderer, Heimito von, 18–19; Dr. Horn, 178–79; Galen of Pergamon, 6–7; Lacan, Jacques, 7; pouch stab and, 200–201; Stoic anger control, Laurence Sterne, and, 10; *Tristram Shandy* (Sterne), 8–9
angry outcries, 95–6. *See also* outbursts: constraints, 96–97; health benefits, 95–100; Herder, Johann Gottfried, 114–15; *The Merowingians, or The Total Family* (Doderer), 173–74; morbid matter, 99–100; Reil, Johann Christoph, 96; treatment in *Siebenkäs* (Jean Paul), 100
animal magnetism, 118–19

animism, 118–19
Anna O. *See* psychoanalysis
anthropology: Platner, Ernst, 73; *Tristram Shandy* (Sterne), 65–66
Anthropology for Physicians and the Worldwise (Platner), 73
Anthropology from a Pragmatic Point of View (Kant), 95–97
anthropomorphism, 5–6, 9–12; laughter and, 113–15; malicious objects and, 159; outbursts and, 114–15; rhetoric of, 155–56; symbolization and, 158–59
anticipation: fantasy and, 254; *Siebenkäs* (Jean Paul), 74–75; reciprocal, 83–84
anticipatory ideas, 235
apperception, 204, 212–13, 216–17
Aristotle: on anger, 38, 99; and *The Athenian Constitution*, 206; and Bernay's interpretation, 184–89; *doxa*, 250; *phantasia*, 250
Ars Semper Gaudendi ex Sola Consideratione Divinae Providentiae et per Adventuales Conciones Exposita (Sarasa), 86–87
"The Art of Being Constantly Cheerful" (Jean Paul), 86–87
The Art of Reading Books (Bergk), 105–6
assignment of a thing, 5
ataraxia, 87–88; energetic discharge and, 100
Auch Einer (Vischer), 12; *amplificatio*, 170–71; Bildungsroman, 148; demons in objects, 12–13; *The Merowingians, or the Total Family* (Doderer), 209; mythology of demons, 160–61; sounds, 169–71; space, 134–36; sublime, 145–47; walking-in-the-way, 137–39

backside of things, 237–38
"The Bare Room" (Doderer), 214–15
Basics of Psychotechnology (Münsterberg), 228–29
becoming, ignition and, 187–88
being, becoming, 187–88
Being and Time (Heidegger), 148–53
Beresford, James, *The Miseries of Human Life, or, The Groans of Samuel Sensitive, and Timothy Testy*, 86–87
Bergk, J.A., *The Art of Reading Books*, 105–6
Besonnenheit, 102–6, 115
Bestand, 136
Bildungsroman, *Auch Einer* (Vischer), 148
blasphemy, 35–36
Bloch, Ernst, *Traces*, 237–38
blood flow, angry outbursts and, 95–96
body-building soul, 98
The Book of the Church of Rochester through Bishop Ernulfus, 41–47
bungled actions, 201–2
bureaucracy, 217, 222

Cannon, Walter, *The Wisdom of the Body*, 241–42, 277
Cassirer, Ernst, "Form and Technology," 236
catharsis, 16–18; cathartic psychotherapy, 189; definition, 184; ecstatic catharsis, 185; laughter, resemblance to cursing, 36; music, 198; productive, 185; profanity and, 43–44
cathartic discharges, 186; psychoanalysis and, 188–89
cause and effect, 15–16; ignitions and, 179–80
Certeau, Michel de, *The Practice of Everyday Life*, 124–25
Civilization and Its Discontents (Freud), 230–31
clairvoyance, 119
closing doors, 3–4
clothing, 126–30; as protection against malicious environment, 29–31; "The Origin of the Work of Art" (Heidegger), 127–28
cognition, interruption and, 142–43
collective in a false society, 219
comedy: *Aesthetics* (Vischer), 143–47; grotesque, 143; Stierle, Karlheinz, 106; tendentious jokes, 16–17
The Comet (Jean Paul), 92–3; addenda, 101–2; Frohauf Süptitz, 68–69, 106-7

composure guided by reason, 87–88
concrete *versus* ideal, 139–40
Conjectural Biography (Jean Paul), writing, 71–72
consciousness, self-consciousness, 103–4
craftsmen, 126–27
crisscrossing, 140–42
culture, primitive tendencies in, 128–29
cursing, 32–3; accident *versus* judgment, 39–40; blasphemy, 35–36; *The Book of the Church of Rochester through Bishop Ernulf*, 41–47; catharsis and, 43–44; laughter and, 36; involuntary respiration, 34–36; malediction, 41–42; medical reasons, 43; naturalness, 97; Phutatorius, 36–38; Protestantism and, 45–47; satirization in *Siebenkäs* (Jean Paul), 99–100; secularization, 46; technology of the self, 47; twelve-penny oath, 249–50; Walter Shandy's speculation on origins, 36; ZOUNDS, 32–35
cybernetics, 239–43

"Das Ding" (Heidegger), 166
déclic, anger and, 195
demons, 84–85; *Auch Einer* (Vischer), 160–61; in objects, 12–13; of technology, 238–39
destruction, anger and, 165–66
devil, anger and, 100
diabolical tendencies of objects, 128
dialectic of enlightenment, 200–201
die Tücke des Objekts, 143
Dionysian humans, self-ignition and, 187–88
directing forces, 181
discipline, 175
dishonorable discharge of objects, 204–6
disruptive power of things, 142–43
distracted attention, 74–76
disturbances of everyday life, 8–9
disturbances *versus* thoughts of disturbance, 11
divinity of man, 232
Doderer, Heimito von, 2–3. See also *The Merowingians, or The Total Family*: anger, 18–19; apperception, 204, 216–17; army service, 218–19; *Auch Einer* (Vischer), 209; "The Bare Room," 214–15; as ethical imperative, 216; and feet, 176–77; German bureaucracy, 222; "The Language of the Poet," 197–98;

Index

The Lighted Windows, or the Humanization of the Bureaucrat Julius Zihal, 196–97; management, 178–89; Nazism, 274; objects *versus* objectivity, 203–4; on Omar Chajjâm, 195–6; pouch stab, 190–201; powerless, 208; Proust and memory, 273; pseudological space, 19–20; psychology characterization, 213–14; rage, 19–20; recalcitrant objects, punishment for, 204–7; refusal to apperceive, 212–13; *Repertory: A Comprehension-Book of Greater and Lesser Life-Things*, 19, 173–74, 194–96; "Rosa Chymica Austriaco-Hispanica," 220–21; "Sexuality and the Total State," 19; statistics, 175–78; *The Strudlhof Steps or Melzer and the Depth of the Years*, 195–96
doors: ajar, 27–8; *Auch Einer* (Vischer), 12; doorbells, 14–15; Freud, Sigmund, 13–14; opening/closing, 3–4; *Tristram Shandy*, 11, 23–25
doxa, 250
dreams, 95; readers and writers, 106
dressage, 175

eccentrics, 94
ecstatic catharsis, 185
The Ego in Freud's Theory and in the Technique of Psychoanalysis, 1954-1955 (Lacan), 241–42
eigentlich, 132–3
emotional economy of man, 182
energetic imperative, 18, 225–27
energy: ethics and, 226; humans as transformers, 227–28; *Principles of Scientific Management* (Taylor), 227; sciences, 225; self-regulation and, 227; Social Energeticism, 228
energy release: accident *versus* judgment, 39–40; blasphemy, 35–36; blood flow and, 95–96; cathartic discharges, 186; constraints, 96–7; cursing, 32–33; naturalness, 97; Walter Shandy's speculation on origins, 36; health benefits, 95–100; involuntary respiration, 34–36; laughter, tendentious jokes, 16–17; music and, 17–18, 181–82; Phutatorius, 36–38; *pointe*, 193; self-ignition, 183, 185; tendentious jokes and, 16–17; transfiguration, 188; ZOUNDS, 32–35

enraged man, 219–20
enthusiastic mysticism, 189
epigrams, 195–96
equipment, 1, 4–6, 19–25, 127–31
Ernulphus, swearing and, 41–47
Essay concerning Human Understanding (Locke), 50–51
ethical function of projection, 159
ethical imperative of apperception, 216
ethics: energetic imperative and, 226–27; energy and, 226; *Tristram Shandy*, 65–66
everyday life: disturbances of, *Tristram Shandy*, 8–9; knowledge and, 10; *The Psychopathology of Everyday Life* (Freud), 13–14; reason and, 10; rise in numbers of objects/equipment, 23
evolution of things, 236
excess, 108–9
execution of objects, 161–62, 201–2; throwing things, 166–68
expectations, 81–82
extravagance, 260–61

false sense of individuality, 94
fantasy: anticipation and, 254; vexations and, 80–81
Fashion and Garb (Vischer), 126–27
feet measurement, anger and, 176–77
fetishization, 246
"Form and Technology" (Cassirer), 236
Foucault, Michel: dressage, 175; *The History of Sexuality*, 228; technologies of the self, 7–8; theatrical representation of psychotherapy, 9, 92–94
Freud, Sigmund: anticipatory ideas, 235; bungled actions, 201–2; catharsis and, 16; "Civilization and Its Discontents," 230–31; *The Ego in Freud's Theory and in the Technique of Psychoanalysis, 1954-1955* (Lacan), 241–42; happiness in modernity, 231; omnipotence of thoughts, 199; parapraxis, 201–2; *The Psychopathology of Everyday Life*, 13–14; *Studies on Hysteria*, 188; technology, 230–33; tendentious jokes, 16–17; shaggy-dog story, 194
friction, tribology, 25
function of projection, 159

Galen of Pergamon, anger management and, 6–7

The Gay Science (Nietzsche), catharsis and music, 198; ignition, 180-81
grotesque comedy and, 143
grounding, 131-33
groundlessness, anger and, 173

happiness in modernity, 231
harmony between humans and things, 11
health: anger expression and, 95-100; ignition and, 180
Heidegger, Martin: *Being and Time*, 148-53; "Das Ding," 166; eigentlich, 132-33; equipment, 4-5, 19-21, 127-31, 148-53; ground, 173; malicious objects, 148-53; *Old Shoes with Laces* (van Gogh), 132-33; open spaces, 133-34; "The Origin of the Work of Art," 127-28; recalcitrant objects, 4-5; roots in being, 131-32; space, 135-56; "What is a Thing?," 135-56
The History of Sexuality (Foucault), 228
holistic treatment of mental illness, 98
homeostasis, 240-42
The Human Use of Human Beings (Wiener), 240
humans: divinity and, 232; language *versus* animal cries, 115; perception of bodies, 115-16; technology's intrusion, 238-39; as transformers of energy, 227-28
humor. *See also* comedy: annoyances and, 12; beginning, 106-7; grotesque comedy, 143; interruption and, 142-43; projective, 111-21; reading and, 112
hypochondria of scholars, 72-73
hysteria, 190

idealization, idyll and, 89-90
ideal *versus* concrete, 139-40
idée fixe, 90-2
idyll: idealization and, 89-90; Jean Paul, 77-8, 88-89; *The School for Aesthetics*, 89-90
ignition, 15; becoming, 187-88; catharsis and, 16; Doderer, Heimito von, 194-95; health and, 180; Mayer, Julius Robert, 179-80; music and, 181-82; Nietzsche, Friedrich, 18, 180-83, 186-87, 247-48; passionate discharges, 182; psychic phenomena, suppression, 180; rage and, 180; self-ignition, 183-87

illusion, 92-94
imagination: Jean Paul, 12, 77, 94-95; literary, protected inner world and, 106; Mauser, Wolfram, 73-74; opinions and, 40-41; powers of, Stoicism and, 37-38; transformation of negative affects and, 87-88
impelling forces, 181
impertinent constitution of space, 134-35
incantation, 198
inconsistent soul of man, 10
individuality, false sense, 94
inner freedom of *Besonnenheit*, 106
insight withdrawal, technology and, 15
intensification: Jean Paul, 108-9; *pointe*, 193
interruption, 142-47, 156
invention of new objects, 235-36
The Invisible Lodge (Jean Paul), 109-10
involuntary respiration of cursing, 34-36; accident *versus* judgment, 39-40; blasphemy, 35-36

Jean Paul: addenda, 101-2; affects, 81-2; animism, 118-19; anticipation, 74-75; anthropomorphism, 12; "The Art of Being Constantly Cheerful," 86-87; body-building soul, 98; clairvoyance, 119; *The Comet*, 92-93; *Conjectural Biography*, writing, 71-2; demons, 84-85; dissociation, 107-8; distracted attention, 74-76; excess, 108-9; expectations, 81-82; fantasy and vexations, 80-81; Fichte's philosophy, 107-8; figurative wit, 113-14; Frohauf Süptitz, 68-69; heroes, humor and, 11-12; idyll, 77-8, 88-89; ill-fitting clothing and, 110-11; imagination, 12, 77, 94-95; intensification, 108-9; *The Invisible Lodge*, 109-10; Kant, Immanuel, and, 95-96; "The Libel of Bailiff Josuah Freudal against His Accursed Demons," 119-21; *The Life of Quintus Fixlein*, 84-85; happiness, 90-1; "Little Book of Joy or *Ars Semper Gaudendi*," 12; marriage, 71-72, 74-75; philosophical physician, 92-93; pleasure and, 255; poetics and ethics, 12; projection, 13; quotidian, 74-75; satirization of curses, 99-100; *The School for*

Index

Aesthetics, 70, 88–90, 103–5; self-reflection, 82; *Siebenkäs*, 10; Sterne, Laurence, and, 9–10; *Titan*, transformation of negative affects, 87–88; Vischer, Friedrich Theodor, and, 116–17; writing, 67–71

Kant, Immanuel: *Anthropology from a Pragmatic Point of View*, 95–7; Ostwald, Wilhelm, and, 226; outbursts, 95–97; space, 135–36; Stoicism and, 95–96
katharsis. *See* catharsis
know thyself, 106
knowledge, poetics of, malicious object, 2
Kraepelin, Emil, 193

Lacan, 54, 233; and Heidegger 7, 166
language: animating objects, 157–58; Gütersloh, Albert Paris, 215–16; magic origins, 198; poetic language, 197–98
"The Language of the Poet" (Doderer), 197–98
Latus Clavus, 52–54
laughter, 32, 122; anthropomorphizing and, 113; beginning of humor and, 107; catharsis and, resemblance to cursing, 36; fashion and, 249; personification and, 113; *pointe*, 193; response to recalcitrance of reality, 101–11; tendentious jokes, 16–17
Laughter: An Essay on the Meaning of the Comic (Bergson), 75–76
laws of thermodynamics, rules of morality and, 226
"The Libel of Bailiff Josuah Freudal against His Accursed Demons" (Jean Paul), 119–21
The Life and Opinions of Tristram Shandy, Gentleman. *See Tristram Shandy* (Sterne)
The Life of Quintus Fixlein (Jean Paul), 84–85; happiness, 90–91
The Lighted Windows, or the Humanization of the Bureaucrat Julius Zihal (Doderer), 196–97
literary imagination, protected inner world and, 106
literature: categories of discourse and, 2; literary knowledge of object, 2; malicious, 2
"Little Book of Joy or *Ars Semper Gaudendi*" (Jean Paul), 12
Locke, John, *Essay concerning Human Understanding*, 50–51

"Machines and Organisms" (Ostwald), 227–28
magic origins of language, 198
magical sphere, 238
magnetism, 118–19
malediction, cursing, 41–42
malice, 5
malicious environment, protection through clothing, 29–31
malicious literature, 2
malicious objects, 1; anthropomorphism and, 6, 159; *Being and Time* (Heidegger), 148–53; comedy, 116–17; Doderer *versus* Vischer, 209–10; metaphorical regulation, 235; metaphysics, 13; mythology of, 155; as poetics of knowledge, 2; reason and, 143–48; revenge against, 161–71; Vischer, Friedrich Theodor, 86
marriage, 71–75
materia peccans, 100
Mayer, Julius Robert, 15–16, 179–81
medical cursing, 43
medical theory of anger, 99
medico-ethical therapy, music, 17–18
The Merowingians, or The Total Family (Doderer), 18–19; *Auch Einer* (Vischer), 209; Dr. Bachmeyer, rage, 172–74; Dr. Horn, 174–79; German bureaucracy, 222; pouch stab, 190–201; statistics of anger, 175–78
metaphor, 113–15; symbolization and, 158–59
metaphorical regulation, 235
mind/body connection, 31
The Miseries of Human Life, or, The Groans of Samuel Sensitive, and Timothy Testy (Beresford), 86–7
morality, laws of thermodynamics and, 226
moral management as psychotherapy, 9–10
morbid matter, anger expression and, 99–100
music: cathartic qualities, 198; energy release and, 17–18, 181–82; medico-ethical therapy, 17–18
"My Autobiography" (Vischer), 13–14

nervous geometries, 234
Nestroy, Johann, *The Two Sleepwalkers or the Necessary and the Superfluous*, 213

Nietzsche, Friedrich: affects, 184, 186; answering one's own letters, 186–87; art and, 159; catharsis, 17–18, 198; directing forces, 181; emotional economy of man, 182; *The Gay Science*, 180–81, 198; ignition, 18, 180–87, 247–48; impelling forces, 181; primitive mind *versus* modern, 203; projection and, 159; tragedy, 184; Turin breakdown, 247

object agency, 245
objects. *See also* recalcitrant object: agency, 153–61; animation, language, 157–58; antagonistic demons and, 12–13; assignment, 5; "Das Ding" (Heidegger), 166; diabolical tendencies, 128; *die Tücke des Objekts*, 143; execution of, 161–62, 201–2; throwing things, 166–68; fetishization, 246; harmony with humans, 11; history of, 3; interruption and, 143; invention of, 235–36; literary knowledge of, 2; object agency, 4; *versus* objectivity, 203–4; rage against, 165–6; revenge against, 161–63, 204–7; throwing things, 163–71; rise in amounts in everyday life, 23; symbolization, 153–61
Old Shoes with Laces (van Gogh), 128–33
omnipotence of thoughts, 199
"On Ignition" (Mayer), 15–16
On the Sublime and the Comical (Vischer), 143–44
open spaces, 133–34
orators, 59–60
"The Origin of the Work of Art" (Heidegger), 127–28
Ostwald, Wilhelm, 18, 225–28
Othello, 147–48
outbursts, 114–15. *See also* energy release: blood flow and, 95–6; constraints, 96–97; health benefits, 95–100; laughter, tendentious jokes, 16–17; *The Merowingians, or The Total Family* (Doderer), 173–74

parapraxis, 201–2
passionate discharges. *See also* energy release; outbursts: catharsis, 186; ignition, 182; music and, 181–2; *pointe*, 193; self-ignition and, 185; tragedy, 185; transfiguration, 188
passions, definition, 38

Patrick, G.T.W., "The Psychology of Profanity," 43
perception of bodies by humans, 115–16
personal space, "Podo-Booetism" article (Vischer), 122–25
personification, 113–15
phantasia, 250
philosophers, Laurence Sterne and, 65–66
philosophical physician, 92–93, 98
Philosophy of Money (Simmel), 234
Phutatorius, 30; accident *versus* judgment, 39–40; opinions, imagination and, 40–41; outburst, 32; theories on, 36–38; ZOUNDS, 32–35
plains, 62–66
Platner, Ernst, *Anthropology for Physicians and the Worldwise*, 73
Plato, 106
pleasure, 255
"Podo-Booetism" article (Vischer), 122–24; primitive tendencies in culture and society, 128–29
poetry: "The Language of the Poet" (Doderer), 197–98; open spaces and, 133–34; poetic symbolization, 157–58; poetics of knowledge, malicious object as, 2
pointe, 193. *See also* punchline
pouch stab, 190–201
powerless rage, 208
"Practical Philosophy" (Ostwald), 226–27
The Practice of Everyday Life (Certeau), 124–25
present moment, Stoics and, 82–83
pressure release. *See* energy release; outbursts
primitive mind *versus* modern, 203, 232
primitive tendencies in culture and society, 128–29
Principles of Scientific Management (Taylor), 227
productive catharsis, 185
profanity. *See* cursing
projection, 13–14. *See also* symbolization: ethical function, 159; interruption and, 156
projective humor, 111–21
Protestantism, cursing and, 45–47
Prytaneum, 205–6
pseudological space, 19–20
psychic abilities, 228
psychic disorders, ignition and, 182–83
psychic energy release, 16–18
psychic healing method, 98

psychic phenomena, ignition and, 180
psychoanalysis: abreaction, 188–89; cathartic, 189; cathartic discharges and, 188–89; hysteria, 190; pouch stab, 190–201
psychology: applied psychology, 229; Doderer's characterization, 213–14
"The Psychology of Profanity" (Patrick), 43
The Psychopathology of Everyday Life (Freud), 13–14
psychotechnology, 228–30
psychotherapy: Galenic model of bodily humors and, 98; moral management as, 9–10; theatrical representation, 92–94
punchline, 193–94. *See also pointe*

quotidian, 74–75

rage, 19–20, 137–38. *See also* anger: against objects, 165–66; enraged man, 219–20; groundlessness and, 173; ignition and, 180; *The Merowingians, or The Total Family* (Doderer), 172–74; powerless, 208
rancor, 96–97
reading: attentiveness and, 105–6; dreams, 106; humor and, 112; *The Lighted Windows, or the Humanization of the Bureaucrat Julius Zihal* (Doderer), 196–97
reality, virtuality and, 236–37
reason: malicious objects and, 143–48; Walter Shandy and, 26
recalcitrance: anger and, *déclic*, 195; cursing outburst, 32–33; environment of *Tristram Shandy*, 8–9; equipment, 129–30; objects, 4–5; punishment, 204–7; reactions to, 1–2; *Tristram Shandy*, 8; of reality, laughter as response, 101–11; writing, 67–84
Reil, Johann Christoph, 78–79; dreams, 95; life *versus* stage, 95; outbursts, 96; psychic healing method, 98; readers and writers, 106; *Rhapsodies on the Application of Psychic Treatment to Mental Disturbances*, 103–4
Repertory: A Comprehension-Book of Greater and Lesser Life-Things (Doderer), 19, 173–74, 194–96
"Restitutions" (Derrida), 128
revenge against malicious objects, 161–71

Rhapsodies on the Application of Psychic Treatment to Mental Disturbances (Reil), 103–4
rhetoric: anthropomorphism and, 155–56; artwork and, 196; decorum, 49–51; language animating objects, 157–58; orators, 59–60; personification and, 114–15; *Tristram Shandy*, 65–66; Tristram's, 58–66; veiling/unveiling objects, 47, 49
rhythm in music, 182
roots in being, 131–32
"Rosa Chymica Austriaco-Hispanica" (Doderer), 220–21
running amok, 176
Rütlisprung, sublime and, 145

The Sacrament of Language: An Archaeology of the Oath (Agamben), 35–36
Sarasa, Alfons Anton de, *Ars Semper Gaudendi ex Sola Consideratione Divinae Providentiae et per Adventuales Conciones Exposita*, 86–87
scene of writing, 67–68
The School for Aesthetics (Jean Paul), 13, 70, 88-90; *Besonnenheit*, 103–5
science: classifications, 225; of friction, tribology as, 25
secularization: of accidents, 23; of cursing, 46
self-affections, cathartic, 179–90
self-command, ataraxia, 87–88
self-consciousness, *Besonnenheit* and, 103–4
self-government: ataraxia, 87–88; energy and, 227
self-ignition, 183–88
self-reflection. *See also Besonnenheit*: Stoicism and, 82; Süptitz *(The Comet)*, 106–7
self-sublation, 144–45
Seneca, anger and, 253
A Sentimental Journey (Sterne), 62–63
"Sexuality and the Total State" (Doderer), 19; apperception, 216–17; refusal to apperceive, 212–13
shaggy-dog story (Freud), 194
shortest stories, 193–94
Siebenkäs (Jean Paul), 10; anger treatment, 100; anticipation, 74–75; cursing, satirization, 99–100; fantasy and vexations, 80–81; reciprocal, 83–84; Stiefel, *Besonnenheit* and, 104–5; writing, 67–73

Simmel, Georg, *Philosophy of Money*, 234
sneezes, 146–47
Social Darwinism, 228
Social Energeticism, 228
society, primitive tendencies in, 128–9
sophrosyne, 106
soul's location in brain, 29
sounds, *Auch Einer* (Vischer), 169–71
space, 134–36, 140–42
spring metaphor in *Tristram Shandy*, 27–28
stage, affects and, 189–90
statistics, anger and, 175–78
Sterne, Laurence, 22. *See also Tristram Shandy*: Germany's fascination with, 246; inconsistent soul of man, 10; Jean Paul, and, 9–10; metaphors, 31; philosophers and, 65–66; *A Sentimental Journey*, 62–63; Stoic anger control and, 10; words as things, 47–48
Stiefelknecht, 109–10
Stoicism, 76, 95; affects and, 81–82; anger control, 10, 248; ataraxia, 87–88, 96; auxiliary causes, 108; composure guided by reason, 87–88; energetic discharge and, 100; idyll and, 84–95; imagination's powers and, 37–38; present focus and, 80–81, 82–83; self-reflection, 82; self-tyranny, 185, 188; Shandean people, 31–32; sustaining causes, 108
The Strudlhof Steps or Melzer and the Depth of the Years (Doderer), 195–96
Studies on Hysteria (Breuer and Freud), 188
sublime, 143–47
superstitious persons, 202–3
suppression of anger, 97–98
swearing. *See* cursing
symbolization, 153–61

Taylor, Frederick Winslow, *Principles of Scientific Management*, 227
technology: cybernetics, 239–43; demons of, 238–39; "Form and Technology" (Cassirer), 236; Freud's prosthesis, 232–33; intrusion into lifeworld of humans, 238–39; technologies of the self, 7–8, 228–32; withdrawal of insight, 15
technology of the self, 21, 79; and anthropomorphism, 238; and curse, 32, 47; and cybernetics 178, 239; and psychotechnology, 228–30; and reading, 197
temperance, 106
tendentious jokes: psychic energy release and, 16–17; shaggy-dog story, 194
theatrical representation, 92–94
theory of mind, 78–79
things, 246; backside of, 237–8; evolution of, 236
thoughts of disturbance *versus* disturbance, 11
throwing things, 163–71
time, *Siebenkäs* (Jean Paul), 82–83
Tissot, Samuel Auguste David, *Treatise on the Health of Men of Letters*, 72–73
Titan (Jean Paul), 107–8
tools (Zeug), 1, 127–28
torment, opinions and, 38
Traces (Bloch), 237–38
tragedy, 184–85
transformation of energy, humans and, 227–28
traveling incarceration, 124–25
Treatise on the Health of Men of Letters (Tissot), 72–73
tribology, 249; science of friction, 25
Tristram Shandy (Sterne): accidents: *versus* judgments, 39–40; anger management, 8–9; anthropology, 65–66; circumcision, 54–55; conception, 52; cursing for medical reasons, 43; door ajar, 27–28; door hinges, 23–25; Dr. Slop, anger, 56–58; Ernulphus and swearing, 41–47; ethics, 65–66; France and, 61–62; garments, 48–49; Jenny, 48; knots, 26; *Latus Clavus*, 52–54; Nanette, 63–66; Nanette, garments, 63–66; malicious environment, protection from, 29–31; mind/body connection, 31; oratory, 60–61 overview, 22; parlor door, 23–29; Phutatorius, 30, 36–38; Plain Stories, 62–64; procreation, 52–53; reason and, 26; recalcitrant environment, 8–9; religion, Walter and, 26–27; rhetoric, 65–66; sermon cottidianus, 66; Shandean people, 31–32; sleep, 10–11, 25; soul's location, 29; speculation on cursing's origins, 36; spring metaphor, 27–28; THINGS, 47–48; Tristram, breeches, 52–58; Tristram's circumcision, 54–55; *Tristrapedia*, 24; Uncle Toby,

Index

religion and, 26–27; Walter and, 27; Walter Shandy, accidents and, 27; Yorick, 49–51
"Tristram Shandy's Law of Gravity" (Burckhardt), 61–62
Truth and Fiction (Goethe), 67–68
twelve-penny oath, 249–50
The Two Sleepwalkers or the Necessary and the Superfluous (Nestroy), 213
tyranny, 185

Unglück, 231

van Gogh, *Old Shoes with Laces*, 128–33
Verdinglichung, 122–23
vexations: aesthetic pleasure and, 85; cursing in response, Kant, Immanuel, on, 96–97; demons assailing humans, 84; fantasy and, 80–81; pleasure in, 85
violent destruction, anger and, 165–56
virtuality, 234–39
Vischer, Friedrich Theodor, 5. *See also Auch Einer* (Vischer): Aesthetics, sublime, 143–47; *Another One: A Traveling Acquaintance*, 124–25; anthropomorphism, 10; boots and shoes, 125–56; on craftsmen, 126–27; criticism of Jean Paul, 116–17; *die Tücke des Objekts*, 143; disruptive power of things, 142–43; equipment, recalcitrant, 129–30; *Fashion and Garb*, 126–27; fury, 137–38; garments, 125–26; ideal *versus* concrete, 139–40; malicious objects, 86; "Mein Lebensgang," 141–42; "My Autobiography," 13–14; objects, diabolical tendencies, 128; personal space, 122–24; "Podo-Booetism" article, 122–24; primitive tendencies in culture and society, 128–29; projection, 13–14; *Punch* magazine article, 122–23; self-sublation, 144–45; sublime, 143–47; *On the Sublime and the Comical*, 143–44; temporal-spatial position, 140; *Verdinglichung*, 122–23

walking-in-the-way, 137–39
Wiener, Norbert, *The Human Use of Human Beings*, 240
The Wisdom of the Body (Cannon), 241–42, 277
wit, 50–51
withdrawal of insight, technology and, 15
"What is a Thing?" (Heidegger), 135–36
words: as incantation, 198; as things, 47–48
worn insides of equipment, 131
writing: dreams, 106; Goethe on, 67–68; heightened attentiveness, 105–6; hypochondria of scholars, 72–73; Jean Paul, 67–72; present moment and, 82–83; scene of, 67–68; shortest story, 193–94; *Treatise on the Health of Men of Letters* (Tissot), 72–73

ZOUNDS, 32–36